2014-2015 Supplement

National Security Law
Fifth Edition

and

Counterterrorism Law
Second Edition

2014-2015 Supplement

National Security Law
Fifth Edition

and

Counterterrorism Law
Second Edition

Stephen Dycus
Professor of Law
Vermont Law School

William C. Banks
Board of Advisors Distinguished Professor
Syracuse University

Peter Raven-Hansen
Glen Earl Weston Research Professor of Law
George Washington University

Stephen I. Vladeck
Professor of Law and Associate Dean for Scholarship
American University Washington College of Law

Wolters Kluwer
Law & Business

To contact Customer Service, e-mail customer.service@wolterskluwer.com, call 1-800-234-1660, fax 1-800-901-9075, or mail correspondence to:

Wolters Kluwer Law & Business
Attn: Order Department
PO Box 990
Frederick, MD 21705

Printed in the United States of America.

1 2 3 4 5 6 7 8 9 0

ISBN 978-1-4548-4050-3

Certified Chain of Custody
Product Line Contains At Least
20% Certified Forest Content
www.sfiprogram.org
SFI-00756

About Wolters Kluwer Law & Business

Wolters Kluwer Law & Business is a leading global provider of intelligent information and digital solutions for legal and business professionals in key specialty areas, and respected educational resources for professors and law students. Wolters Kluwer Law & Business connects legal and business professionals as well as those in the education market with timely, specialized authoritative content and information-enabled solutions to support success through productivity, accuracy and mobility.

Serving customers worldwide, Wolters Kluwer Law & Business products include those under the Aspen Publishers, CCH, Kluwer Law International, Loislaw, ftwilliam.com and MediRegs family of products.

CCH products have been a trusted resource since 1913, and are highly regarded resources for legal, securities, antitrust and trade regulation, government contracting, banking, pension, payroll, employment and labor, and healthcare reimbursement and compliance professionals.

Aspen Publishers products provide essential information to attorneys, business professionals and law students. Written by preeminent authorities, the product line offers analytical and practical information in a range of specialty practice areas from securities law and intellectual property to mergers and acquisitions and pension/benefits. Aspen's trusted legal education resources provide professors and students with high-quality, up-to-date and effective resources for successful instruction and study in all areas of the law.

Kluwer Law International products provide the global business community with reliable international legal information in English. Legal practitioners, corporate counsel and business executives around the world rely on Kluwer Law journals, looseleafs, books, and electronic products for comprehensive information in many areas of international legal practice.

Loislaw is a comprehensive online legal research product providing legal content to law firm practitioners of various specializations. Loislaw provides attorneys with the ability to quickly and efficiently find the necessary legal information they need, when and where they need it, by facilitating access to primary law as well as state-specific law, records, forms and treatises.

ftwilliam.com offers employee benefits professionals the highest quality plan documents (retirement, welfare and non-qualified) and government forms (5500/PBGC, 1099 and IRS) software at highly competitive prices.

MediRegs products provide integrated health care compliance content and software solutions for professionals in healthcare, higher education and life sciences, including professionals in accounting, law and consulting.

Wolters Kluwer Law & Business, a division of Wolters Kluwer, is headquartered in New York. Wolters Kluwer is a market-leading global information services company focused on professionals.

Contents

Preface   *xv*
Teacher's Guide for National Security Law (5th edition)   *xix*
Teacher's Guide for Counterterrorism Law (2d edition)   *xxvii*
Table of Cases   *xxxiii*

Remarks by the President at the United States Military Academy   1
    Commencement Ceremony, May 28, 2014

Clapper v. Amnesty International USA (S. Ct. 2013)   7

Kiobel v. Royal Dutch Petroleum Co. (S. Ct. 2013)   19

Note on Extraterritoriality   36

Note on *United States v. Hamdan (Hamdan II)* (D.C.   37
    Cir. 2012)

Leon Panetta, Secretary of Defense, *Remarks to the Business*   38
    Executives for National Security, Oct. 11, 2012

Harold Hongju Koh, *International Law in Cyberspace*,   41
    Sept. 18, 2012

Presidential Policy Directive PPD-20, *U.S. Cyber Operations*   46
    Policy (n.d.)

Notes and Questions   51

Text of a Letter from the President to the Speaker of the House
of Representatives and the President Pro Tempore of the
Senate, June 16, 2014   52

Remarks by the President in Address to the Nation on Syria,
Sept. 10, 2013   53

United Nations Security Council Resolution 2118,
Sept. 27, 2013   54

Notes   56

Remarks by the President on the Situation in Iraq,
June 19, 2014   56

Remarks by the President at the National Defense
University, May 23, 2013   58

U.S. Policy Standards and Procedures for the Use of Force
in Counterterrorism Operations Outside the United States
and Areas of Active Hostilities, May 22, 2013   62

Department of Justice, White Paper: Lawfulness of a Lethal
Operation Directed Against a U.S. Citizen Who Is a
Senior Operational Leader of Al-Qa'ida or an Associated
Force, Draft Nov. 8, 2011   66

U.S. Department of Justice, Office of Legal Counsel,
Applicability of Federal Criminal Laws and the
Constitution to Contemplated Lethal Operations
Against Shaykh Anwar al-Aulaqi, July 16, 2010   78

Note on "Gang of Four" Notifications   83

Office of the Director of National Intelligence, Intelligence
Community Directive No. 112: Congressional
Notification, Nov. 16, 2011   84

Contents

Note on FY 2013 Intelligence Budget 87

Introduction: The Fourth Amendment and National Security 87

Note on *United States v. Jones* (S. Ct. 2012) 88

Note on FISC "Raw Take" Order 91

Note Updating FISA Reporting Data 92

Note on NSA's STELLARWIND Program 92

Office of the Inspector General, National Security Agency/ 93
Central Security Service, *1109-0002 Working Draft*,
Mar. 24, 2009

Note on FISA Amendments Act Renewal 99

Notes on the Snowden Leaks and PRISM 99

NSA Director of Civil Liberties and Privacy Office, 103
*NSA's Implementation of Foreign Intelligence
Surveillance Act Section 702*, April 16, 2014

Case Title Redacted (FISA Ct. n.d.) 114

Notes and Questions 119

Note on Third-Party Records 126

Note on Section 215 "Metadata" 127

In re Application of the FBI for an Order Requiring the 130
Production of Tangible Things from [REDACTED]
(FISA Ct. Aug. 29, 2013)

Presidential Policy Directive/PPD-28, *Signals Intelligence* 142
Activities, Jan. 17, 2014

Notes and Questions 152

Note on *In re National Security Letter* (N.D. Cal. 2013) 160

The Metadata Program Goes to Court 161

Notes and Questions 165

Reforming FISA by Reforming the FISA Court? 168

Notes and Questions 170

United States v. Cotterman (9th Cir. 2013) 175

Ibrahim v. Department of Homeland Security (9th Cir. 2012) 189

Ibrahim v. Department of Homeland Security, 198
   (N.D. Cal. Jan. 14, 2014)

Notes and Questions 215

Note on *Hernandez v. United States* (5th Cir. June 30, 2014) 218

Al-Zahrani v. Rodriguez (D.C. Cir. 2012) 220

Note on Jurisdiction-Stripping and *Bivens* Claims 223

National Defense Authorization Act for Fiscal Year 2012, 224
   §§1021-1022, Dec. 31, 2011

Presidential Signing Statement on H.R. 1540, Dec. 31, 2011 226

Hedges v. Obama (2d Cir. July 17, 2013) 227

Notes and Questions 239

The Next Generation of Guantánamo Litigation 241

Contents

Notes and Questions   244

Aamer v. Obama (D.C. Cir. Feb. 11, 2014)   245

Notes and Questions   254

In re Guantanamo Bay Detainee Litigation (D.D.C. 2013)   257

Notes and Questions   268

Department of Justice, *Closure of Investigation into the Interrogation of Certain Detainees*, Aug. 30, 2012   270

Note on Senate Intelligence Committee, *Study of the Central Intelligence Agency's Detention and Interrogation*, Dec. 13, 2012   272

Note on *Al Shimari v. CACI Int'l, Inc.* (E.D. Va. 2013)   274

Padilla v. Yoo (9th Cir. 2012)   274

Notes and Questions   284

Note on Remedies from International Courts   287

United States v. Brehm (4th Cir. 2012)   288

Notes and Questions   291

Ibrahim v. Department of Homeland Security (Ibrahim II) (N.D. Cal. 2012)   293

United States v. Rosen (E.D. Va. 2007)   298

National Security Criminal Procedure: *Miranda*, Presentment, and Speedy Trial   304

Federal Bureau of Investigation, *Custodial Interrogation*   305
    for Public Safety and Intelligence-Gathering Purposes
    of Operational Terrorists Inside the United States,
    Oct. 21, 2010

Notes and Questions   307

United States v. Abdulmutallab (E.D. Mich. 2011)   310

Notes and Questions   313

United States v. Ghailani (2nd Cir. Oct. 24, 2013)   316

Notes and Questions   326

Note on *Hamdan v. United States (Hamdan II)*   328
    (D.C. Cir. 2012)

Al Bahlul v. United States (D.C. Cir. July 14, 2014)   329

Notes and Questions   344

Attorney General Eric Holder, Remarks at Northwestern   347
    University School of Law, Mar. 5, 2012

Note on Public Access to Military Trials   349

Office of the Director of National Intelligence,   350
    Intelligence Community Directive 119: Media
    Contacts, Mar. 20, 2014

Note on "Injury of the United States"   352

Department of Justice, *Report on Review of News*   353
    Media Policies, July 12, 2013

United States v. Sterling (4th Cir. July 19, 2013)   356

Contents

Notes and Questions   369

Note on *Rothstein v. UBS AG* (2d Cir. 2013)   370

Note on "Proximate Causation"   370

Note on Finding the Property   371

* * *

Preface

The past year has yielded many developments in our very dynamic field — rich fodder for teachers and students alike. The most important of these are reflected in this *Supplement*, along with other materials not available when the latest editions of our casebooks went to press three years ago.

The continuing disclosures by former NSA contractor employee Edward Snowden keep changing what we know — or think we know — about the scope and legality of government surveillance. Snowden's leaks and related news accounts have, in turn, prompted the release of a growing number of judicial opinions, as well as agency, NGO, and media reports about telephony metadata, cell tower, laptop, and related electronic intelligence collection and analysis. These include Presidential Policy Directive/PPD-28: Signals Intelligence Activities, opinions of the Foreign Intelligence Surveillance Court on "upstream collection" and §702 and on telephony metadata collection under §215, and dueling district court opinions on the legality of the latter.

This year's *Supplement* also includes notes on intervention in Syria and Iraq (Iraq III?), U.S. principles for cyber operations, and excerpts from a 2010 Office of Legal Counsel memorandum on targeted killing, as well as an important new No-Fly decision that highlights some of the risks in airport screening.

The issues generated by military detention continue to generate complex case law. We include here a Second Circuit decision treating the relationship of §1021 of the FY 2012 NDAA to the 2001 AUMF, as well as decisions in what we call the next generation of Guantánamo litigation, with extensive Notes and Questions.

Trials of suspected terrorists also continue to pose legal challenges, which we consider in new decisions treating the applicability of *Miranda* warnings, the Speedy Trial Act, and the constitutional guarantee against *ex post facto* laws. One of these, a badly fractured *en banc* opinion by the D.C. Circuit in *Al Bahlul v. United States*, was issued the day before this *Supplement* went to press.

This *Supplement* serves two closely related casebooks: *National Security Law* (5th ed.) and *Counterterrorism Law* (2d ed.). This Preface is followed immediately by two Teacher's Guides, one for each book, which indicate the placement of supplemental materials in each casebook. Each document listed is accompanied by a reference to one or both casebooks. For example, a recent "No-Fly" decision in *Ibrahim v. Department of Homeland Security* appears with this instruction: **[NSL p. 692, CTL p. 305. Insert after "b. Watch Lists and Other Identification-Related Databases" and before Note 1.].** "NSL" refers to *National Security Law* (5th ed.), "CTL" to *Counterterrorism Law* (2d ed.).

At least one of our adopters, a U.S. government employee, has informed us that he is forbidden to read any leaked documents that have not been officially declassified. The same stricture may apply to some students. With the documents now in the public domain and readily available to friends and enemies alike (and the subject of broad media analysis — much of it inaccurate), we believe that it would be pointless and irresponsible to ignore them here. Review of them in the classroom will help us understand what our government is doing in an area fraught with serious privacy and constitutional concerns, correct serious inaccuracies in the public discussion so far, and perhaps contribute indirectly to the development of better policy that is adopted and executed in accordance with the rule of law. Teachers and students will have to decide for themselves whether and how to use these materials.

As important new developments arise during the coming year, we will continue to document them by posting edited new materials on the websites for the two casebooks, from which they may be downloaded by teachers and shared with students. The website for *National Security Law (5th ed.)* is at http://www.aspenlawschool.com/books/dycus_nationalsecurity/; for *Counterterrorism Law (2d ed.)* at http://www.aspenlawschool.com/ books/ dycus_counterterrorism/.

As always, we are extremely grateful to our adopters, fellow members of the National Security Law Section of the Association of American Law Schools, fellow members of the Editorial Board of the *Journal of National Security Law & Policy*, fellow casebook authors (our collaborators in building the field), members of the ABA Standing Committee on Law and National Security, and our many friends in the national security community. We also wish to thank our research assistants. Finally, we wish to express our gratitude to John Devins and Carol McGeehan of Wolters Kluwer Law & Business for their continued encouragement and support.

Stephen Dycus
William C. Banks
Peter Raven-Hansen
Stephen I. Vladeck

July 2014

* * *

Teacher's Guide for National Security Law (5th Edition)

*Casebook
Page*

*Page in this
Supplement*

Chapter 1. Introduction

Page 4   Remarks by the President at the United States   1
Military Academy Commencement
Ceremony, May 28, 2014

Chapter 6. The Courts' National Security Powers

Page 137   *Clapper v. Amnesty International USA*   7
(S. Ct. 2013)

Chapter 7. The Domestic Effect of International Law

Page 195   *Kiobel v. Royal Dutch Petroleum Co.*   19
(S. Ct. 2013)
Page 200   Note on Extraterritoriality   36
Page 209   Note on *United States v. Hamdan (Hamdan II)*   37
(D.C. Cir. 2012)

Chapter 8. The Right to Wage War (jus ad bellum)

Page 233   Leon Panetta, Secretary of Defense, *Remarks to*   38
the Business Executives for National Security,
Oct. 11, 2012

Page 233   Harold Hongju Koh, *International Law in*   41
               Cyberspace, Sept. 18, 2012
Page 233   Presidential Policy Directive PPD-20, *U.S. Cyber*   46
               Operations Policy (n.d.)
Page 233   Notes and Questions   51

Chapter 11.   The War Powers Resolution

Page 322   Text of a Letter from the President to the Speaker   52
               of the House of Representatives and the President
               Pro Tempore of the Senate, June 16, 2014

Chapter 12.   Collective Self-Defense

Page 342   Remarks by the President in Address to the   53
               Nation on Syria, Sept. 10, 2013
Page 342   United Nations Security Council Resolution   54
               2118, Sept. 27, 2013
Page 342   Notes   56

Chapter 13.   Unilateral Self-Defense and Rescue

Page 367   Remarks by the President on the Situation in   56
               Iraq, June 19, 2014

Chapter 14.   Targeting Terrorists

Page 403   Remarks of the President at the National Defense   58
               University, May 23, 2013

Page 403   *U.S. Policy Standards and Procedures for the*   62
               Use of Force in Counterterrorism Operations
               Outside the United States and Areas of Active
               Hostilities, May 22, 2013

Page 410   Department of Justice, *White Paper: Lawfulness*   66
            of a Lethal Operation Directed Against a U.S.
            Citizen Who Is a Senior Operational Leader of
            Al-Qa'ida or an Associated Force,
            Draft Nov. 8, 2011
Page 410   U.S. Department of Justice, Office of Legal   78
            Counsel, *Applicability of Federal Criminal*
            Laws and the Constitution to Contemplated
            Lethal Operations Against Shaykh Anwar
            al-Aulaqi, July 16, 2010

Chapter 16. Organization and Authority of the Intelligence Community

Page 464   Note on "Gang of Four" Notifications   83
Page 464   Office of the Director of National Intelligence,   84
            Intelligence Community Directive No. 112:
            Congressional Notification, Nov. 16, 2011
Page 469   Note on FY 2013 Intelligence Budget   87

Chapter 20. The Fourth Amendment and National Security

Page 554   Introduction: The Fourth Amendment and   87
            National Security
Page 579   Note on *United States v. Jones*   88
            (S. Ct. 2012)

Chapter 21. Congressional Authority for Foreign Intelligence Surveillance

Page 596   Note on FISC "Raw Take" Order   91
Page 607   Note Updating FISA Reporting Data   92

Chapter 22. Programmatic Electronic Surveillance for Foreign Intelligence

Page 613   Note on NSA's STELLARWIND Program   92
Page 613   Office of the Inspector General, National Security   93
            Agency/Central Security Service, *1109-0002*
            Working Draft, Mar. 24, 2009
Page 629   Note on FISA Amendments Act Renewal   99
Page 632   Notes and Questions on the Snowden Leaks   99
            and PRISM
Page 632   NSA Director of Civil Liberties and Privacy   103
            Office, *NSA's Implementation of Foreign*
            Intelligence Surveillance Act Section 702,
            April 16, 2014
Page 632   *Case Title Redacted* (FISA Ct. n.d.)   114
Page 632   Notes and Questions   119

Chapter 23. Third-Party Records and Data Mining

Page 649   Note on Third-Party Records   126
Page 668   Note on Section 215 "Metadata"   127
Page 668   *In re Application of the FBI for an Order*   130
            Requiring the Production of Tangible Things
            from [REDACTED] (FISA Ct. Aug. 29, 2013)
Page 668   Presidential Policy Directive/PPD-28, *Signals*   142
            Intelligence Activities, Jan. 17, 2014
Page 668   Notes and Questions   152
Page 671   Note on *In re National Security Letter*   160
            (N.D. Cal. 2013)
Page 677   The Metadata Program Goes to Court   161
Page 677   Notes and Questions   165
Page 677   Reforming FISA by Reforming the FISA Court?   168
Page 677   Notes and Questions   170

Chapter 24. Screening for Security

Page 680	*United States v. Cotterman* (9th Cir. 2013)	175
Page 692	*Ibrahim v. Department of Homeland Security* (9th Cir. 2012)	189
Page 692	*Ibrahim v. Department of Homeland Security*, (N.D. Cal. Jan. 14, 2014)	198
Page 694	Notes and Questions	215

Chapter 25. Surveillance Abroad

Page 720	Note on *Hernandez v. United States* (5th Cir. June 30, 2014)	218

Chapter 28. The Great Writ: Habeas Corpus After 9/11

Page 810	*Al-Zahrani v. Rodriguez* (D.C. Cir. 2012)	220
Page 810	Note on Jurisdiction-Stripping and *Bivens* Claims	223

Chapter 30. Military Detention After 9/11

Page 876	National Defense Authorization Act for Fiscal Year 2012, §§1021-1022, Dec. 31, 2011	224
Page 876	Presidential Signing Statement on H.R. 1540, Dec. 31, 2011	226
Page 876	*Hedges v. Obama* (2nd Cir. July 17, 2013)	227
Page 876	Notes and Questions	239
Page 892	The Next Generation of Guantánamo Litigation	241
Page 892	Notes and Questions	244
Page 892	*Aamer v. Obama* (D.C. Cir. Feb. 11, 2014)	245
Page 892	Notes and Questions	254
Page 892	*In re Guantanamo Bay Detainee Litigation* (D.D.C. 2013)	257
Page 892	Notes and Questions	268

Chapter 32. Case Study: Coercive Interrogation by U.S. Forces After 9/11

Page 944   Department of Justice, *Closure of Investigation*   270
into the Interrogation of Certain Detainees,
Aug. 30, 2012

Page 944   Note on Report of Senate Intelligence Committee,   272
*Study of the Central Intelligence Agency's
Detention and Interrogation*, Dec. 13, 2012

Page 951   Note on *Al Shimari v. CACI Int'l, Inc.* (E.D.   274
Va. 2013)

Page 951   *Padilla v. Yoo* (9th Cir. 2012)   274

Page 951   Notes and Questions   284

Chapter 33. Extraordinary Rendition

Page 974   Note on Remedies from International Courts   287

Chapter 34. Criminalizing Terrorism and Material Support

Page 1015 *United States v. Brehm* (4th Cir. 2012)   288

Page 1015 Notes and Questions   291

Chapter 35. Prosecuting Accused Terrorists and Their Supporters in Criminal Courts

Page 1032 *Ibrahim v. Department of Homeland Security*   293
(Ibrahim II) (N.D. Cal. 2012)

Page 1032 *United States v. Rosen* (E.D. Va. 2007)   298

Page 1051 National Security Criminal Procedure: 304
Miranda, Presentment, and Speedy Trial

Page 1051 Federal Bureau of Investigation, *Custodial*   305
*Interrogation for Public Safety and Intelligence-
Gathering Purposes of Operational Terrorists
Inside the United States*, Oct. 21, 2010

Page 1051   Notes and Questions   307
Page 1051   *United States v. Abdulmutallab* (E.D.   310
            Mich. 2011)
Page 1051   Notes and Questions   313
Page 1051   *United States v. Ghailani* (2nd Cir.   316
            Oct. 24, 2013)
Page 1051   Notes and Questions   326

Chapter 36. Trial by Military Commission

Page 1104   Note on *Hamdan v. United States (Hamdan II)*   328
            (D.C. Cir. 2012)
Page 1104   *Al Bahlul v. United States* (D.C. Cir.   329
            July 14, 2014)
Page 1104   Notes and Questions   344
Page 1113   Attorney General Eric Holder, Remarks at   347
            Northwestern University School of Law,
            Mar. 5, 2012

Chapter 41. Other Grounds for Access to National Security Information

Page 1240   Note on Public Access to Military Trials   349

Chapter 42. Restraining Unauthorized Disclosures

Page 1262   Office of the Director of National Intelligence,   350
            *Intelligence Community Directive 119: Media
            Contacts*, Mar. 20, 2014
Page 1274   Note on "Injury of the United States"   352

Chapter 43. Restraints on Publication of National Security Information

Page 1309   Department of Justice, *Report on Review of   353
            News Media Policies*, July 12, 2013

Page 1309   *United States v. Sterling* (4th Cir. July 19, 2013)   356
Page 1309   Notes and Questions   369

Teacher's Guide for Counterterrorism Law (2d Edition)

Casebook Page		Page in this Supplement

Chapter 1. Defining Terrorism and Counterterrorism

Page 1	Remarks by the President at the United States Military Academy Commencement Ceremony, May 28, 2014	1

Chapter 3. Waging War on Terrorists

Page 89	Leon Panetta, Secretary of Defense, *Remarks to the Business Executives for National Security*, Oct. 11, 2012	38
Page 89	Harold Hongju Koh, *International Law in Cyberspace*, Sept. 18, 2012	41
Page 89	Presidential Policy Directive PPD-20, *U.S. Cyber Operations Policy* (n.d.)	46
Page 89	Notes and Questions	51

Chapter 4. Targeting Terrorists

Page 117	Remarks of the President at the National Defense University, May 23, 2013 (targeting)	58

Page 117   *U.S. Policy Standards and Procedures for the*   62
            Use of Force in Counterterrorism Operations
            Outside the United States and Areas of Active
            Hostilities, May 22, 2013
Page 124   Department of Justice, *White Paper: Lawfulness*   66
            of a Lethal Operation Directed Against a U.S.
            Citizen Who Is a Senior Operational Leader of
            Al-Qa'ida or an Associated Force,
            Draft Nov. 8, 2011
Page 124   U.S. Department of Justice, Office of Legal   78
            Counsel, *Applicability of Federal Criminal*
            Laws and the Constitution to Contemplated
            Lethal Operations Against Shaykh Anwar
            al-Aulaqi, July 16, 2010

Chapter 6. The Fourth Amendment and Counterterrorism

Page 167   Introduction: The Fourth Amendment and   87
            National Security
Page 192   Note on *United States v. Jones*   88
            (S. Ct. Jan. 2012)

Chapter 7. Congressional Authority for Foreign Intelligence Surveillance

Page 209   Note on FISC "Raw Take" Order   91
Page 220   Note Updating FISA Reporting Data   92

Chapter 8. Programmatic Electronic Surveillance for Foreign Intelligence

Page 226   Note on NSA's STELLARWIND Program   92
Page 226   Office of the Inspector General, National Security   93
            Agency/Central Security Service, *1109-0002*
            Working Draft, Mar. 24, 2009
Page 242   Note on FISA Amendments Act Renewal   99

Page 245   Notes on the Snowden Leaks and PRISM   99
Page 245   NSA Director of Civil Liberties and Privacy   103
           Office, *NSA's Implementation of Foreign
           Intelligence Surveillance Act Section 702,*
           April 16, 2014
Page 245   *Case Title Redacted* (FISA Ct. n.d.)   114
Page 245   Notes and Questions   119

Chapter 9. Third-Party Records and Data Mining

Page 262   Note on Third-Party Records   126
Page 281   Note on Section 215 "Metadata"   127
Page 281   *In re Application of the FBI for an Order   130
           Requiring the Production of Tangible Things
           from [REDACTED]* (FISA Ct. Aug. 29, 2013)
Page 281   Presidential Policy Directive/PPD-28, *Signals   142
           Intelligence Activities,* Jan. 17, 2014
Page 281   Notes and Questions   152
Page 284   Note on *In re National Security Letter*   160
           (N.D. Cal. 2013)
Page 290   The Metadata Program Goes to Court   161
Page 290   Notes and Questions   165
Page 290   Reforming FISA by Reforming the FISA Court?   168
Page 290   Notes and Questions   170

Chapter 10. Screening for Security

Page 293   *United States v. Cotterman* (9th Cir. 2013)   175
Page 305   *Ibrahim v. Department of Homeland Security*   189
           (9th Cir. 2012)
Page 305   *Ibrahim v. Department of Homeland Security,*   198
           (N.D. Cal. Jan. 14, 2014)
Page 307   Notes and Questions   215

Chapter 11. *Surveillance Abroad*

Page 333   Note on *Hernandez v. United States* (5th Cir.   218
            June 30, 2014)

Chapter 14. *The Great Writ: Habeas Corpus After 9/11*

Page 424   *Al-Zahrani v. Rodriguez* (D.C. Cir. 2012)   220
Page 424   Note on Jurisdiction-Stripping and   223
            Bivens Claims

Chapter 16. *Military Detention After 9/11*

Page 490   National Defense Authorization Act for Fiscal   224
            Year 2012, §§1021-1022, Dec. 31, 2011
Page 490   Presidential Signing Statement on H.R. 1540,   226
            Dec. 31, 2011
Page 490   *Hedges v. Obama* (2nd Cir. July 17, 2013)   227
Page 490   Notes and Questions   239
Page 506   The Next Generation of Guantánamo Litigation   241
Page 506   Notes and Questions   244
Page 506   *Aamer v. Obama* (D.C. Cir. Feb. 11, 2014)   245
Page 506   Notes and Questions   254
Page 506   *In re Guantanamo Bay Detainee   257
            Litigation* (D.D.C. 2013)
Page 506   Notes and Questions   268

Chapter 18. *Case Study: Coercive Interrogation by U.S. Forces After 9/11*

Page 558   Department of Justice, *Closure of Investigation   270
            into the Interrogation of Certain Detainees*,
            Aug. 30, 2012

Page 558   Note on Senate Intelligence Committee,   272
            Study of the Central Intelligence Agency's
            Detention and Interrogation, Dec. 13, 2012
Page 565   Note on *Al Shimari v. CACI Int'l, Inc.* (E.D.   274
            Va. 2013)
Page 565   *Padilla v. Yoo* (9th Cir. 2012)   274
Page 565   Notes and Questions   284

Chapter 19. Extraordinary Rendition

Page 588   Note on Remedies from International Courts   287

Chapter 20. Criminalizing Terrorism and Material Support

Page 629   *United States v. Brehm* (4th Cir. 2012)   288
Page 629   Notes and Questions   291

Chapter 21. Prosecuting Accused Terrorists and Their Supporters in Criminal Courts

Page 646   *Ibrahim v. Department of Homeland Security*   293
            (Ibrahim II) (N.D. Cal. 2012)
Page 646   *United States v. Rosen* (E.D. Va. 2007)   298
Page 665   National Security Criminal Procedure: 304
            Miranda, Presentment, and Speedy Trial
Page 665   Federal Bureau of Investigation, *Custodial*   305
            Interrogation for Public Safety and Intelligence-
            Gathering Purposes of Operational Terrorists
            Inside the United States, Oct. 21, 2010
Page 665   Notes and Questions   307
Page 665   *United States v. Abdulmutallab* (E.D. Mich. 2011)   310
Page 665   Notes and Questions   313
Page 665   *United States v. Ghailani* (2d Cir.   316
            Oct. 24, 2013)
Page 665   Notes and Questions   326

Chapter 22. Trial by Military Commission

Page 718   Note on *Hamdan v. United States (Hamdan II)*   328
            (D.C. Cir. 2012)
Page 718   *Al Bahlul v. United States* (D.C. Cir.   329
            July 14, 2014)
Page 718   Notes and Questions   344
Page 727   Attorney General Eric Holder, Remarks at   347
            Northwestern University School of Law,
            Mar. 5, 2012

Chapter 26. Suing Terrorists and Their Supporters

Page 836   Note on *Rothstein v. UBS AG* (2d Cir. 2013)   370
Page 837   Note on "Proximate Causation"   370
Page 839   *Kiobel v. Royal Dutch Petroleum Co.*   19
            (S. Ct. 2013)
Page 851   Note on Finding the Property   371

Table of Cases

Aamer v. Obama (D.C. Cir. Feb. 11, 2014)   245

Abdulmutallab, United States v. (E.D. Mich. 2011)   310

ACLU v. Clapper (S.D.N.Y. 2013)   161-168

ACLU v. United States (Ct. Mil. Comm'n Rev. 2013)   349

Al Bahlul v. United States (D.C. Cir. July 14, 2014)   38, 329

Al Bahlul v. United States (D.C. Cir. 2013)   329

Al Janko v. Gates (D.C. Cir. Jan. 17, 2014)   223

Al Maqaleh v. Gates (D.C. Cir. 2010)   255

Al Shimari v. CACI Int'l, Inc. (E.D. Va. 2013)   274

Al Shimari v. CACI Premier Tech., Inc. (4th Cir. June 30, 2014)   36, 274

Al-Zahrani v. Rodriguez (D.C. Cir. 2012)   220

Ali, United States v. (C.A.A.F. 2012)   292

Application of the FBI for an Order Requiring the Production of Tangible Things from [REDACTED], In re (FISA Ct. Aug. 29, 2013)   130

Application of the United States for an Order Directing a Provider of Elec. Comm'n Serv. to Disclose Records to the Government, In re (3d Cir. 2010)   158

Application of the United States for Historical Cell Site Data, In re (5th Cir. 2013)   91, 157

Argentina v. NML Capital, Ltd. (S. Ct. June 16, 2014)   371

Bowen v. Mich. Acad. of Family Physicians (S. Ct. 1986)   167

Brehm, United States v. (4th Cir. 2012)   288

Case Title Redacted (FISA Ct. n.d.)   114

Center for Const'l Rights v. Lind (D. Md. 2013)   350

Center for Const'l Rights v. United States (C.A.A.F. 2013)   349

Clapper v. Amnesty International USA (S. Ct. 2013)   7, 162, 240

Corley v. United States (S. Ct. 2009)   314

Cotterman, United States v. (9th Cir. 2013)   175

County of Riverside v. McLaughlin (S. Ct. 1991)   314

Davis, United States v. (11th Cir. June 11, 2014)   91

Dhiab v. Obama (D.D.C. May 23, 2014)   256

El-Masri v. United States (4th Cir. 2007)   287

EPIC, In re (S. Ct. 2013)   167

Ghailani, United States v. (2d Cir. Oct. 24, 2013)   316

Guantanamo Bay Detainee Continuing Access to Counsel, In re (D.D.C. 2012)   256

Guantanamo Bay Detainee Litigation, In re (D.D.C. 2013)   257

Hamdan v. Rumsfeld (S. Ct. 2006)   328

Hamdan, United States v. (Hamdan II) (D.C. Cir. 2012)   37, 328

Hamdan, United States v. (Ct. Mil. Comm'n Rev. 2011)   328

Harlow v. Fitzgerald (S. Ct. 1982)   284

Hedges v. Obama (2d Cir. July 17, 2013)   227, 239-241

Hedges v. *Obama* (S.D.N.Y. 2012)   239

Hernandez v. United States (5th Cir. June 30, 2014)   218-220

Hollingsworth v. Perry (S. Ct. 2013)   173

Hope v. Pelzer (S. Ct. 2002)   285

Hussain v. Obama (S. Ct. Apr. 21, 2014)   270

Ibrahim v. Department of Homeland Security (9th Cir. 2012)   189

Ibrahim v. Department of Homeland Security (Ibrahim II)   293
   (N.D. Cal. 2012)

Ibrahim v. Department of Homeland Security (N.D. Cal.   198
   Jan. 14, 2014)

Iran Nat'l Airlines Corp. v. Marschalk Co. (S. Ct. 1981)   174

Jones, United States v. (S. Ct. Jan. 2012)   88-91, 126-127,
   154-155, 158, 164

Katz v. United States (S. Ct. 1967)   89

Kiobel v. Royal Dutch Petroleum Co. (S. Ct. 2013)   19

Kiyemba v. Obama. (D.C. Cir. 2009)   254

Klayman v. Obama (D.D.C. 2013)   161-168

Latif v. Holder (D. Ore. June 24, 2014)   216-218

Latif v. Holder (D. Ore. 2013)   216

Mallory v. United States (S. Ct. 1957)   314

Maqaleh v. Hagel (D.C. Cir. 2013)   255

Matthews v. Eldridge (S. Ct. 1976)   216

McNabb v. United States (S. Ct. 1943)   314

Miller, United States v. (S. Ct. 1976)   126

Miranda v. Arizona (S. Ct. 1966)   305

Name redacted (FISA Ct. Oct. 3, 2011)   153, 154, 171

National Security Letter, In re (N.D. Cal. 2013)   160

New York v. Quarles (S. Ct. 1984)   305, 307-309

Padilla v. Yoo (9th Cir. 2012)   274

Paroline v. United States (S. Ct. Apr. 23, 2014)   371

Orders of This Court Interpreting Section 215 of the PATRIOT Act, In re (FISA Ct. Sept. 13, 2013)   175

Paul v. Davis (S. Ct. 1976)   216

Pearson v. Callahan (S. Ct. 2009)   286

Quirin, Ex parte (S. Ct. 1942)   37

Riley v. California (S. Ct. June 25, 2014)   90-91

Rosen, United States v. (E.D. Va. 2007)   298

Rothstein v. UBS AG (2d Cir. 2013)   370, 371

Table of Cases

Sanders v. United States (S. Ct. 1963)   269

Saucier v. Katz (S. Ct. 2001)   285

Smith v. Maryland (S. Ct. 1979)   126, 154-155, 164-165, 167-168

Sosa v. Alvarez-Machain (S. Ct. 2004)   37

Sterling, United States v. (4th Cir. July 19, 2013)   356

Stern v. Marshall (S. Ct. 2011)   345

Summers v. Tice (Cal. 1948)   371

Tarhuni v. Holder (D. Ore. Mar. 26, 2014)   216

Tex. Alliance for Home Care Servs. v. Sebilius (D.C. Cir. 2012)   166

Toscanino, United States v. (2d Cir. 1974)   327-328

Webster v. Doe (S. Ct. 1988)   163, 167, 223

Williams v. Jacquez (E.D. Cal. 2011)   315

* * *

Remarks by the President at the United States Military Academy Commencement Ceremony
May 28, 2014

. . . When I first spoke at West Point in 2009, we still had more than 100,000 troops in Iraq. We were preparing to surge in Afghanistan. Our counterterrorism efforts were focused on al Qaeda's core leadership — those who had carried out the 9/11 attacks. . . .

Four and a half years later, as you graduate, the landscape has changed. We have removed our troops from Iraq. We are winding down our war in Afghanistan. Al Qaeda's leadership on the border region between Pakistan and Afghanistan has been decimated, and Osama bin Laden is no more. . . .

In fact, by most measures, America has rarely been stronger relative to the rest of the world. . . . The odds of a direct threat against us by any nation are low and do not come close to the dangers we faced during the Cold War. . . .

But the world is changing with accelerating speed. This presents opportunity, but also new dangers. We know all too well, after 9/11, just how technology and globalization has put power once reserved for states in the hands of individuals, raising the capacity of terrorists to do harm. Russia's aggression toward former Soviet states unnerves capitals in Europe, while China's economic rise and military reach worries its neighbors. From Brazil to India, rising middle classes compete with us, and governments seek a greater say in global forums. And even as developing nations embrace democracy and market economies, 24-hour news and social media makes it impossible to ignore the continuation of sectarian conflicts and failing states and popular uprisings that might have received only passing notice a generation ago. . . .

. . . At least since George Washington served as Commander-in-Chief, there have been those who warned against foreign entanglements that do not touch directly on our security or economic wellbeing. Today, according to self-described realists, conflicts in Syria or Ukraine or the Central African Republic are not ours to solve. And not surprisingly, after costly wars and continuing challenges here at home, that view is shared by many Americans.

1

A different view from interventionists from the left and right says that we ignore these conflicts at our own peril; that America's willingness to apply force around the world is the ultimate safeguard against chaos, and America's failure to act in the face of Syrian brutality or Russian provocations not only violates our conscience, but invites escalating aggression in the future.

And each side can point to history to support its claims. But I believe neither view fully speaks to the demands of this moment. It is absolutely true that in the 21st century American isolationism is not an option. We don't have a choice to ignore what happens beyond our borders. If nuclear materials are not secure, that poses a danger to American cities. As the Syrian civil war spills across borders, the capacity of battle-hardened extremist groups to come after us only increases. Regional aggression that goes unchecked — whether in southern Ukraine or the South China Sea, or anywhere else in the world — will ultimately impact our allies and could draw in our military. We can't ignore what happens beyond our boundaries.

And beyond these narrow rationales, I believe we have a real stake, an abiding self-interest, in making sure our children and our grandchildren grow up in a world where schoolgirls are not kidnapped and where individuals are not slaughtered because of tribe or faith or political belief. I believe that a world of greater freedom and tolerance is not only a moral imperative, it also helps to keep us safe.

But to say that we have an interest in pursuing peace and freedom beyond our borders is not to say that every problem has a military solution. Since World War II, some of our most costly mistakes came not from our restraint, but from our willingness to rush into military adventures without thinking through the consequences — without building international support and legitimacy for our action; without leveling with the American people about the sacrifices required. Tough talk often draws headlines, but war rarely conforms to slogans. As General Eisenhower, someone with hard-earned knowledge on this subject, said at this ceremony in 1947: "War is mankind's most tragic and stupid folly; to seek or advise its deliberate provocation is a black crime against all men." . . .

. . . America must always lead on the world stage. If we don't, no one else will. The military that you have joined is and always will be the backbone of that leadership. But U.S. military action cannot be the only — or even primary — component of our leadership in every instance. Just because we have the best hammer does not mean that every problem is a nail. And because the costs associated with military action are so high, you should expect every civilian leader — and especially your Commander-in-Chief — to be clear about how that awesome power should be used. . . .

First, let me repeat a principle I put forward at the outset of my presidency: The United States will use military force, unilaterally if necessary, when our core interests demand it — when our people are threatened, when our livelihoods are at stake, when the security of our allies is in danger. In these circumstances, we still need to ask tough questions about whether our actions are proportional and effective and just. International opinion matters, but America should never ask permission to protect our people, our homeland, or our way of life.

On the other hand, when issues of global concern do not pose a direct threat to the United States, when such issues are at stake — when crises arise that stir our conscience or push the world in a more dangerous direction but do not directly threaten us — then the threshold for military action must be higher. In such circumstances, we should not go it alone. Instead, we must mobilize allies and partners to take collective action. We have to broaden our tools to include diplomacy and development; sanctions and isolation; appeals to international law; and, if just, necessary and effective, multilateral military action. In such circumstances, we have to work with others because collective action in these circumstances is more likely to succeed, more likely to be sustained, less likely to lead to costly mistakes.

This leads to my second point: For the foreseeable future, the most direct threat to America at home and abroad remains terrorism. But a strategy that involves invading every country that harbors terrorist networks is naïve and unsustainable. I believe we must shift our counterterrorism strategy — drawing on the successes and shortcomings of our experience in Iraq and Afghanistan — to more effectively partner with countries where terrorist networks seek a foothold.

And the need for a new strategy reflects the fact that today's principal threat no longer comes from a centralized al Qaeda leadership. Instead, it comes from decentralized al Qaeda affiliates and extremists, many with agendas focused in countries where they operate. And this lessens the possibility of large-scale 9/11-style attacks against the homeland, but it heightens the danger of U.S. personnel overseas being attacked, as we saw in Benghazi. It heightens the danger to less defensible targets, as we saw in a shopping mall in Nairobi.

So we have to develop a strategy that matches this diffuse threat — one that expands our reach without sending forces that stretch our military too thin, or stir up local resentments. We need partners to fight terrorists alongside us. . . .

. . . I am calling on Congress to support a new Counterterrorism Partnerships Fund of up to $5 billion, which will allow us to train, build capacity, and facilitate partner countries on the front lines. And these resources will give us flexibility to fulfill different missions, including training security forces in Yemen who have gone on the offensive against al Qaeda; supporting a multinational force to keep the peace in Somalia; working with European allies to train a functioning security force and border patrol in Libya; and facilitating French operations in Mali.

A critical focus of this effort will be the ongoing crisis in Syria. As frustrating as it is, there are no easy answers, no military solution that can eliminate the terrible suffering anytime soon. As President, I made a decision that we should not put American troops into the middle of this increasingly sectarian war, and I believe that is the right decision. But that does not mean we shouldn't help the Syrian people stand up against a dictator who bombs and starves his own people. And in helping those who fight for the right of all Syrians to choose their own future, we are also pushing back against the growing number of extremists who find safe haven in the chaos.

So with the additional resources I'm announcing today, we will step up our efforts to support Syria's neighbors — Jordan and Lebanon; Turkey and Iraq — as they contend with refugees and confront terrorists working across Syria's borders. I will work with Congress to ramp up support for those in the Syrian opposition who offer the best alternative to terrorists and brutal dictators. And we will continue to coordinate with our friends and allies in Europe and the Arab World to push for a political resolution of this crisis, and to make sure that those countries and not just the United States are contributing their fair share to support the Syrian people.

Let me make one final point about our efforts against terrorism. The partnerships I've described do not eliminate the need to take direct action when necessary to protect ourselves. When we have actionable intelligence, that's what we do — through capture operations like the one that brought a terrorist involved in the plot to bomb our embassies in 1998 to face justice; or drone strikes like those we've carried out in

Yemen and Somalia. There are times when those actions are necessary, and we cannot hesitate to protect our people.

But as I said last year, in taking direct action we must uphold standards that reflect our values. That means taking strikes only when we face a continuing, imminent threat, and only where there is . . . near certainty of no civilian casualties. For our actions should meet a simple test: We must not create more enemies than we take off the battlefield.

I also believe we must be more transparent about both the basis of our counterterrorism actions and the manner in which they are carried out. . . . [W]hen we cannot explain our efforts clearly and publicly, we face terrorist propaganda and international suspicion, we erode legitimacy with our partners and our people, and we reduce accountability in our own government.

And this issue of transparency is directly relevant to a third aspect of American leadership, and that is our effort to strengthen and enforce international order.

After World War II, America had the wisdom to shape institutions to keep the peace and support human progress — from NATO and the United Nations, to the World Bank and IMF. These institutions are not perfect, but they have been a force multiplier. They reduce the need for unilateral American action and increase restraint among other nations.

Now, just as the world has changed, this architecture must change as well. At the height of the Cold War, President Kennedy spoke about the need for a peace based upon, "a gradual evolution in human institutions." And evolving these international institutions to meet the demands of today must be a critical part of American leadership.

Now, there are a lot of folks, a lot of skeptics, who often downplay the effectiveness of multilateral action. For them, working through international institutions like the U.N. or respecting international law is a sign of weakness. I think they're wrong. Let me offer just two examples why.

In Ukraine, Russia's recent actions recall the days when Soviet tanks rolled into Eastern Europe. But this isn't the Cold War. Our ability to shape world opinion helped isolate Russia right away. Because of American leadership, the world immediately condemned Russian actions; Europe and the G7 joined us to impose sanctions; NATO reinforced our commitment to Eastern European allies; the IMF is helping to stabilize Ukraine's economy; OSCE monitors brought the eyes of the world to unstable parts of Ukraine. And this mobilization of world opinion and international institutions served as a counterweight to Russian propaganda and Russian troops on the border and armed militias in ski masks. . . .

Similarly, despite frequent warnings from the United States and Israel and others, the Iranian nuclear program steadily advanced for years. But at the beginning of my presidency, we built a coalition that imposed sanctions on the Iranian economy, while extending the hand of diplomacy to the Iranian government. And now we have an opportunity to resolve our differences peacefully. . . .

Keep in mind, not all international norms relate directly to armed conflict. We have a serious problem with cyber-attacks, which is why we're working to shape and enforce rules of the road to secure our networks and our citizens. In the Asia Pacific, we're supporting Southeast Asian nations as they negotiate a code of conduct with China on maritime disputes in the South China Sea. And we're working to resolve these disputes through international law. That spirit of cooperation needs to energize the global effort to combat climate change — a creeping national security crisis that will help shape your time in uniform, as we are called on to respond to refugee flows and natural disasters and conflicts over water and food, which is why next year I intend to make sure America is out front in putting together a global framework to preserve our planet. . . .

I believe in American exceptionalism with every fiber of my being. But what makes us exceptional is not our ability to flout international norms and the rule of law; it is our willingness to affirm them through our actions. And that's why I will continue to push to close Gitmo — because American values and legal traditions do not permit the indefinite detention of people beyond our borders. That's why we're putting in place new restrictions on how America collects and uses intelligence — because we will have fewer partners and be less effective if a perception takes hold that we're conducting surveillance against ordinary citizens. America does not simply stand for stability or the absence of conflict, no matter what the cost. We stand for the more lasting peace that can only come through opportunity and freedom for people everywhere.

Which brings me to the fourth and final element of American leadership: Our willingness to act on behalf of human dignity. America's support for democracy and human rights goes beyond idealism — it is a matter of national security. Democracies are our closest friends and are far less likely to go to war. Economies based on free and open markets perform better and become markets for our goods. Respect for human rights is an antidote to instability and the grievances that fuel violence and terror. . . .

[NSL p. 137. Insert at the end of Note 2.]

Clapper v. Amnesty International USA

United States Supreme Court, 2013
133 S. Ct. 1138

Justice ALITO delivered the opinion of the Court. Section 702 of the Foreign Intelligence Surveillance Act of 1978, 50 U.S.C. §1881a (2006 ed., Supp. V), allows the Attorney General and the Director of National Intelligence to acquire foreign intelligence information by jointly authorizing the surveillance of individuals who are not "United States persons"[1] and are reasonably believed to be located outside the United States. Before doing so, the Attorney General and the Director of National Intelligence normally must obtain the Foreign Intelligence Surveillance Court's approval. Respondents are United States persons whose work, they allege, requires them to engage in sensitive international communications with individuals who[m] they believe are likely targets of surveillance under §1881a. Respondents seek a declaration that §1881a is unconstitutional, as well as an injunction against §1881a-authorized surveillance. The question before us is whether respondents have Article III standing to seek this prospective relief.

Respondents assert that they can establish injury in fact because there is an objectively reasonable likelihood that their communications will be acquired under §1881a at some point in the future. But respondents' theory of *future* injury is too speculative to satisfy the well established requirement that threatened injury must be "certainly impending." *E.g., Whitmore v. Arkansas,* 495 U.S. 149, 158 (1990). And even if respondents could demonstrate that the threatened injury is certainly impending, they still would not be able to establish that this injury is fairly traceable to §1881a. As an alternative argument, respondents contend that they are suffering *present* injury because the risk of §1881a-authorized surveillance already has forced them to take costly and burdensome measures to protect the confidentiality of their international communications. But respondents cannot manufacture standing by choosing to make expenditures based on hypothetical future

---

1. The term "United States person" includes citizens of the United States, aliens admitted for permanent residence, and certain associations and corporations. 50 U.S.C. §1801(i); see §1881(a).

harm that is not certainly impending. We therefore hold that respondents lack Article III standing.

I

A

In 1978, after years of debate, Congress enacted the Foreign Intelligence Surveillance Act (FISA) to authorize and regulate certain governmental electronic surveillance of communications for foreign intelligence purposes. See 50 U.S.C. §1801 *et seq.* . . .

When Congress enacted the FISA Amendments Act of 2008 (FISA Amendments Act), 122 Stat. 2436, it left much of FISA intact, but it "established a new and independent source of intelligence collection authority, beyond that granted in traditional FISA." [1 D. Kris & J. Wilson, National Security Investigations & Prosecutions (2d ed.2012)] §9:11, at 349–350. As relevant here, §702 of FISA, 50 U.S.C. §1881a (2006 ed., Supp. V), which was enacted as part of the FISA Amendments Act, supplements pre-existing FISA authority by creating a new framework under which the Government may seek the FISC's authorization of certain foreign intelligence surveillance targeting the communications of non-U.S. persons located abroad. Unlike traditional FISA surveillance, §1881a does not require the Government to demonstrate probable cause that the target of the electronic surveillance is a foreign power or agent of a foreign power. And, unlike traditional FISA, §1881a does not require the Government to specify the nature and location of each of the particular facilities or places at which the electronic surveillance will occur. . . .

B

Respondents are attorneys and human rights, labor, legal, and media organizations whose work allegedly requires them to engage in sensitive and sometimes privileged telephone and e-mail communications with colleagues, clients, sources, and other individuals located abroad. Respondents believe that some of the people with whom they exchange foreign intelligence information are likely targets of surveillance under §1881a. Specifically, respondents claim that they communicate by telephone and e-mail with people the Government "believes or believed to be associated with terrorist organizations," "people located in geographic areas that are a special focus" of the Government's counterterrorism or diplomatic efforts, and activists who oppose governments that are supported by the United States Government.

Respondents claim that §1881a compromises their ability to locate witnesses, cultivate sources, obtain information, and communicate confidential information to their clients. Respondents also assert that they "have ceased engaging" in certain telephone and e-mail conversations. According to respondents, the threat of surveillance will compel them to travel abroad in order to have in-person conversations. In addition, respondents declare that they have undertaken "costly and burdensome measures" to protect the confidentiality of sensitive communications.

C

On the day when the FISA Amendments Act was enacted, respondents filed this action seeking (1) a declaration that §1881a, on its face, violates the Fourth Amendment, the First Amendment, Article III, and separation-of-powers principles and (2) a permanent injunction against the use of §1881a. . . .

II

Article III of the Constitution limits federal courts' jurisdiction to certain "Cases" and "Controversies." As we have explained, "[n]o principle is more fundamental to the judiciary's proper role in our system of government than the constitutional limitation of federal-court jurisdiction to actual cases or controversies." *DaimlerChrysler Corp. v. Cuno,* 547 U.S. 332, 341 (2006) (internal quotation marks omitted); *Raines v. Byrd,* 521 U.S. 811, 818 (1997); see, *e.g., Summers v. Earth Island Institute,* 555 U.S. 488, 492-493 (2009). "One element of the case-or-controversy requirement" is that plaintiffs "must establish that they have standing to sue." *Raines, supra,* at 818.

The law of Article III standing, which is built on separation-of-powers principles, serves to prevent the judicial process from being used to usurp the powers of the political branches. *Summers, supra,* at 492-493. In keeping with the purpose of this doctrine, "[o]ur standing inquiry has been especially rigorous when reaching the merits of the dispute would force us to decide whether an action taken by one of the other two branches of the Federal Government was unconstitutional." *Raines, supra,* at 819-820. "Relaxation of standing requirements is directly

related to the expansion of judicial power," *United States v. Richardson,*
418 U.S. 166, 188 (1974) (Powell, J., concurring), and we have often
found a lack of standing in cases in which the Judiciary has been
requested to review actions of the political branches in the fields of
intelligence gathering and foreign affairs, see, *e.g., Richardson, supra,* at
167-170 (plaintiff lacked standing to challenge the constitutionality of a
statute permitting the Central Intelligence Agency to account for its
expenditures solely on the certificate of the CIA Director); [*Schlesinger
v. Reservists Comm. to Stop the War,* 418 U.S. 208 (1974)], at 209-211
(plaintiffs lacked standing to challenge the Armed Forces Reserve
membership of Members of Congress); *Laird v. Tatum,* 408 U.S. 1, 11-
16 (1972) (plaintiffs lacked standing to challenge an Army intelligence-
gathering program).

   To establish Article III standing, an injury must be "concrete,
particularized, and actual or imminent; fairly traceable to the challenged
action; and redressable by a favorable ruling." *Monsanto Co. v. Geertson
Seed Farms,* 561 U.S. ——, —— (2010) (slip op., at 7). "Although
imminence is concededly a somewhat elastic concept, it cannot be
stretched beyond its purpose, which is to ensure that the alleged injury is
not too speculative for Article III purposes — that the injury is *certainly*
impending." *Id.,* at 565, n.2 (internal quotation marks omitted). Thus, we
have repeatedly reiterated that "threatened injury must be *certainly
impending* to constitute injury in fact," and that "[a]llegations of
possible future injury" are not sufficient. *Whitmore,* 495 U.S., at 158
(emphasis added; internal quotation marks omitted).

III

A

   Respondents assert that they can establish injury in fact that is fairly
traceable to §1881a because there is an objectively reasonable likelihood
that their communications with their foreign contacts will be intercepted
under §1881a at some point in the future. This argument fails. As an
initial matter, the . . . "objectively reasonable likelihood" standard is
inconsistent with our requirement that "threatened injury must be
certainly impending to constitute injury in fact." *Whitmore, supra,* at 158
(internal quotation marks omitted). Furthermore, respondents' argument
rests on their highly speculative fear that: (1) the Government will
decide to target the communications of non-U.S. persons with whom

they communicate; (2) in doing so, the Government will choose to invoke its authority under §1881a rather than utilizing another method of surveillance; (3) the Article III judges who serve on the Foreign Intelligence Surveillance Court will conclude that the Government's proposed surveillance procedures satisfy §1881a's many safeguards and are consistent with the Fourth Amendment; (4) the Government will succeed in intercepting the communications of respondents' contacts; and (5) respondents will be parties to the particular communications that the Government intercepts. As discussed below, respondents' theory of standing, which relies on a highly attenuated chain of possibilities, does not satisfy the requirement that threatened injury must be certainly impending. Moreover, even if respondents could demonstrate injury in fact, the second link in the above-described chain of contingencies — which amounts to mere speculation about whether surveillance would be under §1881a or some other authority — shows that respondents cannot satisfy the requirement that any injury in fact must be fairly traceable to §1881a.

First, it is speculative whether the Government will imminently target communications to which respondents are parties. Section 1881a expressly provides that respondents, who are U.S. persons, cannot be targeted for surveillance under §1881a. Accordingly, it is no surprise that respondents fail to offer any evidence that their communications have been monitored under §1881a, a failure that substantially under-mines their standing theory. Indeed, respondents do not even allege that the Government has sought the FISC's approval for surveillance of their communications. Accordingly, respondents' theory necessarily rests on their assertion that the Government will target *other individuals* — namely, their foreign contacts.

Yet respondents have no actual knowledge of the Government's §1881a targeting practices. Instead, respondents merely speculate and make assumptions about whether their communications with their foreign contacts will be acquired under §1881a. For example, journalist Christopher Hedges states: "I have no choice but to *assume* that any of my international communications *may* be subject to government surveillance, and I have to make decisions . . . in light of that *assumption*." . . . "The party invoking federal jurisdiction bears the burden of establishing" standing — and, at the summary judgment stage, such a party "can no longer rest on . . . 'mere allegations,' but must 'set forth' by affidavit or other evidence 'specific facts.'" [*Lujan v. Defenders of Wildlife,* 504 U.S. 555 (1992)], at 561. Respondents, however, have set forth no specific facts demonstrating that the communications of their foreign contacts will be targeted. Moreover, because §1881a at most *authorizes* — but does not *mandate* or *direct* — the surveillance that respondents fear, respondents' allegations are necessarily conjectural. Simply put, respondents can only speculate as to how the Attorney General and the Director of National Intelligence will exercise their discretion in determining which communications to target.[4]

Second, even if respondents could demonstrate that the targeting of their foreign contacts is imminent, respondents can only speculate as to whether the Government will seek to use §1881a authorized surveillance (rather than other methods) to do so. The Government has numerous other methods of conducting surveillance, none of which is challenged here. Even after the enactment of the FISA Amendments Act, for example, the Government may still conduct electronic surveillance of persons abroad under the older provisions of FISA so long as it satisfies the applicable requirements, including a demonstration of probable cause to believe that the person is a foreign power or agent of a foreign power. See §1805. The Government may also obtain information from the intelligence services of foreign nations. And, although we do not reach the question, the Government contends that it can conduct FISA-exempt human and technical surveillance programs that are governed by Executive Order 12333. See Exec. Order No. 12333, §§1.4, 2.1-2.5. Even if respondents could demonstrate that their foreign contacts will imminently be targeted — indeed, even if they could show that

---

4. It was suggested at oral argument that the Government could help resolve the standing inquiry by disclosing to a court, perhaps through an *in camera* proceeding, (1) whether it is intercepting respondents' communications and (2) what targeting or minimization procedures it is using. This suggestion is puzzling. As an initial matter, it is *respondents'* burden to prove their standing by pointing to specific facts, *Lujan v. Defenders of Wildlife*, 504 U.S. 555, 561 (1992), not the Government's burden to disprove standing by revealing details of its surveillance priorities. Moreover, this type of hypothetical disclosure proceeding would allow a terrorist (or his attorney) to determine whether he is currently under U.S. surveillance simply by filing a lawsuit challenging the Government's surveillance program. Even if the terrorist's attorney were to comply with a protective order prohibiting him from sharing the Government's disclosures with his client, the court's postdisclosure decision about whether to dismiss the suit for lack of standing would surely signal to the terrorist whether his name was on the list of surveillance targets.

interception of their own communications will imminently occur — they would still need to show that their injury is fairly traceable to §1881a. But, because respondents can only speculate as to whether any (asserted) interception would be under §1881a or some other authority, they cannot satisfy the "fairly traceable" requirement.

Third, even if respondents could show that the Government will seek the Foreign Intelligence Surveillance Court's authorization to acquire the communications of respondents' foreign contacts under §1881a, respondents can only speculate as to whether that court will authorize such surveillance. In the past, we have been reluctant to endorse standing theories that require guesswork as to how independent decisionmakers will exercise their judgment. . . .

Fourth, even if the Government were to obtain the Foreign Intelligence Surveillance Court's approval to target respondents' foreign contacts under §1881a, it is unclear whether the Government would succeed in acquiring the communications of respondents' foreign contacts. And fifth, even if the Government were to conduct surveillance of respondents' foreign contacts, respondents can only speculate as to whether *their own communications* with their foreign contacts would be incidentally acquired.

In sum, respondents' speculative chain of possibilities does not establish that injury based on potential future surveillance is certainly impending or is fairly traceable to §1881a.[5]

---

5. Our cases do not uniformly require plaintiffs to demonstrate that it is literally certain that the harms they identify will come about. In some instances, we have found standing based on a "substantial risk" that the harm will occur, which may prompt plaintiffs to reasonably incur costs to mitigate or avoid that harm. *Monsanto Co. v. Geertson Seed Farms,* 561 U.S. ——, —— (2010) (slip op., at 11–12). But to the extent that the "substantial risk" standard is relevant and is distinct from the "clearly impending" requirement, respondents fall short of even that standard, in light of the attenuated chain of inferences necessary to find harm here. In addition, plaintiffs bear the burden of pleading and proving concrete facts showing that the defendant's actual action has caused the substantial risk of harm. Plaintiffs cannot rely on speculation about "'the unfettered choices made by independent actors not before the court.'" *Defenders of Wildlife,* 504 U.S., at 562.

B

Respondents' alternative argument — namely, that they can establish standing based on the measures that they have undertaken to avoid §1881a-authorized surveillance — fares no better. Respondents assert that they are suffering ongoing injuries that are fairly traceable to §1881a because the risk of surveillance under §1881a requires them to take costly and burdensome measures to protect the confidentiality of their communications. Respondents claim, for instance, that the threat of surveillance sometimes compels them to avoid certain e-mail and phone conversations, to "tal[k] in generalities rather than specifics," or to travel so that they can have in-person conversations. . . .

. . . Respondents' contention that they have standing because they incurred certain costs as a reasonable reaction to a risk of harm is unavailing — because the harm respondents seek to avoid is not certainly impending. In other words, respondents cannot manufacture standing merely by inflicting harm on themselves based on their fears of hypothetical future harm that is not certainly impending. See *Pennsylvania v. New Jersey,* 426 U.S. 660, 664 (1976) (*per curiam*). Any ongoing injuries that respondents are suffering are not fairly traceable to §1881a. . . .

Another reason that respondents' present injuries are not fairly traceable to §1881a is that [under FISA authority that predated §1881a], they had a similar incentive to engage in many of the countermeasures that they are now taking. . . .

Because respondents do not face a threat of certainly impending interception under §1881a, the costs that they have incurred to avoid surveillance are simply the product of their fear of surveillance, and our decision in *Laird* makes it clear that such a fear is insufficient to create standing. See 408 U.S., at 10–15. The plaintiffs in *Laird* argued that their exercise of First Amendment rights was being "chilled by the mere existence, without more, of [the Army's] investigative and data-gathering activity." *Id.,* at 10. While acknowledging that prior cases had held that constitutional violations may arise from the chilling effect of "regulations that fall short of a direct prohibition against the exercise of First Amendment rights," the Court declared that none of those cases involved a "chilling effect aris[ing] merely from the individual's knowledge that a governmental agency was engaged in certain activities or from the individual's concomitant fear that, armed with the fruits of those activities, the agency might in the future take some *other* and additional action detrimental to that individual." *Id.,* at 11. Because "[a]llegations of a subjective 'chill' are not an adequate substitute for a claim of specific present objective harm or a threat of specific future harm," *id.,* at 13–14, the plaintiffs in *Laird* [lacked] — and respondents here [lack —] standing.

For the reasons discussed above, respondents' self-inflicted injuries are not fairly traceable to the Government's purported activities under §1881a, and their subjective fear of surveillance does not give rise to standing.

IV . . .

B

Respondents also suggest that they should be held to have standing because otherwise the constitutionality of §1881a could not be challenged. It would be wrong, they maintain, to "insulate the government's surveillance activities from meaningful judicial review." Respondents' suggestion is both legally and factually incorrect. First, "'[t]he assumption that if respondents have no standing to sue, no one would have standing, is not a reason to find standing.'" [*Valley Forge Christian College v. Americans United for Separation of Church and State, Inc.,* 454 U.S. 464 (1982)], at 489.

Second, our holding today by no means insulates §1881a from judicial review. . . . Congress created a comprehensive scheme in which the Foreign Intelligence Surveillance Court evaluates the Government's certifications, targeting procedures, and minimization procedures — including assessing whether the targeting and minimization procedures comport with the Fourth Amendment. §§1881a(a), (c)(1), (i)(2), (i)(3). Any dissatisfaction that respondents may have about the Foreign Intelligence Surveillance Court's rulings — or the congressional delineation of that court's role — is irrelevant to our standing analysis.

Additionally, if the Government intends to use or disclose information obtained or derived from a §1881a acquisition in judicial or administrative proceedings, it must provide advance notice of its intent, and the affected person may challenge the lawfulness of the acquisition. §§1806(c), 1806(e), 1881e(a) (2006 ed. and Supp. V). Thus, if the Government were to prosecute one of respondent-attorney's foreign clients using §1881a-authorized surveillance, the Government would be required to make a disclosure. Although the foreign client might not have a viable Fourth Amendment claim, see, *e.g., United States v. Verdugo-Urquidez,* 494 U.S. 259, 261 (1990), it is possible that the monitoring of the target's conversations with his or her attorney would provide grounds for a claim of standing on the part of the attorney. Such an attorney would certainly have a stronger evidentiary basis for establishing standing than do respondents in the present case. In such a situation, unlike in the present case, it would at least be clear that the Government had acquired the foreign client's communications using §1881a-authorized surveillance.

Finally, any electronic communications service provider that the Government directs to assist in §1881a surveillance may challenge the lawfulness of that directive before the FISC. §1881a(h)(4), (6). Indeed, at the behest of a service provider, the Foreign Intelligence Surveillance Court of Review previously analyzed the constitutionality of electronic surveillance directives issued pursuant to a now-expired set of FISA amendments. See *In re Directives Pursuant to Section 105B of Foreign Intelligence Surveillance Act,* 551 F.3d 1004, 1006-1016 (2008) (holding that the provider had standing and that the directives were constitutional). . . .

We hold that respondents lack Article III standing because they cannot demonstrate that the future injury they purportedly fear is certainly impending and because they cannot manufacture standing by incurring costs in anticipation of non-imminent harm. . . .

Justice BREYER, with whom Justice GINSBURG, Justice SOTOMAYOR, and Justice KAGAN join, dissenting. The plaintiffs' standing depends upon the likelihood that the Government, acting under the authority of 50 U.S.C. §1881a (2006 ed., Supp. V), will harm them by intercepting at least some of their private, foreign, telephone, or e-mail conversations. In my view, this harm is not "speculative." Indeed it is as likely to take place as are most future events that commonsense inference and ordinary knowledge of human nature tell us will happen. This Court has often found the occurrence of similar future events sufficiently certain to support standing. I dissent from the Court's contrary conclusion. . . .

III

Several considerations, based upon the record along with common-sense inferences, convince me that there is a very high likelihood that Government, *acting under the authority of §1881a,* will intercept at least some of the communications just described. First, the plaintiffs have engaged, and continue to engage, in electronic communications of a kind that the 2008 amendment, but not the prior Act, authorizes the Government to intercept. These communications include discussions with family members of those detained at Guantanamo, friends and acquaintances of those persons, and investigators, experts and others with knowledge of circumstances related to terrorist activities. These persons are foreigners located outside the United States. They are not "foreign power[s]" or "agent[s] of . . . foreign power[s]." And the plaintiffs state that they exchange with these persons "foreign intelligence information," defined to include information that "relates to" "international terrorism" and "the national defense or the security of the United States." See 50 U.S.C. §1801 (2006 ed. and Supp. V).

Second, the plaintiffs have a strong *motive* to engage in, and the Government has a strong *motive* to listen to, conversations of the kind described. A lawyer representing a client normally seeks to learn the circumstances surrounding the crime (or the civil wrong) of which the client is accused. . . . Journalists and human rights workers have strong similar motives to conduct conversations of this kind.

At the same time, the Government has a strong motive to conduct surveillance of conversations that contain material of this kind. The Government, after all, seeks to learn as much as it can reasonably learn about suspected terrorists (such as those detained at Guantanamo), as well as about their contacts and activities, along with those of friends and family members. And the Government is motivated to do so, not simply by the desire to help convict those whom the Government believes guilty, but also by the critical, overriding need to protect America from terrorism.

Third, the Government's *past behavior* shows that it has sought, and hence will in all likelihood continue to seek, information about alleged terrorists and detainees through means that include surveillance of electronic communications. As just pointed out, plaintiff Scott McKay states that the Government (under the authority of the pre–2008 law) "intercepted some 10,000 telephone calls and 20,000 email communications involving [his client] Mr. Al–Hussayen."

Fourth, the Government has the *capacity* to conduct electronic surveillance of the kind at issue. . . .

Of course, to exercise this capacity the Government must have intelligence court authorization. But the Government rarely files requests that fail to meet the statutory criteria. . . .

The upshot is that (1) similarity of content, (2) strong motives, (3) prior behavior, and (4) capacity all point to a very strong likelihood that the Government will intercept at least some of the plaintiffs' communications, including some that the 2008 amendment, §1881a, but not the pre-2008 Act, authorizes the Government to intercept. . . .

Consequently, we need only assume that the Government is doing its job (to find out about, and combat, terrorism) in order to conclude that there is a high probability that the Government will intercept at least some electronic communication to which at least some of the plaintiffs are parties. The majority is wrong when it describes the harm threatened plaintiffs as "speculative."

IV

A

The majority more plausibly says that the plaintiffs have failed to show that the threatened harm is *"certainly impending."* But, as the majority appears to concede, *certainty* is not, and never has been, the touchstone of standing. The future is inherently uncertain. Yet federal courts frequently entertain actions for injunctions and for declaratory relief aimed at preventing future activities that are reasonably likely or highly likely, but not absolutely certain, to take place. And that degree of certainty is all that is needed to support standing here. The Court's use of the term "certainly impending" is not to the contrary. Sometimes the Court has used the phrase "certainly impending" as if the phrase described a *sufficient,* rather than a *necessary,* condition for jurisdiction. See *Pennsylvania v. West Virginia,* 262 U.S. 553, 593 (1923) ("If the injury is certainly impending that is enough"). On other occasions, it has used the phrase as if it concerned *when,* not *whether,* an alleged injury would occur. Thus, in *Lujan,* 504 U.S., at 564, n.2, the Court considered a threatened future injury that consisted of harm that plaintiffs would suffer when they "soon" visited a government project area that (they claimed) would suffer environmental damage. . . .

On still other occasions, recognizing that "'imminence' is concededly a somewhat elastic concept," *Lujan, supra,* at 565, n.2, the Court has referred to, or used (sometimes along with "certainly impending") other phrases such as "reasonable probability" that suggest less than absolute, or literal certainty. See *Babbitt, supra,* at 298 (plaintiff "must demonstrate a *realistic danger* of sustaining a direct injury" (emphasis added)). Taken together the case law uses the word "certainly" as if it emphasizes, rather than literally defines, the immediately following term "impending."

B . . .

3

The majority cannot find support in cases that use the words "certainly impending" to *deny* standing. . . .

4

In sum, as the Court concedes, the word "certainly" in the phrase "certainly impending" does not refer to absolute certainty. As our case law demonstrates, what the Constitution requires is something more akin to "reasonable probability" or "high probability." The use of some such standard is all that is necessary here to ensure the actual concrete injury that the Constitution demands. The . . . standard is readily met in this case. . . .

_____

[NSL p. 195, insert after *Sosa v. Alvarez-Machain*. CTL p. 839, insert after Note 11.]

Kiobel v. Royal Dutch Petroleum Co.
Supreme Court of the United States, 2013
133 S. Ct. 1659

Chief Justice ROBERTS delivered the opinion of the Court. Petitioners, a group of Nigerian nationals residing in the United States, filed suit in federal court against certain Dutch, British, and Nigerian corporations. Petitioners sued under the Alien Tort Statute, 28 U.S.C. §1350, alleging that the corporations aided and abetted the Nigerian Government in committing violations of the law of nations in Nigeria. The question presented is whether and under what circumstances courts may recognize a cause of action under the Alien Tort Statute, for violations of the law of nations occurring within the territory of a sovereign other than the United States.

I

Petitioners were residents of Ogoniland, an area of 250 square miles located in the Niger delta area of Nigeria and populated by roughly half a million people. When the complaint was filed, respondents Royal Dutch Petroleum Company and Shell Transport and Trading Company, p.l.c., were holding companies incorporated in the Netherlands and England, respectively. Their joint subsidiary, respondent Shell Petroleum Development Company of Nigeria, Ltd. (SPDC), was incorporated in Nigeria, and engaged in oil exploration and production in Ogoniland. According to the complaint, after concerned residents of Ogoniland began protesting the environmental effects of SPDC's practices, respondents enlisted the Nigerian Government to violently suppress the burgeoning demonstrations. Throughout the early 1990's, the complaint alleges, Nigerian military and police forces attacked Ogoni villages, beating, raping, killing, and arresting residents and destroying or looting property. Petitioners further allege that respondents aided and abetted these atrocities by, among other things, providing the Nigerian forces with food, transportation, and compensation, as well as by allowing the Nigerian military to use respondents' property as a staging ground for attacks.

Following the alleged atrocities, petitioners moved to the United States where they have been granted political asylum and now reside as legal residents. They filed suit in the United States District Court for the Southern District of New York, alleging jurisdiction under the Alien Tort Statute and requesting relief under customary international law. The ATS provides, in full, that "[t]he district courts shall have original jurisdiction of any civil action by an alien for a tort only, committed in violation of the law of nations or a treaty of the United States." 28 U.S.C. §1350. According to petitioners, respondents violated the law of nations by aiding and abetting the Nigerian Government in committing (1) extrajudicial killings; (2) crimes against humanity; (3) torture and cruel treatment; (4) arbitrary arrest and detention; (5) violations of the rights to life, liberty, security, and association; (6) forced exile; and (7) property destruction. The District Court dismissed [portions of the complaint]. . . .

The Second Circuit dismissed the entire complaint, reasoning that the law of nations does not recognize corporate liability. 621 F.3d 111 (2010). We granted certiorari to consider that question. 565 U.S. —— (2011). After oral argument, we directed the parties to file supplemental briefs addressing an additional question: "Whether and under what circumstances the [ATS] allows courts to recognize a cause of action for violations of the law of nations occurring within the territory of a sovereign other than the United States." 565 U.S. —— (2012). We heard oral argument again and now affirm the judgment below, based on our answer to the second question.

II

Passed as part of the Judiciary Act of 1789, the ATS was invoked twice in the late 18th century, but then only once more over the next 167 years. Act of Sept. 24, 1789, §9, 1 Stat 77; see *Moxon v. The Fanny,* 17 F. Cas. 942 (No. 9,895) (DC Pa. 1793); *Bolchos v. Darrel,* 3 F. Cas. 810 (No. 1,607) (DC SC 1795); *O'Reilly de Camara v. Brooke,* 209 U.S. 45 (1908); *Khedivial Line, S.A.E. v. Seafarers' Int'l Union,* 278 F.2d 49, 51–52 (C.A.2 1960) (*per curiam*). The statute provides district courts with jurisdiction to hear certain claims, but does not expressly provide any causes of action. We held in *Sosa v. Alvarez-Machain,* 542 U.S. 692, 714 (2004), however, that the First Congress did not intend the provision to be "stillborn." The grant of jurisdiction is instead "best read as having been enacted on the understanding that the common law would provide a cause of action for [a] modest number of international law violations." *Id.,* at 724. We thus held that federal courts may "recognize private claims [for such violations] under federal common law." *Id.,* at 732. The Court in *Sosa* rejected the plaintiff's claim in that case for "arbitrary arrest and detention," on the ground that it failed to state a violation of the law of nations with the requisite "definite content and acceptance among civilized nations." *Id.,* at 699, 732.

The question here is not whether petitioners have stated a proper claim under the ATS, but whether a claim may reach conduct occurring in the territory of a foreign sovereign. Respondents contend that claims under the ATS do not, relying primarily on a canon of statutory interpretation known as the presumption against extraterritorial application. That canon provides that "[w]hen a statute gives no clear indication of an extraterritorial application, it has none," *Morrison v. National Australia Bank Ltd.,* 561 U.S. ——, —— (2010), and reflects the "presumption that United States law governs domestically but does not rule the world," *Microsoft Corp. v. AT & T Corp.,* 550 U.S. 437, 454 (2007).

This presumption "serves to protect against unintended clashes between our laws and those of other nations which could result in international discord." *EEOC v. Arabian American Oil Co.,* 499 U.S. 244, 248 (1991) (*Aramco*). As this Court has explained:

> "For us to run interference in . . . a delicate field of international relations there must be present the affirmative intention of the Congress clearly expressed. It alone has the facilities necessary to make fairly such an important policy decision where the possibilities of international discord are so evident and retaliative action so certain." *Benz v. Compania Naviera Hidalgo, S. A.,* 353 U.S. 138 (1957). The presumption against extraterritorial application helps ensure that the Judiciary does not erroneously adopt an interpretation of U.S. law that carries foreign policy consequences not clearly intended by the political branches.

We typically apply the presumption to discern whether an Act of Congress regulating conduct applies abroad. See, *e.g., Aramco, supra,* at 246 ("These cases present the issue whether Title VII applies extraterritorially to regulate the employment practices of United States employers who employ United States citizens abroad"); *Morrison, supra,* at —— (noting that the question of extraterritorial application was a "merits question," not a question of jurisdiction). The ATS, on the other hand, is "strictly jurisdictional." *Sosa,* 542 U.S., at 713. It does not directly regulate conduct or afford relief. It instead allows federal courts to recognize certain causes of action based on sufficiently definite norms of international law. But we think the principles underlying the canon of interpretation similarly constrain courts considering causes of action that may be brought under the ATS.

Indeed, the danger of unwarranted judicial interference in the conduct of foreign policy is magnified in the context of the ATS, because the question is not what Congress has done but instead what courts may do. This Court in *Sosa* repeatedly stressed the need for judicial caution in considering which claims could be brought under the ATS, in light of foreign policy concerns. As the Court explained, "the potential [foreign policy] implications . . . of recognizing . . . causes [under the ATS] should make courts particularly wary of impinging on the discretion of the Legislative and Executive Branches in managing foreign affairs." *Id.,* at 727; see also *id.,* at 727-728 ("Since many attempts by federal courts to craft remedies for the violation of new norms of international law would raise risks of adverse foreign policy consequences, they should be undertaken, if at all, with great caution");

id., at 727 ("[T]he possible collateral consequences of making international rules privately actionable argue for judicial caution"). These concerns, which are implicated in any case arising under the ATS, are all the more pressing when the question is whether a cause of action under the ATS reaches conduct within the territory of another sovereign.

These concerns are not diminished by the fact that *Sosa* limited federal courts to recognizing causes of action only for alleged violations of international law norms that are "'specific, universal, and obligatory.'" *Id.,* at 732 (quoting *In re Estate of Marcos, Human Rights Litigation,* 25 F.3d 1467, 1475 (C.A.9 1994)). As demonstrated by Congress's enactment of the Torture Victim Protection Act of 1991, 106 Stat. 73, note following 28 U.S.C. §1350, identifying such a norm is only the beginning of defining a cause of action. See *id.,* §3 (providing detailed definitions for extrajudicial killing and torture); *id.,* §2 (specifying who may be liable, creating a rule of exhaustion, and establishing a statute of limitations). Each of these decisions carries with it significant foreign policy implications.

The principles underlying the presumption against extraterritoriality thus constrain courts exercising their power under the ATS.

III

Petitioners contend that even if the presumption applies, the text, history, and purposes of the ATS rebut it for causes of action brought under that statute. It is true that Congress, even in a jurisdictional provision, can indicate that it intends federal law to apply to conduct occurring abroad. See, *e.g.,* 18 U.S.C. §1091(e) (2006 ed., Supp. V) (providing jurisdiction over the offense of genocide "regardless of where the offense is committed" if the alleged offender is, among other things, "present in the United States"). But to rebut the presumption, the ATS would need to evince a "clear indication of extraterritoriality." *Morrison,* 561 U.S., at ——. It does not.

To begin, nothing in the text of the statute suggests that Congress intended causes of action recognized under it to have extraterritorial reach. The ATS covers actions by aliens for violations of the law of nations, but that does not imply extraterritorial reach — such violations affecting aliens can occur either within or outside the United States. Nor does the fact that the text reaches "*any* civil action" suggest application to torts committed abroad; it is well established that generic terms like "any" or "every" do not rebut the presumption against extraterritoriality.

Petitioners make much of the fact that the ATS provides jurisdiction over civil actions for "torts" in violation of the law of nations. They claim that in using that word, the First Congress "necessarily meant to provide for jurisdiction over extraterritorial transitory torts that could arise on foreign soil." For support, they cite the common-law doctrine that allowed courts to assume jurisdiction over such "transitory torts," including actions for personal injury, arising abroad. See *Mostyn v. Fabrigas,* 1 Cowp. 161, 177, 98 Eng. Rep. 1021, 1030 (1774) (Mansfield, L.) ("[A]ll actions of a transitory nature that arise abroad may be laid as happening in an English county"); *Dennick v. Railroad Co.,* 103 U.S. 11, 18 (1881) ("Wherever, by either the common law or the statute law of a State, a right of action has become fixed and a legal liability incurred, that liability may be enforced and the right of action pursued in any court which has jurisdiction of such matters and can obtain jurisdiction of the parties").

Under the transitory torts doctrine, however, "the only justification for allowing a party to recover when the cause of action arose in another civilized jurisdiction is a well founded belief that it was a cause of action in that place." *Cuba R. Co. v. Crosby,* 222 U.S. 473, 479 (1912) (majority opinion of Holmes, J.). The question under *Sosa* is not whether a federal court has jurisdiction to entertain a cause of action provided by foreign or even international law. The question is instead whether the court has authority to recognize a cause of action under U.S. law to enforce a norm of international law. The reference to "tort" does not demonstrate that the First Congress "necessarily meant" for those causes of action to reach conduct in the territory of a foreign sovereign. In the end, nothing in the text of the ATS evinces the requisite clear indication of extraterritoriality.

Nor does the historical background against which the ATS was enacted overcome the presumption against application to conduct in the territory of another sovereign. See *Morrison, supra,* at —— (noting that "[a]ssuredly context can be consulted" in determining whether a cause of action applies abroad). We explained in *Sosa* that when Congress passed the ATS, "three principal offenses against the law of nations" had been identified by Blackstone: violation of safe conducts, infringement of the rights of ambassadors, and piracy. 542 U.S., at 723, 724; see 4 W. Blackstone, Commentaries on the Laws of England 68 (1769). The first two offenses have no necessary extraterritorial application. Indeed, Blackstone — in describing them — did so in terms of conduct occurring within the forum nation. See *ibid.* (describing the right of safe conducts for those "who are here"); 1 *id.,* at 251 (1765) (explaining that safe conducts grant a member of one society "a right to intrude into another"); *id.,* at 245-248 (recognizing the king's power to "receiv[e] ambassadors at home" and detailing their rights in the state "wherein they are appointed to reside").

Two notorious episodes involving violations of the law of nations occurred in the United States shortly before passage of the ATS. Each concerned the rights of ambassadors, and each involved conduct within the Union. In 1784, a French adventurer verbally and physically assaulted Francis Barbe Marbois — the Secretary of the French Legion — in Philadelphia. The assault led the French Minister Plenipotentiary to lodge a formal protest with the Continental Congress and threaten to leave the country unless an adequate remedy were provided. *Respublica v. De Longschamps,* 1 Dall. 111 (O.T. Phila.1784); *Sosa, supra,* at 716-717, and n.11. And in 1787, a New York constable entered the Dutch Ambassador's house and arrested one of his domestic servants. See Casto, The Federal Courts' Protective Jurisdiction over Torts Committed in Violation of the Law of Nations, 18 Conn. L. Rev. 467, 494 (1986). At the request of Secretary of Foreign Affairs John Jay, the Mayor of New York City arrested the constable in turn, but cautioned that because "'neither Congress nor our [State] Legislature have yet passed any act respecting a breach of the privileges of Ambassadors,'" the extent of any available relief would depend on the common law. See Bradley, The Alien Tort Statute and Article III, 42 Va. J. Int'l L. 587, 641-642 (2002) (quoting 3 Dept. of State, The Diplomatic Correspondence of the United States of America 447 (1837)). The two cases in which the ATS was invoked shortly after its passage also concerned conduct within the territory of the United States. See *Bolchos,* 3 F. Cas. 810 (wrongful seizure of slaves from a vessel while in port in the United States); *Moxon,* 17 F. Cas. 942 (wrongful seizure in United States territorial waters).

These prominent contemporary examples — immediately before and after passage of the ATS — provide no support for the proposition that Congress expected causes of action to be brought under the statute for violations of the law of nations occurring abroad.

The third example of a violation of the law of nations familiar to the Congress that enacted the ATS was piracy. Piracy typically occurs on the high seas, beyond the territorial jurisdiction of the United States or any other country. See 4 Blackstone, *supra,* at 72 ("The offence of piracy, by common law, consists of committing those acts of robbery and depredation upon the high seas, which, if committed upon land, would have amounted to felony there"). This Court has generally treated the high seas the same as foreign soil for purposes of the presumption against extraterritorial application. See, *e.g., Sale v. Haitian Centers Council, Inc.,* 509 U.S. 155, 173-174 (1993) (declining to apply a provision of the Immigration and Nationality Act to conduct occurring on the high seas); *Argentine Republic v. Amerada Hess Shipping Corp.,* 488 U.S. 428, 440 (1989) (declining to apply a provision of the Foreign Sovereign Immunities Act of 1976 to the high seas). Petitioners contend that because Congress surely intended the ATS to provide jurisdiction for actions against pirates, it necessarily anticipated the statute would apply to conduct occurring abroad.

Applying U.S. law to pirates, however, does not typically impose the sovereign will of the United States onto conduct occurring within the territorial jurisdiction of another sovereign, and therefore carries less direct foreign policy consequences. Pirates were fair game wherever found, by any nation, because they generally did not operate within any jurisdiction. See 4 Blackstone, *supra,* at 71. We do not think that the existence of a cause of action against them is a sufficient basis for concluding that other causes of action under the ATS reach conduct that does occur within the territory of another sovereign; pirates may well be a category unto themselves. See *Morrison,* 561 U.S., at ——— ("[W]hen a statute provides for some extraterritorial application, the presumption against extraterritoriality operates to limit that provision to its terms"). . . .

Finally, there is no indication that the ATS was passed to make the United States a uniquely hospitable forum for the enforcement of international norms. As Justice Story put it, "No nation has ever yet pretended to be the custos morum of the whole world. . . ." *United States v. The La Jeune Eugenie,* 26 F. Cas. 832, 847 (No. 15,551) (CC. Mass. 1822). It is implausible to suppose that the First Congress wanted their fledgling Republic — struggling to receive international recognition — to be the first. Indeed, the parties offer no evidence that any nation, meek or mighty, presumed to do such a thing.

The United States was, however, embarrassed by its potential inability to provide judicial relief to foreign officials injured in the United States. Bradley, 42 Va. J. Int'l L., at 641. Such offenses against ambassadors violated the law of nations, "and if not adequately redressed could rise to an issue of war." *Sosa,* 542 U.S., at 715. The ATS ensured that the United States could provide a forum for adjudicating such incidents. See *Sosa, supra,* at 715-718, and n.11. Nothing about this historical context suggests that Congress also intended federal common law under the ATS to provide a cause of action for conduct occurring in the territory of another sovereign.

Indeed, far from avoiding diplomatic strife, providing such a cause of action could have generated it. Recent experience bears this out. See *Doe v. Exxon Mobil Corp.*, 654 F.3d 11, 77-78 (C.A.D.C. 2011) (Kavanaugh, J., dissenting in part) (listing recent objections to extraterritorial applications of the ATS by Canada, Germany, Indonesia, Papua New Guinea, South Africa, Switzerland, and the United Kingdom). Moreover, accepting petitioners' view would imply that other nations, also applying the law of nations, could hale our citizens into their courts for alleged violations of the law of nations occurring in the United States, or anywhere else in the world. The presumption against extraterritoriality guards against our courts triggering such serious foreign policy consequences, and instead defers such decisions, quite appropriately, to the political branches.

We therefore conclude that the presumption against extraterritoriality applies to claims under the ATS, and that nothing in the statute rebuts that presumption. "[T]here is no clear indication of extraterritoriality here," *Morrison*, 561 U.S., at ——, and petitioners' case seeking relief for violations of the law of nations occurring outside the United States is barred.

IV

On these facts, all the relevant conduct took place outside the United States. And even where the claims touch and concern the territory of the United States, they must do so with sufficient force to displace the presumption against extraterritorial application. See *Morrison*, 561 U.S. ——. Corporations are often present in many countries, and it would reach too far to say that mere corporate presence suffices. If Congress were to determine otherwise, a statute more specific than the ATS would be required.

The judgment of the Court of Appeals is affirmed.

It is so ordered.

Justice KENNEDY, concurring. The opinion for the Court is careful to leave open a number of significant questions regarding the reach and interpretation of the Alien Tort Statute. In my view that is a proper disposition. Many serious concerns with respect to human rights abuses committed abroad have been addressed by Congress in statutes such as the Torture Victim Protection Act of 1991 (TVPA), 106 Stat. 73, note following 28 U.S.C. §1350, and that class of cases will be determined in the future according to the detailed statutory scheme Congress has enacted. Other cases may arise with allegations of serious violations of international law principles protecting persons, cases covered neither by the TVPA nor by the reasoning and holding of today's case; and in those disputes the proper implementation of the presumption against extraterritorial application may require some further elaboration and explanation.

Justice ALITO, with whom Justice THOMAS joins, concurring. I concur in the judgment and join the opinion of the Court as far as it goes. Specifically, I agree that when Alien Tort Statute (ATS) "claims touch and concern the territory of the United States, they must do so with sufficient force to displace the presumption against extraterritorial application." *Ante,* at 14. This formulation obviously leaves much unanswered, and perhaps there is wisdom in the Court's preference for this narrow approach. I write separately to set out the broader standard that leads me to the conclusion that this case falls within the scope of the presumption.

In *Morrison v. National Australia Bank Ltd.,* 561 U.S. —— (2010), we explained that "the presumption against extraterritorial application would be a craven watchdog indeed if it retreated to its kennel whenever *some* domestic activity is involved in the case." *Id.,* at ——. We also reiterated that a cause of action falls outside the scope of the presumption — and thus is not barred by the presumption — only if the event or relationship that was "the 'focus' of congressional concern" under the relevant statute takes place within the United States. *Ibid.* (quoting *EEOC v. Arabian American Oil Co.,* 499 U.S. 244, 255 (1991)). For example, because "the focus of the [Securities] Exchange Act [of 1934] is not upon the place where the deception originated, but upon purchases and sales of securities in the United States," we held in *Morrison* that §10(b) of the Exchange Act applies "only" to "transactions in securities listed on domestic exchanges, and domestic transactions in other securities." 561 U.S., at ——.

The Court's decision in *Sosa v. Alvarez–Machain,* 542 U.S. 692 (2004), makes clear that when the ATS was enacted, "congressional concern" was "'focus[ed],'" *Morrison, supra,* at —— , on the "three principal offenses against the law of nations" that had been identified by Blackstone: violation of safe conducts, infringement of the rights of ambassadors, and piracy, *Sosa,* 542 U.S., at 723-724. The Court therefore held that "federal courts should not recognize private claims under federal common law for violations of any international law norm with less definite content and acceptance among civilized nations than the historical paradigms familiar when [the ATS] was enacted." *Id.,* at 732. In other words, only conduct that satisfies *Sosa*'s requirements of definiteness and acceptance among civilized nations can be said to have been "the 'focus' of congressional concern," *Morrison, supra,* at ———, when Congress enacted the ATS. As a result, a putative ATS cause of action will fall within the scope of the presumption against extraterri-toriality — and will therefore be barred — unless the domestic conduct is sufficient to violate an international law norm that satisfies *Sosa*'s requirements of definiteness and acceptance among civilized nations.

Justice BREYER, with whom Justice GINSBURG, Justice SOTOMAYOR and Justice KAGAN join, concurring in the judgment. I agree with the Court's conclusion but not with its reasoning. . . .

Unlike the Court, I would not invoke the presumption against extraterritoriality. Rather, guided in part by principles and practices of foreign relations law, I would find jurisdiction under this statute where (1) the alleged tort occurs on American soil, (2) the defendant is an American national, or (3) the defendant's conduct substantially and adversely affects an important American national interest, and that includes a distinct interest in preventing the United States from becoming a safe harbor (free of civil as well as criminal liability) for a torturer or other common enemy of mankind. See *Sosa v. Alvarez-Machain,* 542 U.S. 692, 732 (2004) ("'[F]or purposes of civil liability, the torturer has become — like the pirate and slave trader before him — *hostis humani generis,* an enemy of all mankind.'" (quoting *Filartiga v. Pena-Irala,* 630 F.2d 876, 890 (C.A.2 1980) (alteration in original))). See also 1 Restatement (Third) of Foreign Relations Law of the United States §§402, 403, 404 (1986). In this case, however, the parties and relevant conduct lack sufficient ties to the United States for the ATS to provide jurisdiction.

I

A

Our decision in *Sosa* frames the question. In *Sosa* the Court specified that the Alien Tort Statute (ATS), when enacted in 1789, "was intended as jurisdictional." 542 U.S., at 714. We added that the statute gives today's courts the power to apply certain "judge-made" damages law to victims of certain foreign affairs-related misconduct, including "three specific offenses" to which "Blackstone referred," namely "violation of safe conducts, infringement of the rights of ambassadors, and piracy." *Id.,* at 715. We held that the statute provides today's federal judges with the power to fashion "a cause of action" for a "modest number" of claims, "based on the present-day law of nations," and which "rest on a norm of international character accepted by the civilized world and defined with a specificity comparable to the features" of those three "18th-century paradigms." *Id.,* at 724-725.

. . . Adjudicating any such claim must, in my view, also be consistent with those notions of comity that lead each nation to respect the sovereign rights of other nations by limiting the reach of its own laws and their enforcement. *Id.,* at 761 (Breyer, J., concurring in part and concurring in judgment).

Recognizing that Congress enacted the ATS to permit recovery of damages from pirates and others who violated basic international law norms as understood in 1789, *Sosa* essentially leads today's judges to ask: Who are today's pirates? See 542 U.S., at 724-725 (majority opinion). We provided a framework for answering that question by setting down principles drawn from international norms and designed to limit ATS claims to those that are similar in character and specificity to piracy. *Id.,* at 725.

In this case we must decide the extent to which this jurisdictional statute opens a federal court's doors to those harmed by activities belonging to the limited class that *Sosa* set forth *when those activities take place abroad.* To help answer this question here, I would refer both to *Sosa* and, as in *Sosa,* to norms of international law.

B

In my view the majority's effort to answer the question by referring to the "presumption against extraterritoriality" does not work well. That presumption "rests on the perception that Congress ordinarily legislates with respect to domestic, not foreign matters." *Morrison v. National Australia Bank Ltd.,* 561 U.S. ——, —— (2010). The ATS, however, was enacted with "foreign matters" in mind. The statute's text refers explicitly to "alien[s]," "treat[ies]," and "the law of nations." 28 U.S.C. §1350. The statute's purpose was to address "violations of the law of nations, admitting of a judicial remedy and at the same time threatening serious consequences in international affairs." *Sosa,* 542 U.S., at 715. And at least one of the three kinds of activities that we found to fall within the statute's scope, namely piracy, *ibid.,* normally takes place abroad. See 4 W. Blackstone, Commentaries on the Law of England 72 (1769). The majority cannot wish this piracy example away by emphasizing that piracy takes place on the high seas. See *ante,* at 10. That is because the robbery and murder that make up piracy do not normally take place in the water; they take place on a ship. And a ship is like land, in that it falls within the jurisdiction of the nation whose flag it flies. See *McCulloch v. Sociedad Nacional de Marineros de Honduras,* 372 U.S. 10, 20-21 (1963); 2 Restatement §502, Comment *d* ("[F]lag state has jurisdiction to prescribe with respect to any activity aboard the ship"). Indeed, in the early 19th century Chief Justice Marshall described piracy as an "offenc[e] against the nation under whose flag the vessel sails, and within whose particular jurisdiction all on board the vessel are." *United States v. Palmer,* 3 Wheat. 610, 632 (1818). See *United States v. Furlong,* 5 Wheat. 184, 197, 5 L.Ed. 64 (1820) (a crime committed "within the jurisdiction" of a foreign state and a crime committed "in the vessel of another nation" are "the same thing").

The majority nonetheless tries to find a distinction between piracy at sea and similar cases on land. . . . But, as I have just pointed out, "[a]pplying U.S. law to pirates" *does* typically involve applying our law to acts taking place within the jurisdiction of another sovereign. Nor can the majority's words "territorial jurisdiction" sensibly distinguish land from sea for purposes of isolating adverse foreign policy risks, as the Barbary Pirates, the War of 1812, the sinking of the *Lusitania,* and the Lockerbie bombing make all too clear.

The majority also writes, "Pirates were fair game wherever found, by any nation, because they generally did not operate within any jurisdiction." *Ibid.* I very much agree that pirates were fair game "wherever found." Indeed, that is the point. That is why we asked, in *Sosa,* who are today's pirates? Certainly today's pirates include torturers and perpetrators of genocide. And today, like the pirates of old, they are "fair game" where they are found. Like those pirates, they are "common enemies of all mankind and all nations have an equal interest in their apprehension and punishment." 1 Restatement §404 Reporters' Note 1, p. 256 (quoting *In re Demjanjuk,* 612 F. Supp. 544, 556 (N.D. Ohio 1985) (internal quotation marks omitted)). See *Sosa, supra,* at 732. And just as a nation that harbored pirates provoked the concern of other nations in past centuries, so harboring "common enemies of all mankind" provokes similar concerns today.

Thus the Court's reasoning, as applied to the narrow class of cases that *Sosa* described, fails to provide significant support for the use of any presumption against extraterritoriality; rather, it suggests the contrary.

In any event, as the Court uses its "presumption against extraterritorial application," it offers only limited help in deciding the question presented, namely "'under what circumstances the Alien Tort Statute . . . allows courts to recognize a cause of action for violations of the law of nations occurring within the territory of a sovereign other than the United States.'" 565 U.S. —— (2012). The majority echoes in this jurisdictional context *Sosa's* warning to use "caution" in shaping federal common-law causes of action. *Ante,* at 5. But it also makes clear that a statutory claim might sometimes "touch and concern the territory of the United States . . . with sufficient force to displace the presumption." *Ante,* at 14. It leaves for another day the determination of just when the presumption against extraterritoriality might be "overcome." *Ante,* at 8.

II

In applying the ATS to acts "occurring within the territory of a[nother] sovereign," I would assume that Congress intended the statute's jurisdictional reach to match the statute's underlying substantive grasp. That grasp, defined by the statute's purposes set forth in *Sosa,* includes compensation for those injured by piracy and its modern-day equivalents, at least where allowing such compensation avoids "serious" negative international "consequences" for the United States. 542 U.S., at 715. And just as we have looked to established international substantive norms to help determine the statute's substantive reach, *id.,* at 729, so we should look to international jurisdictional norms to help determine the statute's jurisdictional scope.

The Restatement (Third) of Foreign Relations Law is helpful. Section 402 recognizes that, subject to §403's "reasonableness" requirement, a nation may apply its law (for example, federal common law, see 542 U.S., at 729-730) not only (1) to "conduct" that "takes place [or to persons or things] within its territory" but also (2) to the "activities, interests, status, or relations of its nationals outside as well as within its territory," (3) to "conduct outside its territory that has or is intended to have substantial effect within its territory," and (4) to certain foreign "conduct outside its territory . . . that is directed against the security of the state or against a limited class of other state interests." In addition, §404 of the Restatement explains that a "state has jurisdiction to define and prescribe punishment for certain offenses recognized by the community of nations as of universal concern, such as piracy, slave trade," and analogous behavior.

Considering these jurisdictional norms in light of both the ATS's basic purpose (to provide compensation for those injured by today's pirates) and *Sosa*'s basic caution (to avoid international friction), I believe that the statute provides jurisdiction where (1) the alleged tort occurs on American soil, (2) the defendant is an American national, or (3) the defendant's conduct substantially and adversely affects an important American national interest, and that includes a distinct interest in preventing the United States from becoming a safe harbor (free of civil as well as criminal liability) for a torturer or other common enemy of mankind.

I would interpret the statute as providing jurisdiction only where distinct American interests are at issue. Doing so reflects the fact that Congress adopted the present statute at a time when, as Justice Story put it, "No nation ha[d] ever yet pretended to be the custos morum of the whole world." *United States v. La Jeune Eugenie,* 26 F. Cas. 832, 847 (No. 15,551) (CC Mass. 1822). That restriction also should help to minimize international friction. Further limiting principles such as exhaustion, *forum non conveniens,* and comity would do the same. So would a practice of courts giving weight to the views of the Executive Branch. See *Sosa,* 542 U.S., at 733, n.21; *id.,* at 761 (opinion of Breyer, J.).

As I have indicated, we should treat this Nation's interest in not becoming a safe harbor for violators of the most fundamental international norms as an important jurisdiction-related interest justifying application of the ATS in light of the statute's basic purposes — in particular that of compensating those who have suffered harm at the hands of, *e.g.,* torturers or other modern pirates. Nothing in the statute or its history suggests that our courts should turn a blind eye to the plight of victims in that "handful of heinous actions." *Tel-Oren v. Libyan Arab Republic,* 726 F.2d 774, 781 (C.A.D.C. 1984) (Edwards, J., concurring).

To the contrary, the statute's language, history, and purposes suggest that the statute was to be a weapon in the "war" against those modern pirates who, by their conduct, have "declar[ed] war against all mankind." 4 Blackstone 71.

International norms have long included a duty not to permit a nation to become a safe harbor for pirates (or their equivalent). . . .

More recently two lower American courts have, in effect, rested jurisdiction primarily upon that kind of concern. In *Filartiga,* 630 F.2d 876, an alien plaintiff brought a lawsuit against an alien defendant for damages suffered through acts of torture that the defendant allegedly inflicted in a foreign nation, Paraguay. Neither plaintiff nor defendant was an American national and the actions underlying the lawsuit took place abroad. The defendant, however, "had . . . resided in the United States for more than ninth months" before being sued, having overstayed his visitor's visa. *Id.,* at 878-879. Jurisdiction was deemed proper because the defendant's alleged conduct violated a well-established international law norm, and the suit vindicated our Nation's interest in not providing a safe harbor, free of damages claims, for those defendants who commit such conduct.

In *Marcos,* the plaintiffs were nationals of the Philippines, the defendant was a Philippine national, and the alleged wrongful act, death by torture, took place abroad. *In re Estate of Marcos, Human Rights Litigation,* 25 F.3d 1467, 1469, 1475 (C.A.9 1994); *In re Estate of Marcos Human Rights Litigation,* 978 F.2d 493, 495-496, 500 (C.A.9 1992). A month before being sued, the defendant, "his family, . . . and others loyal to [him] fled to Hawaii," where the ATS case was heard. *Marcos,* 25 F.3d, at 1469. As in *Filartiga,* the court found ATS jurisdiction.

And in *Sosa* we referred to both cases with approval, suggesting that the ATS allowed a claim for relief in such circumstances. 542 U.S., at 732. Not surprisingly, both before and after *Sosa,* courts have consistently rejected the notion that the ATS is categorically barred from extra-territorial application.

Application of the statute in the way I have suggested is consistent with international law and foreign practice. . . .

Many countries permit foreign plaintiffs to bring suits against their own nationals based on unlawful conduct that took place abroad.

Other countries permit some form of lawsuit brought by a foreign national against a foreign national, based upon conduct taking place abroad and seeking damages. Certain countries, which find "universal" criminal "jurisdiction" to try perpetrators of particularly heinous crimes such as piracy and genocide, see Restatement §404, also permit private persons injured by that conduct to pursue *"actions civiles,"* seeking civil damages in the criminal proceeding. . . .

At the same time Congress has ratified treaties obliging the United States to find and punish foreign perpetrators of serious crimes committed against foreign persons abroad. See Convention on the Prevention and Punishment of Crimes Against Internationally Protected Persons, Including Diplomatic Agents, Dec. 28, 1973, 28 U.S.T.1975, T.I.A.S. No. 8532; Convention for the Suppression of Unlawful Acts Against the Safety of Civil Aviation, Sept. 23, 1971, 24 U.S.T. 565, T.I.A.S. No. 7570; Convention for the Suppression of Unlawful Seizure of Aircraft, Dec. 16, 1970, 22 U.S.T. 1641, T.I.A.S. No. 7192.

And Congress has sometimes authorized civil damages in such cases. See generally note following 28 U.S.C. §1350 (Torture Victim Protection Act of 1991 (TVPA) (private damages action for torture or extrajudicial killing committed under authority of a foreign nation)); S. Rep. No. 102-249, p. 4 (1991) (ATS "should not be replaced" by TVPA); H.R. Rep. No. 102-367, pt. 1, p. 4 (TVPA intended to "enhance the remedy already available under" the ATS). But cf. *Mohamad v. Palestinian Authority,* 566 U.S. —— (2012) (TVPA allows suits against only natural persons). . . .

Thus, the jurisdictional approach that I would use is analogous to, and consistent with, the approaches of a number of other nations. It is consistent with the approaches set forth in the Restatement. Its insistence upon the presence of some distinct American interest, its reliance upon courts also invoking other related doctrines such as comity, exhaustion, and *forum non conveniens,* along with its dependence (for its workability) upon courts obtaining, and paying particular attention to, the views of the Executive Branch, all should obviate the majority's concern that our jurisdictional example would lead "other nations, also applying the law of nations," to "hale our citizens into their courts for alleged violations of the law of nations occurring in the United States, or anywhere else in the world." *Ante,* at 13.

Most importantly, this jurisdictional view is consistent with the substantive view of the statute that we took in *Sosa.* This approach would avoid placing the statute's jurisdictional scope at odds with its substantive objectives, holding out "the word of promise" of compensation for victims of the torturer, while "break[ing] it to the hope."

III

Applying these jurisdictional principles to this case, however, I agree with the Court that jurisdiction does not lie. The defendants are two foreign corporations. Their shares, like those of many foreign corporations, are traded on the New York Stock Exchange. Their only presence in the United States consists of an office in New York City (actually owned by a separate but affiliated company) that helps to explain their business to potential investors. The plaintiffs are not United States nationals but nationals of other nations. The conduct at issue took place abroad. And the plaintiffs allege, not that the defendants directly engaged in acts of torture, genocide, or the equivalent, but that they helped others (who are not American nationals) to do so.

Under these circumstances, even if the New York office were a sufficient basis for asserting general jurisdiction, it would be farfetched to believe, based solely upon the defendants' minimal and indirect American presence, that this legal action helps to vindicate a distinct American interest, such as in not providing a safe harbor for an "enemy of all mankind." Thus I agree with the Court that here it would "reach too far to say" that such "mere corporate presence suffices." *Ante,* at 14.

I consequently join the Court's judgment but not its opinion.

[NSL p. 200. Insert before "d. The Continuing Incorporation Debate," and renumber "d" as "e."]

d. Extraterritoriality

After *Kiobel*, the Alien Tort Statute is going to apply to claims that arise overseas only when plaintiffs can show that such claims nevertheless "touch and concern" the territory of the United States. If that relationship to the United States is sufficiently close, the case is a "foreign-squared" case rather than a foreign-cubed case, like *Kiobel* itself. In one important early case clarifying *Kiobel*'s scope, the Fourth Circuit ruled that claims brought against private military contractors by non-citizens detained and allegedly tortured at the Abu Ghraib prison in Iraq could go forward notwithstanding *Kiobel*. *See Al Shimari v. CACI Premier Tech., Inc.,* No. 13-1937, 2014 WL 2922840 (4th Cir. June 30, 2014). In particular, the Court of Appeals identified six grounds on which *Kiobel* could be distinguished: (1) "the plaintiffs' claims allege acts of torture committed by United States citizens who were employed by an American corporation, CACI, which has corporate headquarters located in Fairfax County, Virginia"; (2) "[t]he alleged torture occurred at a military facility operated by United States government personnel"; (3) "the employees who allegedly participated in the acts of torture were hired by CACI in the United States to fulfill the terms of a contract that CACI executed with the United States Department of the Interior"; (4) "[t]he contract between CACI and the Department of the Interior was issued by a government office in Arizona, and CACI was authorized to collect payments by mailing invoices to government accounting offices in Colorado"; (5) "[u]nder the terms of the contract, CACI interrogators were required to obtain security clearances from the United States Department of Defense"; and (6) "[t]he plaintiffs also allege that CACI's managers located in the United States were aware of reports of misconduct abroad, attempted to 'cover up' the misconduct, and 'implicitly, if not expressly, encouraged' it." *Id.* at *9-10. Do these distinctions suggest that *Al-Shimari* is the exception that proves the sweeping scope of *Kiobel*'s rule, or might some of them be far more important than the others — and, thus, the key to future ATS claims?

————————————

[NSL p. 209. Insert as new Note 1a.]

   1a. *What Standard Is Congress Incorporating?* In 10 U.S.C. §821, Congress recognized the jurisdiction of military commissions "with respect to offenders or offenses that by statute or by the law of war may be tried by military commissions." *See Ex parte Quirin*, 317 U.S. 1, 27-28 (1942), NSL p. 823. In *Hamdan v. United States (Hamdan II)*, 696 F.3d 1238 (D.C. Cir. 2012), the court held that, with this language, Congress necessarily incorporated the *international* laws of war, and not the "U.S. common law of war." *See id.* at 1248 n.8. *Hamdan II* then turned to how courts should assess *whether* a specific offense was recognized as part of that body of international law. Picking up on the themes of his *Al-Bihani* concurrence, Judge Kavanaugh stressed that "the imprecision of customary international law calls for significant caution by U.S. courts before permitting civil or criminal liability premised on violation of such a vague prohibition." *Id.* at 1250 n.10. He analogized to the Supreme Court's interpretation of the Alien Tort Statute in *Sosa v. Alvarez-Machain*, 542 U.S. 692 (2004), NSL p. 189, to hold that "imposing liability on the basis of a violation of 'international law' or the 'law of nations' or the 'law of war' generally must be based on norms firmly grounded in international law." 696 F.3d at 1250 n.10. But *Sosa* had ruled that "any claim based on the present-day law of nations [must] rest on a norm of international character accepted by the civilized world and defined with a specificity comparable to the features of the 18th-century paradigms we have recognized." 542 U.S. at 725. Does it make sense to apply the "firmly grounded" standard to military commissions, thereby preventing military commission trials based upon crimes (like material support and conspiracy) that are well-established *civilian* criminal offenses?

Note that *Hamdan II*'s analysis of §821 was arguably overruled by the D.C. Circuit in *Al Bahlul v. United States*, No. 11-1324 (D.C. Cir. July 14, 2014) (en banc), this *Supplement* p. 329. The majority in *Al Bahlul* held that §821 also incorporates offenses against the "domestic common law of war," but only reached that conclusion under "plain error" review. *See id.*, slip op. at 36-39. *Al Bahlul* thus leaves open whether, under *de novo* review, *Hamdan II*'s adoption of the *Sosa* test will govern the scope of §821.

[NSL p. 233, CTL p. 89. Insert at end of chapter.]

C. CYBER WAR

Leon Panetta, Secretary of Defense, Remarks to the Business Executives for National Security
New York City, Oct. 11, 2012
http://www.defense.gov/transcripts/transcript.aspx?transcriptid=5136

Cyberspace is the new frontier — full of possibilities to help advance security and prosperity in the 21st century. Yet with these possibilities also come new perils. The Internet is open and highly accessible — as it should be. But that also presents a new terrain for warfare where adversaries can seek to do harm to our country, our economy and our citizens. . . .

A cyber attack perpetrated by nation states or violent extremist groups could be as destructive as the terrorist attack of 9/11. Such a destructive cyber terrorist attack could paralyze the nation. . . .

. . . [W]e know that foreign cyber actors are probing America's critical infrastructure networks.

They are targeting the computer control systems that operate chemical, electricity and water plants, and those that guide transportation throughout the country.

We know of specific instances where intruders have successfully gained access to these control systems. We also know they are seeking to create advanced tools to attack these systems and cause panic, destruction, and even the loss of life. . . .

An aggressor nation or extremist group could gain control of critical switches and derail passenger trains, or trains loaded with lethal chemicals. They could contaminate the water supply in major cities, or shut down the power grid across large parts of the country.

The most destructive scenarios involve cyber actors launching several attacks on our critical infrastructure at once, in combination with a physical attack on our country. Attackers could also seek to disable or degrade critical military systems and communications networks.

The collective result of these kinds of attacks could be "cyber Pearl Harbor": an attack that would cause physical destruction and loss of life, paralyze and shock the nation, and create a profound new sense of vulnerability. . . .

The Department of Defense, in large part through the capabilities of the National Security Agency, has developed the world's most sophisticated system to detect cyber intruders or attackers. And we are acting aggressively to get ahead of this problem — putting in place measures to stop cyber attacks dead in their tracks. . . .

Our mission is to defend this nation. We defend. We deter. And if called upon, we take decisive action. In the past, we have done so through operations on land and at sea, in the skies and in space. In this new century, the United States military must help defend the nation in cyberspace as well.

If a foreign adversary attacked U.S. soil, the American people expect their national defense forces to respond. If a crippling cyber attack were launched against our nation, the American people must be protected. And if the Commander-in-Chief orders a response, the Defense Department must be ready to act. . . .

. . . DoD is already in an intense daily struggle against thousands of cyber actors who probe the Defense Department's networks millions of times per day. Through the innovative efforts of our cyber operators, we are enhancing the department's cyber defense programs. These systems rely on sensors and software to hunt down malicious code before it harms our systems. We actively share our own experience defending our systems with those running the nation's critical private sector networks.

In addition to defending the department's networks, we also help deter attacks. Our cyber adversaries will be far less likely to hit us if they know we will be able to link them to the attack, or that their effort will fail against our strong defenses. The department has made significant advances in solving a problem that makes deterring cyber adversaries more complex: the difficulty of identifying the origins of an attack.

Over the last two years, the department has made significant investments in forensics to address this problem of attribution, and we are seeing returns on those investments. Potential aggressors should be aware that the United States has the capacity to locate them and hold them accountable for actions that harm America or its interests.

But we won't succeed in preventing a cyber attack through improved defenses alone. If we detect an imminent threat of attack that will cause significant physical destruction or kill American citizens, we need to have the option to take action to defend the nation when directed by the president.

For these kinds of scenarios, the department has developed the capability to conduct effective operations to counter threats to our national interests in cyberspace. . . .

. . . [W]e will only do so in a manner consistent with the policy principles and legal frameworks that the department follows for other domains, including the law of armed conflict. . . .

Harold Hongju Koh, Legal Adviser, U.S. Department of State, International Law in Cyberspace

Remarks at USCYBERCOM Inter-Agency Legal
Conference, Ft. Meade, MD, Sept. 18, 2012
transcript available at http://www.state.gov/s/l/releases/remarks/197924.htm

. . . [H]ow do we apply old laws of war to new cyber-circumstances, staying faithful to enduring principles, while accounting for changing times and technologies? . . .

I. International Law in Cyberspace: What We Know . . .

Question 1: Do established principles of international law apply to cyberspace?
Answer 1: Yes, international law principles do apply in cyberspace. . . .

. . . [T]he United States has made clear our view that established principles of international law do apply in cyberspace.

Question 2: Is cyberspace a law-free zone, where anything goes?
Answer 2: Emphatically no.

Cyberspace is not a "law-free" zone where anyone can conduct hostile activities without rules or restraint. Think of it this way. This is not the first time that technology has changed and that international law has been asked to deal with those changes. In particular, because the tools of conflict are constantly evolving, one relevant body of law — international humanitarian law, or the law of armed conflict — affirmatively anticipates technological innovation, and contemplates that its existing rules will apply to such innovation. To be sure, new technologies raise new issues and thus, new questions. . . . But to those who say that established law is not up to the task, we must articulate and build consensus around how it applies and reassess from there whether and what additional understandings are needed. . . .

Question 3: Do cyber activities ever constitute a use of force?
Answer 3: Yes.

Cyber activities may in certain circumstances constitute uses of force within the meaning of Article 2(4) of the UN Charter and customary international law.

In analyzing whether a cyber operation would constitute a use of force, most commentators focus on whether the direct physical injury and property damage resulting from the cyber event looks like that which would be considered a use of force if produced by kinetic weapons. *Cyber activities that proximately result in death, injury, or significant destruction would likely be viewed as a use of force.* In assessing whether an event constituted a use of force in or through cyberspace, we must evaluate factors: including the context of the event, the actor perpetrating the action (recognizing challenging issues of attribution in cyberspace), the target and location, effects and intent, among other possible issues. Commonly cited examples of cyber activity that would constitute a use of force include, for example: (1) operations that trigger a nuclear plant meltdown; (2) operations that open a dam above a populated area causing destruction; or (3) operations that disable air traffic control resulting in airplane crashes. Only a moment's reflection makes you realize that this is common sense: if the physical consequences of a cyber attack work the kind of physical damage that dropping a bomb or firing a missile would, that cyber attack should equally be considered a use of force.

Question 4: May a State ever respond to a computer network attack by exercising a right of national self-defense?
Answer 4: Yes.

A State's national right of self-defense, recognized in Article 51 of the UN Charter, may be triggered by computer network activities that amount to an armed attack or imminent threat thereof. . . .

Question 5: Do *jus in bello* rules apply to computer network attacks?
Answer 5: Yes.

In the context of an armed conflict, the law of armed conflict applies to regulate the use of cyber tools in hostilities, just as it does other tools. The principles of necessity and proportionality limit uses of force in self-defense and would regulate what may constitute a lawful response under the circumstances.

There is no legal requirement that the response to a cyber armed attack take the form of a cyber action, as long as the response meets the requirements of necessity and proportionality.

Question 6: Must attacks distinguish between military and nonmilitary objectives?
Answer 6: Yes.

The *jus in bello* principle of *distinction* applies to computer network attacks undertaken in the context of an armed conflict. The principle of distinction applies to cyber activities that amount to an "attack" — as that term is understood in the law of war — in the context of an armed conflict. As in any form of armed conflict, the principle of distinction requires that the intended effect of the attack must be to harm a legitimate *military* target. We must distinguish military objectives — that is, objects that make an effective contribution to military action and whose destruction would offer a military advantage — from civilian objects, which under international law are generally protected from attack.

Question 7: Must attacks adhere to the principle of proportionality?
Answer 7: Yes.

The *jus in bello* principle of *proportionality* applies to computer network attacks undertaken in the context of an armed conflict. The principle of proportionality prohibits attacks that may be expected to cause incidental loss to civilian life, injury to civilians, or damage to civilian objects that would be excessive in relation to the concrete and direct military advantage anticipated. Parties to an armed conflict must assess what the expected harm to civilians is likely to be, and weigh the risk of such collateral damage against the importance of the expected military advantage to be gained. In the cyber context, this rule requires parties to a conflict to assess: (1) the effects of cyber weapons on both military and civilian infrastructure and users, including shared physical infrastructure (such as a dam or a power grid) that would affect civilians; (2) the potential physical damage that a cyber attack may cause, such as death or injury that may result from effects on critical infrastructure; and (3) the potential effects of a cyber attack on civilian objects that are not military objectives, such as private, civilian computers that hold no military significance, but may be networked to computers that are military objectives.

Question 8: How should States assess their cyber weapons?
Answer 8: States should undertake a legal review of weapons,
    including those that employ a cyber capability.

Such a review should entail an analysis, for example, of whether a
particular capability would be *inherently indiscriminate*, i.e., that it
could not be used consistent with the principles of distinction and
proportionality. The U.S. Government undertakes at least two stages of
legal review of the use of weapons in the context of armed conflict —
first, an evaluation of new weapons to determine whether their use
would be per se prohibited by the law of war; and second, specific
operations employing weapons are always reviewed to ensure that each
particular operation is also compliant with the law of war.

Question 9: In this analysis, what role does State sovereignty play?
Answer 9: States conducting activities in cyberspace must take into
    account the sovereignty of other States, including outside the
    context of armed conflict.

The physical infrastructure that supports the internet and cyber
activities is generally located in sovereign territory and subject to the
jurisdiction of the territorial State. Because of the interconnected,
interoperable nature of cyberspace, operations targeting networked
information infrastructures in one country may create effects in another
country. Whenever a State contemplates conducting activities in
cyberspace, the sovereignty of other States needs to be considered.

Question 10: Are States responsible when cyber acts are undertaken
    through proxies?
Answer 10: Yes.

States are legally responsible for activities undertaken through
"proxy actors," who act on the State's instructions or under its direction
or control. The ability to mask one's identity and geography in
cyberspace and the resulting difficulties of timely, high-confidence
attribution can create significant challenges for States in identifying,
evaluating, and accurately responding to threats. But putting attribution
problems aside for a moment, established international law does address
the question of proxy actors. States are legally responsible for activities
undertaken through putatively private actors, who act on the State's

instructions or under its direction or control. If a State exercises a sufficient degree of control over an ostensibly private person or group of persons committing an internationally wrongful act, the State assumes responsibility for the act, just as if official agents of the State itself had committed it. These rules are designed to ensure that States cannot hide behind putatively private actors to engage in conduct that is internationally wrongful.

II. International Law in Cyberspace:
Challenges and Uncertainties . . .

Unresolved Question 3: How do we address the problem of *attribution* in cyberspace?

As I mentioned earlier, cyberspace significantly increases an actor's ability to engage in attacks with "plausible deniability," by acting through proxies. I noted that legal tools exist to ensure that States are held accountable for those acts. What I want to highlight here is that many of these challenges — in particular, those concerning attribution — are as much questions of technical and policy nature rather than exclusively or even predominantly questions of law. Cyberspace remains a new and dynamic operating environment, and we cannot expect that all answers to the new and confounding questions we face will be *legal* ones. . . .

Presidential Policy Directive/PPD-20, U.S. Cyber Operations Policy [1]

No date

I. Definitions (U) . . .

Cyberspace: The interdependent network of information technology infrastructures that includes the Internet, telecommunications networks, computers, information or communications systems, networks, and embedded processors and controllers. (U)

Network Defense: Programs, activities, and the use of tools necessary to facilitate them conducted on a computer, network, or information or communications system by the owner or with the consent of the owner and, as appropriate, the users for the primary purpose of protecting (1) that computer, network, or system; (2) data stored on, processed on, or transiting that computer, network, or system; or (3) physical and virtual infrastructure controlled by that computer, network, or system. . . . (U)

Cyber Effect: The manipulation, disruption, denial, degradation, or destruction of computers, information or communications systems, networks, physical or virtual infrastructure controlled by computers or information systems, or information resident thereon. (U)

Cyber Collection: Operations and related programs or activities conducted by or on behalf of the United States Government, in or through cyberspace, for the primary purpose of collecting intelligence — including information that can be used for future operations — from computers, information or communications systems, or networks with the intent to remain undetected. . . . (C/NF)

TOP SECRET/NOFORN
Reason: 1.4(a)(c)(e)(g)
Declassify on: 10/16/37

[1. Published by *The Guardian* on June 7, 2013, at http://www.guardian.co. uk/world/interactive/2013/jun/07/obama-cyber-directive-full-text.]

Defensive Cyber Effects Operations (DCEO): Operations and related programs or activities — other than network defense or cyber collection — conducted by or on behalf of the United States Government, in or through cyberspace, that are intended to enable or produce cyber effects outside United States Government networks for the purpose of defending or protecting against imminent threats or ongoing attacks or malicious cyber activity against U.S. national interests from inside or outside cyberspace. (C/NF) . . .

Offensive Cyber Effects Operations (OCEO): Operations and related programs or activities — other than network defense, cyber collection, or DCEO — conducted by or on behalf of the United States Government, in or through cyberspace, that are intended to enable or produce cyber effects outside United States Government networks. (C/NF) . . .

Significant Consequences: Loss of life, significant responsive actions against the United States, significant damage to property, serious adverse U.S. foreign policy consequences, or serious economic impact on the United States. (U) . . .

Emergency Cyber Action: A cyber operation undertaken at the direction of the head of a department or agency with appropriate authorities who has determined that such action is necessary, pursuant to the requirements of this directive, to mitigate an imminent threat or ongoing attack against U.S. national interests from inside or outside cyberspace and under circumstances that at the time do not permit obtaining prior Presidential approval to the extent that such approval would otherwise be required. (S/NF)

II. Purpose and Scope (U) . . .

The United States Government shall conduct all cyber operations consistent with the U.S. Constitution and other applicable laws and policies of the United States, including Presidential orders and directives. (C/NF)

The United States Government shall conduct DCEO and OCEO under this directive consistent with its obligations under international law, including with regard to matters of sovereignty and neutrality, and, as applicable, the law of armed conflict. (C/NF)

This directive pertains to cyber operations, including those that support or enable kinetic, information, or other types of operations. Most of this directive is directed exclusively to DCEO and OCEO. (S/NF) . . .

III. Guiding Principles for DCEO and OCEO (U)

DCEO and OCEO may raise unique national security and foreign policy concerns that require additional coordination and policy considerations because cyberspace is globally connected. DCEO and OCEO, even for subtle or clandestine operations, may generate cyber effects in locations other than the intended target, with potential unintended or collateral consequences that may affect U.S. national interests in many locations. (S/NF) . . .

The United States Government shall reserve the right to act in accordance with the United States' inherent right of self defense as recognized in international law, including through the conduct of DCEO. (C/NF)

The United States Government shall conduct neither DCEO nor OCEO that are intended or likely to produce cyber effects within the United States unless approved by the President. A department or agency, however, with appropriate authority may conduct a particular case of DCEO that is intended or likely to produce cyber effects within the United States if it qualifies as an Emergency Cyber Action as set forth in this directive and otherwise complies with applicable laws and policies, including Presidential orders and directives. (C/NF)

The United States Government shall obtain consent from countries in which cyber effects are expected to occur or those countries hosting U.S. computers and systems used to conduct DCEO or OCEO unless:

> Military actions approved by the President and ordered by the Secretary of Defense authorize nonconsensual DCEO or OCEO . . . ;
> DCEO is undertaken in accordance with the United States' inherent right of self defense as recognized in international law, and the United States Government provides notification afterwards in a manner consistent with the protection of U.S. military and intelligence capabilities and foreign policy considerations and in accordance with applicable law; or
> The President — on the recommendation of the Deputies Committee and, as appropriate, the Principals Committee — determines that an exception to obtaining consent is necessary, takes into account overall U.S. national interests and equities, and meets a high threshold of need and effective outcomes relative to the risks created by such an exception. (S/NF) . . .

The United States Government, to ensure appropriate application of these principles, shall make all reasonable efforts, under circumstances prevailing at the time, to identify the adversary and the ownership and geographic location of the targets and related infrastructure where DCEO or OCEO will be conducted or cyber effects are expected to occur, and to identify the people and entities, including U.S. persons, that could be affected by proposed DCEO or OCEO. (S/NF)

Additional Considerations for DCEO (U) . . .

> The United States Government shall reserve use of DCEO to protect U.S. national interests in circumstances when network defense or law enforcement measures are insufficient or cannot be put in place in time to mitigate a threat, and when other previously approved measures would not be more appropriate, or if a Deputies or Principals Committee review determines that proposed DCEO provides an advantageous degree of effectiveness, timeliness, or efficiency compared to other methods commensurate with the risks;
> The United States Government shall conduct DCEO with the least intrusive methods feasible to mitigate a threat; . . . (S/NF)

Offensive Cyber Effects Operations (U)

OCEO can offer unique and unconventional capabilities to advance U.S. national objectives around the world with little or no warning to the adversary or target and with potential effects ranging from subtle to severely damaging. The development and sustainment of OCEO capabilities, however, may require considerable time and effort if access and tools for a specific target do not already exist. (TS/NF)

The United States Government shall identify potential targets of national importance where OCEO can offer a favorable balance of effectiveness and risk as compared with other instruments of national power, establish and maintain OCEO capabilities integrated as appropriate with other U.S. offensive capabilities, and execute those capabilities in a manner consistent with the provisions of this directive. (TS/NF)

IV. Cyber Operations with Significant Consequences (U)

Specific Presidential approval is required for any cyber operations — including cyber collection, DCEO, and OCEO — determined by the head of a department or agency to conduct the operation to be reasonably likely to result in "significant consequences" as defined in this directive. . . . (S/NF)

V. Threat Response Operations (U) . . .

Emergency Cyber Actions (C/NF)

The Secretary of Defense is hereby authorized to conduct, or a department or agency head with appropriate authorities may conduct, under procedures approved by the President, Emergency Cyber Actions necessary to mitigate an imminent threat or ongoing attack using DCEO if circumstances at the time do not permit obtaining prior Presidential approval (to the extent that such approval would otherwise be required) and the department or agency head determines that:

> An emergency action is necessary in accordance with the United States inherent right of self-defense as recognized in international law to prevent imminent loss of life or significant damage with enduring national impact on the Primary Mission Essential Functions of the United States Government,[5] U.S. critical infrastructure and key resources, or the mission of U.S. military forces;
> Network defense or law enforcement would be insufficient or unavailable in the necessary timeframe, and other previously approved activities would not be more appropriate;
> The Emergency Cyber Actions are reasonably likely not to result in significant consequences;
> The Emergency Cyber Actions will be conducted in a manner intended to be nonlethal in purpose, action, and consequence;
> The Emergency Cyber Actions will be limited in magnitude, scope, and duration to that level of activity necessary to mitigate the threat or attack;
> The Emergency Cyber Actions, when practicable, have been coordinated with appropriate departments and agencies . . . ; and
> The Emergency Cyber Actions are consistent with the U.S. Constitution and other applicable laws and policies of the United States, including Presidential orders and directives. (S/NF) . . .

---

5. As defined in NSPD-51/HSPD-20 on "National Continuity Policy" of May 9, 2007. (U)

Department and agency heads shall report Emergency Cyber Actions to the President through the National Security Advisor as soon as feasible. . . . (S/NF) . . .

NOTES AND QUESTIONS

1. *Cyber Warfare in Practice.* In March 2013, the head of the Defense Department's newly created Cyber Command, Gen. Keith B. Alexander, told Congress that 13 teams of computer programmers and experts would be prepared to respond in kind to a major attack on U.S. computer networks. Mark Mazzetti & David E. Sanger, *Security Chief Says Cyberattacks Will Meet With Retaliation*, N.Y. Times, Mar. 13, 2013. "We believe our [cyber] offense is the best in the world," he said. "When authorized to deliver offensive cyber effects, our technological and operational superiority delivers unparalleled effects against our adversaries' systems." He also declared that "in almost all circumstances the Armed Services Committees should be informed in a timely manner of significant offensive cyber operations conducted by CYBERCOM." *US Cyber Offense Is "The Best in the World"*, Secrecy News, Aug. 26, 2013. But in public testimony he did not describe criteria for initiating such operations, and he failed to define the terms "almost," "timely," and "significant."

A short time later the Chairman of the Joint Chiefs of Staff reportedly issued an "execute order" to initiate an offensive military cyber operation, although the contents of the order, including the identity of the target and other details, are classified. Advance approval of the President or Defense Secretary apparently was required. *U.S. Military Given Secret "Execute Order" on Cyber Operations*, Secrecy News, Mar. 13, 2014.

U.S. intelligence services reportedly conducted 231 offensive cyber operations in 2011. Barton Gellman & Ellen Nakashima, *U.S. Spy Agencies Mounted 231 Offensive Cyber-Operations in 2011, Documents Show*, Wash. Post, Aug. 30, 2013. According to the news account, NSA programs with code names like GENIE and TURBINE are designed to implant secret malware in millions of computers that could then be used to conduct cyber espionage or mount offensive attacks. The story is based on information contained in a summary budget for the intelligence community leaked by Edward Snowden, although portions of the document describing cyber operations have not been published.

2. *Preemptive Cyber War?* PPD-20 authorizes emergency cyber operations with the approval of a department or agency head to mitigate "an imminent threat . . . against U.S. national interests." A number of criteria are set forth in Art. V of the directive. Do you think they satisfy the prerequisites for an act of self-defense as described in U.N. Charter Art. 51? See NSL pp. 362-363. Would it be wise to try to specify additional criteria? If so, what would you add?

[NSL p. 322. Insert at the end of the chapter.]

Text of a Letter from the President to the Speaker of the House of Representatives and the President Pro Tempore of the Senate
June 16, 2014

Dear Mr. Speaker: (Dear Mr. President:)

Starting on June 15, 2014, up to approximately 275 U.S. Armed Forces personnel are deploying to Iraq to provide support and security for U.S. personnel and the U.S. Embassy in Baghdad. This force is deploying for the purpose of protecting U.S. citizens and property, if necessary, and is equipped for combat. This force will remain in Iraq until the security situation becomes such that it is no longer needed.

This action has been directed consistent with my responsibility to protect U.S. citizens both at home and abroad, and in furtherance of U.S. national security and foreign policy interests, pursuant to my constitutional authority to conduct U.S. foreign relations and as Commander in Chief and Chief Executive.

I am providing this report as part of my efforts to keep the Congress fully informed, consistent with the War Powers Resolution (Public Law 93-148). I appreciate the support of the Congress in these actions.

Sincerely,
Barack Obama

[NSL p. 342. Insert at the end of Chapter 12.]

D. SYRIA

Remarks by the President in Address
to the Nation on Syria
Sept. 10, 2013

THE PRESIDENT: . . . Over the past two years, what began as a series of peaceful protests against the repressive regime of Bashar al-Assad has turned into a brutal civil war. Over 100,000 people have been killed. Millions have fled the country. In that time, America has worked with allies to provide humanitarian support, to help the moderate opposition, and to shape a political settlement. But I have resisted calls for military action, because we cannot resolve someone else's civil war through force, particularly after a decade of war in Iraq and Afghanistan.

The situation profoundly changed, though, on August 21st, when Assad's government gassed to death over a thousand people, including hundreds of children. The images from this massacre are sickening: Men, women, children lying in rows, killed by poison gas. Others foaming at the mouth, gasping for breath. A father clutching his dead children, imploring them to get up and walk. On that terrible night, the world saw in gruesome detail the terrible nature of chemical weapons, and why the overwhelming majority of humanity has declared them off-limits — a crime against humanity, and a violation of the laws of war. . . .

. . . The question now is what the United States of America, and the international community, is prepared to do about it. Because what happened to those people — to those children — is not only a violation of international law, it's also a danger to our security.

Let me explain why. If we fail to act, the Assad regime will see no reason to stop using chemical weapons. As the ban against these weapons erodes, other tyrants will have no reason to think twice about acquiring poison gas, and using them. Over time, our troops would again face the prospect of chemical warfare on the battlefield. And it could be easier for terrorist organizations to obtain these weapons, and to use them to attack civilians. . . .

. . . [A]fter careful deliberation, I determined that it is in the national security interests of the United States to respond to the Assad regime's use of chemical weapons through a targeted military strike. The purpose of this strike would be to deter Assad from using chemical weapons, to degrade his regime's ability to use them, and to make clear to the world that we will not tolerate their use.

That's my judgment as Commander-in-Chief. But I'm also the President of the world's oldest constitutional democracy. So even though I possess the authority to order military strikes, I believed it was right, in the absence of a direct or imminent threat to our security, to take this debate to Congress. I believe our democracy is stronger when the President acts with the support of Congress. And I believe that America acts more effectively abroad when we stand together. . . .

. . . I will not put American boots on the ground in Syria. I will not pursue an open-ended action like Iraq or Afghanistan. I will not pursue a prolonged air campaign like Libya or Kosovo. This would be a targeted strike to achieve a clear objective: deterring the use of chemical weapons, and degrading Assad's capabilities. . . .

. . . [O]ver the last few days, we've seen some encouraging signs. In part because of the credible threat of U.S. military action, as well as constructive talks that I had with President Putin, the Russian government has indicated a willingness to join with the international community in pushing Assad to give up his chemical weapons. The Assad regime has now admitted that it has these weapons, and even said they'd join the Chemical Weapons Convention, which prohibits their use. . . .

I have, therefore, asked the leaders of Congress to postpone a vote to authorize the use of force while we pursue this diplomatic path. . . . I've spoken to the leaders of two of our closest allies, France and the United Kingdom, and we will work together in consultation with Russia and China to put forward a resolution at the U.N. Security Council requiring Assad to give up his chemical weapons, and to ultimately destroy them under international control. . . .

United Nations Security Council Resolution 2118
U.N. Doc. S/RES 2118 (Sept. 27, 2013)

The Security Council . . .

Reaffirming that the proliferation of chemical weapons, as well as their means of delivery, constitutes a threat to international peace and security,

Recalling that the Syrian Arab Republic on 22 November 1968 acceded to the Protocol for the Prohibition of the Use in War of Asphyxiating, Poisonous or Other Gases and of Bacteriological Methods of Warfare, signed at Geneva on 17 June 1925,

Noting that on 14 September 2013, the Syrian Arab Republic deposited with the Secretary-General its instrument of accession to the Convention on the Prohibition of the Development, Production, Stockpiling and Use of Chemical Weapons and on their Destruction (Convention) and declared that it shall comply with its stipulations and observe them faithfully and sincerely, applying the Convention provisionally pending its entry into force for the Syrian Arab Republic, . . .

Deeply outraged by the use of chemical weapons on 21 August 2013 in Rif Damascus, as concluded in the [report of the United Nations Mission to Investigate Allegations of the Use of Chemical Weapons in the Syrian Arab Republic], condemning the killing of civilians that resulted from it, affirming that the use of chemical weapons constitutes a serious violation of international law, and stressing that those responsible for any use of chemical weapons must be held accountable, . . .

Welcoming the Framework for Elimination of Syrian Chemical Weapons dated 14 September 2013, in Geneva, between the Russian Federation and the United States of America (S/2013/565), with a view to ensuring the destruction of the Syrian Arab Republic's chemical weapons programme in the soonest and safest manner, and expressing its commitment to the immediate international control over chemical weapons and their components in the Syrian Arab Republic,

Welcoming the decision of the Executive Council of the Organization for the Prohibition of Chemical Weapons (OPCW) of 27 September 2013 establishing special procedures for the expeditious destruction of the Syrian Arab Republic's chemical weapons programme and stringent verification thereof, . . .

1. *Determines* that the use of chemical weapons anywhere constitutes a threat to international peace and security; . . .

4. *Decides* that the Syrian Arab Republic shall not use, develop, produce, otherwise acquire, stockpile or retain chemical weapons, or transfer, directly or indirectly, chemical weapons to other States or non-State actors;

5. *Underscores* that no party in Syria should use, develop, produce, acquire, stockpile, retain, or transfer chemical weapons;

6. *Decides* that the Syrian Arab Republic shall comply with all aspects of the decision of the OPCW Executive Council of 27 September 2013 . . . .

20. *Decides* that all Member States shall prohibit the procurement of chemical weapons, related equipment, goods and technology or assistance from the Syrian Arab Republic by their nationals, or using their flagged vessels or aircraft, whether or not originating in the territory of the Syrian Arab Republic; . . .

22. *Decides* to remain actively seized of the matter.

NOTES

Since the President's speech in September, U.S. officials have acknowledged that the CIA and State Department have sent both non-lethal and lethal aid to selected Syrian rebels, as well as humanitarian assistance to displaced persons in nations surrounding Syria. For extensive background and a review of domestic and international legal issues, see Christopher M. Blanchard, Carla E. Humud & Mary Beth D. Nikitin, *Armed Conflict in Syria: Overview and U.S. Response* (Cong. Res. Serv. RL33487), May 5, 2014; Christopher M. Blanchard & Jeremy M. Sharp, *Possible U.S. Intervention in Syria: Issues for Congress* (Cong. Res. Serv. R43201), Sept. 12, 2013.

————————

[NSL p. 367. Insert after Note 2.]

5. Back in Iraq?

Remarks by the President on the Situation in Iraq
June 19, 2014

. . . I just met with my national security team to discuss the situation in Iraq. We've been meeting regularly to review the situation since ISIL, a terrorist organization that operates in Iraq and Syria, made advances inside of Iraq. . . . ISIL poses a threat to the Iraqi people, to the region, and to U.S. interests. . . .

First, we are working to secure our embassy and personnel operating inside of Iraq. As President, I have no greater priority than the safety of our men and women serving overseas. So I've taken some steps to relocate some of our embassy personnel, and we've sent reinforcements to better secure our facilities.

Second, at my direction, we have significantly increased our intelligence, surveillance, and reconnaissance assets so that we've got a better picture of what's taking place inside of Iraq. And this will give us a greater understanding of what ISIL is doing, where it's located, and how we might support efforts to counter this threat.

Third, the United States will continue to increase our support to Iraqi security forces. We're prepared to create joint operation centers in Baghdad and northern Iraq to share intelligence and coordinate planning to confront the terrorist threat of ISIL. Through our new Counter-terrorism Partnership Fund, we're prepared to work with Congress to provide additional equipment. We have had advisors in Iraq through our embassy, and we're prepared to send a small number of additional American military advisors — up to 300 — to assess how we can best train, advise, and support Iraqi security forces going forward.

American forces will not be returning to combat in Iraq, but we will help Iraqis as they take the fight to terrorists who threaten the Iraqi people, the region, and American interests as well.

Fourth, in recent days, we've positioned additional U.S. military assets in the region. Because of our increased intelligence resources, we're developing more information about potential targets associated with ISIL. And going forward, we will be prepared to take targeted and precise military action, if and when we determine that the situation on the ground requires it. If we do, I will consult closely with Congress and leaders in Iraq and in the region. . . .

Finally, the United States will lead a diplomatic effort to work with Iraqi leaders and the countries in the region to support stability in Iraq. . . . And just as all Iraq's neighbors must respect Iraq's territorial integrity, all of Iraq's neighbors have a vital interest in ensuring that Iraq does not descend into civil war or become a safe haven for terrorists.

Above all, Iraqi leaders must rise above their differences and come together around a political plan for Iraq's future. Shia, Sunni, Kurds — all Iraqis — must have confidence that they can advance their interests and aspirations through the political process rather than through violence. National unity meetings have to go forward to build consensus across Iraq's different communities. Now that the results of Iraq's recent election has been certified, a new parliament should convene as soon as possible. The formation of a new government will be an opportunity to begin a genuine dialogue and forge a government that represents the legitimate interests of all Iraqis.

. . . [T]he United States will not pursue military options that support one sect inside of Iraq at the expense of another. There's no military solution inside of Iraq, certainly not one that is led by the United States. But there is an urgent need for an inclusive political process, a more capable Iraqi security force, and counterterrorism efforts that deny groups like ISIL a safe haven.

And going forward, we will continue to consult closely with Congress. We will keep the American people informed. We will remain vigilant. And we will continue to do everything in our power to protect the security of the United States and the safety of the American people.

———————————

[NSL p. 403, CTL p. 117. Insert after Note 7.]

Remarks by the President at the National Defense University
May 23, 2013

. . . [D]espite our strong preference for the detention and prosecution of terrorists, sometimes this approach is foreclosed. Al Qaeda and its affiliates try to gain a foothold in some of the most distant and unforgiving places on Earth. They take refuge in remote tribal regions. They hide in caves and walled compounds. They train in empty deserts and rugged mountains.

In some of these places — such as parts of Somalia and Yemen — the state has only the most tenuous reach into the territory. In other cases, the state lacks the capacity or will to take action. It is also not possible for America to simply deploy a team of Special Forces to capture every terrorist. And even when such an approach may be possible, there are places where it would pose profound risks to our troops and local civilians — where a terrorist compound cannot be breached without triggering a firefight with surrounding tribal communities that pose no threat to us, or when putting U.S. boots on the ground may trigger a major international crisis.

To put it another way, our operation in Pakistan against Osama bin Laden cannot be the norm. . . .

It is in this context that the United States has taken lethal, targeted action against al Qaeda and its associated forces, including with remotely piloted aircraft commonly referred to as drones. As was true in previous armed conflicts, this new technology raises profound questions — about who is targeted, and why; about civilian casualties, and the risk of creating new enemies; about the legality of such strikes under U.S. and international law; about accountability and morality.

Let me address these questions. To begin with, our actions are effective. Don't take my word for it. In the intelligence gathered at bin Laden's compound, we found that he wrote, "we could lose the reserves to the enemy's air strikes. We cannot fight air strikes with explosives." Other communications from al Qaeda operatives confirm this as well. Dozens of highly skilled al Qaeda commanders, trainers, bomb makers, and operatives have been taken off the battlefield. Plots have been disrupted that would have targeted international aviation, U.S. transit systems, European cities and our troops in Afghanistan. Simply put, these strikes have saved lives.

Moreover, America's actions are legal. We were attacked on 9/11. Within a week, Congress overwhelmingly authorized the use of force. Under domestic law, and international law, the United States is at war with al Qaeda, the Taliban, and their associated forces. We are at war with an organization that right now would kill as many Americans as they could if we did not stop them first. So this is a just war — a war waged proportionally, in last resort, and in self-defense.

And yet as our fight enters a new phase, America's legitimate claim of self-defense cannot be the end of the discussion. To say a military tactic is legal, or even effective, is not to say it is wise or moral in every instance. For the same human progress that gives us the technology to strike half a world away also demands the discipline to constrain that power — or risk abusing it. That's why, over the last four years, my Administration has worked vigorously to establish a framework that governs our use of force against terrorists – insisting upon clear guidelines, oversight and accountability that is now codified in Presidential Policy Guidance that I signed yesterday. . . .

Beyond the Afghan theater, we only target al Qaeda and its associated forces. Even then, the use of drones is heavily constrained. America does not take strikes when we have the ability to capture individual terrorists — our preference is always to detain, interrogate, and prosecute them. America cannot take strikes wherever we choose — our actions are bound by consultations with partners, and respect for state sovereignty. America does not take strikes to punish individuals — we act against terrorists who pose a continuing and imminent threat to the American people, and when there are no other governments capable of effectively addressing the threat. And before any strike is taken, there must be near-certainty that no civilians will be killed or injured — the highest standard we can set. . . .

Where foreign governments cannot or will not effectively stop terrorism in their territory, the primary alternative to targeted, lethal action is the use of conventional military options. As I've said, even small Special Operations carry enormous risks. Conventional airpower or missiles are far less precise than drones, and likely to cause more civilian casualties and local outrage. And invasions of these territories lead us to be viewed as occupying armies; unleash a torrent of unintended consequences; are difficult to contain; and ultimately empower those who thrive on violent conflict. So it is false to assert that putting boots on the ground is less likely to result in civilian deaths, or to create enemies in the Muslim world. The result would be more U.S. deaths, more Blackhawks down, more confrontations with local populations, and an inevitable mission creep in support of such raids that could easily escalate into new wars. . . .

This is not to say that the risks [of drone strikes] are not real. Any U.S. military action in foreign lands risks creating more enemies, and impacts public opinion overseas. Our laws constrain the power of the President, even during wartime, and I have taken an oath to defend the Constitution of the United States. The very precision of drones strikes, and the necessary secrecy involved in such actions can end up shielding our government from the public scrutiny that a troop deployment invites. It can also lead a President and his team to view drone strikes as a cure-all for terrorism.

For this reason, I've insisted on strong oversight of all lethal action. After I took office, my Administration began briefing all strikes outside of Iraq and Afghanistan to the appropriate committees of Congress. Let me repeat that — not only did Congress authorize the use of force, it is briefed on every strike that America takes. That includes the one instance when we targeted an American citizen: Anwar Awlaki, the chief of external operations for AQAP.

This week, I authorized the declassification of this action, and the deaths of three other Americans in drone strikes, to facilitate transparency and debate on this issue, and to dismiss some of the more outlandish claims. For the record, I do not believe it would be constitutional for the government to target and kill any U.S. citizen — with a drone, or a shotgun — without due process. Nor should any President deploy armed drones over U.S. soil.

But when a U.S. citizen goes abroad to wage war against America —
and is actively plotting to kill U.S. citizens; and when neither the United
States, nor our partners are in a position to capture him before he carries
out a plot — his citizenship should no more serve as a shield than a
sniper shooting down on an innocent crowd should be protected from a
swat team. . . .

. . . I would have detained and prosecuted Awlaki if we captured him
before he carried out a plot. But we couldn't. And as President, I would
have been derelict in my duty had I not authorized the strike that took
out Awlaki.

Of course, the targeting of any Americans raises constitutional
issues that are not present in other strikes — which is why my
Administration submitted information about Awlaki to the Department
of Justice months before Awlaki was killed, and briefed the Congress
before this strike as well. But the high threshold that we have set for
taking lethal action applies to all potential terrorist targets, regardless of
whether or not they are American citizens. This threshold respects the
inherent dignity of every human life. . . .

Going forward, I have asked my Administration to review proposals
to extend oversight of lethal actions outside of war zones that go beyond
our reporting to Congress. Each option has virtues in theory, but poses
difficulties in practice. For example, the establishment of a special court
to evaluate and authorize lethal action has the benefit of bringing a third
branch of government into the process, but raises serious constitutional
issues about presidential and judicial authority. Another idea that's been
suggested — the establishment of an independent oversight board in the
executive branch — avoids those problems, but may introduce a layer of
bureaucracy into national-security decision-making, without inspiring
additional public confidence in the process. Despite these challenges, I
look forward to actively engaging Congress to explore these — and
other — options for increased oversight. . . .

[NSL p. 403, CTL p. 117. Insert after Note 7.]

U.S. Policy Standards and Procedures for the Use of Force in Counterterrorism Operations Outside the United States and Areas of Active Hostilities

May 22, 2013

available at http://www.whitehouse.gov/the-press-office/2013/05/23/fact-sheet-president-s-may-23-speech-counterterrorism

Since his first day in office, President Obama has been clear that the United States will use all available tools of national power to protect the American people from the terrorist threat posed by al-Qa'ida and its associated forces. The President has also made clear that, in carrying on this fight, we will uphold our laws and values and will share as much information as possible with the American people and the Congress, consistent with our national security needs and the proper functioning of the Executive Branch. To these ends, the President has approved, and senior members of the Executive Branch have briefed to the Congress, written policy standards and procedures that formalize and strengthen the Administration's rigorous process for reviewing and approving operations to capture or employ lethal force against terrorist targets outside the United States and outside areas of active hostilities. Additionally, the President has decided to share, in this document, certain key elements of these standards and procedures with the American people so that they can make informed judgments and hold the Executive Branch accountable. . . .

Preference for Capture

The policy of the United States is not to use lethal force when it is feasible to capture a terrorist suspect, because capturing a terrorist offers the best opportunity to gather meaningful intelligence and to mitigate and disrupt terrorist plots. Capture operations are conducted only against suspects who may lawfully be captured or otherwise taken into custody by the United States and only when the operation can be conducted in accordance with all applicable law and consistent with our obligations to other sovereign states.

Standards for the Use of Lethal Force

Any decision to use force abroad — even when our adversaries are terrorists dedicated to killing American citizens — is a significant one. Lethal force will not be proposed or pursued as punishment or as a substitute for prosecuting a terrorist suspect in a civilian court or a military commission. Lethal force will be used only to prevent or stop attacks against U.S. persons, and even then, only when capture is not feasible and no other reasonable alternatives exist to address the threat effectively. In particular, lethal force will be used outside areas of active hostilities only when the following preconditions are met:

First, there must be a legal basis for using lethal force, whether it is against a senior operational leader of a terrorist organization or the forces that organization is using or intends to use to conduct terrorist attacks.

Second, the United States will use lethal force only against a target that poses a continuing, imminent threat to U.S. persons. It is simply not the case that all terrorists pose a continuing, imminent threat to U.S. persons; if a terrorist does not pose such a threat, the United States will not use lethal force.

Third, the following criteria must be met before lethal action may be taken:

1) Near certainty that the terrorist target is present;

2) Near certainty that non-combatants[6] will not be injured or killed;

3) An assessment that capture is not feasible at the time of the operation;

---

6. Non-combatants are individuals who may not be made the object of attack under applicable international law. The term "non-combatant" does not include an individual who is part of a belligerent party to an armed conflict, an individual who is taking a direct part in hostilities, or an individual who is targetable in the exercise of national self-defense. Males of military age may be non-combatants; it is not the case that all military-aged males in the vicinity of a target are deemed to be combatants.

4) An assessment that the relevant governmental authorities in the country where action is contemplated cannot or will not effectively address the threat to U.S. persons; and

5) An assessment that no other reasonable alternatives exist to effectively address the threat to U.S. persons.

Finally, whenever the United States uses force in foreign territories, international legal principles, including respect for sovereignty and the law of armed conflict, impose important constraints on the ability of the United States to act unilaterally — and on the way in which the United States can use force. The United States respects national sovereignty and international law.

U.S. Government Coordination and Review

Decisions to capture or otherwise use force against individual terrorists outside the United States and areas of active hostilities are made at the most senior levels of the U.S. Government, informed by departments and agencies with relevant expertise and institutional roles. Senior national security officials — including the deputies and heads of key departments and agencies — will consider proposals to make sure that our policy standards are met, and attorneys — including the senior lawyers of key departments and agencies — will review and determine the legality of proposals.

These decisions will be informed by a broad analysis of an intended target's current and past role in plots threatening U.S. persons; relevant intelligence information the individual could provide; and the potential impact of the operation on ongoing terrorism plotting, on the capabilities of terrorist organizations, on U.S. foreign relations, and on U.S. intelligence collection. Such analysis will inform consideration of whether the individual meets both the legal and policy standards for the operation.

Other Key Elements

U.S. Persons. If the United States considers an operation against a terrorist identified as a U.S. person, the Department of Justice will conduct an additional legal analysis to ensure that such action may be conducted against the individual consistent with the Constitution and laws of the United States.

Reservation of Authority. These new standards and procedures do not limit the President's authority to take action in extraordinary circumstances when doing so is both lawful and necessary to protect the United States or its allies.

Congressional Notification. Since entering office, the President has made certain that the appropriate Members of Congress have been kept fully informed about our counterterrorism operations. Consistent with this strong and continuing commitment to congressional oversight, appropriate Members of the Congress will be regularly provided with updates identifying any individuals against whom lethal force has been approved. In addition, the appropriate committees of Congress will be notified whenever a counterterrorism operation covered by these standards and procedures has been conducted.

———————

[NSL p. 410, CTL p. 124. Insert at end of chapter.]

E. Targeting a U.S. Citizen

United States citizen Anwar Al-Aulaqi was a terrorist leader of Al Qaeda in the Arabian Peninsula (AQAP). After news reports that Al-Aulaqi had been placed on a kill list by the United States, Nasser Al-Aulaqi filed suit on behalf of his son against the President and other senior officials and sought to enjoin the government from carrying out the planned killing of Anwar Al-Aulaqi unless they present "a concrete, specific, and imminent threat to life or physical safety, and there are no means other than lethal force that could reasonably be employed to neutralize that threat." *Al-Aulaqi v. Obama*, 727 F. Supp. 2d 1 (D.D.C. 2010). The court dismissed the suit after finding that Nasser Al-Aulaqi did not have standing to assert his son's constitutional rights, and ruling that some of the issues presented were non-justiciable political questions.

On September 30, 2011, missiles from one or more pilotless U.S. drones struck the vehicle Anwar Al-Aulaqi was riding in and killed him and at least three others. A separate U.S. drone strike inadvertently killed Al-Aulaqi's son and at least six others two weeks later in a mission that did not kill its intended target. Al-Aulaqi's father and mother thereafter sued various U.S. officials for damages in their personal capacities and claimed that the officials violated the Fifth Amendment rights of the decedents by authorizing the drone strikes. After finding the case justiciable and agreeing that the complaint states a plausible procedural and substantive due process claim on behalf of Anwar Al-Aulaqi, the court dismissed the lawsuit because "special factors" precluded implying a judicial remedy for a constitutional violation under *Bivens v. Six Unknown Named Agents of the Federal Bureau of Narcotics*, 403 U.S. 388, 389 (1971), *Al-Aulaqi v. Panetta*, 2014 WL 1352452 (D.D.C. 2014). The *Bivens* problems are considered at NSL p. 973, CTL p. 587.

The legal bases for targeting Al-Aulaqi were provided in the following DOJ White Paper:

Department of Justice, White Paper: Lawfulness of a Lethal Operation Directed Against a U.S. Citizen Who Is a Senior Operational Leader of Al-Qa'ida or an Associated Force

Draft Nov. 8, 2011
available at www.fas.org/irp/eprint/doj-lethal.pdf

This white paper sets forth a legal framework for considering the circumstances in which the U.S. government could use lethal force in a foreign country outside the area of active hostilities against a U.S. citizen who is a senior operational leader of al-Qa'ida or an associated force[1] of al-Qa'ida — that is, an al-Qa'ida leader actively engaged in planning operations to kill Americans. The paper does not attempt to determine the minimum requirements necessary to render such an operation lawful; nor does it assess what might be required to render a lethal operation against a U.S. citizen lawful in other circumstances, including an operation against enemy forces on a traditional battlefield or an operation against a U.S. citizen who is not a senior operational leader of such forces. . . .

---

1. An associated force of al-Qa'ida includes a group that would qualify as a co-belligerent under the laws of war.

I.

The United States is in an armed conflict with al-Qa'ida and its associated forces, and Congress has authorized the President to use all necessary and appropriate force against those entities. *See* Authorization for Use of Military Force ("AUMF"), Pub. L. No. 107-40, §2(a), 115 Stat. 224, 224 (2001). In addition to the authority arising from the AUMF, the President's use of force against al-Qa'ida and associated forces is lawful under other principles of U.S. and international law, including the President's constitutional responsibility to protect the nation and the inherent right to national self-defense recognized in international law (*see, e.g.*, U.N. Charter art. 51). It was on these bases that the United States responded to the attacks of September 11, 2001, and "[t]hese domestic and international legal authorities continue to this day." Harold Hongju Koh, Legal Adviser, U.S. Department of State, Address to the Annual Meeting of the American Society of International Law: The Obama Administration and International Law (Mar. 25, 2010) ("2010 Koh ASIL Speech").

Any operation of the sort discussed here would be conducted in a foreign country against a senior operational leader of al-Qa'ida or its associated forces who poses an imminent threat of violent attack against the United States. A use of force under such circumstances would be justified as an act of national self-defense. In addition, such a person would be within the core of individuals against whom Congress has authorized the use of necessary and appropriate force. The fact that such a person would also be a U.S. citizen would not alter this conclusion. The Supreme Court has held that the military may constitutionally use force against a U.S. citizen who is a part of enemy forces. See *Hamdi*, 542 U.S. 507, 518 (2004) (plurality opinion); *id.* at 587, 597 (Thomas, J., dissenting); *Ex Parte Quirin*, 317 U.S. at 37-38. Like the imposition of military detention, the use of lethal force against such enemy forces is an "important incident of war." *Hamdi*, 542 U.S. at 518 (plurality opinion) (quotation omitted). Accordingly, the Department does not believe that U.S. citizenship would immunize a senior operational leader of al-Qa'ida or its associated forces from a use of force abroad authorized by the AUMF or in national self-defense.

In addition, the United States retains its authority to use force against al-Qa'ida and associated forces outside the area of active hostilities when it targets a senior operational leader of the enemy forces who is actively engaged in planning operations to kill Americans. The

United States is currently in a non-international armed conflict with al-Qa'ida and its associated forces. *See Hamdan v. Rumsfeld*, 548 U.S. 557, 628-31 (2006) (holding that a conflict between a nation and a transnational non-state actor, occurring outside the nation's territory, is an armed conflict "not of an international character" (quoting Common Article 3 of the Geneva Conventions) because it is not a "clash between nations"). Any U.S. operation would be part of this non-international armed conflict, even if it were to take place away from the zone of active hostilities. . . . None of the three branches of the U.S. Government has identified a strict geographical limit on the permissible scope of the AUMF's authorization.

Claiming that for purposes of international law, an armed conflict generally exists only when there is "protracted armed violence between governmental authorities and organized armed groups," *Prosecutor v. Tadic*, Case No. IT-94-1AR72, Decision on the Defence Motion for Interlocutory Appeal on Jurisdiction, ¶70 (Int'l Crim. Trib. for the Former Yugoslavia, App. Chamber Oct. 2, 1995), some commenters have suggested that the conflict between the United States and al-Qa'ida cannot lawfully extend to nations outside Afghanistan in which the level of hostilities is less intense or prolonged than in Afghanistan itself. *See, e.g.*, Mary Ellen O'Connell, *Combatants and the Combat Zone*, 43 U. Rich. L. Rev. 845, 857-59 (2009). There is little judicial or other authoritative precedent that speaks directly to the question of the geographic scope of a non-international armed conflict in which one of the parties is a transnational, non-state actor and where the principal theater of operations is not within the territory of the nation that is a party to the conflict. Thus, in considering this potential issue, the Department looks to principles and statements from analogous contexts.

The Department has not found any authority for the proposition that when one of the parties to an armed conflict plans and executes operations from a base in a new nation, an operation to engage the enemy in that location cannot be part of the original armed conflict, and thus subject to the laws of war governing that conflict, unless the hostilities become sufficiently intense and protracted in the new location. That does not appear to be the rule of the historical practice, for instance, even in a traditional international conflict. *See* John R. Stevenson, Legal Adviser, Department of State, United States Military Action in Cambodia: Questions of International Law, Address before the Hammarskjold Forum of the Association of the Bar of the City of New York (May 28, 1970), *in* 3 *The Vietnam War and International Law: The*

Widening Context 23, 28-30 (Richard A. Falk, ed. 1972) (arguing that in an international armed conflict, if a neutral state has been unable for any reason to prevent violations of its neutrality by the troops of one belligerent using its territory as a base of operations, the other belligerent has historically been justified in attacking those enemy forces in that state). Particularly in a non-international armed conflict, where terrorist organizations may move their base of operations from one country to another, the determination of whether a particular operation would be part of an ongoing armed conflict would require consideration of the particular facts and circumstances in each case, including the fact that transnational non-state organizations such as al-Qa'ida may have no single site serving as their base of operations. . . .

II.

The Department assumes that the rights afforded by Fifth Amendment's Due Process Clause, as well as the Fourth Amendment, attach to a U.S. citizen even while he is abroad. *See Reid v. Covert*, 354 U.S. 1, 5-6 (1957) (plurality opinion); *United States v. Verdugo-Urquidez*, 494 U.S. 259, 269-70 (1990); *see also In re Terrorist Bombings of U.S. Embassies in East Africa*, 552 F.3d 157, 170 n.7 (2d Cir. 2008). The U.S. citizenship of a leader of al-Qa'ida or its associated forces, however, does not give that person constitutional immunity from attack. . . .

A.

The Due Process Clause would not prohibit a lethal operation of the sort contemplated here. In *Hamdi*, a plurality of the Supreme Court used the *Mathews v. Eldridge* balancing test to analyze the Fifth Amendment due process rights of a U.S. citizen who had been captured on the battlefield in Afghanistan and detained in the United States, and who wished to challenge the government's assertion that he was part of enemy forces. The Court explained that the "process due in any given instance is determined by weighing 'the private interest that will be affected by the official action' against the Government's asserted interest, 'including the function involved' and the burdens the Government would face in providing greater process." *Hamdi*, 542 U.S. at 529 (plurality opinion) (quoting *Mathews v. Eldridge*, 424 U.S. 319, 335 (1976)). The due process balancing analysis applied to determine the Fifth Amendment rights of a U.S. citizen with respect to law-of-war detention supplies the framework for assessing the process due a U.S. citizen who is a senior operational leader of an enemy force planning violent attacks against Americans before he is subjected to lethal targeting.

In the circumstances considered here, the interests on both sides would be weighty. *See Hamdi*, 542 U.S. at 529 (plurality opinion) ("It is beyond question that substantial interests lie on both sides of the scale in this case."). An individual's interest in avoiding erroneous deprivation of his life is "uniquely compelling." *See Ake v. Oklahoma*, 470 U.S. 68, 178 (1985). No private interest is more substantial. At the same time, the government's interest in waging war, protecting its citizens, and removing the threat posed by members of enemy forces is also compelling. *Cf. Hamdi*, 542 U.S. at 531 (plurality opinion) ("On the other side of the scale are the weighty and sensitive governmental interests in ensuring that those who have in fact fought with the enemy during a war do not return to battle against the United States."). As the *Hamdi* plurality observed, in the "circumstances of war," "the risk of erroneous deprivation of a citizen's liberty in the absence of sufficient process . . . is very real," *id.* at 530 (plurality opinion), and, of course, the risk of an erroneous deprivation of a citizen's life is even more significant. But, "the realities of combat" render certain uses of force "necessary and appropriate," including force against U.S. citizens who have joined enemy forces in the armed conflict against the United States and whose activities pose an imminent threat of violent attack against the United States — and "due process analysis need not blink at those realities." *id.* at 531 (plurality opinion). These same realities must also be considered in assessing "the burdens the Government would face in providing greater process" to a member of enemy forces. *Id.* at 529, 531 (plurality opinion).

In view of these interests and practical considerations, the United States would be able to use lethal force against a U.S. citizen, who is located outside the United States and is an operational leader continually planning attacks against U.S. persons and interests, in at least the following circumstances: (1) where an informed, high-level official of the U.S. government has determined that the targeted individual poses an imminent threat of violent attack against the United States; (2) where a capture operation would be infeasible — and where those conducting the operation continue to monitor whether capture becomes feasible; and (3) where such an operation would be conducted consistent with applicable law of war principles. In these circumstances, the "realities" of the conflict and the weight of the government's interest in protecting its citizens from an imminent attack are such that the Constitution would not require the government to provide further process to such a U.S. citizen before using lethal force. *Cf. Hamdi*, 542 U.S. at 535 (plurality opinion) (noting that the Court "accord[s] the greatest respect and consideration to the judgments of military authorities in matters relating to the actual prosecution of war, and . . . the scope of that discretion necessarily is wide").

Certain aspects of this legal framework require additional explication. *First*, the condition that an operational leader present an "imminent" threat of violent attack against the United States does not require the United States to have clear evidence that a specific attack on U.S. persons and interests will take place in the immediate future. Given the nature of, for example, the terrorist attacks on September 11, in which civilian airliners were hijacked to strike the World Trade Center and the Pentagon, this definition of imminence, which would require the United States to refrain from action until preparations for an attack are concluded, would not allow the United States sufficient time to defend itself. The defensive options available to the United States may be reduced or eliminated if al-Qa'ida operatives disappear and cannot be found when the time of their attack approaches. Consequently, with respect to al-Qa'ida leaders who are continually planning attacks, the United States is likely to have only a limited window of opportunity within which to defend Americans in a manner that has both a high likelihood of success and sufficiently reduces the probabilities of civilian causalities. Furthermore, a "terrorist 'war' does not consist of a massive attack across an international border, nor does it consist of one isolated incident that occurs and is then past. It is a drawn out, patient, sporadic pattern of attacks. It is very difficult to know when or where the next incident will occur." Gregory M. Travalio, *Terrorism, International Law, and the Use of Military Force*, 18 Wis. Int'l L.J. 145, 173 (2000). Delaying action against individuals continually planning to kill Americans until some theoretical end stage of the planning for a particular plot would create an unacceptably high risk that the action would fail and that American casualties would result.

By its nature, therefore, the threat posed by al-Qa'ida and its associated forces demands a broader concept of imminence in judging when a person continually planning terror attacks presents an imminent threat, making the use of force appropriate. In this context, imminence must incorporate considerations of the relevant window of opportunity, the possibility of reducing collateral damage to civilians, and the likelihood of heading off future disastrous attacks on Americans. Thus, a decision maker determining whether an al-Qa'ida operational leader presents an imminent threat of violent attack against the United States must take into account that certain members of al-Qa'ida (including any potential target of lethal force) are continually plotting attacks against the United States; that al-Qa'ida would engage in such attacks regularly to the extent it were able to do so; that the U.S. government may not be aware of all al-Qa'ida plots as they are developing and thus cannot be confident that none is about to occur; and that, in light of these predicates, the nation may have a limited window of opportunity within which to strike in a manner that both has a high likelihood of success and reduces the probability of American casualties.

With this understanding, a high-level official could conclude, for example, that an individual poses an "imminent threat" of violent attack against the United States where he is an operational leader of al-Qa'ida or an associated force and is personally and continually involved in planning terrorist attacks against the United States. Moreover, where the al-Qa'ida member in question has recently been involved in activities posing an imminent threat of violent attack against the United States, and there is no evidence suggesting that he has renounced or abandoned such activities, that member's involvement in al-Qa'ida's continuing terrorist campaign against the United States would support the conclusion that the member poses an imminent threat.

Second, regarding the feasibility of capture, capture would not be feasible if it could not be physically effectuated during the relevant window of opportunity or if the relevant country were to decline to consent to a capture operation. Other factors such as undue risk to U.S. personnel conducting a potential capture operation also could be relevant. Feasibility would be a highly fact-specific and potentially time-sensitive inquiry.

Third, it is a premise here that any such lethal operation by the United States would comply with the four fundamental law-of-war principles governing the use of force: necessity, distinction, proportionality, and humanity (the avoidance of unnecessary suffering). For example, it would not be consistent with those principles to continue an operation if anticipated civilian casualties would be excessive in relation to the anticipated military advantage. An operation consistent with the laws of war could not violate the prohibitions against treachery and perfidy, which address a breach of confidence by the assailant. These prohibitions do not, however, categorically forbid the use of stealth or surprise, nor forbid attacks on identified individual soldiers or officers. And the Department is not aware of any other law-of-war grounds precluding use of such tactics. Relatedly, "there is no prohibition under the laws of war on the use of technologically advanced weapons systems in armed conflict — such as pilotless aircraft or so-called smart bombs — as long as they are employed in conformity with applicable laws of war." 2010 Koh ASIL Speech. Further, under this framework, the United States would also be required to accept a surrender if it were feasible to do so. . . .

B.

Similarly, assuming that a lethal operation targeting a U.S. citizen abroad who is planning attacks against the United States would result in a "seizure" under the Fourth Amendment, such an operation would not violate that Amendment in the circumstances posited here. The Supreme Court has made clear that the constitutionality of a seizure is determined by "balanc[ing] the nature and quality of the intrusion on the individual's Fourth Amendment interests against the importance of the governmental interests alleged to justify the intrusion." *Tennessee v. Garner*, 471 U.S. 1, 8 (1985) (internal quotation marks omitted). . . .

C.

Finally, the Department notes that under the circumstances described in this paper, there exists no appropriate judicial forum to evaluate these constitutional considerations. It is well-established that "[m]atters intimately related to foreign policy and national security are rarely proper subjects for judicial intervention," *Haig v. Agee*, 453 U.S. 280, 292 (1981), because such matters "frequently turn on standards that defy judicial application," or "involve the exercise of a discretion demonstrably committed to the executive or legislature," *Baker v. Carr*, 369 U.S. 186, 211 (1962). Were a court to intervene here, it might be required inappropriately to issue an ex ante command to the President and officials responsible for operations with respect to their specific tactical judgment to mount a potential lethal operation against a senior operational leader of al-Qa'ida or its associated forces. And judicial enforcement of such orders would require the Court to supervise

inherently predictive judgments by the President and his national
security advisors as to when and how to use force against a member of
an enemy force against which Congress has authorized the use of force.

III.

Section 1119(b) of title 18 provides that a "person who, being a
national of the United States, kills or attempts to kill a national of the
United States while such national is outside the United States but within
the jurisdiction of another country shall be punished as provided under
sections 1111, 1112, and 1113." 18 U.S.C. §1119(b) (2006). Because the
person who would be the target of the kind of operation discussed here
would be a U.S. citizen, it might be suggested that section 1119(b)
would prohibit such an operation. Section 1119, however, incorporates
the federal murder and manslaughter statutes, and thus its prohibition
extends only to "unlawful killing[s]," 18 U.S.C. §§1111(a), 1112(a)
(2006). Section 1119 is best construed to incorporate the "public
authority" justification, which renders lethal action carried out by a
government official lawful in some circumstances. . . .

A. . . .

Guidance as to the meaning of the phrase "unlawful killing" in
sections 1111 and 1112 — and thus for purposes of section 1119(b) —
can be found in the historical understandings of murder and
manslaughter. That history shows that states have long recognized
justifications and excuses to statutes criminalizing "unlawful" killings. . . .
Accordingly, section 1119 does not proscribe killings covered by a
justification traditionally recognized under the common law or state and
federal murder statutes. . . .

B.

The public authority justification is well-accepted, and it may be
available even in cases where the particular criminal statute at issue does
not expressly refer to a public authority justification. Prosecutions where
such a "public authority" justification is invoked are understandably
rare, and thus there is little case law in which courts have analyzed the
scope of the justification with respect to the conduct of government
officials. Nonetheless, discussions in the leading treatises and in the

Model Penal Code demonstrate its legitimacy. *See* 2 Wayne R. LaFave, *Substantive Criminal Law* §10.2(b), at 135 (2d ed. 2003). . . .

The public authority justification would not excuse all conduct of public officials from all criminal prohibitions. The legislature may design some criminal prohibitions to place bounds on the kinds of governmental conduct that can be authorized by the Executive. Or the legislature may enact a criminal prohibition in order to limit the scope of the conduct that the legislature has otherwise authorized the Executive to undertake pursuant to another statute. But the generally recognized public authority justification reflects that it would not make sense to attribute to Congress the intent to criminalize all covered activities undertaken by public officials in the legitimate exercise of their otherwise lawful authorities, even if Congress clearly intends to make those same actions a crime when committed by persons not acting pursuant to public authority. In some instances, therefore, the best interpretation of a criminal prohibition is that Congress intended to distinguish persons who are acting pursuant to public authority from those who are not, even if the statute does not make that distinction express.

The touchstone for the analysis whether section 1119 incorporates not only justifications generally, but also the public authority justification in particular, is the legislative intent underlying this statute. Here, the statute should be read to exclude from its prohibitory scope killings that are encompassed by traditional justifications, which include the public authority justification. The statutory incorporation of two other criminal statutes expressly referencing "unlawful" killings is one indication. Moreover, there are no indications that Congress had a contrary intention. Nothing in the text or legislative history of sections 1111-1113 of title 18 suggests that Congress intended to exclude the established public authority justification from those justifications that Congress otherwise must be understood to have imported through the use of the modifier "unlawful" in those statutes. Nor is there anything in the text or legislative history of section 1119 itself to suggest that Congress intended to abrogate or otherwise affect the availability of this traditional justification for killings. . . .

The Department thus concludes that section 1119 incorporates the public authority justification. . . .

C. . . .

The United States is currently in the midst of a congressionally authorized armed conflict with al-Qa'ida and associated forces, and may act in national self-defense to protect U.S. persons and interests who are under continual threat of violent attack by certain al-Q'aida operatives planning operations against them. The public authority justification would apply to a lethal operation of the kind discussed in this paper if it were conducted in accord with applicable law of war principles. As one legal commentator has explained, "if a soldier intentionally kills an enemy combatant in time of war and within the rules of warfare, he is not guilty of murder," whereas, for example, if that soldier intentionally kills a prisoner of war — a violation of the laws of war — "then he commits murder." 2 LaFave, *Substantive Criminal Law* §10.2(c), at 136. . . .

The fact that an operation may target a U.S. citizen does not alter this conclusion. . . .

. . . [T]he Department believes that the use of lethal force addressed in this white paper would constitute a lawful killing under the public authority doctrine if conducted in a manner consistent with the fundamental law of war principles governing the use of force in a non-international armed conflict. Such an operation would not violate the assassination ban in Executive Order No. 12333. Section 2.11 of Executive Order No. 12333 provides that "[n]o person employed by or acting on behalf of the United States Government shall engage in, or conspire to engage in, assassination." 46 Fed. Reg. 59,941, 59, 952 (Dec. 4, 1981). A lawful killing in self-defense is not an assassination. In the Department's view, a lethal operation conducted against a U.S. citizen whose conduct poses an imminent threat of violent attack against the United States would be a legitimate act of national self-defense that would not violate the assassination ban. Similarly, the use of lethal force, consistent with the laws of war, against an individual who is a legitimate military target would be lawful and would not violate the assassination ban.

IV.

The War Crimes Act, 18 U.S.C. §2441 (2006) makes it a federal crime for a member of the Armed Forces or a national of the United States to "commit[] a war crime." *Id.* §2441(a). The only potentially applicable provision of section 2441 to operations of the type discussed herein makes it a war crime to commit a "grave breach" of Common Article 3 of the Geneva Conventions when that breach is committed "in the context of and in association with an armed conflict not of an international character." *Id.* §2441(c)(3). As defined by the statute, a "grave breach" of Common Article 3 includes "[m]urder," described in pertinent part as "[t]he act of a person who intentionally kills, or conspires or attempts to kill . . . one or more persons taking no active part in the hostilities, including those placed out of combat by sickness, wounds, detention, or any other cause." *Id.* §2441(d)(1)(D).

Whatever might be the outer bounds of this category of covered persons, Common Article 3 does not alter the fundamental law of war principle concerning a belligerent party's right in an armed conflict to target individuals who are part of an enemy's armed forces or eliminate a nation's authority to take legitimate action in national self-defense. The language of Common Article 3 "makes clear that members of such armed forces [of both the state and non-state parties to the conflict] . . . are considered as 'taking no active part in the hostilities' only once they have disengaged from their fighting function ('have laid down their arms') or are placed *hors de combat*; mere suspension of combat is insufficient." International Committee of the Red Cross, *Interpretive Guidance on the Notion of Direct Participation in Hostilities Under International Humanitarian Law* 28 (2009). An operation against a senior operational leader of al-Qa'ida or its associated forces who poses an imminent threat of violent attack against the United States would target a person who is taking "an active part in hostilities" and therefore would not constitute a "grave breach" of Common Article 3. . . .

———————————

The 2011 Department of Justice White Paper was based in substantial part on a 2010 memorandum by the Office of Legal Counsel. In 2014, a court ordered disclosure of a partially redacted version of the memorandum pursuant to a Freedom of Information Act request, at *New York Times Co. v. Dep't of Justice*, Nos. 13-422 (L), 13-4445 (CON), 2014 WL 2838861, at app. (2d Cir. June 23, 2014). In the following excerpt, we have omitted portions of the memorandum that are most redundant with the 2011 White Paper.

U.S. Department of Justice, Office of Legal Counsel, Applicability of Federal Criminal Laws and the Constitution to Contemplated Lethal Operations Against Shaykh Anwar al-Aulaqi

July 16, 2010

[Redacted] . . . .

III.

Given that section 1119 incorporates the public authority justification, we must next analyze whether the contemplated DoD and CIA operations would be encompassed by that justification. In particular, we must analyze whether that justification would apply even though the target of the contemplated operations is a United States citizen. . . .

A. . . .

In applying this variant of the public authority justification to the contemplated DoD operation, we note as an initial matter that DoD would undertake the operation pursuant to Executive war powers that Congress has expressly authorized. *See Youngstown Sheet & Tube Co. v. Sawyer,* 343 U.S. 579, 635 (1952) (Jackson, J., concurring) ("When the President acts pursuant to an express or implied authorization of Congress, his authority is at its maximum, for it includes all that he possesses in his own right plus all that Congress can delegate."). By authorizing the use of force against "organizations" that planned, authorized, and committed the September 11th attacks, Congress clearly authorized the President's use of "necessary and appropriate" force against al-Qaida forces, because al-Qaida carried out the September 11th attacks. *See* Authorization for Use of Military Force ("AUMF"), Pub. L. No. 107-40, 115 Stat. 224, §2(a) (2001) (providing that the President may "use all necessary and appropriate force against those nations, organizations, or persons he determines planned, authorized, committed or aided the terrorist attacks that occurred on September 11, 2001, or harbored such organizations or persons, in order to prevent any future acts of international terrorism against the United States by such nations, organizations, or persons,"). And, as we have explained, a decision-maker could reasonably conclude that this leader of AQAP forces is part of al-Qaida forces. Alternatively, and as we have further explained, *supra* at 10 n.5, the AUMF applies with respect to forces "associated with" al-Qaida that are engaged in hostilities against the U.S. or its coalition partners, and a decision-maker could reasonably conclude that the AQAP forces of which al-Aulaqi is a leader are "associated with" al Qaida forces for purposes of the AUMF. On either view, DoD would carry out its contemplated operation against a leader of an organization that is within the scope of the AUMF, and therefore DoD would in that respect be operating in accord with a grant of statutory authority.

Based upon the facts represented to us, moreover, the target of the contemplated operation has engaged in conduct as part of that organization that brings him within the scope of the AUMF. High-level government officials have concluded, on the basis of al-Aulaqi's activities in Yemen, that al-Aulaqi is a leader of AQAP whose activities in Yemen pose a "continued and imminent threat" of violence to United States persons and interests. Indeed, the facts represented to us indicate that al-Aulaqi has been involved, through his operational and leadership roles within AQAP, in an abortive attack within the United States and continues to plot attacks intended to kill Americans from his base of operations in Yemen. The contemplated DoD operation, therefore, would be carried out against someone who is within the core of individuals against whom Congress has authorized the use of necessary and appropriate force. . . .

Here, unlike in *Hamdan* [*v. Rumsfeld*, 548 U.S. 557 (2006)]*,* the contemplated DoD operation would occur in Yemen, a location that is far from the most active theater of combat between the United States and al-Qaida. That does not affect our conclusion, however, that the combination of facts present here would make the DoD operation in Yemen part of the non-international armed conflict with al-Qaida. To be sure, *Hamdan* did not directly address the geographic scope of the noninternational armed conflict between the United States and al-Qaida that the Court recognized, other than to implicitly hold that it extended to Afghanistan, where Hamdan was apprehended. *See* 548 U.S. at 566; *see also id.* at 641-42 (Kennedy, J., concurring in part) (referring to Common Article 3 as "applicable to our Nation's armed conflict with al Qaeda in Afghanistan"). The Court did, however, specifically reject the argument that non-international armed conflicts are necessarily limited to internal conflicts. The Common Article 3 term "conflict not of an international character," the Court explained, bears its "literal meaning" — namely, that it is a conflict that "does not involve a clash between nations." *Id.* at 630 (majority opinion). . . .

For present purposes, in applying the more context-specific approach to determining whether an operation would take place within the scope of a particular armed conflict, it is sufficient that the facts as they have been represented to us here, in combination, support the judgment that DoD's operation in Yemen would be conducted as part of the non-international armed conflict between the United States and al-Qaida. Specifically, DoD proposes to target a leader of AQAP, an organized enemy force that is either a component of al-Qaida or that is a co-belligerent of that central party to the conflict and engaged in hostilities against the United States as part of the same comprehensive armed conflict, in league with the principal enemy. Moreover, DoD would conduct the operation in Yemen, where, according to the facts related to us, AQAP has a significant and organized presence, and from which AQAP is conducting terrorist training in an organized manner and has executed and is planning to execute attacks against the United States. Finally, the targeted individual himself, on behalf of that force, is continuously planning attacks from that Yemeni base of operations against the United States, as the conflict with al-Qaida continues. Taken together, these facts support the conclusion that the DoD operation would be part of the non-international armed conflict the Court recognized in *Hamdan*.

There remains the question whether DoD would conduct its operation in accord with the rules governing targeting in a non-international armed conflict — namely, international humanitarian law, commonly known as the laws of war. *See* Dinstein, *Conduct of Hostilities* at 17 (international humanitarian law "takes a middle road, allowing belligerent States much leeway (in keeping with the demands of military necessity) and yet circumscribing their freedom of action (in the name of humanitarianism"). The 1949 Geneva Conventions to which the United States is a party do not themselves directly impose extensive restrictions on the conduct of a non-international armed conflict — with the principal exception of Common Article 3, *see Hamdan,* 548 U.S. at 630-31. But the norms specifically described in those treaties "are not exclusive, and the laws and customs of war also impose limitations on the conduct of participants in non-international armed conflict." . . .

In particular, the "fundamental rules" and "intransgressible principles of international customary law," Advisory Opinion of 8 July 1996 on the Legality of the Threat or Use of Nuclear Weapons IT 79,

1996 I.C.J. 226, 257 ("Nuclear Weapons Advisory Opinion"), which apply to all armed conflicts, include the "four fundamental principles that are inherent to all targeting decisions" — namely, military necessity, humanity (the avoidance of unnecessary suffering), proportionality, and distinction. . . .

DoD represents that it would conduct its operation against al-Aulaqi in compliance with these fundamental law-of-war norms. *See* Chairman of the Joint Chiefs of Staff, Instruction 5810.01D, *Implementation of the DoD Law of War Program* ¶14.a, at 1 (Apr. 30, 2010) ("It is DOD policy that . . . [m]embers of the DOD Components comply with the law of war during all armed conflicts, however such conflicts are characterized, and in all other military operations."). In particular, the targeted nature of the operation would help to ensure that it would comply with the principle of distinction, and DoD has represented to us that it would make every effort to minimize civilian casualties and that the officer who launches the ordnance would be required to abort a strike if he or she concludes that civilian casualties will be disproportionate or that such a strike will in any other respect violate the laws of war. *See DoD May 18 Memorandum for OLC,* at 1 ("Any official in the chain of command has the authority and duty to abort" a strike "if he or she concludes that civilian casualties will be disproportionate or that such a strike will otherwise violate the laws of war."). . . .

In light of all these circumstances, we believe DoD's contemplated operation against al-Aulaqi would comply with international law, including the laws of war applicable to this armed conflict, and would fall within Congress's authorization to use "necessary and appropriate force" against al-Qaida. In consequence, the operation should be understood to constitute the lawful conduct of war and thus to be encompassed by the public authority justification. Accordingly, the contemplated attack, if conducted by DoD in the mariner described, would not result in an "unlawful" killing and thus would not violate section 1119(b).

B.

We next consider whether the CIA's contemplated operation against al-Aulaqi in Yemen would be covered by the public authority justification. . . .

Specifically, we understand that the CIA, like DoD, would carry out the attack against an operational leader of an enemy force, as part of the

United States's ongoing non-international armed conflict with al-Qaida.

[Redacted] the CIA — would conduct the operation in a manner that accords with the rules of international humanitarian law governing this armed conflict, and in circumstances [sic].[44] . . .

Accordingly, we conclude that, just as the combination of circumstances present here supports the judgment that the public authority justification would apply to the contemplated operation by the

---

44. If the killing by a member of the armed forces would comply with the law of war and otherwise be lawful, actions of CIA officials facilitating that killing should also not be unlawful. *See, e.g., Shoot Down Opinion* at 165 n.33 ("[O]ne cannot be prosecuted for aiding and abetting the commission of an act that is not itself a crime.") (citing *Shuttlesworth v. City of Birmingham*, 373 U.S. 262 (1963)).

Nor would the fact that CIA personnel would be involved in the operation itself cause the operation to violate the laws of war. It is true that CIA personnel, by virtue of their not being part of the armed forces, would not enjoy the immunity from prosecution under the domestic law of the countries in which they act for their conduct in targeting and killing enemy forces in compliance with the laws of war — an immunity that the armed forces enjoy by virtue of their status. *See Report of the Special Rapporteur* ¶71, at 22; *see also* Dinstein, *Conduct of Hostilities*, at 31. Nevertheless, lethal activities conducted in accord with the laws of war, and undertaken in the course of lawfully authorized hostilities, do not violate the laws of war by virtue of the fact that they are carried out in part by government actors who are not entitled to the combatant's privilege. The contrary view "arises . . . from a fundamental confusion between acts punishable under international law and acts with respect to which international law affords no protection." Statements in the Supreme Court's decision in *Ex parte Quirin*, 317 U.S. 1 (1942), are sometimes cited for the contrary view. *See, e.g., id.* at 36 n.12 (suggesting that passing through enemy lines in order to commit "any hostile act" while not in uniform "renders the offender liable to trial for violation of the laws of war"); *id.* at 31 (enemies who come secretly through the lines for purposes of waging war by destruction of life or property "without uniform" not only are "generally not to be entitled to the status of prisoners of war," but also "to be offenders against the law of war subject to trial and punishment by military tribunals"). Because the Court in *Quirin* focused on conduct taken behind enemy lines, it is not clear whether the Court in these passages intended to refer only to conduct that would constitute perfidy or treachery. To the extent the Court meant to suggest more broadly that any hostile acts performed by unprivileged belligerents are for that reason violations of the laws of war, the authorities the Court cited (the Lieber Code and Colonel Winthrop's military law treatise) do not provide clear support. . . . .

armed forces, the combination of circumstances also supports the judgment that the CIA's operation, too, would be encompassed by that justification. The CIA's contemplated operation, therefore, would not result in an "unlawful" killing under section 1111 and thus would not violate section 1119. . . .

Please let us know if we can be of further assistance.

———————

[NSL p. 464. Insert at the end of Note 2.]

Over time, an informal system of congressional oversight has developed regarding certain particularly sensitive *non-covert action intelligence* (mostly collection) activities. So-called "Gang of Four" notifications of such activities are given to the chairs and ranking Members of the two congressional intelligence committees, when "the intelligence community believes a particular intelligence activity to be of such sensitivity that a restricted notification is warranted in order to reduce the risk of disclosure, inadvertent or otherwise." John Rollins & Rebecca S. Lange, *"Gang of Four" Congressional Intelligence Notifications* (Cong. Res. Serv. R40698), Nov. 19, 2012. Other non-covert action activities are generally briefed to the full committees.

———————

[NSL p. 464. Insert after Note 2.]

In November 2011, Director of National Intelligence James Clapper issued an Intelligence Community Directive that elaborates on reporting required by statute to keep the congressional intelligence committees "fully and currently informed of the intelligence activities of the United States" (see p. 504). The Directive adds to statutory obligations by requiring agencies of the Intelligence Community to report in writing, to report on intelligence failures, and to resolve any doubts in favor of reporting. But it does not apply to separately prescribed reporting of covert actions (see p. 505).

Office of the Director of National Intelligence, Intelligence Community Directive Number 112: Congressional Notification

Nov. 16, 2011
http://www.dni.gov/electronic_reading_room/ICD_112.pdf

C. APPLICABILITY . . .

3. This Directive does not apply to reporting of covert actions to the Congressional intelligence committees, to statutory reporting requirements for IC Inspectors General, or to routine informational briefings.

D. POLICY . . .

2. The provisions of this Directive shall be interpreted with a presumption of notification in fulfillment of the statutory requirement to keep the Congressional intelligence committees fully and currently informed of all intelligence activities.

3. It is IC policy that IC elements shall, in a timely manner, keep the Congressional intelligence committees fully informed, in writing, of all significant anticipated intelligence activities, significant intelligence failures, significant intelligence activities, and illegal activities. . . .

5. Determining whether written notification should be provided of a particular intelligence activity is a judgment based on all the facts and circumstances known to the IC element, and on the nature and extent of previous notifications or briefings to Congress on the same matter. Not every intelligence activity warrants written notification. Facts and circumstances of intelligence activities change over time; therefore, IC elements must continually assess whether there is an obligation to report a matter pursuant to the National Security Act and this Directive.

6. As required by the National Security Act, Congress must receive written notification of significant anticipated intelligence activities and significant intelligence failures. General guidelines for determining the types of intelligence activities that warrant written notification follow:

a. Significant anticipated intelligence activities include:

(1) intelligence activities that entail, with reasonable foreseeability, significant risk of exposure, compromise, and loss of human life;

(2) intelligence activities that are expected to have a major impact on important foreign policy or national security interests;

(3) an IC element's transfer, to a recipient outside that IC element, of defense articles, personnel services, or "controlled equipment" valued in excess of $1 million as provided in Section 505 of the National Security Act;

(4) extensive organizational changes in an IC element;

(5) deployment of new collection techniques that represent a significant departure from previous operations or activities or that result from evidence of significant foreign developments;

(6) significant activities undertaken pursuant to specific direction of the President or the National Security Council (this is not applicable to covert action, which is covered by Section 503 of the National Security Act); or

(7) significant acquisition, reprogramming, or non-routine budgetary actions that are of Congressional concern and that are not otherwise reportable under the National Intelligence Program Procedures for Reprogramming and Transfers.

b. Significant intelligence failures are failures that are extensive in scope, continuing in nature, or likely to have a serious impact on United States (US) national security interests and include:

(1) the loss or compromise of classified information on such a scale or over such an extended period as to indicate a systemic loss or compromise of classified intelligence information that may pose a substantial risk to US national security interests;

(2) a significant unauthorized disclosure of classified intelligence infonnation that may pose a substantial risk to US national security interests;

(3) a potentially pervasive failure, interruption, or compromise of a collection capability or collection system; or

(4) a conclusion that an intelligence product is the result of foreign deception or denial activity, or otherwise contains major errors in analysis, with a significant impact on US national security policies, programs, or activities.

7. As a matter of policy, IC elements shall provide Congress written notification of other significant intelligence activities and illegal activities. General guidelines for determining these types of intelligence activities warranting notification follow.

a. Significant intelligence activities include:

(1) substantial changes in the capabilities or known vulnerabilities of US intelligence operations or intelligence systems or resources;

(2) programmatic developments likely to be of Congressional interest, such as major cost overruns, a major modification of, or the termination of a significant contract;

(3) developments that affect intelligence programs, projects, or activities that are likely to be of Congressional concern because of their substantial impact on national security or foreign policy;

(4) the loss of life in the performance of an intelligence activity; or

(5) significant developments in, or the resolution of, a matter previously reported under these procedures.

b. Illegal activities include:

(1) An intelligence activity believed to be in violation of US law, including any corrective action taken or planned in connection with such activity;

(2) Significant misconduct by an employee of an IC element or asset that is likely to seriously affect intelligence activities or otherwise is of congressional concern, including human rights violations; or

(3) Other serious violations of US criminal law by an employee of an IC element or asset, which in the discretion of the head of an IC element warrants congressional notification.

8. Criteria described in Sections D.6 and D.7 above are not exhaustive. The absence of any of these criteria shall not be seen as determinative. Each potential determination shall be addressed on its particular merits. If it is unclear whether a notification is appropriate, IC elements should decide in favor of notification. . . .

———————————

[NSL p. 469. Insert at the of Note 6.]

On August 29, 2013, the *Washington Post* published portions of the budget proposal for the intelligence community for FY 2013, containing never-before-disclosed details of funding for individual agencies, as well as activities of those agencies, at least in broad terms. *See* Barton Gellman & Greg Miller, *U.S. Spy Network's Successes, Failures and Objectives Detailed in "Black Budget" Summary*, Wash. Post, Aug. 29, 2013. *See also $52.6 Billion: The Black Budget*, Wash. Post, Aug. 29, 2013. The document, leaked by Edward Snowden, is replete with full-color pie-charts and graphs. It offers an unprecedented snapshot of each member of the entire community, including numbers of employees. An accompanying news story provides useful analysis of the numbers and their significance.

———————————

[NSL p. 554, CTL p. 167. Substitute for paragraph at top of each page.]

In 1978, Congress codified a foreign intelligence collection authority in the Foreign Intelligence Surveillance Act (FISA). In NSL Chapter 21/CTL Chapter 7, we turn to this statutory authority for electronic surveillance and, eventually, "black bag jobs" (surreptitious entry). We see that FISA originally authorized court orders for individually targeted surveillance based on probable cause to believe that the target was a foreign power or its agent.

Beginning in 2005, media stories, first about the so-called Terrorist Surveillance Program and later about an NSA program called "PRISM," awakened many Americans to the fact that our government was conducting some kind of surveillance in the United States of the contents of Internet and telephone traffic to or from foreign targets. NSL Chapter 22/CTL Chapter 8 examines the 2008 extension of FISA procedures to permit this kind of "programmatic surveillance" without individualized targeting, or what one might call wholesale instead of retail electronic surveillance.

When we mail a letter through the U.S. postal system, we have no reasonable expectation that the addresses on the outside of the envelope will be private, because we know that postal workers can see them (and must see the destination address to deliver the letter). But we do reasonably expect that no one other than the addressee will open our letter and read the contents. In a pair of early cases, the Supreme Court recognized this distinction between what could be called "envelope" information and "content" information. The Court denied traditional Fourth Amendment protection to dialed telephone numbers and certain bank records that customers necessarily disclose to their phone companies and banks. In NSL Chapter 23/CTL Chapter 9, we take up statutory authority for government collection of what we call "third-party records" — tangible and electronic transactional data held by private third parties, including "telephony" (telephone metadata like calling and called numbers, as well as time and duration of calls), telephone customer transactional data (including billing records, names, and addresses), and a broad range of other data (including credit card records), using court orders under USA Patriot Act §215, national security letters pursuant to several statutes, and subpoenas. We consider whether the original envelope-contents distinction still makes sense for contemporary digital data, such as stored Internet search requests, and whether expectations of privacy are different for searchable data sets in the aggregate than they are for individual items of information.

In NSL Chapter 24/CTL Chapter 10, we shift our focus from collecting the data "dots" to connecting them. Dots are connected for the purpose of profiling and "watchlisting" terrorist suspects and for screening access to transportation systems, critical infrastructure, and other possible targets for terrorism.

Finally, in NSL Chapter 25/CTL Chapter 11, we again shift our focus, this time from domestic intelligence collection to the U.S. law governing national security surveillance abroad. U.S. persons and even aliens with a substantial connection to the United States have constitutionally protected expectations of privacy when they travel abroad, but not necessarily the same expectations they have at home. The Fourth Amendment has never been interpreted to protect expectations of privacy by aliens abroad who have no connection to the United States, however. For this reason, traditional "spying" abroad on such aliens has not been subject to constitutional regulation, although it may, of course, be illegal in the foreign country where it occurs. This chapter explores the implications of these differences.

[NSL p. 579, CTL p. 192. Insert at the end of Note 6.]

The GPS issue was confronted by the Court in *United States v. Jones*, 132 S. Ct. 945 (2012), where the Justices unanimously concluded that Jones was searched when police attached a GPS device to the undercarriage of his car and tracked his movements for four weeks. Yet none of the three opinions expressly required that police obtain a warrant for GPS tracking, and the opinions yielded no clear indication of the nature or degree of suspicion that is required to attach a GPS device and monitor the target's movements.

The opinion of the Court by Justice Scalia ruled that the government's installation of the GPS device was a trespass, a physical intrusion of private property that would have constituted a "search" when the Fourth Amendment was ratified in 1791. Eschewing the *Katz* "reasonable expectation of privacy" formula, Justice Scalia wrote that Fourth Amendment rights are based on the privacy that existed when the Fourth Amendment was adopted. According to Justice Scalia, to constitute a Fourth Amendment violation, in addition to the trespass, the government must have "attempt[ed] to find something or to obtain information." 132 S. Ct. at 951 n.5.

As the concurring Justices noted, the property-based approach of the majority did nothing to guide law enforcement or intelligence officials or the lower courts in determining the permissible uses of new surveillance technologies. Concurring in the judgment for himself and Justices Ginsburg, Breyer, and Kagan, Justice Alito would have applied *Katz* to decide *Jones*. *Id.* at 957-964. For Justice Alito, the long-term monitoring of Jones' movements, not the installation of the device on his car, violated his privacy. Justice Alito asked whether "GPS tracking in a particular case involve[s] a degree of instrusion that a reasonable person would not have anticipated." *Id.* at 964. Separately, Justice Sotomayor approved Justice Scalia's opinion, but also supported Justice Alito's *Katz*-based approach. She argued that the courts should take into account that "GPS monitoring generates a precise, comprehensive record of a person's public movements that reflects a wealth of detail about her familial, political, professional, religious, and sexual associations." *Id.* at 955.

Is an intrusiveness assessment any different from one based on a reasonable expectation of privacy? As Justice Alito noted, if an auto manufacturer installed a GPS in the cars it produces, the Court's theory would not protect the owner. What should be the Fourth Amendment rule for pre-installed GPS tracking? For the same tracking when GPS is pre-installed on cell phones? Or when some form of ID card, such as drivers' licenses or passports, is embedded with GPS capabilities, allowing the government to track every citizen's movements?

In *Knotts*, police discovered the location of a secluded drug lab by enclosing a beeper in a can of chloroform sold to one of the defendants. The can carrying the chloroform transmitted signals that enabled the police to track the defendant's car after earlier efforts to find the lab failed. *Knotts*, 460 U.S. at 278. Why isn't the GPS device used by the police in *Jones* simply an advanced beeper? The *Knotts* Court was careful to note that the beeper provided only location information, and that a car driving down the road is subject to scrutiny in that public space. The Court found no constitutional difference between traditional visual surveillance and this then-new form of electronic surveillance. *Id.* 460 U.S. at 281. Why should *Jones* be decided differently than *Knotts*?

In June 2014, the Supreme Court unanimously held that the police must normally obtain a warrant before searching cell phones. *Riley v. California*, 134 S. Ct. 2473 (June 25, 2014). In the two cases under review, police had searched cell phones incident to the arrest of suspects without obtaining warrants. The Court found that the categorical rule from *United States v. Robinson* (NSL p. 555, CTL p. 168), that a search incident to arrest requires no additional justification, should not apply to searches of data on cell phones. The Court noted that a cell phone cannot itself be used as a weapon, and that any government interests in preventing the destruction of data on a cell phone have not been demonstrated to date and may be met by other means than a warrantless search.

The Court recognized the important privacy concerns implicated by cell phones:

> Modern cell phones, as a category, implicate privacy concerns far beyond those implicated by the search of a cigarette pack, a wallet, or a purse. . . .
>
> Cell phones differ in both a quantitative and a qualitative sense from other objects that might be kept on an arrestee's person. The term "cell phone" is itself misleading shorthand; many of these devices are in fact minicomputers that also happen to have the capacity to be used as a telephone. They could just as easily be called cameras, video players, rolodexes, calendars, tape recorders, libraries, diaries, albums, televisions, maps, or newspapers. . . .
>
> . . . [A] cell phone search would typically expose to the government far *more* than the most exhaustive search of a house: A phone not only contains in digital form many sensitive records previously found in the home; it also contains a broad array of private information never found in a home in any form –- unless the phone is. [*Riley, supra*, 134 S. Ct. 2488-2489, 2491.]

It reasoned that the exigent circumstances exception may still justify a warrantless search of a particular phone and that, in any case, a search may be carried out after obtaining a warrant. The Court also sidestepped an important question that arises in connection with bulk metadata, analyzed *infra*: "[T]hese cases do not implicate the question whether the collection or inspection of aggregated digital information amounts to a search under other circumstances." *Id.* at 2489 n.1.

Speaking of cell phones, does the government's warrantless gathering of cell phone site location information violate a reasonable expectation of privacy? The Eleventh Circuit Court of Appeals recently said yes, in the context of the use of such evidence in a criminal proceeding, creating a split among the circuits and possible appeal to the Supreme Court. In *United States v. Davis*, No. 12-12928, 2014 WL 2599917 (11th Cir. June 11, 2014), the government argued that gathering of cell site location information (a record of calls made by a provider's customer, revealing which cell tower carried the call and thus the approximate location of the customer) is factually distinguishable from the GPS data at issue in *Jones*. The court agreed that the two are distinguishable, but found that the cell phone, unlike an automobile, "can accompany its owner anywhere. Thus, the exposure of cell site location information can convert what would otherwise be a private event into a public one." According to the court, "cell site data is more like communications data than it is like GPS information. . . . [I]t is private in nature rather than being public data that warrants privacy protection only when its collection creates a sufficient mosaic to expose that which would otherwise be private." *Id.* *8. The Fifth Circuit earlier found that compelling cell site location data pursuant to a statutory "reasonable grounds" basis was not "per se unconstitutional." *In re Application of U.S. for Historical Cell Site Data*, 724 F.3d 600, 602 (5th Cir. 2013).

[NSL p. 596, CTL p. 209. Insert at the end of Note 4.c.]

Less than a year after the 9/11 attacks, the FISC approved a "Raw Take" order that allowed counterterrorism analysts at the NSA, FBI, and CIA to share unfiltered personal information as an exception to FISA's minimization requirements. The FISC apparently sided with the Justice Department's request to interpret those requirements as not applicable to the sharing or retention of information "between and among counterintelligence components of the government." In 2012, the FISC expanded the sharing to include the National Counterterrorism Center (NCTC). Charlie Savage & Laura Poitras, *How a Court Secretly Evolved, Extending U.S. Spies' Reach*, N.Y. Times, Mar. 11, 2014.

————————

[NSL p. 607, CTL p. 220. Insert after the first paragraph of C. FISA Trends.]

Of 1,655 applications submitted to the FISC in calendar year 2013 for authority to conduct electronic surveillance and/or physical searches for foreign intelligence purposes, none was denied, although unspecified modifications were made to 34 proposed orders. *See* Letter from Peter J. Kadzig, Deputy Assistant Attorney General, to Honorable Joseph R. Biden, Jr. (Apr. 30, 2014), *available at* www.justice.gov/nsd/foia/foia_library/2013fisa-ltr.pdf. Far more substantial disclosures of surveillance activity were made by NSA contractor Edward Snowden since June 2013. Government declassification of pertinent intelligence records has nearly kept pace with the Snowden disclosures. These developments are treated in the next chapter. A new website for the Foreign Intelligence Surveillance Court contains significantly more useful information than DOJ's annual reports to Congress. *See* http://www.fisc.uscourts.gov/.

An additional new website created by the ODNI after the Snowden disclosures released annual statistics for the use of FISA authorities under traditional FISA and the specialized authorities examined in the next two chapters. The calendar year 2013 statistics, with some explanatory commentary, may be found here: http://icontherecord.tumblr.com/transparency/odni_transparencyreport_cy2013.

————————

[NSL p. 613, CTL p. 226, add to Note 1.]

A somewhat different and more detailed description of the TSP was provided in a 2009 draft NSA Inspector General report published in June 2013 by the London *Guardian* newspaper and *The Washington Post* in the wave of disclosures of classified documents by former NSA contractor Edward Snowden. What was later called the TSP was created as the President's Surveillance Program (PSP) on October 4, 2001, without FISC orders, on the basis of the President's putative constitutional powers. PSP included four components under the code name STELLARWIND — collection of contents and metadata from telephone calls and emails. Robert O'Harrow Jr. & Ellen Nakashima, *President's Surveillance Program Worked with Private Sector to Collect Data after September 11, 2001*, Wash. Post, June 27, 2013.

According to the following excerpt from the 57-page draft report, NSA began collecting data from U.S. telephone numbers on communications links to some foreign countries a few days after 9/11.

TOP SECRET//STLW//COMINT/ORCON/NOFORN

Office of the Inspector General, National Security Agency/Central Security Service, 1109-0002 Working Draft [1]

Mar. 24, 2009

available at http://www.guardian.co.uk/world/interactive/2013/jun/27/nsa-inspector-general-report-document-data-collection

. . . Actions Taken After 9/11

On 14 September 2001, three days after terrorist attacks in the United States, [the NSA Director, General Michael] Hayden approved the targeting of terrorist-associated foreign telephone numbers on communication links between the United States and foreign countries where terrorists were known to be operating. Only specified, pre-approved numbers were allowed to be tasked for collection against U.S.-originating links. He authorized this collection at Special Collection Service and Foreign Satellite sites with access to links between the United States and countries of interest, including Afghanistan. According to the Deputy General Counsel, General Hayden determined by 26 September that any Afghan telephone number in contact with a U.S. telephone number on or after 26 September was presumed to be of foreign intelligence value and could be disseminated to the FBI.

[1. This document was published online in Glenn Greenwald & Spencer Ackerman, *NSA Collected US Email Records in Bulk for More than Two Years under Obama*, The Guardian, June 27, 13, 2013, http://www.guardian.co.uk/world/2013/jun/27/nsa-data-mining-authorised-obama.]

NSA OGC said General Hayden's action was a lawful exercise of his power under Executive Order (E.O.) 12333, United States Intelligence Activities, as amended. The targeting of communication links with one end in the United States was a more aggressive use of E.O. 12333 authority than that exercised by former Directors. General Hayden was operating in a unique environment in which it was a widely held belief that additional terrorist attacks on U.S. soil were imminent. General Hayden said this was a "tactical decision."

On 2 October 2001, General Hayden briefed the House Permanent Select Committee on Intelligence (HPSCI) on this decision and later informed members of the Senate Select Committee on Intelligence (SSCI) by telephone. He had also informed DCI George Tenet.

At the same time NSA was assessing collection gaps and increasing efforts against terrorist targets immediately after the 11 September attacks, it was responding to Department of Defense (DOD), Director of Central Intelligence Community Management Staff questions about its ability to counter the new threat.

Need to Expand NSA Authority

General Hayden said that soon after he told Mr. Tenet about NSA actions to counter the threat, Mr. Tenet shared the information with the "Oval Office." Mr. Tenet relayed that the Vice President wanted to know if NSA could be doing more. General Hayden replied that nothing else could be done within existing NSA authorities. In a follow-up telephone conversation, Mr. Tenet asked General Hayden what could be done if he had additional authorities. General Hayden said that these discussions were not documented.

NSA Identifies SIGINT Collection Gaps

To respond to the Vice President, General Hayden met with NSA personnel who were already working to identify and fill SIGINT collection gaps in light of the recent terrorist attacks. General Hayden stated that he met with personnel to identify which additional authorities would be operationally useful and technically feasible. In particular, discussions focused on how NSA might bridge the "international gap." An NSA Technical Director described that gap in these terms:

"Here is NSA standing at the U.S. border looking outward for foreign threats. There is the FBI looking within the United States for domestic threats. But no one was looking at the foreign threats coming into the United States. That was a huge gap that NSA wanted to cover."

Possible Solutions. Among other things, NSA considered how to tweak transit collection — the collection of communications transiting through but not originating or terminating in the United States. NSA personnel also resurfaced a concept proposed in 1999 to address the Millennium Threat. NSA proposed that it would perform contact chaining on metadata it had collected. Analysts would chain through masked U.S. telephone numbers to discover foreign connections to those numbers, without specifying, even for analysts, the U.S. number involved. In December 1999, the Department of Justice Office of Intelligence Policy Review (OIPR) told NSA that the proposal fell within one of the FISA definitions of electronic surveillance and, therefore, was not permissible when applied to metadata associated with presumed U.S. persons (i.e., U.S. telephone numbers not approved for targeting by the FISC).

Collection gaps not adequately filled by FISA authorized intercept. NSA determined that FISA authorization did not allow sufficient flexibility to counter the new terrorist threat. First, it believed that because of technological advances, the jurisdiction of the FISC went beyond the original intent of the statute. For example, most communications signals no longer flowed through radio or via phone systems as they did in 1978 when the FISA was written. By 2001, Internet communications were used worldwide, undersea cables carried huge volumes of communications, and a large amount of the world's communications passed through the United States. Because of language used in the Act in 1978, NSA was required to obtain court orders to target email accounts used by non-U.S. persons outside the United States if it intended to intercept the communications at a webmail service within the United States. Large numbers of terrorists were using such accounts in 2001.

Second, NSA believed that the FISA process was unable to accommodate the number of terrorist targets or the speed with which they changed their communications. From the time NSA sent FISA requests to the OIPR until the time data arrived at NSA, the average wait was between four and six weeks. Terrorists could have changed their telephone numbers or internet addresses before NSA received FISC approval to target them. NSA believed the large number of terrorist targets and their frequently changing communications would have overwhelmed the existing FISA process.

Emergency FISA provision not an option. NSA determined that even using emergency FISA court orders would not provide the speed and flexibility needed to counter the terrorist threat. First, although the emergency authorization provision permitted 72 hours of surveillance without obtaining a court order, it did not — as many believed — allow the Government to undertake surveillance immediately. Rather, the Attorney General had to ensure that emergency surveillance would ultimately be acceptable to the FISC. He had to be certain the court would grant a warrant before initiating emergency surveillance. Additionally, before NSA surveillance requests were submitted to the Attorney General, they had to be reviewed by NSA intelligence officers, NSA attorneys, and Department of Justice attorneys. Each reviewer had to be satisfied that standards had been met before the request proceeded to the next review group, and each request was certified by a senior official in the DoD, usually the Secretary or Deputy Secretary. From the time NSA sent a request to Justice's OIPR until the time data arrived at NSA, the average wait was between a day and a day and a half. In the existing threat environment with U.S. interests at risk, NSA deemed the wait too long.

Early Efforts to Amend FISA

Given the limitations of FISA, there were early efforts to amend the statute. For example, shortly after 11 September, the HPSCI asked NSA for technical assistance in drafting a proposal to amend Section of FISA that would give the President the authority to conduct electronic surveillances without a court order for the purpose of obtaining foreign intelligence information. On 20 September 2001, the NSA General Counsel wrote to Judge Alberto Gonzales, Counsel to the President, asking whether the proposal had merit. We found no record of a response.

We could not determine why early efforts to amend FISA were abandoned. Anecdotal evidence suggests that government officials feared the public debate surrounding any changes to FISA would compromise intelligence sources and methods.

NSA identifies SIGINT collection gaps to Vice President's Office.

Because early discussions about expanding NSA's authority were not documented, we do not have records of specific topics discussed or people who attended General Hayden's meetings with White House representatives. General Hayden stated that after consulting with NSA personnel, he described to the White House how NSA collection of communications on a wire inside the United States was constrained by the FISA statute. Specifically, NSA could not collect from a wire in the United States, without a court order, either content or metadata from communications links with either one or both ends in the United States. Furthermore, General Hayden pointed out that communications metadata did not have the same level of constitutional protection as content and that access to metadata of communications with one end in the United States would significantly enhance NSA's analytic capabilities. General Hayden suggested that the ability to collect communications with one end in the United States without a court order would increase NSA's speed and agility. General Hayden stated that after two additional meetings with the Vice President, the Vice President asked him to work with his Counsel, David Addington.

Presidential Authorization Drafted and Signed

According to General Hayden, the Vice President's Counsel, David Addington, drafted the first Authorization. General Hayden described himself as the "subject matter expert" but stated that no other NSA personnel participated in the drafting process, including the General Counsel. He also said that Department of Justice (DOJ) representatives were not involved in any of the discussions that he attended and he did not otherwise inform them.

General Hayden said he was "surprised with a small 's'" when the Authorization was signed on 4 October 2001, and that it only changed the location from which NSA could collect communications. Rules for minimizing U.S. person information still had to be followed.

SIGINT Activity Authorized by the President

On 4 October 2001, the President delegated authority through the Secretary of Defense to the Director of NSA to conduct specified electronic surveillance on targets related to Afghanistan and international terrorism for 30 days. Because the surveillance included wire and cable communications carried into or out of the United States, it would otherwise have required FISC authority.

The Authorization allowed NSA to conduct four types of collection activity:

- Telephony content
- Internet content
- Telephony metadata
- Internet metadata

NSA could collect the content and associated metadata of telephony and Internet communications for which there was probable cause to believe that one of the communicants was in Afghanistan or that one communicant was engaged in or preparing for acts of international terrorism. In addition, NSA was authorized to acquire telephony and Internet metadata for communications with at least one communicant outside the United States or for which no communicant was known to be a citizen of the United States. NSA was also allowed to retain, process, analyze and disseminate intelligence from the communications acquired under the authority.

Subsequent Changes to the Authorization

After the first Presidential authorization, the specific terms, wording, or interpretation of the renewals periodically changed. . . .

––––––––––––––––––

The report goes on to state that 3,018 people inside the United States had the contents of their phone or emails targeted between October 2001 and January 17, 2007, while 34,646 targets, or 92 percent of the total, were outside the United States. The Vice President's Counsel, David Addington, apparently prepared the PSP authorization for the President and obtained Attorney General and OLC approval. When the NSA General Counsel asked Addington if he could see the legal opinion authorizing PSP, he was turned down. NSA Director Hayden did not ask to see or read it. During the period when the leadership at OLC changed hands in 2003, and OLC head Jack Goldsmith joined senior DOJ officials in refusing to approve a reauthorization of the TSP in 2004, NSA lawyers were briefed on the PSP and provided comments on revised OLC opinions concerning the legality of PSP. *Id.* at 21-22. As early as June 2002, more than 500 people were cleared into PSP, including select members of Congress and two FISC judges. *Id.* at 24.

After the *New York Times* story broke in December 2005, the new NSA Director, Gen. Keith B. Alexander, briefed all FISC judges on PSP in January 2006. *Id.* at 37. When FISC judges then took over responsibility for reviewing PSP, the metadata components of STELLARWIND were authorized under pen register/trap and trace and business records orders, *id.* at 39-40, and the contents collection components were authorized under foreign and domestic content orders, on the theory that the U.S. gateway or cable head that foreign targets used for communications were "facilit[ies]" under traditional FISA definitions. *Id.* at 41.

––––––––––––––––

[NSL p. 629, CTL p. 242. Insert at the end of Note 3.]

Congress acted to extend the FAA on December 28, 2012, three days before it was set to expire. It was extended for five years, until December 31, 2017. FISA Amendments Act Reauthorization Act of 2012, Pub. L. No. 112-238, 126 Stat. 1631. Although the Senate debated several amendments that would have addressed instances of inadvertent over-collection of U.S. persons communications under the FAA, all were defeated.

––––––––––––––––

[NSL p. 632, CTL p. 245. Insert at end of chapter.]

c. The Snowden Leaks

Beginning in June 2013, former NSA contractor Edward Snowden disclosed to *The Guardian* and *The Washington Post* a series of classified documents that shed light on many details of some foreign intelligence collection programs implemented by NSA and other agencies after the 9/11 attacks.

One of the NSA programs first reported by *The Washington Post* is code-named PRISM. PRISM was launched as a result of agreements between the government and several U.S.-based Internet companies that permit NSA to monitor the contents of online communications of non-U.S. persons believed to be physically located outside the United States. Barton Gellman & Laura Poitras, *Documents: U.S. Mining Data from 9*

Leading Internet Firms; Companies Deny Knowledge, Wash. Post, June 6, 2013. According to briefing slides obtained by *The Post* and intended for senior NSA analysts, PRISM has become one of the most important sources of intelligence, including those that contribute to the President's Daily Brief. *Id.*

The leaked slides list the U.S. companies that have cooperated in PRISM operations: Microsoft, Yahoo, Google, Facebook, PalTalk, AOL, Skype, YouTube, and Apple. *Id.* Although NSA could conceivably extract anything at will from a company's data stream, following FAA §702 (50 U.S.C. §1881a) requirements and the resulting directives, NSA analysts apparently send "selectors" (such as an email address) about non-U.S. persons believed to be abroad to a United States-based communications provider, and the provider is compelled to give communications sent to or from that selector to the government. PRISM collection does not include acquisition of telephone calls. Although NSA receives all data collected through PRISM, the CIA and FBI each receive a portion of PRISM collection. The President's Civil Liberties Oversight Board, *Report on the Surveillance Program Operated Pursuant to Section 702 of the Foreign Intelligence Surveillance Act* (PCLOB Report), July 2, 2014, http://www.pclob.gov/All%20Documents/ Report%20on%20the%20Section%20702%20Program/PCLOB-Section-702-Report.pdf. Through contact chaining — building a list or network by modeling the communication patterns of targeted entities and their associates from communications sent or received by the target's selector — NSA would typically search two "hops," or degrees of separation from the target. *See* Office of the Inspector General, National Security Agency/Central Security Service, *1109-0002 Working Draft*, Mar. 24, 2009, *supra* p. 93, at 13.

A release by DNI James Clapper declared that "PRISM is not an undisclosed collection or data mining program. It is an internal government computer system used to facilitate the government's statutorily authorized collection of foreign intelligence information from electronic communication service providers under court supervision. . . . The Government cannot target anyone under the court-approved procedures [prescribed by the FAA] unless there is an appropriate, and documented, foreign intelligence purpose for the acquisition. . . ." Director of National Intelligence, *Facts on the Collection of Intelligence Pursuant to Section 702 of the Foreign Intelligence Surveillance Act*, June 8, 2013, http://www.dni.gov/index.php/newsroom/press-releases/191-press-releases-2013/871-facts-on-the-collection-of-intelligence-pursuant-to-section-702-of-the-foreign-intelligence-surveillance-act. Director Clapper also stated that PRISM enabled the government to acquire "information on a terrorist organization's strategic planning efforts . . . intelligence regarding proliferation networks . . . [and] significant and unique intelligence regarding potential cyber threats to the United States." *Id.*

A second NSA collection program purportedly based on Section 702 was leaked later in 2013 in an October 3, 2011, opinion by Judge John D. Bates, then Presiding Judge of the FISC. The opinion is available online from several sources, including http://www.lawfareblog.com/wp-content/uploads/2013/08/162016974-FISA-court-opinion-with-exemptions.pdf. The name of the case is entirely redacted, complicating citation, as is much of the text. Most of the 81-page opinion is readable, however. This FISC opinion resulted from a government application for the court's reauthorization of Section 702 collection. Beginning in May 2011, the government clarified its application under Section 702 by explaining that its activities included "upstream collection" of internet communications — tapping the data pipeline as it enters the United States and the Internet "backbone" within the United States, before it is managed by the ISPs. The volume of communications acquired upstream is much smaller than that obtained through PRISM. *The Intelligence Community's Collection Programs Under Title VII of the Foreign Intelligence Surveillance Act*, May 4, 2012, *available at* http://www.dni.gov/files/documents/Ltr to HPSCI Chairman Rogers and Ranking Member Ruppersberger_Scan.pdf. As we learn from Judge Bates, the upstream "transactions" includes telephone calls as well as Internet communications, and they may include "about" communications in which the selector of the targeted person is contained within the communication but the targeted person is not necessarily a participant in the communication. PCLOB Report, *supra.* Apparently, Judge Bates and the FISC had granted prior certifications under Section 702 without being informed of the full extent of NSA collection and its impacts on privacy. Bates wrote that the government's explanation of upstream collection marked "the third instance in less than three years in which the government has disclosed a substantial misrepresentation regarding the scope of a major collection program." At least one prior incident involved the use of collected telephone metadata.

An August 9, 2013, NSA memorandum, *The National Security Agency: Missions, Authorities, Oversight and Partnerships*, http://www.nsa.gov/public_info/_files/speeches_testimonies/2013_08_0

9_the_nsa_story.pdf, usefully reviews the legal basis for NSA intelligence collection. While it offers no new legal justifications, the memo does include new information about the scope and scale of NSA collection (NSA "touches about 1.6%" of daily Internet traffic and selects for review 0.025% of the 1.6%) and about the roles of communications providers and foreign governments.

Also in August 2013, ODNI declassified a May 2012 white paper prepared by ODNI and DOJ for the intelligence committees, but provided to all members of Congress. *The Intelligence Community's Collection Programs Under Title VII of the Foreign Intelligence Surveillance Act*, May 4, 2012, http://www.dni.gov/files/documents/Ltr to HPSCI Chairman Rogers and Ranking Member Ruppersberger_Scan.pdf. Written in anticipation of the renewal of the 2008 FAA, the white paper principally reviews Section 702 and its implementation. The white paper also asserts the importance of Section 702 collection and provides examples of its use, although the only unredacted example involves the FBI's use of an intercepted email to identify Najibullah Zazi (subsequently convicted of planning to bomb a New York City subway) in 2009.

In May 2012 an internal NSA audit, based only on Washington-area NSA facilities, found 2,776 incidents in the proceeding 12 months of unauthorized collection, retention, access to, or distribution of protected communications. *NSAW SID Intelligence Oversight (IO) Quarterly Report — First Quarter Calendar Year 2012 (1 January – 31 March 2012) — EXECUTIVE SUMMARY*, May 3, 2012, http://www2.gwu.edu/~nsarchiv/NSAEBB/NSAEBB436/docs/EBB-044.pdf. Most of the incidents involved "roamers," foreign intelligence targets who entered the United States (thus negating the lawfulness of the targeting), unintentional database query errors, or similar mistakes.

Scores of media reports decried the "thousands of privacy violations," while NSA compliance officers put the number in context. At 20 million agency queries of data each month, the error rate during the examined period in 2012 was asserted to be .00001156666. *See* Jennifer Rubin, *NSA Scandal or Near-Perfection?*, Wash. Post, Aug. 18, 2013. Perhaps the bigger news was the number of queries.

————————

NSA Director of Civil Liberties and Privacy Office, NSA's Implementation of Foreign Intelligence Surveillance Act Section 702

April 16, 2014
available at fas.org/irp/nsa/clpo-702.pdf

SECTION 702 OF FISA

. . . Section 702 of FISA was widely and publicly debated in Congress both during the initial passage in 2008 and the subsequent re-authorization in 2012. It provides a statutory basis for NSA, with the compelled assistance of electronic communication service providers, to target non-U.S. persons reasonably believed to be located outside the U.S. in order to acquire foreign intelligence information. Given that Section 702 only allows for the targeting of non-U.S. persons outside the U.S., it differs from most other sections of FISA. It does not require an individual determination by the U.S. Foreign intelligence Surveillance Court (FISC) that there is probable cause to believe the target is a foreign power or an agent of a foreign power. Instead, the FISC reviews annual topical certifications executed by the Attorney General (AG) and the Director of National Intelligence (DNI) to determine if these certifications meet the statutory requirements. The FISC also determines whether the statutorily required targeting and minimization procedures used in connection with the certifications are consistent with the statute and the Fourth Amendment. The targeting procedures are designed to ensure that Section 702 is only used to target non-U.S. persons reasonably believed to be located outside the U.S.

The minimization procedures are designed to minimize the impact on the privacy on U.S. persons by minimizing the acquisition, retention, and dissemination of non-publicly available U.S. person information that was lawfully, but incidentally acquired under Section 702 by the targeting of non-U.S. persons reasonably believed to be located outside the U.S. Under these certifications the AG and the DNI issue directives to electronic communication service providers (service providers) that require these service providers to "immediately provide the Government with all information . . . or assistance necessary to accomplish the acquisition [of foreign intelligence information] in a manner that will protect the secrecy of the acquisition . . . ." The Government's acquisition of communications under its Section 702 authority thus takes place pursuant to judicial review and with the knowledge of the service providers.

NSA cannot intentionally use Section 702 authority to target any U.S. citizen, any other U.S. person, or anyone known at the time of acquisition to be located within the U.S. The statute also prohibits the use of Section 702 to intentionally acquire any communication as to which the sender and all intended recipients are known at the time of acquisition to be located inside the U.S. Similarly, the statute prohibits the use of Section 702 to conduct ' reverse targeting" (i.e., NSA may not intentionally target a person reasonably believed to be located outside of the U.S. if the purpose of such acquisition is to target a person reasonably believed to be located inside the U.S.). All acquisitions conducted pursuant to Section 702 must be conducted in a manner consistent with the Fourth Amendment. NSA's FISC-approved targeting procedures permit NSA to target a non-U.S. person reasonably believed to be located outside the U.S. if the intended target possesses, is expected to receive, and/or is likely to communicate foreign intelligence information concerning one of the certifications executed by the AG and DNI. Although the purpose of Section 702 is to authorize targeting of non-U.S. persons outside the U.S., the statute's requirement for minimization procedures recognizes that such targeted individuals or entities may communicate about U.S. persons or with U.S. persons. For this reason, NSA also must follow FISC-approved minimization procedures that govern the handling of any such communications.

NSA must report to the Office of the Director of National Intelligence (ODNI) and the Department of Justice (DOJ) any and all instances where it has failed to comply with the targeting and/or minimization procedures. In addition, ODNI and DOJ have access to documentation concerning each of NSA's Section 702 targeting decisions and conduct regular reviews in order to provide independent oversight of NSA's use of the authority. The FISC Rules of Procedure require the Government to notify the Court of all incidents of non-compliance with applicable law or with an authorization granted by the Court. The Government reports Section 702 compliance incidents to the Court via individual notices and quarterly reports. In addition, the Government reports all Section 702 compliance incidents to Congress in the Attorney General's Semiannual Report. Depending on the type or severity of compliance incident, NSA may also promptly notify the Congressional Intelligence Committees, as well as the President's Intelligence Oversight Board of an individual compliance matter.

Existing Privacy and Civil Liberties Protections: Each of the three branches of federal government oversees NSA's use of the Section 702 authorities. NSA provides transparency to its oversight bodies (Congress, DOJ, ODNI, DoD, the President's Intelligence Oversight Board and the FISC) through regular briefings, court filings, and incident reporting. In addition, DOJ and ODNI conduct periodic reviews of NSA's use of the authority and report on those reviews. More recently, at the direction of the President, the Government has provided additional transparency to the public regarding the program by declassifying FISC opinions and related documents. Although FISA surveillance is normally kept secret from the targets of the surveillance, there are exceptions. For example, if the Government intends to use the results of FISA surveillance, to include Section 702 surveillance, in a trial or other proceeding against a person whose communications were collected, the Government must notify the person so the person can challenge whether the communications were acquired lawfully. These protections implement the general Fair Information Practice Principle (FIPP) of transparency.

HOW NSA IMPLEMENTS SECTION 702 OF FISA TRAINING

Training

Before an analyst gains access to any NSA signals intelligence data, the analyst must complete specialized training on the legal and policy guidelines that govern the handling and use of the data. Additional training is required for access to Section 702 data. These annual mandatory training requirements include scenario-based training, required reading, and a final competency test. The analyst must pass this test before being granted access. Furthermore, if a compliance incident involves a mistake or misunderstanding of relevant policies, the analyst is re-trained in order to continue to have access to the data acquired pursuant to Section 702.

Identifying and Tasking a Selector

Next in the Section 702 process is for an NSA analyst to identify a non-U.S. person located outside the U.S. who has and/or is likely to communicate foreign intelligence information as designated in a certification. For example, such a person might be an individual who belongs to a foreign terrorist organization or facilitates the activities of that organization's members. Non-U.S. persons are not targeted unless NSA has reason to believe that they have and/or are likely to communicate foreign intelligence information as designated in a certification; U.S. persons are never targeted.

Once the NSA analyst has identified a person of foreign intelligence interest who is an appropriate target under one of the FISC-approved Section 702 certifications, that person is considered the target. The NSA analyst attempts to determine how, when, with whom, and where the target communicates. Then the analyst identifies specific communications modes used by the target and obtains a unique identifier associated with the target-for example, a telephone number or an email address. This unique identifier is referred to as a selector. The selector is not a "keyword" or particular term (e.g., "nuclear"or "bomb"), but must be a specific communications identifier (e.g., e-mail address).

Next the NSA analyst must verify that there is a connection between the target and the selector and that the target is reasonably believed to be (a) a non-U.S. person and (b) located outside the U.S. This is not a 51% to 49% "foreignness" test. Rather the NSA analyst will check multiple sources and make a decision based on the totality of the information available. If the analyst discovers any information indicating the targeted person may be located in the U.S. or that the target may be a U.S. person, such information must be considered. In other words, if there is conflicting information about the location of the person or the status of the person as a non-U.S. person, that conflict must be resolved before targeting can occur.

For each selector, the NSA analyst must document the following information: (1) the foreign intelligence information expected to be acquired, as authorized by a certification, (2) the information that would lead a reasonable person to conclude the selector is associated with a non-U.S. person, and (3) the information that would similarly lead a reasonable person to conclude that this non-U.S. person is located outside the U.S. This documentation must be reviewed and approved or denied by two senior NSA analysts who have satisfied additional training requirements. The senior NSA analysts may ask for more documentation or clarification, but regardless must verify that all requirements have been met in full. NSA tracks the submission, review, and approval process through the documentation and the senior NSA analysts' determinations are retained for further review by NSA's compliance elements, as well as external oversight reviewers from DOJ and ODNI. Upon approval, the selector may be used as the basis for compelling a service provider to forward communications associated with the given selector. This is generally referred to as "tasking"the selector.

Existing Privacy and Civil Liberties Protections: NSA trains its analysts extensively through a variety of means to ensure that analysts fully understand their responsibilities and the specific scope of this authority. If the analyst fails to meet the training standards, the analyst will not have the ability to use the Section 702 authority for collection purposes. If the analyst fails to maintain ongoing training standards, the analyst will lose the ability to use the Section 702 authority for collection purposes and all ability to retrieve any data previously collected under the authority. NSA requires any authorized and trained analyst seeking to task a selector using Section 702 to document the three requirements for use of the authority-that the target is connected sufficiently to the selector for an approved foreign intelligence purpose, that the target is a non-U.S. person, and that the target is reasonably believed to be located outside the U.S. This documentation must be reviewed, validated, and approved by the senior analysts who have received additional training. These protections implement the general FIPPs of purpose specification, accountability and auditing, and minimization.

Accessing and Assessing Communications Obtained Under Section 702 Authority

Once senior analysts have approved a selector as compliant, the service providers are legally compelled to assist the government by providing the relevant communications. Therefore, tasking under this authority takes place with the knowledge of the service providers. NSA receives information concerning a tasked selector through two different methods.

In the first, the Government provides selectors to service providers through the FBI. The service providers are compelled to provide NSA with communications to or from these selectors. This has been generally referred to as the PRISM program.

In the second, service providers are compelled to assist NSA in the lawful interception of electronic communications to, from, or about tasked selectors. This type of compelled service provider assistance has

generally been referred to as Upstream collection. NSA's FLSC-approved targeting procedures include additional requirements for such collection designed to prevent acquisitions of wholly domestic communications. For example, in certain circumstances NSA's procedures require that it employ an Internet Protocol filter to ensure that the target is
located overseas. The process for approving the selectors for tasking is the same for both PRISM and Upstream collection.

Once NSA has received communications of the tasked selector, NSA must follow additional FISC-approved procedures known as the minimization procedures. These procedures require NSA analysts to review at least a sample of communications acquired from all selectors tasked under Section 702, which occurs on a regular basis to verify that the reasonable belief determination used for tasking remains valid.

The NSA analyst must review a sample of communications received from the selectors to ensure that they are in fact associated with the foreign intelligence target and that the targeted individual or entity is not a U.S. person and is not currently located in the U.S. If the NSA analyst discovers that NSA is receiving communications that are not in fact associated with the intended target or that the user of a tasked selector is determined to be a U.S. person or is located in the U.S., the selector must be promptly "detasked." As a general rule, in the event that the target is a U.S. person or in the U.S., all other selectors associated with the target also must be detasked.

Existing Privacy and Civil Liberties Protections: In addition to extensive training, the analyst is required to review the collection to determine that it is associated with the targeted selector and is providing the expected foreign intelligence shortly after the tasking starts and at least annually thereafter. This review allows NSA to identify possible problems with the collection and provides an additional layer of accountability. In addition, NSA has technical measures that alert the NSA analysts if it appears a selector is being used from the U.S. These protections implement the general FIPPs of purpose specification, minimization, accountability and auditing, data quality, and security.

NSA Processing and Analysis of Communications Obtained Under Section 702 Authority

Communications provided to NSA under Section 702 are processed and retained in multiple NSA systems and data repositories. One data repository, for example, might hold the contents of communications such as the texts of emails and recordings of conversations, while another, may only include metadata, i.e., basic information about the communication, such as the time and duration of a telephone call, or sending and receiving email addresses.

NSA analysts may access communications obtained under Section 702 authority for the purpose of identifying and reporting foreign intelligence. They access the information via "queries,"which may be date-bound, and may include alphanumeric strings such as telephone numbers, email addresses, or terms that can be used individually or in combination with one another. FISC-approved minimization procedures govern any queries done on Section 702-derived information. NSA analysts with access to Section 702-derived information are trained in the proper construction of a query so that the query is reasonably likely to return valid foreign intelligence and minimizes the likelihood of returning non-pertinent U.S. person information. Access by NSA analysts to each repository is controlled, monitored, and audited. There are, for example, automated checks to determine if an analyst has completed all required training prior to returning information responsive to a query. Further, periodic spot checks on queries by NSA analysts are conducted.

Since October 2011 and consistent with other agencies' Section 702 minimization procedures, NSA's Section 702 minimization procedures have permitted NSA personnel to use U.S. person identifiers to query Section 702 collection when such a query is reasonably likely to return foreign intelligence information. NSA distinguishes between queries of communications content and communications metadata. NSA analysts must provide justification and receive additional approval before a content query using a U.S. person identifier can occur. To date, NSA analysts have queried Section 702 content with U.S. person identifiers less frequently than Section 702 metadata. For example, NSA may seek to query a U.S. person identifier when there is an imminent threat to life, such as a hostage situation. NSA is required to maintain records of U.S. person queries and the records are available for review by both DOJ and ODNI as part of the external oversight process for this authority.

Additionally, NSA's procedures prohibit NSA from querying Upstream data with U.S. person identifiers.

Existing Privacy and Civil Liberties Protections: In addition to the training and access controls, NSA maintains audit trails for all queries of the Section 702 data. NSA's Signals Intelligence Directorate's compliance staff routinely reviews a portion of all queries that include U.S. person identifiers to ensure that all such queries are only conducted when appropriate. Personnel from DOJ and ODNI provide an additional layer of oversight to ensure that NSA is querying the data appropriately. These protections implement the general FIPPs of security, accountability and auditing, and data quality.

NSA Dissemination of Intelligence Derived from Communications Obtained under Section 702 Authority

NSA only generates signals intelligence reports when the information meets a specific intelligence requirement, regardless of whether the proposed report contains U.S. person information. Dissemination of information about U.S. persons in any NSA foreign intelligence report is expressly prohibited unless that information is necessary to understand foreign intelligence information or assess its importance, contains evidence of a crime, or indicates a threat of death or serious bodily injury. Even if one or more of these conditions apply, NSA may include no more than the minimum amount of U.S. person information necessary to understand the foreign intelligence or to describe the crime or threat. For example, NSA typically "masks" the true identities of U.S. persons through use of such phrases as "a U.S. person" and the suppression of details that could lead to him or her being successfully identified by the context. Recipients of NSA reporting can request that NSA provide the true identity of a masked U.S. person referenced in an intelligence report if the recipient has a legitimate need to know the identity. Under NSA policy, NSA is allowed to unmask the identity only under certain conditions and where specific additional controls are in place to preclude its further dissemination, and additional approval has been provided by one of seven designated positions at NSA. Additionally, together DOJ and ODNI review the vast majority of disseminations of information about U.S. persons obtained pursuant to Section 702 as part of their oversight process.

Existing Privacy and Civil Liberties Protections: As noted above, NSA only generates signals intelligence reports when the information meets a specific intelligence requirement, regardless of whether the proposed report contains U.S. person information or not. Additionally, NSA's Section 702 minimization procedures require any U.S. person information to be minimized prior to dissemination, thereby reducing the impact on privacy for U.S. persons. The information may only be unmasked in specific instances consistent with the minimization procedures and NSA policy. These protections implement the general FIPPs of minimization and purpose specification.

Retention of Unevaluated Communications Obtained Under Section 702 Authority

The maximum time that specific communications' content or metadata may be retained by NSA is established in the FISC-approved minimization procedures. The unevaluated content and metadata for PRISM or telephony data collected under Section 702 is retained for no more than five years. Upstream data collected from Internet activity is retained for no more than two years. NSA complies with these retention limits through an automated process.

NSA's procedures also specify several instances in which NSA must destroy U.S. person collection promptly upon recognition. In general, these include any instance where NSA analysts recognize that such collection is clearly not relevant to the authorized purpose of the acquisition nor includes evidence of a crime. Additionally, absent limited exceptions, NSA must destroy any communications acquired when any user of a tasked account is found to have been located in the U.S. at the time of acquisition.

Existing Privacy and Civil Liberties Protections: NSA has policies, technical controls, and staff in place to ensure the data is retained in accordance with the FISC-approved procedures. The automated process to delete the collection at the end of the retention period applies to both U.S. person and non U.S. person the information. There is an additional manual process for the destroying information related to U.S. persons where NSA analysts have recognized the collection is clearly not relevant to the authorized purpose of the acquisition nor includes evidence of a crime. These protections implement the general FIPPs of minimization and security.

Organizational Management, Compliance, and Oversight

NSA is subject to rigorous internal compliance and external oversight. Like many other regulated entities, NSA has an enterprise-wide compliance program, led by NSA's Director of Compliance, a position required by statute. NSA's compliance program is designed to provide precision in NSA's activities to ensure that they are consistently conducted in accordance with law and procedure, including in this case the Section 702 certifications and accompanying Section 702 targeting and minimization procedures and additional FISC requirements. As part of the enterprise-wide compliance structure, NSA has compliance elements throughout its various organizations. NSA also seeks to detect incidents of non-compliance at the earliest point possible. When issues of non-compliance arise regarding the way in which NSA carries out the FISC-approved collection, NSA takes corrective action and, in parallel, NSA must report incidents of non-compliance to ODNI and DOJ for further reporting to the FISC and Congress, as appropriate or required.

These organizations, along with the NSA General Counsel, the NSA Inspector General, and most recently the Director of Civil Liberties and Privacy have critical roles in ensuring all NSA operations proceed in accordance with the laws, policies, and procedures governing intelligence activities. Additionally, each individual NSA analyst has a responsibility for ensuring that his or her personal activities are similarly compliant. Specifically, this responsibility includes recognizing and reporting all situations in which he or she may have exceeded his or her authority to obtain, analyze, or report intelligence information under Section 702 authority.

Compliance: NSA reports all incidents in which, for example, it has or may have inappropriately queried the Section 702 data, or in which an analyst may have made typographical errors or dissemination errors. NSA personnel are obligated to report when they believe NSA is not, or may not be, acting consistently with law, policy, or procedure. If NSA is not acting in accordance with law, policy, or procedure, NSA will report through its internal and external intelligence oversight channels, conduct reviews to understand the root cause, and make appropriate adjustments to its procedures.

If NSA discovers that it has tasked a selector that is used by a person in the U.S. or by a U.S. person, then NSA must cease collection immediately and, in most cases must also delete the relevant collected data and cancel or revise any disseminated reporting based on this data. NSA encourages self-reporting by its personnel and seeks to remedy any errors with additional training or other measures as necessary. Following an incident, a range of remedies may occur: admonishment , written explanation of the offense, request to acknowledge a training point that the analyst might have missed during training, and/or required retesting. In addition to reporting described above, any intentional violation of law would be referred to the NSA Office of Inspector General. To date there have been no such instances, as most recently confirmed by the President's Review Group on Intelligence and Communications Technology.

External Oversight: As required by the Section 702 targeting procedures, both DOJ and ODNI conduct routine oversight reviews. Representatives from both agencies visit NSA on a bi-monthly basis. They examine all tasking data sheets that NSA provides to DOJ and ODNJ to determine whether the tasking sheets meet the documentation standards required by NSA's targeting procedures and provide sufficient information for the reviewers to ascertain the basis for NSA's foreign-ness determinations. For those records that satisfy the standards, no additional documentation is requested. For those records that warrant further review, NSA provides additional information to DOJ and ODNI during or following the onsite review. NSA receives feedback from the DOJ and ODNI team and incorporates this information into formal and informal training to analysts. DOJ and ODNI also review the vast majority of disseminated reporting that includes U.S. person information.

Existing Privacy and Civil Liberties Protections: The compliance and oversight processes allow NSA to identify any concerns or problems early in the process so as to minimize the impact on privacy and civil liberties. These protections implement the general FIPPs of transparency to oversight organizations and accountability and auditing. . . .

————————————

The following additional FISC opinion by Presiding Judge Bates, issued in September 2012 in declassified form, assesses efforts by NSA to comply with FISA in the upstream collection portion of its 702 programs. As in the leaked Bates opinion discussed above, the case title has been redacted.

[Case Title Redacted]
Foreign Intelligence Surveillance Court, n.d.
http://www.dni.gov/files/documents/September%202012%20Bates%20Opinion
%20and%20Order.pdf

MEMORANDUM OPINION

This matter is before the Foreign Intelligence Surveillance Court ("FISC" or "Court") on the "Government's Ex Parte Submission of Reauthorization Certification and Related Procedures, Ex Parte Submission of Amended Certifications, and Request for an Order Approving Such Certification and Amended Certifications," which was filed on August 24, 2012.

a. The Scope of NSA's Upstream Collection.

Last year, following the submission of Certifications [redacted] for renewal, the government made a series of submissions to the Court disclosing that it had materially misrepresented the scope of NSA's "upstream collection" under Section 702 (and prior authorities including the Protect America Act). The term "upstream collection" refers to the acquisition of [redacted] Internet communications as they transit the "internet backbone" facilities of [redacted] as opposed to the collection of communications directly [redacted] from Internet service providers like [redacted] *See* Docket Nos. [redacted] Oct. 3, 2011 Memorandum Opinion ("Oct. 3 Op.") at 5 n.3. Since 2006, the government had represented that NSA's upstream collection only acquired discrete communications to or from a facility tasked for acquisition and communications that referenced the [redacted] tasked facility (so-called "about" communications). *See id.* at 15-16. With regard to the latter category, the government had repeatedly assured the Court that NSA only acquired [redacted] specific categories of "about" communications. *Id.*

The government's 2011 submissions made clear, however, that NSA's upstream collection was much broader than the government had previously represented. For the first time, the government explained that NSA's upstream collection results in the acquisition of "Internet transactions" instead of discrete communications to, from or about a tasked selector. *See id.* at 15. Internet transactions, the government would ultimately acknowledge, could and often do contain multiple discrete communications, including wholly domestic non-target communications and other non-target communications to, from, or concerning U.S. persons. *Id.* While the government was able to show that the percentage of wholly domestic non-target communications and other non-target communications to, from, or concerning U.S. persons being acquired was small relative to the total volume of Internet communications acquired by the NSA pursuant to section 702, the acquisition of such communications nonetheless presented a significant issue for the Court in reviewing the procedures. In fact, it appeared that NSA was annually acquiring tens of thousands of Internet transactions containing at least one wholly domestic communication; that many of these wholly domestic communications were not to, from, or about a targeted facility; and that NSA was also likely annually acquiring tens of thousands of additional Internet transactions containing one or more non-target communications to or from U.S. persons or persons in the United States. *Id.* at 33, 37. [redacted]

In October 3 Opinion, the Court approved in large part Certifications [redacted] and the accompanying targeting and minimization procedures. The Court concluded, however, that one aspect of the proposed collection — NSA's upstream collection of Internet transactions containing multiple communications, or "MCTs" — was, in some respects, deficient on statutory and constitutional grounds. The Court concluded that although NSA's targeting procedures met the statutory requirements, the NSA minimization procedures, as the government proposed to apply them to MCTs, did not satisfy the statutory definition of "minimization procedures" with respect to retention. Oct. 3 Op. at 59-63. As applied to the upstream collection of Internet transactions, the Court found that the procedures were not reasonably designed to minimize the retention of U.S. person information consistent with the government's national security needs. *Id.* at 62-63. The Court explained that the net effort of the procedures would have been that thousands of wholly domestic communications, and thousands of other discrete communications that are not to or from a targeted selector but that are to, from, or concerning United States persons, would be retained by NSA for at least five years, despite the fact that they have no direct connection to a targeted selector and, therefore, were unlikely to contain foreign intelligence information. *Id.* at 60-61. For the same reason, the Court concluded that NSA's procedures, as the government proposed to apply then to MCTs, failed to satisfy the requirements of the Fourth Amendment. *Id.* at 78-79. The Court noted that the government might be able to remedy the deficiencies that it had identified, either by tailoring its upstream acquisition or by adopting more stringent post-acquisition safeguards. *Id.* at 61-62, 79.

By operation of the statute, the government was permitted to continue the problematic portion of its collection for 30 days while taking steps to remedy the deficiencies identified in the October 3 order and opinion. *See* 50 U.S.C. §1881a(i)(3)(B). In late October 2011, the government timely submitted amended NSA minimization procedures that included additional provisions regarding NSA's upstream collection. The amended procedures, which took effect on October 31, 2011 ("Oct. 31, 2011 NSA Minimization Procedures"), require NSA to restrict access to the portions of its ongoing upstream collection that are most likely to contain wholly domestic communications and non-target information that is subject to statutory or Fourth Amendment protection. *See* Nov. 30 Op. at 7-9. Segregated Internet transactions can be moved to NSA's general repositories only after having been determined by a specially trained analyst not to contain a wholly domestic communication. *Id.* at 8. Any transaction containing a wholly domestic communication (whether segregated or not) would be purged upon recognition. *Id.* at 8, 9. Any transaction moved from segregation to NSA's general repositories would be permanently marked as having previously been segregated. *Id.* at 8. On the non-segregated side, any discrete communication within an Internet transaction that an analyst wishes to use is subject to additional checks. *Id.* at 8-10. NSA is not permitted to use any discrete, non-target communication that is determined to be to or from a U.S. person or a person who appears to be in the United States, other than to protect against an immediate threat to human life. *Id.* at 9. Finally, all upstream acquisitions are retained for a default maximum period of two, rather than five, years. *Id.* at 10-11.

The Court concluded in the November 30 Opinion that the October 31, 2011 NSA Minimization Procedures adequately remedied the deficiencies that had been identified in the October 3 opinion. *Id.* at 1415. Accordingly, NSA was able to continue its upstream collection of Internet transactions (including MCTs) without interruption, but pursuant to amended procedures that are consistent with statutory and constitutional requirements.

However, issues remained with respect to the past upstream collection residing in NSA's databases. Because NSA's upstream collection almost certainly included at least some acquisitions constituting "electronic surveillance" within the meaning of 50 U.S.C. §1801(f), any overcollection resulting from the government's misrepresentation of the scope of that collection implicates 50 U.S.C. §1809(a)(2). Section 1809(a)(2) makes it a crime to "disclose[] or use[] information obtained under color of law by electronic surveillance, knowing or having reason to know that the information was obtained through electronic surveillance not authorized" by statute. The Court therefore directed the government to make a written submission addressing the applicability of Section 1809(a), which the government did on November 22, 2011. *See* [redacted], Oct. 13, 2011 Briefing Order, and Government's Response to the Court's Briefing Order of Oct. 13, 2011 (arguing that Section 1809(a)(2) does not apply).

Beginning late in 2011, the government began taking steps that had the effect of mitigating any Section 1809(a)(2) problem, including the risk that information subject to the statutory criminal prohibition might be used or disclosed in an application filed before this Court. The government informed the Court in October 2011 that although the amended NSA procedures do not by their terms apply to information acquired before October 31, NSA would apply portions of the procedures to the past upstream collection, including certain limitations on the use or disclosure of such information. *See* Nov. 30 Opinion at 20-21. Although it was not technically feasible for NSA to segregate the past upstream collection in the same way it is now segregating the incoming upstream acquisitions, the government explained that it would apply the remaining components of the amended procedures approved by the Court to the previously-collected data, including (1) the prohibition on using discrete, non-target communications determined to be to or from a U.S. person or a person in the United states, and (2) the two-year age-off requirement. *See id.* at 21.

Thereafter, in April 2012, the government orally informed the Court that NSA had made a "corporate decision" to purge all data in its repositories that can be identified as having been acquired through upstream collection before the October 31, 2011 effective date of the amended NSA minimization procedures approved by the Court in the November 30 Opinion. NSA's effort to purge that information, to the extent it is reasonably feasible to do so, is now complete. *See* Aug. 24 Submission at 9-10.[17]

Finally, NSA has adopted measures to deal with the possibility that it has issued reports based on upstream collection that was unauthorized. NSA has identified [redacted] reports that were issued from the inception of its collection under Section 702 to October 31, 2011, that rely at least in part on information derived from NSA's upstream acquisitions from that period. *See* Sept. 12, 2012 Supplement to the Government's Ex Parte Submission of Reauthorization Certifications at 2 ("Sept. 12 Submission"). The government advises that, of the [redacted] reports, [redacted] have been confirmed to be based entirely upon communications that are to, from or about persons properly targeted under Section 702 and therefore present no issue under Section 1809(a)(2). *See id.* The government is unable to make similar assurances, however, regarding the remaining [redacted] reports. Accordingly, NSA will direct the recipients of those [redacted] reports (both within NSA and outside the agency) not to further use or disseminate information contained therein without first obtaining NSA's express approval. *Id.* at 3-4. Upon receipt of such a request, NSA will review the relevant report to determine whether continued use thereof is appropriate. *Id.* at 4.[18] Finally, the government has informed the Court that it will not use *any* report that cites to upstream collection acquired prior to October 31, 2011 in an application to this Court absent express notice to, and approval of, the Court. Aug. 24 Submission at 24.

---

17. The government has informed the Court that NSA stores some of the past upstream collection in repositories in which it may no longer be identifiable as such. [redacted] *See* Aug. 24 Submission at 14-16. Assuming that NSA cannot with reasonable effort identify information in its repositories as the fruit of an unauthorized electronic surveillance, such information falls outside the scope of Section 1809(a)(2), which by its terms applies only when there is knowledge or "reason to know that the information was obtained through electronic surveillance not authorized" by statute.

18. For instance, NSA may determine that the report is fully supported by cited communications other than the ones obtained through upstream communication. Sept. 12 Submission at 4. In other instances, NSA may revise the report so that it no longer relies upon upstream communications and reissue it. *Id.* If such steps are not feasible because the report cannot be supported without the upstream communication, NSA will cancel the report. *Id.*

Taken together, the remedial steps taken by the government since October 2011 greatly reduce the risk that NSA will run afoul of Section 1809(a)(2) in its handling of the past upstream acquisitions made under color of Section 702. NSA's self-imposed prohibition on using non-target communications to or from a U.S. person or a person in the United States helped to ensure that the fruits of unauthorized electronic surveillance were not used or disclosed while it was working to purge the pre-October 31, 2011 upstream collection. And NSA's subsequent purge of derivative reports further reduce the risk of a problem under Section 1809(a)(2). Finally, the amended NSA minimization procedures provide that in the event, despite NSA's effort to purge the prior upstream collection, the agency discovers an Internet transaction acquired before October 31, 2011, such transaction must be purged upon recognition. *See* Amended NSA Minimization Procedures at 8 §3(c)(3). In light of the foregoing, it appears to the Court that the outstanding issues raised by NSA's upstream collection of Internet transactions have been resolved, subject to the discussion of changes to the minimization procedures that appear below.[19] [redacted]

NOTES AND QUESTIONS

1. *What's the Big Deal?* Is PRISM focused on just what the FAA authorized — realtime collection against non-U.S. persons outside the United States? If so, why would the government object to its disclosure? Who would benefit from knowing the identities of U.S. companies cooperating with NSA under Section 702 agreements?

2. *The Value of PRISM.* In June 18, 2013, testimony before the House Intelligence Committee, the NSA Director, General Keith Alexander, stated that PRISM and a metadata collection program described in this *Supplement, infra* p. 127, have helped "prevent . . . potential terrorist events over 50 times since 9/11." Sean Sullivan, *NSA Head: Surveillance Helped Thwart More than 50 Terror Plots*, Wash. Post, June 18, 2013. Publicly disclosed examples included the cases of

---

19. Under the circumstances, the Court finds it unnecessary to further address the arguments advanced by the government in its November 22, 2011 response to the Court's October 13, 2011 briefing order regarding Section 1809(a), particularly those regarding the scope of prior Section 702 authorizations.

Najibullah Zazi, who pleaded guilty to planning suicide attacks in New York City, and David Headley, a co-conspirator in the 2008 terrorist attacks by Pakistani operatives in Mumbai, India. *Id.* If General Alexander's claims are accurate, do you see any downsides to PRISM?

3. *Just What Does NSA Collect?* Can you tell from the descriptions of PRISM and upstream collection what data are or may be collected by NSA? Does PRISM or upstream collection include email messages, Facebook posts, instant messages? Audio and video chats, or photographs? Facebook reported that in the last six months of 2012 the company provided law enforcement (federal, state, and local, including NSA) the private data of between 18,000 and 19,000 user accounts. Ted Ullyot, *Facebook Releases Data, Including All National Security Requests*, facebook Newsroom, June 14, 2013, http://newsroom.fb.com/ News/636/Facebook-Releases-Data-Including-All-National-Security-Requests. Do you suppose that the extent and nature of the collection varies from company to company? In what ways?

NSA also intercepts "millions of images per day" — including about 55,000 "facial recognition quality images," according to documents leaked by Edward Snowden. James Risen & Laura Poitras, *NSA Collecting Millions of Faces From Web Images*, N.Y. Times, May 31, 2014. Could NSA lawfully collect images of Americans through its Section 702 authorities? If the images are a form of communications content, presumably NSA would require FISC approval to collect images of a United States person. What about someone not a U.S. person reasonably believed to be abroad? Should privacy protections extend to facial recognition technologies and the data they generate?

4. *Targeting — Identify and Tasking a Selector.* NSA apparently relies on Section 702 collection to provide the basis for a form of link analysis, known as contact chaining, in which an analyst begins with some form of Internet identifier — a "selector" — and then mines a data base containing the collected information using algorithms to find other communications linked to the original source.

Does this process satisfy FISA and the Constitution? How about the mining of data collected by NSA "upstream" from the ISPs or similar companies? With upstream collection, NSA has access to virtually all Internet traffic. Does the government's access to this mass of communications content require a Fourth Amendment warrant, in addition to the known procedures for searching and filtering the collected data? Consider the following issues:

(a) *Avoiding U.S. Persons?* Does the process for identifying and tasking a selector described in the NSA Civil Liberties and Privacy Office Report, apparently typically an email address or phone number, sufficiently protect U.S. persons? What guidance would you add?

(b) *Foreign Intelligence and Location.* The phrase "foreign intelligence" is pervasive in describing authorized collection activities, including programmatic collection under FISA. Significantly, the term is still defined by geography: targeting is permitted against those reasonably believed to be outside the United States. Through PRISM, massive quantities of the contents of emails and other electronic communications are collected on the basis of presumed location. But can location abroad reasonably be presumed on the basis of a domain name or the identity of a service provider? If not, then how? Won't the adoption of such a presumption lead inevitably to collection from individuals inside the United States? If it will, does collection on this basis violate the FAA?

(c) *Collection against U.S. Persons.* NSA has reportedly interpreted the FAA to require that in keying in its search terms it need only ensure 51 percent confidence in the target's "foreignness." Gellman & Poitras, *supra.* In theory, then, nearly half of the time NSA could mistakenly target U.S. persons.

A U.S. person is more likely to have her communications collected if she communicates with someone abroad. Given that U.S.-person communications are intermingled with foreign communications collected from U.S. companies' fiber optic cables in the United States, NSA collection has no way of ensuring that only non-U.S.-person communications are scooped up.

NSA slides leaked by Edward Snowden and reported by *The Washington Post* promised that PRISM would soon expand to include cloud computing companies. If so, then U.S. persons communicating with each other domestically could have their communications intercepted, too. Gellman & Poitras, *supra.* In July 2014, *Washington Post* reporters concluded a four month review of approximately 160,000 email and instant message conversations from data provided to them by Snowden. Their review found that 90% of intercepted conversations "were not the intended surveillance targets but were caught in a net the agency had cast for somebody else." Barton Gellman, Julie Tate & Askan Soltani, *In NSA-Intercepted Data, Those Not Targeted Far Outnumber the Foreigners Who Are*, Wash. Post, July 5, 2014. Nearly half of the communications contained names, email addresses or other details marked by the NSA as belonging to U.S. citizens or residents. Is the disparity between the number of communications collected from intelligence targets and those collected incidentally an inevitable feature of Section 702 surveillance? How would you revise the program to cut down on incidental collection and particularly the collection against U.S. persons?

Upstream collection also inevitably acquires information from U.S. persons as a byproduct of contact chaining and the "hops" from the initial non-U.S.-person targets believed to be located abroad.

NSA is increasingly able to store and process massive amounts of data, which are then available at any time to its analysts. Open source software like Hadoop lets NSA preserve aggregated data on agency computers until an analyst needs the information. The analyst can look at what was collected and make the non-U.S.-person/U.S.-person distinctions later. Shane Harris, *The NSA Can't Tell the Difference Between an American and a Foreigner*, Foreign Policy, June 28, 2013, http://www.foreignpolicy.com/articles/2013/06/27/the_nsa_cant_tell_the_ difference_between_an_american_and_a_foreigner. Implicitly, then, the combination of big data and sophisticated software makes it more likely that U.S.-persons communications will be reviewed by NSA analysts.

Does the incidental collection of U.S. person information under the Section 702 programs violate the FAA? The Constitution? If the initial search of a PRISM-created database is conducted entirely by computer, can a computer by itself violate your privacy? *See* Richard A. Posner, *Privacy, Surveillance, and Law*, 75 U. Chi. L. Rev. 245, 254 (2008) ("Computer searches do not invade privacy because computers are not sentient beings.").

(d) *Oversight and Compliance*. Do you believe that the guidelines and training described in the NSA Report will effectively ensure against over-collection against U.S. persons? If not, how would you modify the requirements?

5. *Section 702 Minimization*. Recall that the statutory minimization requirements for programmatic surveillance in the FAA parrot the

language of traditional FISA minimization. Should legal standards for minimization associated with individualized and programmatic electronic collection be different? In August 2013, the ODNI declassified Section 702 minimization procedures approved in October 2011 that had been leaked earlier by Edward Snowden. *Minimization Procedures Used by the National Security Agency in Connection with Acquisitions of Foreign Intelligence Information Pursuant to Section 702 of the Foreign Intelligence Surveillance Act of 1978, as Amended.* http://www.dni.gov/files/documents/Minimization%20Procedures%20us ed%20by%20NSA%20in%20Connection%20with%20FISA%20SECT %20702.pdf. Consider the following issues:

(a) *Culling the U.S. Person Data.* Reviewing the 2014 NSA Civil Liberties and Privacy Office Report, how is Section 702 minimization different from generic FISA minimization? Does minimization fairly protects U.S. persons whose private information is inadvertently collected?

According to the September 2012 FISC opinion by Judge Bates, in what specific respects had NSA been violating FISA and the Constitution in its upstream collection program? Would you say that the revisions made by NSA in response to earlier FISC rulings remedied the violations? Did the changes compromise in any way the capabilities of NSA to collect foreign intelligence? Can you sketch the likely changes to minimization that may have been ordered by the FISC in the redacted portion at the end of its opinion?

(b) *Presidential Policy Directive/PPD-28 and Non-U.S. Persons.* On January 17, 2014, President Obama issued a new PPD proclaiming that "[a]ll persons should be treated with dignity and respect, regardless of their nationality or wherever they might reside, and all persons have legitimate privacy interests in the handling of their personal information. U.S. signals intelligence activities must, therefore, include appropriate safeguards for the personal information of all individuals, regardless of the nationality of the individual to whom the information pertains or where that individual resides." The White House, *Presidential Policy Directive/PPD-28*, Jan. 17, 2014, http://www.whitehouse.gov/the-press-office/2014/01/17/presidential-policy-directive-signals-intelligence-activities. The directive goes on state, however, that the policies and procedures outlined in it apply equally to all persons, regardless of nationality, only "[t]o the maximum extent feasible consistent with national security." *Id.* §4(a). Apart from this wiggle room, the PPD extends minimization procedures to forbid retention or dissemination of non-U.S. person information except to the extent that "dissemination of comparable information concerning U.S. persons would be permitted under section 2.3 of Executive Order 12333." *Id.* §4(a)(i). *See* NSL p. 457, CTL p. 141. Section 2.3 permits retention and dissemination of foreign intelligence information. What, if any, legal impact does this portion of the PPD have on the obligations of NSA or the rights of non-U.S. persons?

(c) *Domestic Communications.* Once identified as domestic communications, data normally will be promptly destroyed. Are you satisfied that the conditions that permit senior NSA officials to retain U.S. person communications are sufficiently attentive to the needs for both foreign intelligence and the privacy of innocent persons? What is the justification for retaining data that may contain U.S. person information for up to five years?

(d) *NSA Management, Compliance, and Oversight.* Are you satisfied with the internal compliance processes at NSA? With the role reserved for Congress and the FISC?

6. *The Role of the FISC.* What legal standards were applied by the FISC in approving the PRISM directives? Upstream collection? Does the FISC have a role in monitoring the PRISM directives? In the October 2011 FISC opinion discussed in the September 2012 opinion by Judge Bates, the FISC ruled that NSA minimization violated the Fourth Amendment. Reviewing Section 702 and the limited role prescribed for the FISC in approving and reviewing programmatic surveillance, can you piece together how the FISC would have had an opportunity to make such a determination? If NSA had not disclosed its misrepresentations to the FISC, would the Court or any other overseer have had the opportunity to correct its violations of FISA and the Constitution?

If the FISC's only role in the directives process is periodic re-approval of the procedures, as opposed to individualized approval of their application, is that role properly characterized as adjudicative? Or is it more administrative (or, perhaps, legislative)? If so, should an Article III court be engaged in such approval?

7. *Constitutional Challenges to Section 702?* Jamshid Muhtorov, a lawful permanent resident, was charged in a federal indictment in Colorado with providing material support to a terrorist organization. After the government informed Muhtorov that it intended to use information obtained or derived from Section 702 surveillance at trial, Muhtorov moved to suppress any such evidence on the ground that Section 702 violates the Fourth Amendment and Article III. Presumably, any foreign intelligence the government plans to use in prosecuting Muhtorov, a U.S. person, was incidentally collected while targeting a person or persons reasonably believed to be abroad.

If the judge orders the government to disclose sufficient details of Muhtorov's surveillance, the defendant may be able to argue that monitoring of his communications was unconstitutional. Can you outline his argument?

It is by no means clear that a challenge to particular surveillance on Fourth Amendment grounds enables a facial challenge to the constitutionality of the statute. Assuming that a court will entertain such a challenge, can you sketch the likely Fourth Amendment argument? The government's response? Could the district court entertain the argument that the administrative role played by the FISC in Section 702 collection is incompatible with that court's Article III authority? *See* Orin Kerr, *Is the Supreme Court Likely to Rule on FISA Section 702?*, Lawfare, Oct. 29, 2013; Marty Lederman, *The Muhtorov Constitutional Challenge to Section 702*, Just Security, Feb. 4, 2014.

8. *Push-Back from the Telecoms.* In the wake of ongoing revelations of NSA surveillance and data collection from a largely cooperative telecommunications industry, companies are building encryption to protect their customers' communications from government eaves-dropping and are refusing to cooperate with government requests when there is no legal obligation or warrant. David E. Sanger & Nicole Perlroth, *Internet Giants Erect Barriers to Spy Agencies*, N.Y. Times, June 6, 2014.

9. *Recommended Reforms.* On July 1, 2014, the President's Civil Liberties Oversight Board (PCLOB) released its Report on Section 702 of FISA. http://www.pclob.gov/All%20Documents/Report%20on%20 the%20Section%20702%20Program/PCLOB-Section-702-Report.pdf. The PCLOB found that "PRISM collection is clearly authorized by the statute," and that "the statute can permissibly be interpreted" to allow

upstream collection. The Board also concluded that the Section 702 collection passes reasonableness review under the Fourth Amendment. Because "certain aspects of the Section 702 program push the program close to the line of constitutional reasonableness" — including incidental collection on U.S. persons and some uses of upstream collection — the Board recommends, among other things, revising targeting procedures to specify criteria for determining the foreign intelligence value of a particular target, revising minimization procedures to better monitor U.S. person queries of collected information, and enhancing the FISC role to include reviewing samples of tasking orders and query terms submitted by the NSA. Are courts competent to manage an expanded scope of judicial review? Can you think of other ways to reform the program to protect against incidental U.S. persons collection and to limit upstream collection?

––––––––––––––

[NSL p. 649, CTL p. 262. Insert after Note 5.]

6. *Requiem for Smith and Miller?* The assumptions underlying *Smith* and *Miller* may be eroding even in the Supreme Court. In a 2012 case in which the Court unanimously sustained a Fourth Amendment challenge to the use of a hidden GPS tracking device on a suspect's vehicle, Justice Sotomayor wrote in a concurring opinion:

> [I]t may be necessary to reconsider the premise that an individual has no reasonable expectation of privacy in information voluntarily disclosed to third parties. *E.g., Smith* [*v. Maryland*, 442 U.S. 735 (1979)], at 742; *United States v. Miller*, 425 U.S. 435 (1976). This approach is ill suited to the digital age, in which people reveal a great deal of information about themselves to third parties in the course of carrying out mundane tasks. People disclose the phone numbers that they dial or text to their cellular providers; the URLs that they visit and the e-mail addresses with which they correspond to their Internet service providers; and the books, groceries, and medications they purchase to online retailers. Perhaps, as Justice Alito notes, some people may find the "tradeoff" of privacy for convenience "worthwhile," or come to accept this "diminution of privacy" as "inevitable," *post*, at 962, and perhaps not. I for one doubt that people would accept without complaint the warrantless disclosure to the Government of a list of every Web site they had visited in the last week, or month, or year. But whatever the societal expectations, they can attain constitutionally protected status only if our Fourth Amendment jurisprudence ceases to treat secrecy as a prerequisite for privacy. I would

not assume that all information voluntarily disclosed to some member of the public for a limited purpose is, for that reason alone, disentitled to Fourth Amendment protection. See *Smith*, at 749 (Marshall, J., dissenting) ("Privacy is not a discrete commodity, possessed absolutely or not at all. Those who disclose certain facts to a bank or phone company for a limited business purpose need not assume that this information will be released to other persons for other purposes"); see also *Katz* [*v. United States*, 389 U.S. 347], at 351–352 ("[W]hat [a person] seeks to preserve as private, even in an area accessible to the public, may be constitutionally protected"). [*United States v. Jones*, 132 S. Ct. 945, 957 (2012).]

[NSL p. 668, CTL p. 281. Add to end of Note 4.]

Before the 2013 disclosure of classified documents by Edward Snowden and the U.S. government's release of redacted and previously classified documents in response, many thought that Section 215 orders were used only case-by-case for individually targeted collection of transactional data. Some critics, however, warned that the Section 215 authority could theoretically be invoked to get the "entire database of a credit card company" or all of the library borrowing records for a certain date. Yet even the most critical probably doubted that this authority would be pushed to (or beyond?) its outer limits. In fact, some believed that collection by national security letters would be far more prevalent.

Many were therefore shocked when documents leaked by Edward Snowden revealed the aggressive use of Section 215 authority for the *bulk* collection and lengthy retention of vast amounts of telephony metadata (essentially data about telephone calls without the contents of those calls) from millions of U.S. persons making calls within the United States.[1] The leaks showed, for the first time, that the government was

---

1. Even before the bulk Section 215 orders, certain "Internet metadata" were collected without any court order or any apparent statutory authority, according to a 2009 report of the Inspector General of the NSA. *See* Office of the Inspector General, National Security Agency/Central Security Service, *1109-0002 Working Draft*, Mar. 24, 2009, *available at* http://www.guardian.co. uk/world/interactive/2013/jun/27/nsa-inspector-general-report-document-data-collection. This collection was temporarily halted by a "palace revolt" by Department of Justice officials, who resisted White House efforts to have the then seriously ill Attorney General John Ashcroft sign an order authorizing the program's continuation. *Id. See* NSL p. 618, Note 10; CTL p. 231, Note 10,

using Section 215 authority not just to access "specific items about specific persons on a case-by-case basis, but also as a means to create giant databases of telephony metadata that might *later* be queried on a case by-case basis." Robert Chesney & Benjamin Wittes, *A Tale of Two NSA Leaks*, New Republic, June 10, 2013, www.newrepublic.com/article/113427/nsa-spyingscandal-one-leak-more-damaging-other# (emphasis added). This use of Section 215 raised serious statutory and constitutional questions.[2]

The FISC defined "telephony metadata" for calls between the United States and abroad and wholly within the United States as "comprehensive communications routing information, including but not limited to session identifying information (e.g., originating and terminating telephone number, International Mobile Subscriber Identity (IMSI) number, International Mobile station Equipment Identity (IMEI) number, etc.), trunk identifier, telephone calling card numbers, and time and duration of call . . . [but not including] the substantive content of any communication, as identified by 18 U.S.C. §2510(8), or the name, address, or financial information of a subscriber or customer." *In re Application of the Federal Bureau of Investigation for an Order Requiring the Production of Tangible Things from Verizon Business Network Services, Inc. on Behalf of MCI Communication Services, Inc. d/b/a Verizon Business Services*, No. BR 13-80 (FISA Court Apr. 25, 2013). (This order, marked "Top Secret," was published online in Glenn Greenwald, *NSA Collecting Phone Records of Millions of Verizon Customers Daily*, The Guardian, June 5, 2013, http://www.guardian.co.uk/world/2013/jun/06/nsa-phone-records-verizon-courtorder.)

A Congressional Research Service report suggests how those data may have been used in conjunction with Section 702 programmatic intercepts:

---

erroneously connecting this controversy to the TSP. The collection effort was then resumed after an order was obtained from the FISC. This effort was reportedly discontinued in 2011 as a result of an interagency review. Office of the Inspector General, *supra*.

2. Subsequent disclosures of FISC opinions on the collection effort reinforced the shock by documenting the NSA's non-compliance with FISC orders, as well as its repeated inaccurate submissions to the FISC.

NSA, using 702 authorities, intercepted an email between an extremist in Pakistan and an individual in the United States. NSA provided this email to the FBI, which identified and began to surveil Colorado-based Najibulla Zazi. NSA then received Zazi's phone number from the FBI, checked it against phone records procured using 215 authorities, and identified one of Zazi's accomplices, an individual named Adis Medunjanin. Zazi and Medunjanin were both subsequently arrested and convicted of planning to bomb the New York City subway.

Marshall Curtis Erwin & Edward C. Liu, *NSA Surveillance Leaks: Background and Issues for Congress* (Cong. Res. Serv. R43134), July 2, 2013, 10. In other words, Section 215 authority had been used to compile a giant database of telephony metadata without any individualized predicate (e.g., evidence suggesting the identity of a foreign agent), which the NSA then queried at a later date using a telephone numbers obtained from email intercepted under Section 702 authority, enabling it to discover calls to or from Zazi's accomplices.

Although the story of Section 215 metadata collection is still evolving at this writing, the following materials help limn the issues. An August 29, 2013, opinion by FISC Judge Claire V. Eagan, excerpted below, addresses some of the statutory and constitutional questions. The opinion accepts many of the arguments made more fully by the United States in *Administration White Paper, Bulk Collection of Telephony Metadata Under Section 215 of the USA Patriot Act*, Aug. 9, 2013, *available at* http://info.publicintelligence.net/DoJ-NSABulk Collection.pdf.

In December 2013, the President's Review Group on Intelligence and Communications Technologies, convened by the President after the Snowden documents began to appear, concluded that the metadata program had not made the nation safer: "Our review suggests that the information contributed to terrorist investigations by the use of . . . telephony meta-data was not essential to preventing attacks." *Liberty and Security in a Changing World*, Dec. 12, 2013, http://www.whitehouse.gov/sites/default/files/docs/2013-12-12_rg_final_report.pdf. The Review Group recommended that "as a general matter, and without senior policy review, the government should not be permitted to collect and store all mass, undigested, non-public personal information about individuals to enable future queries and data-mining for foreign intelligence purposes."

In January 2014, the Privacy and Civil Liberties Oversight Board (PCLOB) issued its *Report on the Telephone Records Program*

Conducted under Section 215 of the USA PATRIOT ACT and on the Operations of the Foreign Intelligence Surveillance Court, Jan. 23, 2014, http://www.pclob.gov/SiteAssets/Pages/default/PCLOB-Report-on-the-Telephone-Records-Program.pdf. The majority of the Board found that Section 215 does not authorize the bulk telephone data collection program and, if it did, such collection is of doubtful constitutionality. The PCLOB Report's conclusions are assessed in Notes and Questions below.

Finally, in a January 17, 2014, speech President Obama ordered a review and eventual transition from the existing Section 215 bulk telephony metadata program. On the same day, the President issued Presidential Policy Directive/PPD-28, *Signals Intelligence Activities*, http://www.whitehouse.gov/the-press-office/2014/01/17/ presidential-policy-directive-signals-intelligence-activities, outlining new policies on signals intelligence. PPD-28 is set out following the excerpted FISC opinion immediately below.

In re Application of the FBI for an Order Requiring the Production of Tangible Things from [REDACTED]

Foreign Intelligence Surveillance Court, Aug. 29, 2013

No. BR-13-109

available at www.uscourts.gov/uscourts/courts/fisc/br13-09-primary-order.pdf

CLAIRE V. EAGAN, Judge:

I. Background

On July 18, 2013, a verified Final "Application for Certain Tangible Things for Investigations to Protect Against International Terrorism" (Application) was submitted to the Court by the Federal Bureau of Investigation (FBI) for an order pursuant to the Foreign Intelligence Surveillance Act of 1978 (FISA or the Act), Title 50, United States Code (U.S.C.), §1861, as amended (also known as Section 215 of the USA PATRIOT Act), requiring the ongoing daily production to the National Security Agency (NSA) of certain call detail records or "telephony metadata" in bulk.[2] The Court . . . GRANTED the application for the reasons stated in this Memorandum Opinion and in a Primary Order issued on July 19, 2013, which is appended hereto. . . .

Specifically, the government requested Orders from this Court to obtain certain business records of specified telephone service providers. Those telephone company business records consist of a very large volume of each company's call detail records or telephony metadata, but expressly exclude the contents of any communication; the name, address, or financial information of any subscriber or customer; or any cell site location information (CSLI). Primary Ord. at 3 n.l.[5] The government requested production of this data on a daily basis for a period of 90 days. The sole purpose of this production is to obtain foreign intelligence information in support of [REDACTED] individual authorized investigations to protect against international terrorism and concerning various international terrorist organizations. See Primary Ord. at 2, 6; App. at 8; and, Ex. A. at 2-3. In granting the government's request, the Court has prohibited the government from accessing the data for any other intelligence or investigative purpose. Primary Ord. at 4.

By the terms of this Court's Primary Order, access to the data is restricted through technical means, through limits on trained personnel with authorized access, and through a query process that requires a reasonable, articulable suspicion (RAS), as determined by a limited set of personnel, that the selection term (*e.g.*, a telephone number) that will be used to search the data is associated with one of the identified

---

2. For purposes of this matter, "'telephony metadata' includes comprehensive communications routing information, including but not limited to session identifying information (*e.g.*, originating and terminating telephone number, International Mobile station Equipment Identity (IMEI) number, International Mobile Subscriber Identity (IMSI) number, etc.), trunk identifier, telephone calling card numbers, and time and duration of call. Telephony metadata does not include the substantive content of any communication, as defined by 18 U.S.C. §2510(8), or the name, address, or financial information of a subscriber or customer." App. at 4. In addition, the Court has explicitly directed that its authorization does not include "the production of cell site location information (CSLI)." Primary Ord. at 3.

5. In the event that the government seeks the production of CSLI as part of the bulk production of call detail records in the future, the government would be required to provide notice and briefing to this Court pursuant to FISC Rule 11. . . .

international terrorist organizations.[7] *Primary Ord.* at 4-9. Moreover, the government may not make the RAS determination for selection terms reasonably believed to be used by U.S. persons solely based on activities protected by the First Amendment. *Id.* at 9; and *see* 50 U.S.C. §1861(a)(1). To ensure adherence to its Orders, this Court has the authority to oversee compliance, *see* 50 U.S.C. §1803(h), and requires the government to notify the Court in writing immediately concerning any instance of non-compliance, *see* FISC Rule 13(b). According to the government, in the prior authorization period there have been no compliance incidents.[8]

Finally, although not required by statute, the government has demonstrated through its written submissions and oral testimony that this production has been and remains valuable for obtaining foreign intelligence information regarding international terrorist organizations.

II. Fourth Amendment

The production of telephone service provider metadata is squarely controlled by the U.S. Supreme Court decision in *Smith v. Maryland*, 442 U.S. 735 (1979). . . . The same type of information [that was at issue in *Smith*] is at issue here.[11] . . .

---

7. A selection term that meets specific legal standards has always been required. This Court has not authorized government personnel to access the data for the purpose of wholesale "data mining" or browsing.

8. The Court is aware that in prior years there have been incidents of non-compliance with respect to NSA's handling of produced information. Through oversight by this Court over a period of months, those issues were resolved.

11. The Court is aware that additional call detail data is obtained via this production than was acquired through the pen register acquisition at issue in *Smith*. Other courts have had the opportunity to review whether there is a Fourth Amendment expectation of privacy in call detail records similar to the data sought in this matter and have found that there is none. *See United States v. Reed*, 575 F.3d 900, 914 (9th Cir. 2009) (finding that because "data about the 'call origination, length, and time of call' . . . is nothing more than pen register and trap and trace data, there is no Fourth Amendment 'expectation of privacy.'") (citing *Smith*, 442 U.S. at 743-44), *cert. denied* 559 U.S. 987, 988 (2010); *United States Telecom Ass'n*, 227 F.3d 450, 454 (D.C. Cir. 2000) (noting pen registers record telephone numbers of outgoing calls and trap and

In *Smith*, the government was obtaining the telephone company's metadata of one person suspected of a crime. *See id*. at 737. Here, the government is requesting daily production of certain telephony metadata in bulk belonging to companies without specifying the particular number of an individual. This Court had reason to analyze this distinction in a similar context in [REDACTED]. In that case, this Court found that "regarding the breadth of the proposed surveillance, it is noteworthy that the application of the Fourth Amendment depends on the government's intruding into some individual's reasonable expectation of privacy." The Court noted that Fourth Amendment rights are personal and individual, *see id*. (citing *Steagald v. United States*, 451 U.S. 204, 219 (1981); *accord., e.g., Rakas v. Illinois*, 439 U.S. 128, 133 (1978) ("'Fourth Amendment rights are personal rights which . . . may not be vicariously asserted.'") (quoting *Alderman v. United States*, 394 U.S. 165, 174 (1969))), and that "[s]o long as no individual has a reasonable expectation of privacy in meta data, the large number of persons whose communications will be subjected to the . . . surveillance is irrelevant to the issue of whether a Fourth Amendment search or seizure will occur." Put another way, where one individual does not have a Fourth Amendment interest, grouping together a large number of similarly-situated individuals cannot result in a Fourth Amendment interest springing into existence *ex nihilo*.

In sum, because the Application at issue here concerns only the production of call detail records or "telephony metadata" belonging to a telephone company, and not the contents of communications, *Smith v. Maryland* compels the conclusion that there is no Fourth Amendment impediment to the collection. Furthermore, for the reasons stated in [REDACTED] and discussed above, this Court finds that the volume of records being acquired does not alter this conclusion. Indeed, there is no legal basis for this Court to find otherwise.

---

trace devices are like caller ID systems, and that such information is not protected by the Fourth Amendment); *United States v. Hallmark*, 911 F.2d 399, 402 (10th Cir. 1990) (recognizing that "[t]he installation and use of a pen register and trap and trace device is not a 'search' requiring a warrant pursuant to the Fourth Amendment," and noting that there is no "'legitimate expectation of privacy' at stake." (citing *Smith*, 442 U.S. at 739-46)).

III. Section 215

Section 215 of the USA PATRIOT Act created a statutory framework, the various parts of which are designed to ensure not only that the government has access to the information it needs for authorized investigations, but also that there are protections and prohibitions in place to safeguard U.S. person information. It requires the government to demonstrate, among other things, that there is "an investigation to obtain foreign intelligence information . . . to [in this case] protect against international terrorism," 50 U.S.C. §1861(a)(1); that investigations of U.S. persons are "not conducted solely upon the basis of activities protected by the first amendment to the Constitution," *id.*; that the investigation is "conducted under guidelines approved by the Attorney General under Executive Order 12333," *id.* §1861(a)(2); that there is "a statement of facts showing that there are reasonable grounds to believe that the tangible things sought are relevant" to the investigation, *id.* §1861(b)(2)(A); that there are adequate minimization procedures "applicable to the retention and dissemination" of the information requested, *id.* §1861(b)(2)(B); and, that only the production of such things that could be "obtained with a subpoena *duces tecum*" or "any other order issued by a court of the United States directing the production of records" may be ordered, *id.* §1861(c)(2)(D), *see infra* Part III.a. (discussing Section 2703(d) of the Stored Communications Act). If the Court determines that the government has met the requirements of Section 215, it shall enter an *ex parte* order compelling production.

This Court must verify that each statutory provision is satisfied before issuing the requested Orders. For example, even if the Court finds that the records requested are relevant to an investigation, it may not authorize the production if the minimization procedures are insufficient. Under Section 215, minimization procedures are "specific procedures that are reasonably designed in light of the purpose and technique of an order for the production of tangible things, to minimize the retention, and prohibit the dissemination, of nonpublicly available information concerning unconsenting United States persons consistent with the need of the United States to obtain, produce, and disseminate foreign intelligence information." *Id.* §1861(g)(2)(A). Congress recognized in this provision that information concerning U.S. persons that is not directly responsive to foreign intelligence needs will be produced under these orders and established postproduction protections for such information. As the Primary Order issued in this matter demonstrates, this Court's authorization includes detailed restrictions on the government through minimization procedures. *See* Primary Ord. at 4-17. Without those restrictions, this Court could not, nor would it, have approved the proposed production. This Court's Primary Order also sets forth the requisite findings under Section 215 for issuing the Orders requested by the government in its Application. *Id.* at 2, 4-17. . . .

a.   **Section 215 of FISA and Section 2703(d) of the Stored Communications Act**

It is instructive to compare Section 215, which is used for foreign intelligence purposes and is codified as part of FISA, with 18 U.S.C. §2703 ("Required disclosure of customer communications or records"), which is used in criminal investigations and is part of the Stored Communications Act (SCA). *See In re Production of Tangible Things From* [REDACTED], Docket No. BR 08-13, Supp. Op. (Dec. 12, 2008) [*available at* https://www.eff.org/document/br-08-13-supp-op-re-sca-121208-final-redactedex-ocr] (discussing Section 215 and Section 2703). Section 2703 establishes a process by which the government can obtain information from electronic communications service providers, such as telephone companies. As with FISA, this section of the SCA provides the mechanism for obtaining either the contents of communications, or non-content records of communications. *See* 18 U.S.C. §§2703(a)-(c).

For non-content records production requests, such as the type sought here, Section 2703(c) provides a variety of mechanisms, including acquisition through a court order under Section 2703(d). Under this section, which is comparable to Section 215, the government must offer to the court "*specific and articulable facts* showing that there are reasonable grounds to believe that . . . the records or other information sought, are relevant and material to an ongoing criminal investigation." *Id.* §2703(d) (emphasis added). Section 215, the comparable provision for foreign intelligence purposes, requires neither "specific and articulable facts" nor does it require that the information be "material." Rather, it merely requires a statement of facts showing that there are reasonable grounds to believe that the records sought are relevant to the investigation. *See* 50 U.S.C. §1861(b)(2)(A). That these two provisions apply to the production of the same type of records from the same type of providers is an indication that Congress intended this Court to apply a different, and in specific respects lower, standard to the government's

Application under Section 215 than a court reviewing a request under Section 2703(d). . . .

Furthermore, Congress provided different measures to ensure that the government obtains and uses information properly, depending on the purpose for which it sought the information. First, Section 2703 has no provision for minimization procedures. However, such procedures are mandated under Section 215 and must be designed to restrict the retention and dissemination of information, as imposed by this Court's Primary Order. Primary Ord. at 4-17; *see* 50 U.S.C. §§1861(c)(1), (g).

Second, Section 2703(d) permits the service provider to file a motion with a court to "quash or modify such order, if the information or records requested are unusually voluminous in nature or compliance with such order otherwise would cause undue burden on such provider." *Id*. Congress recognized that, even with the higher statutory standard for a production order under Section 2703(d), some requests authorized by a court would be "voluminous" and provided a means by which the provider could seek relief using a motion. *Id*. Under Section 215, however, Congress provided a specific and complex statutory scheme for judicial review of an Order from this Court to ensure that providers could challenge both the legality of the required production and the nondisclosure provisions of that Order. 50 U.S.C. §1861(f). This adversarial process includes the selection of a judge from a pool of FISC judges to review the challenge to determine if it is frivolous and to rule on the merits, *id*. §1861(f)(2)(A)(ii), provides standards that the judge is to apply during such review, *id*. §§1861(f)(2)(B)-(C), and provides for appeal to the Foreign Intelligence Surveillance Court of Review and, ultimately, the U.S. Supreme Court, *id*. §1861(f)(3). This procedure, as opposed to the motion process available under Section 2703(d) to challenge a production as unduly voluminous or burdensome, contemplates a substantial and engaging adversarial process to test the legality of this Court's Orders under Section 215. This enhanced process appears designed to ensure that there are additional safeguards in light of the lower threshold that the government is required to meet for production under Section 215 as opposed to Section 2703(d). To date, no holder of records who has received an Order to produce bulk telephony metadata has challenged the legality of such an Order. Indeed, no recipient of any Section 215 Order has challenged the legality of such an Order, despite the explicit statutory mechanism for doing so.

When analyzing a statute or a provision thereof, a court considers the statutory schemes as a whole. . . . Here, the Court finds that Section

215 and Section 2703(d) operate in a complementary manner and are designed for their specific purposes. In the criminal investigation context, Section 2703(d) includes front-end protections by imposing a higher burden on the government to obtain the information in the first instance. On the other hand, when the government seeks to obtain the same type of information, but for a foreign intelligence purpose, Congress provided the government with more latitude at the production stage under Section 215 by not requiring specific and articulable facts or meeting a materiality standard. Instead, it imposed post-production checks in the form of mandated minimization procedures and a structured adversarial process. This is a logical framework and it comports well with the Fourth Amendment concept that the required factual predicate for obtaining information in a case of special needs, such as national security, can be lower than for use of the same investigative measures for an ordinary criminal investigation. *See United States v. United States District Court (Keith)*, 407 U.S. 297, 308-309, 322-323 (1972); and, *In re Sealed Case*, 310 F.3d 717, 745-746 (FISA Ct. Rev. 2002) (differentiating requirements for the government to obtain information obtained for national security reasons as opposed to a criminal investigation). . . .

b. Relevance

Because known and unknown international terrorist operatives are using telephone communications, and because it is necessary to obtain the bulk collection of a telephone company's metadata to determine those connections between known and unknown international terrorist operatives as part of authorized investigations, the production of the information sought meets the standard for relevance under Section 215.

As an initial matter and as a point of clarification, the government's burden under Section 215 is not to prove that the records sought are, in fact, relevant to an authorized investigation. The explicit terms of the statute require "a statement of facts showing that there are *reasonable grounds to believe* that the tangible things sought are relevant . . . ." 50 U.S.C. §1861(b)(2)(A) (emphasis added). In establishing this standard, Congress chose to leave the term "relevant" undefined. It is axiomatic that when Congress declines to define a term a court must give the term its ordinary meaning. *See, e.g., Taniguchi v. Kan Pacific Saipan, Ltd.,* _ U.S. __, 132 S. Ct. 1997, 2002 (2012). Accompanying the government's first application for the bulk production of telephone company metadata was a Memorandum of Law which argued that "[i]nformation is 'relevant' to an authorized international terrorism investigation if it bears upon, or is pertinent to, that investigation." Mem. of Law in Support of App. for Certain Tangible Things for Investigations to Protect Against International Terrorism, Docket No. BR 06-05 (filed May 23, 2006), at 13-14 (quoting dictionary definitions, *Oppenheimer Fund, Inc. v. Sanders*, 437 U.S. 340, 351 (1978), and Fed. R. Evid. 401). This Court recognizes that the concept of relevance here is in fact broad and amounts to a relatively low standard.[21] Where there is no requirement for specific and articulable facts or materiality, the government may meet the standard under Section 215 if it can demonstrate reasonable grounds to believe that the information sought to be produced has some bearing on its investigations of the identified international terrorist organizations.

 . . . As this Court noted in 2010, the "finding of relevance most crucially depended on the conclusion that bulk collection is necessary for NSA to employ tools that are likely to generate useful investigative leads to help identify and track terrorist operatives." [REDACTED] Indeed, in [REDACTED] this Court noted that bulk collections such as these are "necessary to identify the much smaller number of [international terrorist] communications." [REDACTED] As a result, it is this showing of necessity that led the Court to find that "the entire mass of collected metadata is relevant to investigating [international terrorist groups] and affiliated persons." [REDACTED]

This case is no different. The government stated, and this Court is well aware, that individuals associated with international terrorist organizations use telephonic systems to communicate with one another around the world, including within the United States. Ex. A. at 4. The government argues that the broad collection of telephone company

---

21. Even under the higher "relevant and material" standard for 18 U.S.C. §2703(d), discussed above, "[t]he government need not show actual relevance, such as would be required at trial." *In re Application of the United States for an Order Pursuant to 18 U.S.C. §2703(d)*, 830 F. Supp. 2d 114, 130 (E.D. Va. 2011). The petitioners had argued in that case that most of their activity for which records were sought was "unrelated" and that "the government cannot be permitted to blindly request everything that 'might' be useful . . . ." *Id.* (internal quotation omitted). The court rejected this argument, noting that "[t]he probability that some gathered information will not be material is not a substantial objection," and that where no constitutional right is implicated, as is the case here, "there is no need for . . . narrow tailoring." *Id.*

metadata "is necessary to create a historical repository of metadata that enables NSA to find or identify known and *unknown* operatives . . . , some of whom may be in the United States or in communication with U.S. persons." App. at 6 (emphasis added). The government would use such information, in part, "to detect and prevent terrorist acts against the United States and U.S. interests." Ex. A. at 3. The government posits that bulk telephonic metadata is necessary to its investigations because it is impossible to know where in the data the connections to international terrorist organizations will be found. *Id.* at 8-9. The government notes also that "[a]nalysts know that the terrorists' communications are located somewhere" in the metadata produced under this authority, but cannot know where until the data is aggregated and then accessed by their analytic tools under limited and controlled queries. *Id.* As the government stated in its 2006 Memorandum of Law, "[a]ll of the metadata collected is thus relevant, because the success of this investigative tool depends on bulk collection."

The government depends on this bulk collection because if production of the information were to wait until the specific identifier connected to an international terrorist group were determined, most of the historical connections (the entire purpose of this authorization) would be lost. *See* Ex. A. at 7-12. The analysis of past connections is only possible "if the Government has collected and archived a broad set of metadata that contains within it the subset of communications that can later be identified as terrorist-related." Because the subset of terrorist communications is ultimately contained within the whole of the metadata produced, but can only be found after the production is aggregated and then queried using identifiers determined to be associated with identified international terrorist organizations, the whole production is relevant to the ongoing investigation out of necessity.

The government must demonstrate "facts showing that there are reasonable grounds to believe that the tangible things sought are relevant to an authorized investigation." 50 U.S.C. §1861(b)(2)(A). The fact that international terrorist operatives are using telephone communications, and that it is necessary to obtain the bulk collection of a telephone company's metadata to determine those connections between known and unknown international terrorist operatives as part of authorized investigations, is sufficient to meet the low statutory hurdle set out in Section 215 to obtain a production of records. Furthermore, it is important to remember that the relevance finding is only one part of a whole protective statutory scheme. Within the whole of this particular statutory scheme, the low relevance standard is counterbalanced by significant post-production minimization procedures that must accompany such an authorization and an available mechanism for an adversarial challenge in this Court by the record holder. *See supra* Part III.a. Without the minimization procedures set out in detail in this Court's Primary Order, for example, no Orders for production would issue from this Court. See Primary Ord. at 4-17. Taken together, the Section 215 provisions are designed to permit the government wide latitude to seek the information it needs to meet its national security responsibilities, but only in combination with specific procedures for the protection of U.S. person information that are tailored to the production and with an opportunity for the authorization to be challenged. The Application before this Court fits comfortably within this statutory framework.

c. Legislative Re-enactment or Ratification

As the U.S. Supreme Court has stated, "Congress is presumed to be aware of an administrative or judicial interpretation of a statute and to adopt that interpretation when it re-enacts a statute without change." *Lorillard v. Pons*, 434 U.S. 575, 580 (1978) (citing cases and authorities); *see also Forest Groye Sch. Dist. v. T.A.*, 557 U.S. 230, 239-240 (2009) (quoting *Lorillard*, 434 U.S. at 580). This doctrine of legislative re-enactment, also known as the doctrine of ratification, is applicable here because Congress reauthorized Section 215 of the PATRIOT Act without change in 2011. PATRIOT Sunsets Extension Act of 2011, Pub. L. No. 112-14, 125 Stat. 216 (May 26, 2011). This doctrine applies as a presumption that guides a court in interpreting a re-enacted statute. . . . Admittedly, in the national security context where legal decisions are classified by the Executive Branch and, therefore, normally not widely available to Members of Congress for scrutiny, one could imagine that such a presumption would be easily overcome. However, despite the highly-classified nature of the program and this Court's orders, that is not the case here.

Prior to the May 2011 congressional votes on Section 215 re-authorization, the Executive Branch provided the Intelligence Committees of both houses of Congress with letters which contained a "Report on the National Security Agency's Bulk Collection Programs for USA PATRIOT Act Reauthorization" (Report). The Report provided extensive and detailed information to the Committees regarding the nature and scope of this Court's approval of the implementation of Section 215 concerning bulk telephone metadata.[23] The Report noted that "[a]lthough these programs have been briefed to the Intelligence and Judiciary Committees, it is important that other Members of Congress have access to information about th[is] . . . program[] when considering reauthorization of the expiring PATRIOT Act provisions." *Id*. Report at 3. Furthermore, the government stated the following in [letters to the Intelligence Committees]: "We believe that making this document available to all Members of Congress is an effective way to inform the legislative debate about reauthorization of Section 215." *Id*. HPSCI Letter at 1; SSCI Letter at 1. It is clear from the letters that the Report would be made available to all Members of Congress and that HPSCI, SSCI, and Executive Branch staff would also be made available to answer any questions from Members of Congress.[24] *Id*. HPSCI Letter at 2; SSCI Letter at 2.

---

23. Specifically, the Report provided the following information: 1) the Section 215 production is a program "authorized to collect in bulk certain dialing, routing, addressing and signaling information about telephone calls . . . *but not the content of* the calls." Ex. 3, Report at 1 (emphasis in original); 2) this Court's "orders generally require production of the business records (as described above) relating to substantially all of the telephone calls handled by the companies, including both calls made between the United States and a foreign country and calls made entirely within the United States," *id*. at 3 (emphasis added); 3) "Although the program[] collect[s] a large amount of information, the vast majority of that information is never reviewed by any person, because the information is not responsive to the limited queries that are authorized for intelligence purposes," *id*. at 1; 4) "The programs are subject to an extensive regime of internal checks, particularly for U.S. persons, and are monitored by the FISA Court and Congress," *id*.; 5) "Although there have been compliance problems in recent years, the Executive Branch has worked to resolve them, subject to oversight by the FISA Court," *id*.; 6) "Today, under FISA Court authorization pursuant to the 'business records' authority of the FISA (commonly referred to as 'Section 215'), the government has developed a program to close the gap" regarding a terrorist plot, *id*. at 2; 7) "NSA collects and analyzes large amounts of transactional data obtained from certain telecommunications service providers in the United States," *id*.; and, 8) that the program operates "on a very large scale." *Id*.

24. It is unnecessary for the Court to inquire how many of the 535 individual Members of Congress took advantage of the opportunity to learn the facts about how the Executive Branch was implementing Section 215 under this Court's Orders. Rather, the Court looks to congressional action on the whole, not

In light of the importance of the national security programs that were set to expire, the Executive Branch and relevant congressional committees worked together to ensure that each Member of Congress knew or had the opportunity to know how Section 215 was being implemented under this Court's Orders. Documentation and personnel were also made available to afford each Member full knowledge of the scope of the implementation of Section 215 and of the underlying legal interpretation.

The record before this Court thus demonstrates that the factual basis for applying the re-enactment doctrine and presuming that in 2011 Congress intended to ratify Section 215 as applied by this Court is well supported. Members were informed that this Court's "orders generally require production of the business records (as described above) relating to *substantially all of the telephone calls* handled by the companies, including both calls made between the United States and a foreign country and calls made entirely within the United States." Ex. 3, Report at 3 (emphasis added). When Congress subsequently re-authorized Section 215 without change, except as to expiration date, that re-authorization carried with it this Court's interpretation of the statute, which permits the bulk collection of telephony metadata under the restrictions that are in place. Therefore, the passage of the PATRIOT Sunsets Extension Act provides a persuasive reason for this Court to adhere to its prior interpretations of Section 215. . . .

———————————

Presidential Policy Directive/PPD-28, Signals Intelligence Activities
Jan. 17, 2014
http://www.whitehouse.gov/the-press-office/2014/01/17/presidential-policy-directive-signals-intelligence-activities

The United States, like other nations, has gathered intelligence throughout its history to ensure that national security and foreign policy decision makers have access to timely, accurate, and insightful information.

The collection of signals intelligence is necessary for the United States to advance its national security and foreign policy interests and to

———————————

the preparatory work of individual Members in anticipation of legislation. . . .

protect its citizens and the citizens of its allies and partners from harm. At the same time, signals intelligence activities and the possibility that such activities may be improperly disclosed to the public pose multiple risks. These include risks to: our relationships with other nations, including the cooperation we receive from other nations on law enforcement, counterterrorism, and other issues; our commercial, economic, and financial interests, including a potential loss of international trust in U.S. firms and the decreased willingness of other nations to participate in international data sharing, privacy, and regulatory regimes; the credibility of our commitment to an open, interoperable, and secure global Internet; and the protection of intelligence sources and methods.

In addition, our signals intelligence activities must take into account that all persons should be treated with dignity and respect, regardless of their nationality or wherever they might reside, and that all persons have legitimate privacy interests in the handling of their personal information.

In determining why, whether, when, and how the United States conducts signals intelligence activities, we must weigh all of these considerations in a context in which information and communications technologies are constantly changing. The evolution of technology has created a world where communications important to our national security and the communications all of us make as part of our daily lives are transmitted through the same channels. This presents new and diverse opportunities for, and challenges with respect to, the collection of intelligence – and especially signals intelligence. The United States Intelligence Community (IC) has achieved remarkable success in developing enhanced capabilities to perform its signals intelligence mission in this rapidly changing world, and these enhanced capabilities are a major reason we have been able to adapt to a dynamic and challenging security environment.[1]

The United States must preserve and continue to develop a robust and technologically advanced signals intelligence capability to protect our security and that of our partners and allies. Our signals intelligence capabilities must also be agile enough to enable use to focus on fleeting opportunities or emerging crises and to address not only the issues of

---

1. For the purposes of this directive, the terms "Intelligence Community" and "elements of the Intelligence Community" shall have the same meaning as they do in Executive Order 12333 of December 4, 1981, as amended (Executive Order 12333).

today, but also the issues of tomorrow, which we may not be able to foresee.

Advanced technologies can increase risks, as well as opportunities, however, and we must consider these risks when deploying our signals intelligence capabilities. The IC conducts signals intelligence activities with care and precision to ensure that its collection, retention, use, and dissemination of signals intelligence account for these risks. In light of the evolving technological and geopolitical environment, we must continue to ensure that our signals intelligence policies and practices appropriately take into account our alliances and other partnerships; the leadership role that the United States plays in upholding democratic principles and universal human rights; the increased globalization of trade, investment, and information flows; our commitment to an open, interoperable and secure global Internet; and the legitimate privacy and civil liberties concerns of U.S. citizens and citizens of other nations.

Presidents have long directed the acquisition of foreign intelligence and counterintelligence[2] pursuant to their constitutional authority to conduct U.S. foreign relations and to fulfill their constitutional responsibilities as Commander in Chief and Chief Executive. They have also provided direction on the conduct of intelligence activities in furtherance of these authorities and responsibilities, as well as in execution of laws enacted by the Congress. Consistent with this historical practice, this directive articulates principles to guide why, whether, when, and how to United States conducts signals intelligence

---

2. For the purposes of this directive, the terms "foreign intelligence" and "counterintelligence" shall have the same meaning as they have in Executive Order 12333. Thus, "foreign intelligence" means "information relating to the capabilities, intentions, or activities of foreign governments or elements thereof, foreign organizations, foreign persons, or international terrorists," and "counterintelligence" means "information gathered and activities conducted to identify, deceive, exploit, disrupt, or protect against espionage, other intelligence activities, sabotage, or assassinations conducted for or on behalf of foreign powers, organizations, or persons, or their agents, or international terrorist organizations or activities." Executive Order 12333 further notes that "[i]ntelligence includes foreign intelligence and counterintelligence."

activities for authorized foreign intelligence and counterintelligence purposes.[3]

Section 1. Principles Governing the Collection of Signals Intelligence.

Signals intelligence collection shall be authorized and conducted consistent with the following principles:

(a) The collection fo signals intelligence shall be authorized by statute or Executive Order, proclamation, or other Presidential directive, and undertaken in accordance with the Constitution and applicable statutes, Executive Orders, proclamations, and Presidential directives.

(b) Privacy and civil liberties shall be integral considerations in the planning of U.S. signals intelligence activities. The United States shall not collect signals intelligence for the purpose of suppressing or burdening criticism or dissent, or for disadvantaging persons based on their ethnicity, race, gender, sexual orientation, or religion. Signals intelligence shall be collected exclusively where there is a foreign intelligence or counterintelligence purpose to support national and departmental missions and not for any other purposes.

(c) The collection of foreign private commercial information or trade secrets is authorized only to protect the national security of the United States or its partners or allies. It is not an authorized foreign intelligence or counterintelligence purpose to collect such information to afford a competitive advantage[4] to U.S. companies and U.S. business sectors commercially.

(d) Signals intelligence activities shall be as tailored as feasible. In determining whether to collect signals intelligence, the United

---

3. Unless otherwise specified, this directive shall apply to signals intelligence activities conducted in order to collect communications or information about communications, except that it shall not apply to signals intelligence activities undertaken to test or develop signals intelligence capabilities.

4. Certain economic purposes, such as identifying trade or sanctions violations or government influence or direction, shall not constitute competitive advantage.

States shall consider the availability of other information, including from diplomatic and public sources. Such appropriate and feasible alternatives to signals intelligence should be prioritized.

Sec. 2.   Limitations on the Use of Signals Intelligence Collected in Bulk.

Locating new or emerging threats and other vital national security information is difficult, as such information is often hidden within the large and complex system of modern global communications. The United States must consequently collect signals intelligence in bulk[5] in certain circumstances in order to identify these threats. Routine communications and communications of national security interest increasingly transit the same networks, however, and the collection of signals intelligence in bulk may consequently result in the collection of information about persons whose activities are not of foreign intelligence or counterintelligence value. The United States will therefore impose new limits on its use of signals intelligence collected in bulk. These limits are intended to protect the privacy and civil liberties of all persons, whatever their nationality and regardless of where they might reside.

In particular, when the United States collects nonpublicly available signals intelligence in bulk, it shall use that data only for the purposes of detecting and countering: (1) espionage and other threats and activities directed by foreign powers or their intelligence services against the United States and its interests; (2) threats to the United States and its interests from terrorism; (3) threats to the United States and its interests from the development, possession, proliferation, or use of weapons of mass destruction; (4) cybersecurity threats; (5) threats to U.S. or allied Armed Forces or other U.S. or allied personnel; and (6) transnational criminal threats, including illicit finance and sanctions evasion related to the other purposes named in this section. In no event may signals intelligence collected in bulk be used for the purposes of suppressing or burdening criticism or dissent; disadvantaging persons based on their

---

5. The limitations contained in this section do not apply to signals intelligence data that is temporarily acquired to facilitate targeted collection. References to signals intelligence collected in "bulk" mean the authorized collection of large quantities of signals intelligence data which, due to technical or operational considerations, is acquired without the use of discriminants (e.g. specific identifiers, selection terms, etc.).

ethnicity, race, gender, sexual orientation, or religion; affording a competitive advantage to U.S. companies and U.S. business sectors commercially; or achieving any purpose other than those identified in this section.

The Assistant to the President and National Security Advisor (APNSA), in consultation with the Director of National Intelligence (DNI), shall coordinate, on at least an annual basis, a review of the permissible uses of signals intelligence collected in bulk through the National Security Council Principals and Deputies Committee system identified in PPD-1 or any successor document. At the end of this review, I will be presented with recommended additions to or removals from the list of the permissible uses of signals intelligence collected in bulk.

The DNI shall maintain a list of the permissible uses of signals intelligence collected in bulk. This list shall be updated as necessary and made publicly available to the maximum extent feasible, consistent with the national security.

Sec. 3. Refining the Process for Collecting Signals Intelligence.

U.S. intelligence collection activities present the potential for national security damage if improperly disclosed. Signals intelligence collection raises special concerns, given the opportunities and risks created by the constantly evolving technological and geopolitical environment; the unique nature of such collection and the inherent concerns raised when signals intelligence can only be collected in bulk, and the risk of damage to our national security interests and our law enforcement, intelligence-sharing, and diplomatic relationships should our capabilities or activities be compromised. It is, therefore, essential that national security policymakers consider carefully the value of signals intelligence activities in light of the risks entailed in conducting these activities.

To enable this judgment, the heads of departments and agencies that participate in the policy processes for establishing signals intelligence priorities or requirements identified by their departments or agencies and advise the DNI whether each should be maintained, with a copy of the advice provided to the APNSA.

Additionally, the classified Annex to this directive, which supplements the existing policy process for reviewing signals intelligence activities, affirms that determinations about whether and how to conduct signals intelligence activities must carefully evaluate the benefits to our national interests and the risks posed by those activities.[6]

Sec. 4. Safeguarding Personal Information Collected Through Signals Intelligence.

All persons should be treated with dignity and respect, regardless of their nationality or wherever they might reside, and all persons have legitimate privacy interests in the handling of their personal information.[7] U.S. signals intelligence activities must, therefore, include appropriate safeguards for the personal information of all individuals, regardless of the nationality of the individual to whom the information pertains or where that individual resides.[8]

(a) **Policies and Procedures.** The DNI, in consultation with the Attorney General, shall ensure that all elements of the IC establish policies and procedures that apply the following principles for safeguarding personal information collected from signals intelligence activities. To the maximum extent feasible consistent with the national security, these policies and procedures area to be

---

6. Section 3 of this directive, and the directive's classified Annex, do not apply to (1) signals intelligence activities undertaken by or for the Federal Bureau of Investigation in support of predicated investigations other than those conducted solely for purposes of acquiring foreign intelligence; or (2) signals intelligence activities undertaken in support of military operations in an area of active hostilities, covert action, or human intelligence operations.

7. Departments and agencies shall apply the term "personal information" in a manner that is consistent for U.S. persons and non-U.S. persons. Accordingly, for the purposes of this directive, the term "personal information" shall cover the same types of information covered by "information concerning U.S. persons" under section 2.3 of Executive Order 12333.

8. The collection, retention, and dissemination of information concerning "United States persons" is governed by multiple legal and policy requirements, such as those required by the Foreign Intelligence Surveillance Act and Executive Order 12333. For the purposes of this directive, the term "United States person" shall have the same meaning as it does in Executive Order 12333.

applied equally to the personal information of all persons, regardless of nationality:[9]

    i. *Minimization.* The sharing of intelligence that contains personal information is necessary to protect our national security and advance our foreign policy interests, as it enables the United States to coordinate activities across the government. At the same time, however, by setting appropriate limits on such sharing, the United States takes legitimate privacy concerns into account and decreases the risks that personal information will be misused or mishandled. Relatedly, the significance to our national security of intelligence is not always apparent upon an initial review of information: intelligence must be retained for a sufficient period of time for the IC to understand its relevance and use it to meet our national security needs. However, long-term storage of personal information unnecessary to protect our national security is inefficient, unnecessary, and raises legitimate privacy concern. Accordingly, IC elements shall establish policies and procedures reasonably designed to minimize the dissemination and retention of personal information collected from signals intelligence activities.

- Dissemination: Personal information shall be disseminated only if the dissemination of comparable in formation concerning U.S. persons would be permitted under section. 2.3 of Executive Order 12333.

- Retention: Personal information shall be retained only if the retention of comparable information concerning U.S. persons would be permitted under section 2.3 of Executive Order 12333 and shall be subject to the same retention periods as applied to comparable information concerning U.S. persons. Information

---

9. The policies and procedures of affected elements of the IC shall also be consistent with any additional IC policies, standards, procedures, and guidance the DNI, in coordination with the Attorney General, the heads of IC elements, and the heads of any other departments containing such elements, may issue to implement these principles. This directive is not intended to alter the rules applicable to U.S. persons in Executive Order 12333, the Foreign Intelligence Surveillance Act, or other applicable law.

for which no such determination has been made shall not be retained for more than 5 years, unless the DNI expressly determines that continued retention is in the national security interests of the United States.

Additionally, within 180 days of the date of this directive, the DNI, in coordination with the Attorney General, the heads of other elements of the IC, and the heads of departments and agencies containing other elements of the IC, shall prepare a report evaluating possible additional dissemination and retention safeguards for personal information collected through signals intelligence, consistent with technical capabilities and operational needs.

    ii. *Data Security and Access.* When our national security and foreign policy needs require us to retain certain intelligence, it is vital that the United States take appropriate steps to ensure that any personal information contained within that intelligence is secure. Accordingly, personal information shall be processed and stored under conditions that provide adequate protection and prevent access by unauthorized persons, consistent with the applicable safeguards for sensitive information contained in relevant Executive Orders, proclamations, Presidential directives, IC directives, and associated policies. Access to such personal information shall be limited to authorized personnel with a need to know the information to perform their mission, consistent with the personnel security requirements of relevant Executive Orders, IC directives, and associated policies. Such personnel will be provided appropriate and adequate training in the principles set forth in this directive. These persons may access and use the information consistent with applicable laws and Executive Orders and the principles of this directive; personal information for which no determination has been made that it can be permissibly disseminated or retained under section 4 (a) (i) of this directive shall be accessed only in order to make such determinations (or to conduct authorized administrative, security, and oversight functions).

    iii. *Data Quality.* IC elements strive to provide national security policymakers with timely, accurate, and insightful intelligence, and inaccurate records and reporting can not only undermine our national security interests, but also can result in the collection or analysis of information relating to persons whose activities are not of foreign intelligence or counter-intelligence value. Accordingly, personal information shall be included in intelligence products only as consistent with applicable IC standards for accuracy and objectivity, as set forth in relevant IC directives. Moreover, while IC elements should apply the IC Analytic Standards as a whole, particular care should be taken to apply standards relating to the quality and reliability of the information, consideration of alternative sources of information and interpretations of data, and objectivity in performing analysis.

   iv. *Oversight.* The IC has long recognized that effective oversight is necessary to ensure that we are protecting our national security in a manner consistent with our interests and values. Accordingly, the policies and procedures of IC elements, and departments and agencies containing IC elements, shall include appropriate measures to facilitate oversight over the implementation of safeguards protecting personal information, to include periodic auditing against the standards required by this section.

   The policies and procedures shall also recognize and facilitate the performance of oversight by the Inspectors General of IC elements, and departments and agencies containing IC elements, and other relevant oversight entities, as appropriate and consistent with their responsibilities. When a significant compliance issue occurs involving personal information of any person, regardless of nationality, collected as a result of signals intelligence activities, the issue shall, in addition to any existing reporting requirements, be reported promptly to the DNI, who shall determine what, if any, corrective actions are necessary. If the issue involves a non-United States person, the DNI, in consultation with the Secretary of State and the head of the notifying department or agency, shall determine whether steps should be taken to notify the relevant foreign government, consistent with the protection of sources and methods and of U.S. personnel.

(b) _Update and Publication._ Within 1 year of the date of this directive, IC elements shall update or issue new policies and procedures as necessary to implement section 4 of this directive, in coordination with the DNI. To enhance public understanding of, and promote public trust in, the safeguards in place to protect personal information, these updated or newly issued policies and procedures shall be publicly released to the maximum extent possible, consistent with classification requirements.

(c) _Privacy and Civil Liberties Policy Official._ To help ensure that the legitimate privacy interests all people share related to the handling of their personal information are appropriately considered in light of the principles i this section, the APNSA, the Director of the Office of Management and Budget (OMB), and the Director of the Office of Science and Technology Policy (OSTP) shall identify one or more senior officials who will be responsible for working with the DNI, the Attorney General, the heads of other elements of the IC, and the heads of departments and agencies containing other elements of the IC, as appropriate, as they develop the policies and procedures called for in this section.

(d) _Coordinator for International Diplomacy._ The Secretary of State shall identify a senior official within the Department of State to coordinate with the responsible departments and agencies the United States Government's diplomatic and foreign policy efforts related to international information technology issues and to serve as a point of contact for foreign governments who wish to raise concerns regarding signals intelligence activities conducted by the United States. . . .

NOTES AND QUESTIONS

1. _Who Cares?_ Telephony metadata do not include the contents of the calls. Why should we care that the government has records of when we made calls, the numbers we called, or how long the calls lasted? The answer depends on what the government does with that information and how carefully it does it. It queries the accumulated database using identifiers that must themselves satisfy some predicate of relation to an

investigation of terrorism. But suppose the identifiers do not meet the predicate?

A FISC opinion from 2011 reported that "NSA had been routinely running queries of the metadata using querying terms that did not meet the required standard for querying," and that this requirement had been "so frequently and systematically violated that it can fairly be said that this critical element of the overall . . . regime has never functioned effectively." [Name redacted], Memorandum Opinion at 16 n.14, [docket no. unavailable] (FISA Court Oct. 3, 2011) (Bates, J.). If the compliance mechanism is not functioning, what is the risk of a false positive, leading the NSA erroneously to identify a telephone caller as a person of interest? Or suppose that the NSA queries the database for a purpose other than an investigation into terrorism, perhaps (at the FBI's request) for an investigation of a drug conspiracy, a leak, or even a dissident advocacy group?

How would you balance these dangers of improper queries, mission creep, and false positives against the possible future benefit to a terrorism investigation from collecting and retaining the database?

2. *Collection vs. Querying and the Significance (and Limits) of Minimization.* In the August 29, 2013 FISC opinion set out above, note the number of times Judge Eagan defends the significance of the "minimization" requirements, which, among other things, require the government to have (albeit not show to a judge) "reasonable articulable suspicion" (RAS) before querying the collected metadata for specific information concerning U.S. persons — at least those with Fourth Amendment rights. The minimization procedures are, as Judge Eagan explains, meant to ensure that the collected data are used only for permissible purposes — and that the government is not able to use the breadth of its authority under §215 as a pretext for utilizing data for which it would otherwise need a more specific basis.

This point is significant in at least two respects: *First*, it underscores the government's apparent position that there is a materially significant distinction between *collecting* telephony metadata and *querying* it (and that only the latter is a "search" for Fourth Amendment purposes). If, as appears likely, such a distinction is designed to ameliorate Fourth Amendment concerns, are you convinced?

Second, Judge Eagan's repeated focus on minimization also appears to suggest that the government's authority to obtain metadata on such a broad scale is conditioned upon its *compliance* with the minimization requirements. To that end, Judge Eagan notes that there have been "no compliance incidents" in the "prior authorization period" (i.e., the last 90 days), but also alludes (in footnote 7) to a host of (serious) compliance incidents before that. Who is in charge of *enforcing* the minimization requirements? Is the FISC in a position to review the government's compliance directly, or only to compel the government to self-regulate — and report to the FISC if and when there are compliance incidents?

What are the consequences of non-compliance? What if the government affirmatively misleads the FISC about its activities? *See, e.g.*, [Name redacted], Memorandum Opinion at 16 n.14, [docket no. unavailable] (FISA Ct. Oct. 3, 2011) (describing at least three instances in which "the government has disclosed a substantial misrepresentation regarding the scope of a major collection program"). Is there any basis in the statute for denying *subsequent* production orders to the government in response to *prior* minimization violations?

3. *The Straightforwardness — or Not — of the Fourth Amendment Question.* As we suggested in the Notes and Questions after *Smith v. Maryland* (*see* NSL pp. 637-640, CTL pp. 250-253), a broad reading of *Smith does* appear to compel Judge Eagan's conclusion that the Fourth Amendment question arising from the government's use of §215 is, in fact, straightforward. But note the two potential bases on which *Smith* could be distinguished: (1) that the *volume* of collected data matters insofar as it provides the government with information that would not be available in the aggregate to any one of the specific third parties from which the data are being obtained, and (2) that the *variety* of metadata acquired under §215 is broader than the data provided by pen registers in *Smith*. Judge Eagan rejects this second argument in footnote 11. How does she respond to the first argument?

Although each of the phone companies has its own telephony metadata, only the government is able (or at least has undertaken) to build such a comprehensive database of this kind of information. Does anyone communicating by telephone have a reasonable expectation of privacy in light of the fact that the government clearly is *able* to build such a database? *See, e.g., United States v. Jones*, 132 S. Ct. 945, 957-964 (2012) (Alito, J., concurring in the judgment).

Has the reasonableness of any such expectation necessarily changed with recent public disclosures that the government *actually does* build and mine such databases? If so, could the government effectively alter the meaning of the Fourth Amendment by revealing that it possesses the technical capability to collect and analyze non-public information in hitherto unknown ways, and that it is utilizing that capability?

Are your answers to these questions affected by the fact that private concerns routinely collect and share vast amounts of personal data online, and that some of the information ends up in huge databases created by consumer credit reporting companies such as Experian and Equifax? Does it matter for this purpose that consumers typically are required to accept "terms of service" agreements providing for such sharing?

How do you think Justice Marshall, dissenting in *Smith*, would have answered these questions? Might the potentially limitless scope of §215 provoke the very reconsideration of the Court's Fourth Amendment jurisprudence proposed by Justice Sotomayor in *Jones*? *See id.* at 954-957 (Sotomayor, J., concurring). Should Judge Eagan at least have *considered* the fact that five of the Justices in *Jones* (Justice Sotomayor and those who joined Justice Alito's concurrence) expressed concerns about such unstinting devotion to *Smith*?

4. *The Stored Communications Act.* Judge Eagan begins her defense of the government's capacious definition of "relevance" with an extended analogy to the Stored Communications Act. In essence, her argument appears to be that "Congress intentionally created Section 215 to have more ex post review and less ex ante review than its criminal law cousins — thus suggesting a Congressional endorsement of the 'get everything, look through it later' nature of the telephony metadata program." Orin Kerr, *My (Mostly Critical) Thoughts on the August 2013 FISC Opinion on Section 215*, The Volokh Conspiracy, Sept. 17, 2013, http://www.volokh.com/2013/09/17/thoughts-august-2013-fisc-opinion-section-215/. As Professor Kerr explains, however, "it's pretty ironic to say that the higher standard for 2703(d) indicates a congressional wish to have less [ex] ante review in Section 215: Congress raised the standard for 2703(d) orders in 1994 to increase *privacy* protections, so [it is] a bit strange to read that as an implicit endorsement of expanded government power in the Section 215 setting." *Id.* In any event, even if the analogy were not "quite forced," *id.*, wouldn't this argument turn on the robustness of the *ex post* review available under §215? Judge Eagan seems to think so — and offers a detailed summary of the review theoretically available under §215. Are you convinced? Is Judge Eagan's opinion an example of such a robust review?

5. *"Relevance" and the Needle/Haystack Problem*. The heart of Judge Eagan's opinion — and the strongest legal challenge to the metadata program — concerns the scope of "relevance" under §215, and the controversial implications of the government's interpretation thereof. As Judge Eagan describes it, "The government posits that bulk telephonic metadata is necessary to its investigations because it is impossible to know where in the data the connections to international terrorist organizations will be found." In colloquial terms, this argument is often framed as the government needing to have the haystack before it can search for the needle. But isn't there a critical, albeit subtle, distinction between justifying a search of a haystack in order to *find* a needle and justifying it in order to find out if there even *is* a needle? That is, isn't it bootstrapping to argue that telephony metadata is "relevant" under §215 because its collection *might* further ongoing terrorism investigations? Judge Eagan says no. As long as the metadata "bears upon" ongoing terrorism investigations, its collection satisfies §215. And the government's assertion that bulk metadata collection is "necessary" to its counterterrorism efforts is enough for Judge Eagan to carry that (modest) burden. By that logic, wouldn't the collection of virtually *all* data be "relevant"? Moreover,

> [w]hen dealing with a physical object, we naturally treat relevance on an object-by-object basis. Sets of records are different. If Verizon has a database containing billions of phone calls made by millions of customers, is that database a single thing, millions of things, or billions of things? Is relevance measured by each record, each customer, or the relevance of the entire database as a whole? If the entire massive database has a single record that is relevant, does that make the entire database relevant, too?

Chesney & Wittes, *supra* (quoting Orin Kerr at *The Volokh Conspiracy*).

Is there a better, and more circumscribed, definition of "relevance" that the FISC should adopt in these cases? Should the government have to show, for example, specific ways in which collected data *will* be relevant to an ongoing investigation?

6. *Legislative Ratification of Secret Opinions*. Toward the end of her opinion, Judge Eagan concludes that any doubt over the validity of the government's broad interpretation of "relevance" is settled by Congress's "ratification" of that view in the 2011 PATRIOT Sunsets Extension Act. It is certainly true that, in the ordinary case, courts presume that Congress is aware of how statutory language has been

interpreted when it reenacts such language, and makes corresponding assumptions about legislative intent. But are you persuaded by Judge Eagan's efforts to explain why that presumption should also apply here — when the relevant judicial interpretations were provided in secret (and non-precedential) judicial opinions made available to all members of Congress but not their staffs or the public, and only under stringent security procedures? Judge Eagan suggests that the relevant inquiry is simply whether members of Congress had *access* to the relevant FISC opinions, whether or not they read (or understood) them. But shouldn't we ask instead whether the 2011 statute reflected Congress's *informed* decision to codify the interpretation adopted in those opinions? If so, is there any practical way to answer that question?

7. *Judicial Review as a Defense.* Perhaps in response to concerns over the potential breadth of the government's understanding of "relevance," Judge Eagan extols the virtues of the "specific and complex" judicial review scheme provided by §215. But she also notes that "no recipient of any Section 215 Order has challenged the legality of such an Order, despite the explicit statutory mechanism for doing so." Indeed, there is no mechanism for appellate review of this decision *unless* the recipient of a §215 order pursues it. Why do you suppose recipients of §215 orders have not taken advantage of the available judicial review? Even if they did so, do you have faith that recipients such as your phone company could or would fully vindicate your statutory and constitutional rights against the government? If not, how might Congress improve upon this existing review scheme?

8. *Cell-Site Location Information.* Finally, there seems to be something important going on with regard to Cell Site Location Information (CSLI) in footnotes 2 and 5 of the opinion by Judge Eagan. Why might CSLI differ from the rest of the telephony metadata that, per footnote 2, clearly *is* covered by the §215 orders at issue in this case? One possibility is that CSLI data may also include information about conduct undertaken within the privacy of one's home. Might that help to explain why it is carved out here? In that regard, there now appears to be a circuit split over whether — and to what extent — the Fourth Amendment applies to government requests for historical CSLI. *Compare, e.g., United States v. Davis*, No. 12-12928, 2014 WL 2599917 (11th Cir. 2014) (the Fourth Amendment does apply), *In re Application of the United States for Historical Cell Site Data*, 724 F.3d 600 (5th Cir.

2013) (holding that it does not apply), *with In re Application of the United States for an Order Directing a Provider of Elec. Comm'n Serv. to Disclose Records to the Government*, 620 F.3d 304 (3d Cir. 2010) (holding that, in at least some circumstances, judges have the discretion to require warrants before the government can obtain historical CSLI). Should the Fourth Amendment ever apply to CSLI? If so, when? After *Jones*, how do you suppose Justice Alito — or Justice Sotomayor — would answer that question?

9. *The PCLOB Report*. The majority of the five-member PCLOB (see *supra* p. 129) recommended that the government shut down the metadata program. Their report concluded that Section 215 "does not authorize NSA to acquire anything at all. Instead, it permits the FBI to obtain records for its own investigations." They found "the interpretation of Section 215 by the FISA court . . . dangerously overbroad, leading to the implication that virtually all information may be relevant to counterterrorism and therefore subject to collection by the government." Without reaching a firm conclusion on the constitutionality of the program, the majority found that the program "raises serious threats to privacy and civil liberties. . . . The government should end the program."

The two dissenters would not shut down the program, but they agreed that the government should immediately modify the program to reduce how much information is used, how long it is held, and require a "reasonable articulable suspicion" standard for querying the database, subject to approval by a FISC judge. How could the PCLOB and FISC judges have such disparate views on what Section 215 authorizes?

10. *PPD-28*. What is the legal significance of the policies contained in the new signals directive? Consider in particular Section 4 and its commitment to safeguard the personal information of all individuals. Does the directive confer legally enforceable duties on government officials, or rights for non-U.S. persons concerning their personal information? What legal wiggle room is preserved for the government? Some of the categories of personal information that may be disseminated or retained according to Executive Order 12,333 are listed at NSL pp. 457-458, CTL p. 141. How would you advise the DNI and Attorney General to further implement Section 4?

11. *The Administration's Proposal for Reshaping the Section 215 Program*. On March 27, 2014, the White House released *Fact Sheet: The*

Administration's Proposal for Ending the Section 215 Bulk Telephony Metadata Program, http://www.whitehouse.gov/the-press-office/2014/03/27/fact-sheet-administration-s-proposal-ending-section-215-bulk-telephony-m. The President's proposal came in two stages:

a. *Three hops or two?* In his January speech, the President directed the Justice Department, absent an emergency situation, to query the collected metadata only after a FISC judge approves the use of specific numbers for the queries based on national security concerns. Analysts are limited to metadata within two hops of the selection term, instead of three. What difference will it make to the NSA and to those of us making phone calls whether the government uses two or three hops from the selection term?

b. *Reauthorizing the Program.* President Obama proposed legislation that would let the records remain at the telephone companies, rather than being held by the government. The government would obtain the records only pursuant to individual orders from a judge approving the use of specific numbers for queries, and then only within two hops of the selection term being used. The government analysis would occur over a limited period of time before requiring reauthorization from the FISC. Companies would be required to provide technical assistance to the government as needed to provide records in a usable format and in a timely manner. Are these recommendations sound? If they are not enacted, could the President order the changes on his own authority?

c. *Latest Status?* On June 20, 2014, the Justice Department and DNI announced that the government sought and obtained a 90-day reauthorization of the bulk collection program from the FISC, as modified by the changes announced earlier by the President. The order issued by the FISC expires on September 12, 2014. *Joint Statement from the Office of the Director of National Intelligence and the Department of Justice on the Declassification of Renewal of Collection Under Section 501 of the Foreign Intelligence Surveillance Act,* June 20, 2014, http://www.justice.gov/opa/pr/2014/June/14-ag-655.html.

12. *Further Reading.* For further analysis of the legality of bulk collection and of Judge Eagan's reasoning, compare David S. Kris, *On*

the Bulk Collection of Tangible Things, 7 J. Nat'l Sec. L. & Pol'y 209 (2014), with Marty Lederman, *The Kris Paper, and the Problematic FISC Opinion on the Section 215 "Metadata" Collection Program*, Just Security, Oct. 1, 2013, *available at* http://justsecurity.org/2013/ 10/01/kris-paper-legality-section-215-metadata-collection/.

[NSL p. 671; CTL p. 284. Insert after Note 10.]

A federal district court said no in *In re National Security Letter*, 930 F. Supp. 2d 1064 (N.D. Cal. 2013), reasoning that the Second Circuit's creative reconstruction of the statute with the help of the executive branch crossed the line between adjudicating and legislating.

> . . . As an initial matter, the Court finds that it is not within its power to "conform" the NSL nondisclosure provisions, as did the Second Circuit. The statutory provisions at issue — as written, adopted and amended by Congress in the face of a constitutional challenge — are not susceptible to narrowing or conforming constructions to save their constitutionality. . . . [T]he narrow defects in the statutes under review in those cases [in which the courts did so "conform" the statute under challenge] bear little resemblance to the multiple constitutional inadequacies identified by the Court in the NSL nondisclosure provisions. . . .
>
> . . . [Alternatively,] the government asserts that this Court should rely on the "canon of constitutional avoidance." Here, however, the Court cannot ignore express language in the statute in order to come up with "reasonable interpretations" that would be constitutional.
>
> The government also relies on a line of cases where courts accepted limiting constructions offered by the government to avoid striking down content-neutral time, place and manner restrictions on speech. Again, those cases are inapposite to the situation here, where Congress has drafted a very specific statute aimed at preventing speech on a particular subject, and redrafted amendments to it to address identified constitutional deficiencies. In light of the language actually and intentionally used by Congress in amending the statute after it was initially struck down as unconstitutional by two different district courts in the Second Circuit, this Court finds there is no "reasonable construction" that can avoid the constitutional infirmities that have been identified.
>
> The Court also finds that the unconstitutional nondisclosure provisions are not severable. . . .

Id. at 1079-1081.

[NSL p. 677; CTL p. 290. Insert after Section B.]

B1. The Metadata Program Goes to Court

Unsurprisingly, shortly after Edward Snowden's disclosures revealed the existence of the bulk telephony metadata program under Section 215 of the USA Patriot Act, a host of plaintiffs brought civil suits challenging the program's legality. Although the claims varied to some degree, the two central legal objections were that the program exceeded the scope of what Congress had actually *authorized* under Section 215 — a claim ordinarily cognizable under the Administrative Procedure Act (APA) — and that, insofar as the program *was* authorized by Congress, such mass, warrantless collection of the metadata of U.S. persons violates the Fourth Amendment.

In a pair of decisions handed down 10 days apart in December 2013, district court judges in New York and Washington became the first to reach these issues in the context of ordinary civil litigation. *See ACLU v. Clapper*, 959 F. Supp. 2d 724 (S.D.N.Y. 2013); *Klayman v. Obama*, 957 F. Supp. 2d 1 (D.D.C. 2013). The courts split on the ultimate question of whether the metadata program is likely consistent with the Fourth Amendment — after holding that the plaintiffs in both cases (1) had standing, and (2) were precluded by Section 215's "exclusive review" scheme from pursuing their statutory challenge under the APA. Because of the length of the decisions and the fact that they almost surely will not be the last word (appeals of both are already pending), the key elements of each opinion are summarized below, rather than excerpted or reprinted in their entirety.

1. Standing

In *Klayman*, Judge Richard J. Leon rested his conclusion that the plaintiffs have standing to challenge the NSA's collection of their metadata on the fact that they were Verizon business customers, and that their metadata were therefore clearly subject to collection under the by-then-disclosed Section 215 production orders. As he explained, "whereas the plaintiffs in *Clapper* could only speculate as to whether they would be surveilled at all, plaintiffs in this case can point to strong evidence that, as Verizon customers, their telephony metadata has been collected for the last seven years (and stored for the last five) and will continue to be collected barring judicial or legislative intervention." *Klayman*, 957 F. Supp. 2d at 26. Although the government argued that there was no specific proof that the *plaintiffs'* metadata were being collected, Judge Leon concluded that such an argument was belied by the entire defense of the program: "Put simply, the Government wants it both ways. Virtually all of the Government's briefs and arguments to this Court explain how the Government has acted in good faith to create a *comprehensive* metadata database that serves as a potentially valuable tool in combating terrorism — in which case, the NSA *must* have collected metadata" from the nation's largest telecom providers. *Id.* at 27.

Judge Leon also concluded that the plaintiffs had standing to challenge the NSA's *querying* of their metadata, even though it was less obvious that such querying was actually taking place. Again, as he explained, the key was in the way in which the program was structured: "The Government . . . describes the advantages of bulk collection in such a way as to convince me that plaintiffs' metadata — indeed *everyone's* metadata — is analyzed, manually or automatically, whenever the Government runs a query using as the 'seed' a phone number or identifier associated with a phone for which the NSA has not collected metadata (e.g., phones operating through foreign phone companies)." *Id.* at 28. Thus, whether or not the plaintiffs could actually show that their specific records had been accessed, Judge Leon held that those records presumably were being queried, at least in some form.

In the *ACLU* challenge, Judge William H. Pauley III reached similar conclusions as to the plaintiffs' standing, albeit while focusing only on their standing to challenge the government's *collection* of metadata, and rather summarily at that. As he concluded, "Here, there is no dispute the Government collected telephony metadata related to the ACLU's telephone calls. Thus, the standing requirement is satisfied." 959 F. Supp. 2d at 738 (citing *Amnesty Int'l v. Clapper*, 133 S. Ct. 1138, 1153 (2013)).

2. APA Preclusion

Both courts also concluded that the plaintiffs' *statutory* challenges to the metadata program were "precluded" by the exclusive review scheme Congress created in Section 215 — a scheme in which only the *recipient* of a production order (such as Verizon) is entitled to challenge the validity of the order in civil litigation. As Judge Leon concluded in

Klayman, "Stated simply, Congress created a closed system of judicial review of the government's domestic foreign intelligence-gathering, generally, and of Section 1861 production orders, specifically. This closed system includes no role for third parties, such as plaintiffs here, nor courts besides the FISC, such as this District Court. Congress's preclusive intent is therefore sufficiently clear." 957 F. Supp. 2d at 20 (citations omitted). This holding, in Judge Leon's view, followed from the text of Section 215, its legislative history, and the fact that, as Judge Leon concluded, Congress did not intend for third parties to participate in the FISA scheme "at all." *See id.* at 22. Thus, and notwithstanding the strong presumption in *favor* of APA review, Judge Leon held that the plaintiffs' statutory claims were barred.

Judge Pauley reached a similar conclusion in the *ACLU* case. In his words, "section 215 does not provide for any person other than a recipient of an order to challenge the order's legality or otherwise participate in the process." 959 F. Supp. 2d at 741. Moreover, Pauley explained, "Allowing any challenge to a section 215 order by anyone other than a recipient would undermine the Government's vital interest in keeping the details of its telephone metadata collection program secret. It would also — because of the scope of the program — allow virtually any telephone subscriber to challenge a section 215 order." *Id.*

But both courts held that their preclusion analysis did *not* extend to the plaintiffs' *constitutional* claims. Invoking *Webster v. Doe*, 486 U.S. 592 (1988), for the proposition that "where Congress intends to preclude judicial review of constitutional claims its intent to do so must be clear," *id.* at 603, both courts held that Section 215 did not include the requisite "heightened showing" of legislative intent to preclude constitutional claims. Thus, as Judge Leon concluded, although Section 215 did not authorize extra-FISA review of challenges to its orders, "neither does FISA contain any language *expressly barring* all judicial review of third party claims regarding Section 1861 orders — a necessary condition to even raise the question of whether FISA's statutory scheme of judicial review provides the exclusive means of review for constitutional claims relating to Section 1861 production orders." *Klayman*, 957 F. Supp. 2d at 24. Judge Pauley agreed. *See ACLU*, 959 F. Supp. 2d at 742 ("Of course, this says nothing about the ACLU's constitutional claims and it is hard to image a regime where they would be barred. A constitutional claim is precluded only on a 'heightened showing' demonstrating a clear intent to do so. And there is no language in FISA expressly barring a constitutional claim." (citations omitted)). Both courts thus turned to the merits of the Fourth Amendment challenge to bulk telephone metadata collection.

3. Fourth Amendment Challenge

With regard to the plaintiffs' Fourth Amendment challenge, both district courts asked whether the Supreme Court's decision in *Smith v. Maryland*, 442 U.S. 735 (1979), governed the dispute. In *Klayman*, Judge Leon held that it did not. As he explained, the question presented by the metadata program is: "When do present-day circumstances — the evolutions in the Government's surveillance capabilities, citizens' phone habits, and the relationship between the NSA and telecom companies — become so thoroughly unlike those considered by the Supreme Court thirty-four years ago that a precedent like *Smith* simply does not apply? The answer, unfortunately for the Government, is now." 957 F. Supp. 2d at 31. Relying heavily upon the views of the five concurring Justices in *United States v. Jones*, 132 S. Ct. 945 (2012), Judge Leon identified four key distinctions between the collection of bulk telephony metadata and the pen register that the *Smith* Court held did not constitute a search for Fourth Amendment purposes:

> 1. the short-term and forward-looking nature of pen registers, as compared to the "creation and maintenance of a historical database containing *five years'* worth of data," *Klayman*, 957 F. Supp. 2d at 32;
> 2. the relationship between the government and the phone companies — "It's one thing to say that people expect phone companies to occasionally provide information to law enforcement; it is quite another to suggest that our citizens expect all phone companies to operate what is effectively a joint intelligence-gathering operation with the Government." *Id*. at 33;
> 3. "the almost-Orwellian technology that enables the Government to store and analyze the phone metadata of every telephone user in the United States is unlike anything that could have been conceived in 1979." *Id.*; and
> 4. "*most importantly*, not only is the Government's ability to collect, store, and analyze phone data greater now than it was in 1979, but the nature and quantity of the information contained in people's telephony metadata is much greater, as well." *Id*. at 33-34.

Thus, even though "what metadata *is* has not changed over time," *id.* at 35, individuals' expectations of privacy *in* their metadata has. Judge Leon therefore held that the plaintiffs demonstrated a significant likelihood that the metadata program constitutes a "search" for Fourth Amendment purposes, one that he went on to suggest was likely unreasonable, as well. *See id.* at 37-42. As he concluded, "I cannot imagine a more 'indiscriminate' and 'arbitrary invasion' than this systematic and high-tech collection and retention of personal data on virtually every single citizen for purposes of querying and analyzing it without prior judicial approval." *Id.* at 42.

Judge Pauley disagreed, holding that *Smith* still governs the Fourth Amendment question:

> Some ponder the ubiquity of cellular telephones and how subscribers' relationships with their telephones have evolved since *Smith.* While people may "have an entirely different relationship with telephones than they did thirty-four years ago," *Klayman,* 957 F. Supp. 2d at 36, this Court observes that their relationship with their telecommunications providers has not changed and is just as frustrating. Telephones have far more versatility now than when *Smith* was decided, but this case only concerns their use as telephones. The fact that there are more calls placed does not undermine the Supreme Court's finding that a person has no subjective expectation of privacy in telephony metadata. Importantly, "what metadata is has not changed over time," and "[a]s in *Smith,* the types of information at issue in this case are relatively limited: [tele]phone numbers dialed, date, time, and the like." [*Id.*] at 35. Because *Smith* controls, the NSA's bulk telephony metadata collection program does not violate the Fourth Amendment. [*ACLU,* 959 F. Supp. 2d at 752 (citations omitted).]

Judge Pauley also rejected First Amendment challenges to Section 215 not raised in the *Klayman* litigation, holding that, in light of *Clapper,* the plaintiffs could not establish standing to pursue their First Amendment claim. *See id.* at 753-754.

NOTES AND QUESTIONS

1. *Standing and the Ineffectiveness of the Metadata Program.* Note that both decisions rested the plaintiffs' standing on the *comprehensiveness* of the metadata program: For metadata collection to actually have the effect the government desires, it should follow, Judges Leon and Pauley concluded, that the government is collecting *all* of it.

Thus, and unlike in *Clapper*, there is no question that the plaintiffs are "injured." Contrast that reasoning, though, with subsequent news stories suggesting that, in fact, the NSA may only be collecting as little as 20% of telephone metadata — owing, among other things, to technological difficulties caused by the proliferation of cellular phones. *See* Siobhan Gorman, *NSA Collects 20% or Less of U.S. Call Data*, Wall St. J., Feb. 8, 2014; Ellen Nakashima, *NSA Is Collecting Less Than 30 Percent of US Call Data, Officials Say*, Wash. Post, Feb. 8, 2014. Note the potential irony in these reports: On one hand, they underscore charges that the metadata program can't possibly be effective even on its own terms, since the government can hardly have any confidence that it will find a needle by searching only one-fifth of the haystack. On the other hand, though, they may make it far harder for plaintiffs to *challenge* the metadata program in court. They may even provide the government with a successful ground for appealing Judge Leon's ruling in *Klayman*, and for defending against the ACLU's appeal of Judge Pauley's decision.

    2. *Judge Pauley and the Merits of the APA Claim.* Although both Judges Leon and Pauley held that the plaintiffs were "precluded" from pursuing their statutory challenge to the metadata program, Judge Pauley nevertheless proceeded to express his views on its merits — or lack thereof. He concluded that the statutory challenge failed because (1) the government could obtain similar information through a National Security Letter (thereby suggesting that Congress knew how broad an authority it was conferring when it enacted Section 215 with a "relevance" standard); and (2) Congress ratified this understanding when it reauthorized the relevant provisions in 2010 and 2011. *ACLU*, 959 F. Supp. 2d at 742-749. Are these arguments persuasive?

    3. *Third Parties and FISA.* Both judges' APA preclusion arguments pay little more than lip service to "the APA's basic presumption of judicial review," which "will not be cut off unless there is persuasive reason to believe that such was the purpose of Congress." *Tex. Alliance for Home Care Servs. v. Sebilius*, 681 F.3d 402, 408 (D.C. Cir. 2012). But leaving aside the lack of clear evidence rebutting the presumption in favor of APA claims, isn't there a more obvious flaw with Judges Leon and Pauley's analysis of APA preclusion, *i.e.*, the clear *availability* of FISA review to at least *some* third parties — including "aggrieved persons" entitled to sue under 50 U.S.C. §1810, and criminal defendants entitled to seek suppression of FISA-derived evidence the government

seeks to introduce against them at trial? *See, e.g.*, Charlie Savage, *Warrantless Surveillance Challenged by Defendant*, N.Y. Times, Jan. 30, 2014. If so, then isn't it true that "it's not really an 'implied preclusion' argument; it's an 'implied preclusion except for those other two available remedies' argument." *See* Steve Vladeck, *Why the Constitutional Holding in* Klayman *Wasn't Necessary*, Just Security, Dec. 17, 2013 (3:37 p.m.), http://justsecurity.org/ 2013/12/17/ constitutional-holding-klayman-wasnt/. Shouldn't it follow that a regime that isn't *actually* comprehensive can't be deemed preclusive, at least absent some indication that Congress so intended? At the very least, doesn't the availability of at least *some* judicial review to *some* third parties under FISA demand a more nuanced explanation for why *these* plaintiffs may not proceed? Indeed, the government even argued to the Supreme Court that it did not need to entertain a third party's *direct* challenge to a FISC order because such review should be available in district court. *See* Brief for the United States in Opposition at 15, *In re EPIC*, 134 S. Ct. 638 (2013) (mem.) ("[T]he proper way for petitioner to challenge the Telephony Records Program is to file an action in federal district court to enjoin the program, as other parties have done.").

4. *Constitutional Avoidance*. Both Judges Leon and Pauley interpreted Section 215 as not precluding judicial review of the plaintiffs' *constitutional* claims, in order to "avoid the 'serious constitutional question' that would arise if a federal statute were construed to deny any judicial forum for a colorable constitutional claim." *Webster*, 486 U.S. at 603 (citing *Bowen v. Mich. Acad. of Family Physicians*, 476 U.S. 667, 681 n.12 (1986)). But *Webster* is a variation on the constitutional avoidance canon. Didn't both district courts effectively *violate* that canon by holding that Congress barred review of the *statutory* claims in a statute that is hardly explicit on that issue, thereby forcing a ruling on the *constitutional* claims? *See* Vladeck, *supra*.

5. *Another Ground for Distinguishing Smith*? Judge Leon alludes to but does not expressly invoke the argument that while "each of the phone companies has its own telephony metadata, only the government is able (or at least has undertaken) to build such a comprehensive database of this kind of information. Does anyone communicating by telephone have a reasonable expectation of privacy in light of the fact that the government clearly is able to build such a database?" Put

another way, given Judge Leon's focus on the changes in technology and technological capabilities, isn't the most significant basis for distinguishing *Smith* the government's unique ability to aggregate third-party data from *multiple* providers, something that no individual firm (such as Verizon) is in a position to do — and, as significantly, something we very much would not *expect* such third parties to do? Or is Judge Pauley correct that these arguments may constitute *factual* grounds on which to distinguish *Smith*, but not legal ones?

6. *Next Steps.* As this *Supplement* went to press, appeals were pending in both cases to the Second and D.C. Circuits, respectively, and reform proposals were working their way through Congress. Should the courts of appeal wait for Congress? Should Congress wait for the courts? Who, in your view, is in the best position to resolve the two questions raised in these cases: whether Congress actually *authorized* the metadata program, and, if so, whether the program is consistent with the Fourth Amendment?

———————

[NSL p. 677; CTL p. 290. Insert after Section B1.]

C. Reforming FISA by Reforming the FISA Court?

As noted above, FISA created the Foreign Intelligence Surveillance Court (FISC) and Court of Review (FISCR) to entertain and review applications from the government under the various authorities provided by the statute. Because applications under FISA as originally enacted largely resemble applications for search warrants in the context of ordinary criminal prosecutions, the FISC was set up to act *in camera* and *ex parte* in virtually all of its cases.

As Congress has expanded the scope and nature of the government's surveillance powers under FISA, however, it has also modified the FISC's role in reviewing and approving such authorities. For example, when Congress enacted the business-records provision (USA Patriot Act §215) in 2001, it also authorized the recipient of a §215 order to challenge the order before the FISC, and to appeal an adverse decision to the FISCR (and, eventually, the Supreme Court). *See* 50 U.S.C. §1861(f). Similarly, the FISA Amendments Act of 2008 authorizes "[a]n electronic communication service provider receiving a directive issued pursuant to" the Act to challenge that directive before the FISC — and, again, to appeal an adverse decision to the FISCR and the Supreme Court. *See* 50 U.S.C. §1881a(h). Thus, §1861(f) and §1881a(h) opened the door to adversarial proceedings before the FISC. The assumption was that the recipient of a FISC-approved order/directive could use security-cleared counsel to contest the ruling behind closed doors — and thereby serve as a check on the government in cases in which it was not otherwise required to make an individualized probable cause showing to a FISC judge.

In a July 2013 letter, however, FISC Presiding Judge Reggie Walton explained that "[t]o date, no recipient of a production order has opted to invoke" the judicial review available under §1861(f), and "no electronic service communication service provider has opted to challenge a directive issued pursuant to [§1881a]." (The *In re Directives* case excerpted above arose under the now-defunct scheme created by the Protect America Act of 2007.) *See* Letter from Hon. Reggie B. Walton, Presiding Judge, FISC, to Hon. Patrick J. Leahy, Chairman, Sen. Comm. on the Judiciary, at 8-9 (July 29, 2013), *available at* http://www.leahy. senate.gov/download/ honorable-patrick-j-leahy.

The absence of meaningful adversarial process before the FISC has been at the heart of many calls for reform — including two from former FISC judges. Judge James Robertson, for example, testified before the Privacy and Civil Liberties Oversight Board (PCLOB) that he wished there had been a special lawyer with high-level security clearance upon whom he could have called when he was serving on the FISC to provide adversarial briefing and argument, even as an *amicus curiae*. And in an influential *New York Times* op-ed, Judge James Carr went further, suggesting that Congress formally create an office designed to challenge the government's position before FISC whenever an application for a FISA order "raises new issues." *See* Hon. James G. Carr, Op-Ed, *A Better Secret Court*, N.Y. Times, July 22, 2013. As Judge Carr explained,

> Having lawyers challenge novel legal assertions in these secret proceedings would result in better judicial outcomes. Even if the government got its way all or most of the time, the court would have more fully developed its reasons for letting it do so. Of equal importance, the appointed lawyer could appeal a decision in the government's favor to the Foreign Intelligence Surveillance Court of Review — and then to the Supreme Court. No opportunity for such review exists today, because only the government can appeal a FISA court ruling.

Id. Thus, Judge Carr concluded, giving the FISC the power to appoint such a "special advocate" would "give the court's judges the discretion to appoint lawyers to serve not just the interests of the target and the public — but those of the court as well."

Judges Carr and Robertson are not alone. By the end of the summer of 2013, more than a dozen bills had been introduced in Congress reflecting some variation on the "special advocate" theme. The version of the USA FREEDOM Act passed by the House of Representatives in May 2014 includes a provision requiring the FISC to appoint an *amicus curiae* to play an analogous role, "to assist such court in the consideration of any application for an order or review that, in the opinion of the court, presents a novel or significant interpretation of the law, unless the court issues a written finding that such appointment is not appropriate." H.R. 3361, §401, 113th Cong. (2014). In other cases, the bill would preserve the status quo by allowing, but not requiring, the appointment of an *amicus*.

NOTES AND QUESTIONS

1. *Can Adversarial FISA Process Work?* Why do you suppose that, as Judge Walton explained, *no* recipient of a §215 order or a §702 directive had, to date, availed itself of the judicial review provided by §1861(f) or §1881a(h), respectively? What are the incentives for a business that receives such an order to challenge it? What are the disincentives? Would Judge Carr's call for a "special advocate" have less force if, in fact, the adversarial review provided by these two provisions were more robust? Even if there had been cases in which recipients of such FISC demands had challenged them, are you convinced that the recipient of a §215 order or §702 directive has the same interests in seeking judicial review thereof as an individual whose information and/or communications might be obtained *pursuant* to such authority? Does your answer differ at all under FISA as compared to judicial review of national security letters after and in light of *Doe v. Gonzales*? See NSL p. 668, Note 6; CTL p. 281, Note 6.

2. *Can Adversarial FISA Process Work If the Court Is Fooled?* In a 2011 opinion about a Section 702 application, the FISC dropped this footnote about the NSA's applications in 2006 and 2009 for bulk collection of telephony metadata under Section 215:

The Court is troubled that the government's revelations regarding NSA's acquisition of Internet transactions mark the third instance in less than three years in which the government has disclosed a substantial misrepresentation regarding the scope of a major collection program.

In March 2009, the Court concluded that its authorization of NSA's bulk acquisition of telephone call detail records from [REDACTED] in the so-called "big business records" matter "ha[d] been premised on a flawed depiction of how the NSA uses [the acquired] metadata," and that "[t]his misperception by the FISC existed from the inception of its authorized collection in May 2006, buttressed by repeated inaccurate statements made in the government's submissions, and despite a government-devised and Court-mandated oversight regime." Docket [REDACTED]. Contrary to the government's repeated assurances, NSA had been routinely running queries of the metadata using querying terms that did not meet the required standard for querying. The Court concluded that this requirement had been "so frequently and systematically violated that it can fairly be said that this critical element of the overall . . . regime has never functioned effectively." *Id.*

[Name redacted], Memorandum Opinion at 16 n.14, [docket no. unavailable] (FISA Court Oct. 3, 2011) (Bates, J.). How can the adversarial process work if the only party before the court "repeatedly" provides it with inaccurate information and makes "substantial misrepresentations"? How can the FISC check the accuracy of government representations? If the court finds that it has been misled, can or should it impose a sanction? What sanction?

The Office of the Director of National Intelligence responded to the disclosure of these past incidents of non-compliance by explaining that they:

> stemmed in large part from the complexity of the technology employed in connection with the bulk telephony metadata collection program, interaction of that technology with other NSA systems, and a lack of a shared understanding among various NSA components about how certain aspects of the complex architecture supporting the program functioned. These gaps in understanding led, in turn, to unintentional misrepresentations in the way the collection was described to the FISC. As discussed in the documents, there was no single cause of the incidents and, in fact, a number of successful oversight, management, and technology processes in place operated as designed and uncovered these matters.

ODNI Press Release, *DNI Clapper Declassifies Intelligence Community Documents Regarding Collection Under Section 501 of the Foreign*

Intelligence Surveillance Act (FISA) (Sept. 10, 2013), *available at*
http://www.dni.gov/index.php/newsroom/press-releases/191-press-releases-
2013/927-draft-document. In other words, the misrepresentations resulted
from the fact that the NSA itself did not understand what it was doing.
He asserted that in response to these problems, the NSA had undertaken
an "end-to-end review," resulting in numerous remedial steps to enhance
compliance, including assignment of more than 300 personnel to the
NSA compliance program.

If the technology has progressed so rapidly that its designers and
users are flummoxed by its complexity, how can the lay judges on the
FISC understand it? The congressional overseers? Does the FISC's
eventual recognition of its misperceptions and its corrective orders to the
NSA actually suggest that the oversight works, with somewhat irregular
delays?

3. *The Devil in the "Special Advocate" Details.* As Judge Carr's op-
ed notes, both he and fellow former FISC Judge James Robertson have
endorsed some form of "special advocate" to argue against the
government in at least some cases before the FISC — a security-cleared
lawyer who would be in a position to provide the FISC with the
adversarial process that has thus far been all but nonexistent. But the
devil, as always, is in the details. Wouldn't it completely undermine
FISA if the government had to go through adversarial briefing and
argument before obtaining FISC approval under any of its FISA
authorities? And if Congress created an emergency exception for cases
in which such adversarial process would compromise the government's
need to act expeditiously, isn't it likely that such an exception would end
up swallowing the rule?

These concerns help to explain why some, like Judge Carr, would
leave the power to request the intervention of a "special advocate" to the
FISC itself — to be invoked only in cases in which an individual FISC
judge believes that such adversarial presentation would be useful. Other
proposals, such as Senator Blumenthal's FISA Court Reform Act of
2013, S. 1467, 113th Cong. (2013), would also allow the special
advocate to formally seek reconsideration of all FISC rulings within 30
days after they are issued, a compromise that would allow the
government to obtain the authority it seeks at the outset, and then defend
it only after the fact — while also not leaving the availability of
adversarial briefing and argument wholly to the discretion of individual
FISC judges. Which of these approaches seems more satisfying to you?

Is the House-passed version of the USA FREEDOM Act a good compromise, or does it leave too much discretion in the hands of FISC judges, who can sidestep *amicus* participation simply by issuing a secret "written finding that such appointment is not appropriate"? *See* Steve Vladeck, *The USA FREEDOM Act and a FISA "Special Advocate,"* Lawfare, May 20, 2014, http://www.lawfareblog.com/2014/05/the-usa-freedom-act-and-a-fisa-special-advocate/.

4. *Who/Where Is the "Special Advocate"?* Separate from the timing and role of special advocates is the question of their independence. Should these special advocates be private counsel, akin to the habeas lawyers representing Guantánamo detainees? Should they be government lawyers, perhaps in a special office of the Justice Department's National Security Division? And how (and by whom) should they be appointed? The FISA Court Reform Act, to take one example, would create an independent Executive Branch agency — the Office of the Special Advocate — the director of which would be selected by the FISC from a list of candidates submitted by the PCLOB. The constitutionality of such an appointment scheme may well follow from the Supreme Court's decision in *Morrison v. Olson*, 487 U.S. 654 (1988). But is there a better way to ensure that special advocates are in a position meaningfully to challenge the government's position in FISA cases? *See, e.g.*, The Constitution Project, *The Case for a FISA "Special Advocate"* (2014), *available at* http://www.constitutionproject.org/wp-content/uploads/2014/05/The-Case-for-a-FISA-Special-Advocate_FINAL.pdf.

5. *The Article III Objection to a "Special Advocate."* Although a special advocate would not need Article III standing to participate in proceedings before the FISC (where the government is the moving party), it is not clear that the special advocate would have Article III standing to *appeal* a decision by the FISC. After all, unlike the recipient of a §215 order or a §702 directive, the special advocate is not directly affected by an adverse FISC ruling. *See Hollingsworth v. Perry*, 133 S. Ct. 2652 (2013) (holding that parties who intervened in a district court challenge to the constitutionality of a state ballot measure did not have standing to appeal an adverse decision). Could Congress avoid this constitutional objection by expressly charging the special advocate to act on behalf of those whose data and/or communications would be disclosed by the FISC order at issue? *Cf.* 8 U.S.C. §1534(e)(3)(F) (authorizing a "special attorney" to represent a lawful permanent alien in cases before

the Alien Terrorist Removal Court, while barring him from sharing classified information with his client). Would such a solution replace constitutional issues with ethical ones? Might an alternative be to borrow from the age-old procedure by which lower courts certify questions to the Supreme Court — a process that apparently is available without regard to standing? *See, e.g.,* 28 U.S.C. §1254(2); *see also Iran Nat'l Airlines Corp. v. Marschalk Co.*, 453 U.S. 919 (1981) (accepting — and answering — three questions certified by the Second Circuit). For more on the constitutional issues, see Covington & Burling, *The Constitutionality of a Public Advocate for Privacy* (2014), *available at* http://justsecurity.org/wp-content/uploads/2014/06/The-Constitutionality-of-a-Public-Advocate-for-Privacy.pdf.

6. *A Biased Court?* Another theme that has garnered at least some attention is reform of the process by which FISC (and FISCR) judges are selected. Under current law, the judges serve seven-year terms, and are appointed by the Chief Justice of the United States from the pool of active district and circuit judges — and without formal involvement of any other entity or individual. The only other statutory requirements are that the judges hail from at least seven different circuits, and that at least three reside within 20 miles of Washington, D.C. *See* 50 U.S.C. §1803. This has led some to criticize the court's perceived ideological make-up, given that 10 of the court's 11 judges as of July 2013 were appointed to the federal bench by Republican presidents. *See* Charlie Savage, *Roberts's Picks Reshaping Secret Surveillance Court*, N.Y. Times, July 25, 2013. Would it make more sense to reestablish the FISC as a standalone Article III court, with judges specifically nominated by the President and confirmed by the Senate for that role? Are there other ways to diversify the selection of FISC judges short of an independent confirmation process (*e.g.*, having one judge selected by the Chief Judge of each of the eleven "numerical" circuit courts of appeals)? More fundamentally, is there any reason to believe that changing the *composition* of the court would affect the way the court conducts its business?

7. *Another Ground for Reform: More Disclosure of FISC Opinions.* Both as a reform unto itself, and to help inform further reform discussions, one of the other common themes of FISC-reform discussions has been a demand for increased disclosure of FISC opinions. Under Rule 62 of the FISC's Rules of Procedure, the decision

to publish an opinion is up to the issuing judge, who may choose to publish an opinion *sua sponte* or "on motion by a party." In addition, the presiding judge — in consultation with the rest of the court — may direct publication even when the issuing judge has not done so. Importantly, however, Rule 62 (like FISA itself) creates no presumption in favor of publication, which may help to explain why so few FISC opinions had been released to the public prior to 2013.

Should seeking publication of hitherto classified FISC opinions be one of the responsibilities assigned to the "special advocate" in the proposals summarized above? Should interested parties be left to pursue such disclosure through the ordinary mechanisms provided by the Freedom of Information Act (FOIA)? *See* NSL pp. 1197-1225. Or should interested parties be allowed to seek declassification of FISC opinions from the FISC itself? In a September 2013 ruling on a motion brought by the ACLU, a FISC judge ordered the government to identify all FISC opinions involving §215 that were not already the subject of FOIA litigation commenced by the ACLU, and undertake declassification review of such opinions (including the proposal of redactions for those opinions that could otherwise be released to the public). *See In re Orders of This Court Interpreting Section 215 of the PATRIOT Act*, No. Misc. 13-02 (FISA Ct. Sept. 13, 2013). The same decision held that the ACLU had standing to pursue such relief, and that the FISC's rules did not preclude the court from providing it. Given this decision, should potentially interested parties seek release of opinions directly from FISC, rather than collaterally via FOIA, which provides access only to "agency," not judicial, records? Would a regime in which Congress mandated disclosure of all FISC opinions (subject to appropriate redactions) be preferable to such a bifurcated status quo?

———————

[NSL p. 680, CTL p. 293. Replace *United States v. Arnold* with the following opinion.]

United States v. Cotterman

United States Court of Appeals for the Ninth Circuit, Mar. 8, 2013
709 F.3d 952 (en banc), *cert. denied*, 134 S. Ct. 899 (2014)

McKeown, Circuit Judge: Every day more than a million people cross American borders, from the physical borders with Mexico and Canada to functional borders at airports such as Los Angeles (LAX),

Honolulu (HNL), New York (JFK, LGA), and Chicago (ORD, MDW). As denizens of a digital world, they carry with them laptop computers, iPhones, iPads, iPods, Kindles, Nooks, Surfaces, tablets, Blackberries, cell phones, digital cameras, and more. These devices often contain private and sensitive information ranging from personal, financial, and medical data to corporate trade secrets. And, in the case of Howard Cotterman, child pornography. . . .

This watershed case implicates both the scope of the narrow border search exception to the Fourth Amendment's warrant requirement and privacy rights in commonly used electronic devices. The question we confront "is what limits there are upon this power of technology to shrink the realm of guaranteed privacy." *Kyllo v. United States*, 533 U.S. 27, 34 (2001). More specifically, we consider the reasonableness of a computer search that began as a cursory review at the border but transformed into a forensic examination of Cotterman's hard drive. . . .

I. Factual Background and Procedural History . . .

[Cotterman and his wife were crossing the border on their way home to the United States from a vacation in Mexico. During the primary border inspection, a watch list returned a hit, indicating that Cotterman was a sex offender who had been previously convicted on two counts of use of a minor in sexual conduct, two counts of lewd and lascivious conduct upon a child, and three counts of child molestation. This hit raised a question for border agents whether Cotterman was potentially involved in child sex tourism. He was therefore subjected to a secondary inspection of his car which retrieved two laptop computers and three digital cameras. A border agent inspected the electronic devices and found what appeared to be family and other personal photos, along with several password-protected files.

The agents allowed the Cottermans to leave the border but retained the Cottermans' laptops and a digital camera. An agent then took the laptops and cameras 170 miles to an ICE office in Tucson, Arizona, for further forensic examination. Opening the password-protected files, a computer expert found hundreds of images of child pornography.

A grand jury indicted Cotterman for a host of offenses related to child pornography. Cotterman moved to suppress the evidence gathered from his laptop and the fruits of that evidence. The lower court granted the motion, and the government appealed.]

III. The Border Search

The broad contours of the scope of searches at our international borders are rooted in "the long-standing right of the sovereign to protect itself by stopping and examining persons and property crossing into this country." [*United States v. Ramsey*, 431 U.S. 606 (1977),] at 616. Thus, border searches form "a narrow exception to the Fourth Amendment prohibition against warrantless searches without probable cause." *United States v. Seljan*, 547 F.3d 993, 999 (9th Cir. 2008) (en banc) (internal quotation marks and citation omitted). Because "[t]he Government's interest in preventing the entry of unwanted persons and effects is at its zenith at the international border," *United States v. Flores-Montano,* 541 U.S. 149, 152 (2004), border searches are generally deemed "reasonable simply by virtue of the fact that they occur at the border." *Ramsey,* 431 U.S. at 616.

This does not mean, however, that at the border "anything goes." *Seljan,* 547 F.3d at 1000. Even at the border, individual privacy rights are not abandoned but "[b]alanced against the sovereign's interests." *United States v. Montoya de Hernandez,* 473 U.S. 531, 539 (1985). That balance "is qualitatively different . . . than in the interior" and is "struck much more favorably to the Government." *Id.* at 538, 540. Nonetheless, the touchstone of the Fourth Amendment analysis remains reasonableness. The reasonableness of a search or seizure depends on the totality of the circumstances, including the scope and duration of the deprivation.

In view of these principles, the legitimacy of the initial search of Cotterman's electronic devices at the border is not in doubt. . . . But the search here transformed into something far different. The difficult question we confront is the reasonableness, without a warrant, of the forensic examination that comprehensively analyzed the hard drive of the computer.

A. The Forensic Examination Was Not an Extended Border Search

Cotterman urges us to treat the examination as an extended border search that requires particularized suspicion. Although the semantic moniker "extended border search" may at first blush seem applicable here, our jurisprudence does not support such a claim. We have "define[d] an extended border search as any search away from the border where entry is not apparent, but where the dual requirements of reasonable certainty of a recent border crossing and reasonable suspicion of criminal activity are satisfied." *United States v. Guzman-Padilla,* 573 F.3d 865, 878-79 (9th Cir. 2009) (internal quotation marks and citations omitted). The key feature of an extended border search is that an individual can be assumed to have cleared the border and thus regained an expectation of privacy in accompanying belongings.

Cotterman's case is different. Cotterman was stopped and searched at the border. Although he was allowed to depart the border inspection station after the initial search, some of his belongings, including his laptop, were not. The follow-on forensic examination was not an "extended border search." A border search of a computer is not transformed into an extended border search simply because the device is transported and examined beyond the border.

To be sure, our case law has not always articulated the "extended border search" doctrine with optimal clarity. But the confusion has come in distinguishing between facts describing a functional border search and those describing an extended border search, not in defining the standard for a search at the border. The "functional equivalent" doctrine effectively extends the border search doctrine to all ports of entry, including airports. A routine customs search at the "functional equivalent" of the border is "analyzed as a border search" and requires neither probable cause nor reasonable suspicion. This case involves a search initiated at the actual border and does not encounter any of the difficulties surrounding identification of a "functional" border. As to the extended border search doctrine, we believe it is best confined to cases in which, after an apparent border crossing or functional entry, an attenuation in the time or the location of conducting a search reflects that the subject has regained an expectation of privacy. . . .

B. Forensic Examination at the Border Requires Reasonable Suspicion

It is the comprehensive and intrusive nature of a forensic examination — not the location of the examination — that is the key factor triggering the requirement of reasonable suspicion here. The search would have been every bit as intrusive had Agent Owen traveled to the border with his forensic equipment. Indeed, Agent Owen had a laptop with forensic software that he could have used to conduct an examination at the port of entry itself, although he testified it would have been a more time-consuming effort. To carry out the examination of Cotterman's laptop, Agent Owen used computer forensic software to copy the hard drive and then analyze it in its entirety, including data that ostensibly had been deleted. This painstaking analysis is akin to reading a diary line by line looking for mention of criminal activity — plus looking at everything the writer may have erased.

Notwithstanding a traveler's diminished expectation of privacy at the border, the search is still measured against the Fourth Amendment's reasonableness requirement, which considers the nature and scope of the search. Significantly, the Supreme Court has recognized that the "dignity and privacy interests of the person being searched" at the border will on occasion demand "some level of suspicion in the case of highly intrusive searches of the person." *Flores-Montano*, 541 U.S. at 152. Likewise, the Court has explained that "some searches of property are so destructive," "particularly offensive," or overly intrusive in the manner in which they are carried out as to require particularized suspicion. . . .

We are now presented with a case directly implicating substantial personal privacy interests. The private information individuals store on digital devices — their personal "papers" in the words of the Constitution — in stark contrast to the generic and impersonal contents of a gas tank. We rest our analysis on the reasonableness of this search, paying particular heed to the nature of the electronic devices and the attendant expectation of privacy.

The amount of private information carried by international travelers was traditionally circumscribed by the size of the traveler's luggage or automobile. That is no longer the case. Electronic devices are capable of storing warehouses full of information. The average 400-gigabyte laptop hard drive can store over 200 million pages — the equivalent of five floors of a typical academic library. Even a car full of packed suitcases with sensitive documents cannot hold a candle to the sheer, and ever-increasing, capacity of digital storage.

The nature of the contents of electronic devices differs from that of luggage as well. Laptop computers, iPads and the like are simultaneously offices and personal diaries. They contain the most intimate details of our lives: financial records, confidential business documents, medical records and private emails. This type of material implicates the Fourth Amendment's specific guarantee of the people's right to be secure in their "papers." U.S. Const. amend. IV. The express listing of papers "reflects the Founders' deep concern with safeguarding the privacy of thoughts and ideas — what we might call freedom of conscience — from invasion by the government." *Seljan*, 547 F.3d at 1014 (Kozinski, C.J., dissenting). These records are expected to be kept private and this expectation is "one that society is prepared to recognize as 'reasonable.'" *Katz v. United States,* 389 U.S. 347, 361 (Harlan, J., concurring).

Electronic devices often retain sensitive and confidential information far beyond the perceived point of erasure, notably in the form of browsing histories and records of deleted files. This quality makes it impractical, if not impossible, for individuals to make meaningful decisions regarding what digital content to expose to the scrutiny that accompanies international travel. A person's digital life ought not be hijacked simply by crossing a border. When packing traditional luggage, one is accustomed to deciding what papers to take and what to leave behind. When carrying a laptop, tablet or other device, however, removing files unnecessary to an impending trip is an impractical solution given the volume and often intermingled nature of the files. It is also a time-consuming task that may not even effectively erase the files.

The present case illustrates this unique aspect of electronic data. Agents found incriminating files in the unallocated space of Cotterman's laptop, the space where the computer stores files that the user ostensibly deleted and maintains other "deleted" files retrieved from web sites the user has visited. Notwithstanding the attempted erasure of material or the transient nature of a visit to a web site, computer forensic examination was able to restore the files. It is as if a search of a person's suitcase could reveal not only what the bag contained on the current trip, but everything it had ever carried.

With the ubiquity of cloud computing, the government's reach into private data becomes even more problematic. In the "cloud," a user's data, including the same kind of highly sensitive data one would have in "papers" at home, is held on remote servers rather than on the device itself. The digital device is a conduit to retrieving information from the cloud, akin to the key to a safe deposit box. Notably, although the virtual "safe deposit box" does not itself cross the border, it may appear as a seamless part of the digital device when presented at the border. With access to the cloud through forensic examination, a traveler's cache is just a click away from the government.

As Justice Scalia wrote, "It would be foolish to contend that the degree of privacy secured to citizens by the Fourth Amendment has been entirely unaffected by the advance of technology." *Kyllo,* 533 U.S. at 33-34. Technology has the dual and conflicting capability to decrease privacy and augment the expectation of privacy. While the thermal imaging device in *Kyllo* threatened to expose the hour at which "the lady of the house" took her daily "sauna and bath," *id.* at 38, digital devices allow us to carry the very papers we once stored at home. . . .

This is not to say that simply because electronic devices house sensitive, private information they are off limits at the border. The relevant inquiry, as always, is one of reasonableness. But that reasonableness determination must account for differences in property. Unlike searches involving a reassembled gas tank, or small hole in the bed of a pickup truck, which have minimal or no impact beyond the search itself — and little implication for an individual's dignity and privacy interests — the exposure of confidential and personal information has permanence. It cannot be undone. Accordingly, the uniquely sensitive nature of data on electronic devices carries with it a significant expectation of privacy and thus renders an exhaustive exploratory search more intrusive than with other forms of property.

After their initial search at the border, customs agents made copies of the hard drives and performed forensic evaluations of the computers that took days to turn up contraband. It was essentially a computer strip search. An exhaustive forensic search of a copied laptop hard drive intrudes upon privacy and dignity interests to a far greater degree than a cursory search at the border. It is little comfort to assume that the government — for now — does not have the time or resources to seize and search the millions of devices that accompany the millions of travelers who cross our borders. It is the potential unfettered dragnet effect that is troublesome. . . .

International travelers certainly expect that their property will be searched at the border. What they do not expect is that, absent some particularized suspicion, agents will mine every last piece of data on their devices or deprive them of their most personal property for days (or perhaps weeks or even months, depending on how long the search takes). Such a thorough and detailed search of the most intimate details of one's life is a substantial intrusion upon personal privacy and dignity. We therefore hold that the forensic examination of Cotterman's computer required a showing of reasonable suspicion, a modest requirement in light of the Fourth Amendment.

IV. Reasonable Suspicion

Reasonable suspicion is defined as "a particularized and objective basis for suspecting the particular person stopped of criminal activity."

United States v. Cortez, 449 U.S. 411, 417-18 (1981). This assessment is to be made in light of "the totality of the circumstances." *Id.* at 417. "[E]ven when factors considered in isolation from each other are susceptible to an innocent explanation, they may collectively amount to a reasonable suspicion." *United States v. Berber-Tinoco,* 510 F.3d 1083, 1087 (9th Cir. 2007). We review reasonable suspicion determinations de novo, reviewing findings of historical fact for clear error and giving "due weight to inferences drawn from those facts by resident judges and local law enforcement officers." *Ornelas v. United States,* 517 U.S. 690, 699 (1996).

In the district court and in supplemental briefing, the government argued that the border agents had reasonable suspicion to conduct the initial search and the forensic examination of Cotterman's computer. We agree. . . .

[The court cited Cotterman's prior record, his travel patterns, and Mexico's reputation for sex tourism as factors in calculating such suspicion.]

To these factors, the government adds another — the existence of password-protected files on Cotterman's computer. We are reluctant to place much weight on this factor because it is commonplace for business travelers, casual computer users, students and others to password protect their files. Law enforcement "cannot rely solely on factors that would apply to many law-abiding citizens," *Berber-Tinoco,* 510 F.3d at 1087, and password protection is ubiquitous. National standards require that users of mobile electronic devices password protect their files. Computer users are routinely advised — and in some cases, required by employers — to protect their files when traveling overseas.

Although password protection of files, in isolation, will not give rise to reasonable suspicion, where, as here, there are other indicia of criminal activity, password protection of files may be considered in the totality of the circumstances. To contribute to reasonable suspicion, encryption or password protection of files must have some relationship to the suspected criminal activity. Here, making illegal files difficult to access makes perfect sense for a suspected holder of child pornography. When combined with the other circumstances, the fact that Officer Alvarado encountered at least one password protected file on Cotterman's computer contributed to the basis for reasonable suspicion to conduct a forensic examination.

The existence of the password-protected files is also relevant to assessing the reasonableness of the scope and duration of the search of

Cotterman's computer. The search was necessarily protracted because of the password protection that Cotterman employed. . . .

. . . [W]e conclude that the examination of Cotterman's electronic devices was supported by reasonable suspicion and that the scope and manner of the search were reasonable under the Fourth Amendment. Cotterman's motion to suppress therefore was erroneously granted.

Reversed.

CALLAHAN, Circuit Judge, concurring in part, dissenting in part, and concurring in the judgment, with whom CLIFTON, Circuit Judge, joins, and with whom M. SMITH, Circuit Judge, joins as to all but Part II.A: Whether it is drugs, bombs, or child pornography, we charge our government with finding and excluding any and all illegal and unwanted articles and people before they cross our international borders. Accomplishing that Herculean task requires that the government be mostly free from the Fourth Amendment's usual restraints on searches of people and their property. Today the majority ignores that reality by erecting a new rule requiring reasonable suspicion for any thorough search of electronic devices entering the United States. This rule flouts more than a century of Supreme Court precedent, is unworkable and unnecessary, and will severely hamstring the government's ability to protect our borders.

I therefore dissent from Part III of the majority's opinion. I concur in Parts I, II, and IV, and in particular the majority's conclusion in Part IV that the government had reasonable suspicion to conduct the forensic examination of Howard Cotterman's electronic devices. I therefore also concur in the judgment. . . .

II.

. . . Under the border search doctrine, suspicionless border searches are *per se* reasonable. However, the Supreme Court has identified three situations in which they might not be *per se* reasonable, *i.e.,* at least reasonable suspicion is required: (1) "highly intrusive searches of the person;" (2) destructive searches of property; and (3) searches conducted in a "particularly offensive" manner.

Although its opinion is not entirely clear, the majority appears to rely on the first and third exceptions to hold that the search at issue in this case required reasonable suspicion. (There is no claim that the government damaged or destroyed Cotterman's property.) But the exception for "highly intrusive searches of the person," cannot apply here; "papers," even private ones in electronic format, are not a "person." That leaves the exception for searches conducted in a "particularly offensive" manner. The majority relies primarily on the notion that electronic devices are special to conclude that reasonable suspicion was required. The majority is mistaken. . . .

B.

The majority's opinion turns primarily on the notion that electronic devices deserve special consideration because they are ubiquitous and can store vast quantities of personal information. That idea is fallacious and has no place in the border search context. . . .

. . . The fact that electronic devices are capable of storing a lot of personal information does not make an extensive search of them "particularly offensive." We have squarely rejected the idea that the "intrusiveness" of a search depends in whole or in part on the nature of the property being searched. In *United States v. Giberson,* 527 F.3d 882 (9th Cir. 2008), we specifically rebuffed the argument that computers are special for Fourth Amendment purposes by virtue of how much information they store; "neither the quantity of information, nor the form in which it is stored, is legally relevant in the Fourth Amendment context." *Id.* at 888.

. . . If the government may search the contents of a briefcase, car, or mobile home that transits the border, there is no reason it should not also be able to search the contents of a camera, tablet, or laptop that enters the country. All of those things are capable of storing, and often do store, private information. The majority points out that electronic devices can and usually do store much *more* private information than their non-electronic counterparts. But "a port of entry is not a traveler's home," [*United States v. Thirty-Seven (37) Photographs,* 402 U.S. 363 (1971),] at 376, even if a traveler chooses to carry a home's worth of personal information across it. Moreover, a bright-line rule distinguishing electronic from non-electronic devices — of the sort the Supreme Court has made clear has no place in Fourth Amendment jurisprudence — is arbitrary; there is no reason someone carrying a laptop should receive greater privacy protection than someone who chooses (or can only afford) to convey his or her personal information on paper.

In short, today the court erects a new bright-line rule: "forensic examination" of electronic devices "at the border requires reasonable suspicion." The majority never defines "forensic," leaving border agents to wonder exactly what types of searches are off-limits. Even if the majority means to require reasonable suspicion for *any* type of digital forensic border search, no court has ever erected so categorical a rule, based on so general a type of search or category of property, and the Supreme Court has rightly slapped down anything remotely similar. The majority invites — indeed, requires — the Court to do so again.

III. . . .

Apart from being unnecessary, the majority's new limits on the government's border search authority will make it much harder for border agents to do their jobs, for at least two reasons. First, it is common knowledge that border agents at security checkpoints conduct more thorough searches not simply of those persons who arouse suspicion but also of a percentage of travelers on a random basis. Otherwise, a person who appears entirely innocent will have nothing to fear and will not be deterred from carrying something that should not be brought into the country. A checkpoint limited to searches that can be justified by articulable grounds for "reasonable suspicion" is bound to be less effective.

Second, courtesy of the majority's decision, criminals now know they can hide their child pornography or terrorist connections in the recesses of their electronic devices, while border agents, fearing Fourth Amendment or *Bivens* actions, will avoid conducting the searches that could find those illegal articles. The result will be that people and things we wish to keep out of our country will get in — a result hardly in keeping with our "inherent authority to protect, and a paramount interest in protecting," the "territorial integrity" of the United States. The border search doctrine *must* account for the fact that border agents may need time and forensics to bypass "evasive actions" a criminal has taken to hide contraband or other illegal articles from plain view. I would rather leave those difficult decisions "to the discretion of the officers in the field who confront myriad circumstances we can only begin to imagine from the relative safety of our chambers." *United States v. Williams,* 419 F.3d 1029, 1034 (9th Cir.), *cert. denied,* 546 U.S. 1081 (2005). . . .

M. SMITH, Circuit Judge, dissenting, with whom CLIFTON and CALLAHAN, Circuit Judges, join with respect to Part I: I respectfully dissent. Until today, federal courts have consistently upheld suspicionless searches of electronic storage devices at the border. Yet the majority ignores these cases, rewrites long standing Fourth Amendment jurisprudence, and, in narrowing [*United States v. Arnold*, 533 F.3d 1003 (9th Cir. 2008)] creates a circuit split.

While I share some of the majority's concerns about the steady erosion of our personal privacy in this digital age, the majority's decision to create a reasonable suspicion requirement for some property searches at the border so muddies current border search doctrine that border agents will be left to divine on an ad hoc basis whether a property search is sufficiently "comprehensive and intrusive" to require reasonable suspicion, or sufficiently "unintrusive" to come within the traditional border search exception. Requiring border patrol agents to determine that reasonable suspicion exists prior to performing a basic forensic examination of a laptop or other electronic devices discourages such searches, leaving our borders open to electronically savvy terrorists and criminals who may hereafter carry their equipment and data across our borders with little fear of detection. In fact, the majority opinion makes such a legal bouillabaisse out of the previously unambiguous border search doctrine, that I sincerely hope the Supreme Court will grant certiorari, and reverse the holding in this case regarding the level of suspicion necessary to search electronic devices at the border, for the sake of our national security, and the consistency of our national border search law. . . .

I. . . .

C. Expectation of Privacy in Electronic Data at the Border

The majority suggests that travelers at the border have a heightened expectation of privacy in their electronic storage devices, due to the "uniquely sensitive nature of [this] data." There is no question that searches of electronic data are protected by the Fourth Amendment, but we have never found this data to be immune from the border search exception. In fact, these electronic storage devices are hardly a bastion of privacy. When connected to the Internet, they transmit a massive amount of intimate data to the public on an almost constant basis, rendering it unremarkable that they can be searched at the border, where "[t]he government's interest in preventing the entry of unwanted persons and effects is at its zenith." *Flores-Montano,* 541 U.S. at 152.

Indeed, Facebook, for example, now has more than 500 million users, who share more than 25 billion pieces of data each month. Those who opt out of social networking sites are no less susceptible to the ubiquitous Internet cookie, which collects data on users' Internet activities to share or sell with other organizations. Until recently, a federally funded data accumulation system allowed clients to "search tens of billions of data records on individuals and businesses in mere seconds." Considering the steady erosion of our privacy on the Internet, searches of electronic storage devices may be increasingly akin to a well-placed Internet search. Ironically, the majority creates a zone of privacy in electronic devices at the border that is potentially greater than that afforded the Google searches we perform in our own homes, and elsewhere.

The majority muses that "[a] person's digital life ought not be hijacked simply by crossing the border," but it fails to explain why electronic data deserves special protections when we have never extended such protections to the same data in written form. *See Seljan,* 547 F.3d at 1003 ("An envelope containing personal correspondence is not uniquely protected from search at the border."). The documents carried on today's smart phones and laptops are different only in form, but not in substance, from yesterday's papers, carried in briefcases and wallets. The majority contends that electronic devices hold data of a "uniquely sensitive nature" and that, inexplicably, these devices have the "capability to . . . augment the expectation of privacy." *Under the majority's reasoning, the mere process of digitalizing our diaries and work documents somehow increases the "sensitive nature" of the data therein, providing travelers with a greater expectation of privacy in a diary that happens to be produced on an iPad rather than a legal pad.* Such artificial and arbitrary distinctions cannot serve as a reasonable basis for determining privacy rights at the border.

The majority attempts to distinguish electronic devices from papers by the vast amount of data they can hold, noting that "[a] car full of packed suitcases . . . cannot hold a candle to the sheer, and ever-increasing, capacity of digital storage." Yet, "case law does not support a finding that a search which occurs in an otherwise ordinary manner, is 'particularly offensive' simply due to the storage capacity of the object being searched." *Arnold,* 533 F.3d at 1010. The majority contends that it "discuss[es] the typical storage capacity of electronic devices simply to highlight the features that generally distinguish them from traditional baggage." Yet why the majority would bother to distinguish between the storage capacities of electronic devices and traditional luggage is a mystery, unless to support its enhanced protections for electronic devices based on their greater storage capacity.

Mapping our privacy rights by the amount of information we carry with us leads to unreasonable and absurd results. Under the majority's reasoning, a Mini Cooper filled with documents is entitled to less privacy protection at the border than a stretch Rolls-Royce filled with documents; a pickup truck filled with documents is entitled to less protection than an 18 wheeler filled with documents. It appears that those who cannot afford a 64 gigabyte iPad, or the "average" 400 gigabyte hard drive discussed by the majority, will alone be subject to suspicionless searches. The majority's reasoning also protects the rich (who can generally afford more sophisticated devices) to a greater extent than the poor (who are presumably less able to afford those more capable devices.) . . . .

V. Conclusion

Reasonable suspicion has no place in property searches at the border, as the Supreme Court has consistently held. Imposing a reasonable suspicion requirement here forces courts and border patrol agents to engage in just the "sort of decision-making process that the Supreme Court wished to avoid in sanctioning expansive border searches." *Seljan,* 547 F.3d at 1011 (citation omitted) (Callahan, J., concurring). Rather than rewrite the border search exception, as the majority does, I would affirm the district court's application of the extended border search doctrine to Cotterman's case, which appears most appropriate given the extensive lapse in distance and time between the first and the second search. Additionally, I would hold the government to its burden of proof in determining that reasonable suspicion was absent here. Under the doctrine of this case, the majority sweeps in thousands of innocent individuals whose electronic equipment can now be taken away from the border and searched indefinitely, under the border search exception.

I respectfully dissent.

_____

[NSL p. 684, CTL p. 297. Omit Note 4.]

_____

[NSL p. 692, CTL p. 305. Insert after "b. Watch Lists and Other
Identification-Related Databases" and before Note 1.]

Ibrahim v. Department of Homeland Security

United States Court of Appeals, Ninth Circuit, Feb. 8, 2012
669 F.3d 983

W. FLETCHER, Circuit Judge: Plaintiff Rahinah Ibrahim is a citizen
of Malaysia and mother of four children. She was legally in the United
States from 2001 to 2005 as a Ph.D. student at Stanford University. She
alleges that the U.S. government has mistakenly placed her on the "No-
Fly List" and other terrorist watchlists. On January 2, 2005, she
attempted to travel to a Stanford-sponsored conference in Malaysia
where she was to present her doctoral research. She was prevented from
flying and was detained in a holding cell for two hours at the San
Francisco airport. She was allowed to fly to Malaysia the next day, but
she was prevented from returning to the United States after the
conference. Ibrahim has not been permitted to return to the United
States.

Ibrahim brought suit in federal district court seeking, among other
things, injunctive relief under the First and Fifth Amendments, with the
ultimate aim of having her name removed from the government's
watchlists. The district court denied injunctive relief [accepting the
government argument that she had no right to assert claims under the
First and Fifth Amendments because she is an alien who has voluntarily
left the United States.] We reverse and remand for further proceedings.

I. Factual Background . . .

B. The Government's Terrorist Watchlists

Since the terrorist attacks of September 11, 2001, the federal
government has assembled a vast, multi-agency, counterterrorism
bureaucracy that tracks hundreds of thousands of individuals. *See, e.g.,* 6
U.S.C. §§122, 124h, 482, 485; Exec. Order No. 13388, 70 Fed. Reg.
62023 (Oct. 25, 2005). At the heart of this bureaucracy is the Terrorist
Screening Center ("TSC"). Established by the Attorney General in 2003
pursuant to a presidential directive, the mission of TSC is "to
consolidate the Government's approach to terrorism screening and
provide for the appropriate and lawful use of Terrorist Information in

screening processes." *See* Homeland Security Presidential Directive/ HSPD-6. Though administered by the FBI, TSC retains personnel from the Departments of State, Homeland Security, and Defense, and other federal agencies.

TSC manages the Terrorist Screening Database ("TSDB"), the federal government's centralized watchlist of known and suspected terrorists. The National Counterterrorism Center nominates known and suspected international terrorists to the TSDB, while the FBI nominates known and suspected domestic terrorists. TSC distributes subsets of the TSDB to other federal agencies to help implement the government's counterterrorism initiatives. TSA uses two subsets of the TSDB — the No-Fly List and the Selectee List — to screen airline passengers. Individuals on the No-Fly List are prohibited from boarding American carriers or any flight having virtually any contact with U.S. territory or airspace. Individuals on the Selectee List are subject to enhanced security screening before boarding an airplane. The State Department uses a subset of the TSDB to screen visa applicants through the Consular Lookout and Support System.

The evidence and procedures used to nominate individuals to the TSDB are kept secret from the general public, as are the names of those in the TSDB. However, thousands of front line law enforcement officers from federal, state, local, territorial, and tribal agencies have access to the TSDB, as do some private sector entities and individuals. As of January 2011, TSC had also agreed to share information with 22 foreign governments.

Since its inception, the TSDB has grown by more than 700%, from about 158,000 records in June 2004 to over 1.1 million records in May 2009. In 2007, these records contained information on approximately 400,000 individuals. As of 2007, the TSDB was increasing at a rate of 20,000 records per month. TSC makes 400 to 1200 changes to the TSDB every day. It is the "world's most comprehensive and widely shared database of terrorist identities."

In theory, only individuals who pose a threat to civil aviation are put on the No-Fly and Selectee Lists, but the Justice Department has criticized TSC for its "weak quality assurance process." In July 2006 — after the events that gave rise to this lawsuit — there were 71,872 records in the No-Fly List. After an internal review, TSC downgraded 22,412 records from the No-Fly List to the Selectee List and deleted entirely an additional 5,086 records. By January 2007, the TSC had cut the No-Fly List by more than half, to 34,230 records. Tens of thousands of travelers have been misidentified because of misspellings and transcription errors in the nomination process, and because of computer algorithms that imperfectly match travelers against the names on the list. TSA maintains a list of approximately 30,000 individuals who are commonly confused with those on the No-Fly and Selectee Lists. One major air carrier reported that it encountered 9,000 erroneous terrorist watchlist matches every day during April 2008.

Nomination and identification errors are so common that TSC organized a redress unit in 2007 to deal with complaints. The redress procedures have been opaque. A 2006 GAO report stated that an individual who submitted a query to TSC's redress unit received an initial response letter that "neither confirms nor denies the existence of any terrorist watch list records relating to the individual." A 2009 internal DHS report stated, "With few exceptions, redress-seekers receive response letters that do not reveal the basis for their travel difficulties, the action the government took to address those difficulties, or other steps that they may take to help themselves in the future."

When Ibrahim filed suit, TSA managed a Passenger Identity Verification program for travelers who believed that they were mistakenly put on the No-Fly or Selectee List. In place of that program, the Department of Homeland Security ("DHS") now manages the Traveler Redress Inquiry Program ("TRIP"). A 2007 Department of Justice audit commended TSC for accurately resolving redress queries, but noted that 45% of the reviewed records contained an error. The 2009 DHS report was less charitable, concluding that the "TRIP website advises travelers that the program can assist them with resolving a range of travel difficulties. Our review of redress results revealed that those claims are overstated. While TRIP offers effective solutions to some traveler issues, it does not address other difficulties effectively, including the most common — watch list misidentifications in aviation security settings." . . .

IV. Discussion . . .

B. Constitutional Claims

Claim 13 . . . alleges that the placement of Ibrahim's name on the government's terrorist watchlists violates her right to freedom of association under the First Amendment and her rights to equal protection and due process under the Fifth Amendment.

At this point in the litigation, no court has attempted to determine the merits of Ibrahim's claims under the First and Fifth Amendments. The parties have not briefed whether her placement on a terrorist watchlist violates her rights to freedom of association, equal protection, and due process. The only question before us is whether Ibrahim even has the right to assert such claims.

We begin with the uncontested proposition that if Ibrahim had remained in the United States, she would have been able to assert claims under the First and Fifth Amendments to challenge her placement on the government's terrorist watchlists. It is well established that aliens legally within the United States may challenge the constitutionality of federal and state actions. Even aliens who are in the United States illegally may bring constitutional challenges, *see, e.g., Plyler v. Doe,* 457 U.S. 202, 211–12 (1982); *Wong Wing v. United States,* 163 U.S. 228, 237 (1896), including the ability to challenge the revocation of a visa. The question in this case is whether Ibrahim lost the right she otherwise had because she left the United States.

The Supreme Court has held in a series of cases that the border of the United States is not a clear line that separates aliens who may bring constitutional challenges from those who may not. For example, a resident alien who voluntarily leaves the United States on a brief trip with an intent to return is constitutionally entitled to a due process hearing if the government seeks to exclude her upon return to the United States. *See, e.g., Landon v. Plasencia,* 459 U.S. 21, 34 (1982) (resident alien entitled to constitutional due process hearing in exclusion proceedings upon re-entry after a "few days" abroad); *Rosenberg v. Fleuti,* 374 U.S. 449, 450 (1963) (entry after innocent, casual, and brief excursion abroad did not qualify as "entry" for immigration purposes); *Kwong Hai Chew,* 344 U.S. at 593–95 (resident alien entitled to constitutional due process hearing after exclusion following a five-month voyage abroad). *See also Boumediene v. Bush,* 553 U.S. 723 (2008) (aliens held as enemy combatants outside the *de jure* sovereign territory of the United States may petition for habeas corpus to challenge the constitutionality of their detention); *Al Maqaleh v. Gates,* 605 F.3d 84, 95–96 (D.C. Cir. 2010) (location of alien outside the United States is only a factor in determining the extraterritorial reach of the Constitution); *Nat'l Council of Resistance of Iran v. Dep't of State,* 251 F.3d 192 (D.C. Cir. 2001) (a foreign organization with property in the United States entitled to constitutional due process hearing before Secretary of State may classify it as a "foreign terrorist organization");

Cardenas v. Smith, 733 F.2d 909, 915 (D.C. Cir. 1984) (Colombian national outside the United States entitled to assert due process claim against U.S. government based on seizure of her Swiss bank account); *In re Aircrash in Bali, Indonesia on April 22, 1974,* 684 F.2d 1301, 1308 n.6 (9th Cir. 1982) (nonresident aliens suing on same cause of action as citizens have the right to assert takings claim).

In *United States v. Verdugo-Urquidez,* 494 U.S. 259 (1990), the Supreme Court wrote that "aliens receive constitutional protections when they have come within the territory of the United States and developed substantial connections with this country." *Id.* at 271. The Court's statement in *Verdugo-Urquidez* was an elaboration of its earlier language in *Johnson v. Eisentrager,* 339 U.S. 763 (1950), that an alien "is accorded a generous and ascending scale of rights as he increases his identity with our society." *Verdugo-Urquidez,* 494 U.S. at 269 (quoting *Eisentrager,* 339 U.S. at 770) (internal quotations omitted). The Court wrote in *Boumediene* that the right of an alien outside the United States to assert constitutional claims is based on "objective factors and practical concerns" rather than "formalism." 553 U.S. at 764. In determining the constitutional rights of aliens outside the United States, the Court applies a "functional approach" rather than a bright-line rule. *Id.*

A comparison of Ibrahim's case with *Verdugo-Urquidez, Eisentrager*, and *Boumediene* is instructive.

In *Verdugo-Urquidez,* plaintiff had been arrested in Mexico and brought against his will to the Mexico-United States border, where he was turned over to United States authorities and imprisoned in the United States while awaiting trial on narcotics smuggling charges. The Court held that the plaintiff had "no previous *significant voluntary connection* with the United States" and therefore had no right to assert a Fourth Amendment challenge to searches and seizures of his property by United States agents in Mexico. *Verdugo-Urquidez,* 494 U.S. at 271 (emphasis added).

Relying on *Verdugo-Urquidez,* the government insists that Ibrahim left the United States "voluntarily" and that she thereby forfeited any right to assert constitutional claims she might have had if she had remained in the United States. The government mistakes the nature of the *Verdugo-Urquidez* inquiry. Under *Verdugo-Urquidez,* the inquiry is whether the alien has voluntarily established a connection with the United States, not whether the alien has voluntarily left the United States. The circumstances of an alien's departure may cast some light on whether the alien has established, and wishes to maintain, a voluntarily established connection with the United States. But the mere fact that an alien's departure is voluntary tells us very little. In Ibrahim's case, she left the United States to attend a Stanford-sponsored conference to present her academic research, performed in connection with her Ph.D. studies at Stanford, and she expected to return to Stanford after the conference to complete her studies. Ibrahim thus did not intend to sever her established connection to the United States by her voluntary departure, but rather to develop that connection further.

In *Eisentrager,* the plaintiffs were German citizens who had been arrested in China, convicted of violating the laws of war after adversary trials before a U.S. military tribunal in China, and sent to a prison in Germany to serve their sentences. The Supreme Court held that they did not have a right to seek a writ of habeas corpus under our Constitution. The Court summarized:

> [To agree with plaintiffs that they are entitled to seek habeas] we must hold that a prisoner of our military authorities is constitutionally entitled to the writ, even though he (a) is an enemy alien; (b) has never been or resided in the United States; (c) was captured outside of our territory and there held in military custody as a prisoner of war; (d) was tried and convicted by a Military Commission sitting outside the United States; (e) for offenses against laws of war committed outside the United States; (f) and is at all times imprisoned outside the United States.

339 U.S. at 777.

Ibrahim's case is unlike that of the plaintiffs in *Eisentrager.* She has not been convicted of, or even charged with, any violation of law. She is a citizen of a country with which we have never been at war. She contends that the placement of her name on the government's terrorist watchlists is a mistake. Her contention is not implausible, given the frequent mistakes the government has made in placing names on these lists. She has established a substantial voluntary connection with the United States through her Ph.D. studies at a distinguished American university, and she wishes to maintain that connection.

In *Boumediene,* the plaintiffs were aliens who had been designated as enemy combatants and who were detained at the United States Naval Station in Guantanamo. Plaintiffs had not been tried or convicted of any crime. They sought federal habeas corpus. The government argued that because plaintiffs were aliens who had committed acts outside the United States and were being detained outside the United States, they were not entitled to seek habeas relief. The Court rejected the government's proposed bright-line rule, calling it a "formal, sovereignty-based test." 553 U.S. at 764. The Court wrote that while the United States does not have *de jure* sovereignty over the Naval Station at Guantanamo Bay, it "maintains *de facto* sovereignty." *Id.* at 755. Applying a "functional approach," *id.* at 764, the Court held that the plaintiffs in *Boumediene,* unlike the plaintiffs in *Eisentrager*, had a right to seek a writ of habeas corpus.

Ibrahim shares an important similarity with the plaintiffs in *Boumediene.* The *Boumediene* plaintiffs and Ibrahim both sought (or seek) the right to assert constitutional claims in a civilian court in order to correct what they contend are mistakes. In *Boumediene,* plaintiffs sought the right to try to establish they were not, in fact, enemy combatants. Ibrahim seeks the right to try to establish that she does not, in fact, deserve to be placed on the government's watchlists.

The government in *Boumediene* proposed a bright-line "formal sovereignty-based test" under which the absence of *de jure* jurisdiction over Guantanamo would have meant that plaintiffs had no right to seek habeas corpus under the Constitution. The Court disagreed, adopting instead a "functional approach" under which the absence of *de jure* jurisdiction was not determinative. *Id.* at 764. The government proposes a similar bright-line "formal sovereignty-based test" in Ibrahim's case. Under the government's proposed test in this case, any alien, no matter how great her voluntary connection with the United States, immediately loses all constitutional rights as soon as she voluntarily leaves the country, regardless of the purpose of her trip, and regardless of the length of her intended stay abroad. The government's proposed test is not the law. The law that we are bound to follow is, instead, the "functional approach" of *Boumediene* and the "significant voluntary connection" test of *Verdugo-Urquidez.*

Under *Boumediene* and *Verdugo-Urquidez,* we hold that Ibrahim has "significant voluntary connection" with the United States. She voluntarily established a connection to the United States during her four years at Stanford University while she pursued her Ph.D. She voluntarily departed from the United States to present the results of her research at a Stanford-sponsored conference. The purpose of her trip was to further, not to sever, her connection to the United States, and she intended her stay abroad to be brief.

We do not hold that tourists, business visitors, and all student visa holders have the same connection to the United States as Ibrahim. Nor do we hold that Congress is without authority to exclude undesirable aliens from the United States and to prescribe terms and conditions for entry and re-entry of aliens. We hold only that Ibrahim has established "significant voluntary connection" with the United States such that she has the right to assert claims under the First and Fifth Amendments. Like the Court in *Boumediene,* we express no opinion on the validity of the underlying constitutional claims. . . .

Conclusion

We hold that Ibrahim has significant voluntary connection to the United States and she may therefore assert claims against the federal defendants for prospective relief under the First and Fifth Amendments. . . .

We REVERSE in part, [and for reasons not relevant here] AFFIRM in part, and VACATE in part. We REMAND for further proceedings consistent with this opinion. Costs to Appellant.

DUFFY, District Judge: I dissent. . . . The majority relies on a number of cases to show that certain aliens located outside the United States can challenge the constitutionality of U.S. laws. One such case is *Kwong Hai Chew v. Colding,* 344 U.S. 590 (1953). . . . [But in *Kwong,*] [t]he Supreme Court recognized that, while Kwong Hai Chew was on the high seas, he was at all times under the jurisdiction of the United States, as evidenced by the American flag on the S.S. Sir John Franklin.

. . . In the instant case, Petitioner resides in Malaysia and, therefore, does not enjoy the right of constitutional challenge.

Slightly more instructive on the issue of whether aliens located outside of the United States can bring constitutional claims is *Boumediene v. Bush,* 553 U.S. 723 (2008). . . . [In that case,] [t]he Supreme Court's decision did not disregard the extraterritoriality of the claims being asserted, but focused instead on the fact that Boumediene and his fellow petitioners held at Guantánamo Bay were in U.S. custody following capture in, and transfer from, various foreign lands. Here, the Petitioner, knowing that she could be forever banned from returning to this country, voluntarily left and returned to her native land, outside of U.S. jurisdiction. No one can believe that she did not know exactly the consequences of the choice she made.

In *Johnson v. Eisentrager,* 339 U.S. 763 (1950), a group of German nationals sought the writ of habeas corpus after being arrested by the United States Army in China, convicted of violating the laws of war by a Military Commission sitting in China, and imprisoned in Germany. . . .

[L]ike the petitioners in *Eisentrager,* the Petitioner does not find herself under U.S. jurisdiction, whether *de jure* or *de facto,* as did the petitioners in *Boumediene.*

I must also note a crucial distinction between *Boumediene* and *Eisentrager* on the one hand and the present case on the other. The petitioners in the habeas cases cited above sought to challenge their detention at U.S. hands, whereas the Petitioner is not in our custody and therefore can have no grounds on which to seek similar relief. . . .

The majority distinguishes *Verdugo-Urquidez* by finding that Petitioner "established a substantial voluntary connection with the United States through her studies at a distinguished American university." I cannot come to the same conclusion. If we were to hold today that Petitioner may assert her constitutional claims because she formed a "substantial voluntary connection with the United States" while here on a student visa, then we would be hard pressed not to allow all alien students who studied in the United States and subsequently left the country to bring constitutional claims in our courts.

. . . If this were sufficient to vest constitutional rights in an alien located outside of the United States to bring actions in the United States against the government, there would be a significant number of aliens in the world just waiting to get into court. For example, a visitor to this country who overstays his visa, makes a livelihood in this country for a substantial amount of time, and chooses voluntary departure when caught as an illegal alien, could fit within the class of people who would have such rights. He would have been in the country for a "substantial time" and would have friends and contacts in this country — as would most illegal aliens. As such, he would most likely have the desire and intention to return to this country.

As this example shows, the majority holding is too broad, while the government's bright line argument based on extraterritoriality is too narrow and hidebound for use in the modern world.

In the case at bar, however, there is no need to set forth a definitive test because the simple answer is that Petitioner has not shown a "substantial voluntary connection" with the United States, which is the measurement the majority believes the precedent would require. The Petitioner does not suggest that she ever worked in or paid taxes to the United States or indeed did anything (except study at a university) to indicate that she ever made a conscious decision to live in this country or to accept any of the responsibilities of a permanent resident. She merely came to acquire the education available and thereby improve her position in her own native country. Obviously, the Petitioner is quite content in having advanced from assistant professor at the University Putra Malaysia prior to obtaining her doctorate to associate professor and Deputy Dean of that university now. At all times that she was in the United States, her main objective was to personally benefit from this country. Any contribution the Petitioner made to the United States was incidental to this objective. That, to my mind, is totally insufficient to constitute a substantial voluntary connection. . . .

———————

Ibrahim v. Department of Homeland Security

United States District Court, Northern Dist. of California, No. C 06-00545 WHA
Jan. 14, 2014 (unsealed Apr. 15, 2014)

WILLIAM ALSUP, J.:

INTRODUCTION

In this terrorist-watchlist challenge, a nonimmigrant alien seeks relief after having been barred airplane-boarding privileges and after having been denied a visa to return to the United States. This order includes the findings of fact and conclusions of law following a five-day bench trial. Some but not all of the relief sought is granted. . . .

FINDINGS OF FACT

[An overview of the facts appears at p. 189, *supra*.]

Plaintiff . . .

5. Government counsel has conceded at trial that Dr. Ibrahim is not a threat to our national security. She does not pose (and has not posed) REDACTED This the government admits and this order finds. . . .

7. In November 2004,FBI Special Agent Kevin Michael Kelley, located in San Jose, nominated Dr. Ibrahim, who was then at Stanford, to various federal watchlists using the NCIC Violent Gang and Terrorist Organizations File Gang Member Entity Form ("VGTOF"). VGTO, also known as Violent Gang and Terrorist Organization, was an office within the FBI's National Crime Information Center ("NCIC"). VGTOF was a file within the FBI's NCIC.

Agent Kelley misunderstood the directions on the form and erroneously nominated Dr. Ibrahim to the TSA's no-fly list REDACTED He did not intend to do so. This was a mistake, he admitted at trial. He intended to nominate her to the REDACTED He checked the wrong boxes, filling out the form exactly the opposite way from the instructions on the form. He made this mistake even though the form stated, "It is recommended the subject NOT be entered into the following selected terrorist screening databases." An excerpt of Agent Kelley's nomination is provided below:

It is recommended the subject NOT be entered into the following selected terrorist screening databases

REDACTED	Consular Lookout and Support System (CLASS)
REDACTED	Interagency Border Information System (IBIS)
☐	TSA No Fly List
REDACTED	TSA Selectee List
REDACTED	TUSCAN
REDACTED	TACTICS

Figure 1. VGTOF Form (November 2004.)

Based on the way Agent Kelley checked the boxes on the form, plaintiff was placed on the no-fly list REDACTED So, the way in which plaintiff got on the no-fly list in the first place was human error by the FBI. Agent Kelley did not learn of this error until his deposition in September 2013. . . .

Events from January 2005 to March 2005

11. In early January 2005, Dr. Ibrahim planned to fly from San Francisco to Hawaii and then to Los Angeles and thence to Kuala Lumpur. Her plans were to attend a conference in Hawaii (sponsored by Stanford University) from January 3 to January 6 and to present her research findings at the conference.

12. On January 2, 2005, Dr. Ibrahim arrived at the San Francisco airport with her daughter, Rafeah, then fourteen. At the time, Dr. Ibrahim was still recovering from her hysterectomy surgery performed three months earlier and thus requested wheelchair assistance to the airport gate.

13. The trouble started when Dr. Ibrahim arrived at the United Airlines counter. The police were called by airline staff. She was handcuffed and arrested. She was escorted to a police car (while handcuffed) and transported to a holding cell by male police officers. There, a female police officer asked her if she had any weapons and attempted to remove her hiijab.

14. She was held for approximately two hours. Paramedics were called so that medication related to her hysterectomy surgery could be administered.

15. Eventually, an aviation security inspector with the Department of Homeland Security informed Dr. Ibrahim that she was released and her name had been removed from the no-fly list. The police were satisfied that there were insufficient grounds for making a criminal complaint against her. The trial record shows no evidence that would have justified a detention or arrest. She was told that she could fly to Hawaii the next day. She did, voluntarily. She was, however, given an unusual red boarding pass (in addition to her regular boarding pass) with "SSSS," meaning Secondary Security Screening Selection, printed on it.

16. Dr. Ibrahim flew to Hawaii and presented her research findings at the conference. From there, she flew to Los Angeles and then to Kuala Lumpur. That was in January 2005.

17. The next trouble came two months later. In March 2005, Dr. Ibrahim planned to visit the United States to meet with one of her Stanford thesis advisors and her friend, Professor Paulson, who was very ill. She was not permitted to board the flight to the United States. She was told her F-1 student visa had been revoked, which in fact it had been, as will be detailed below. The ticket cost was approximately one month's salary at the time. The record is unclear as to the extent to which she was able to get reimbursed. So, even though she had been told she was off the no-fly list, she was now being told that she could not come to the United States, regardless of how she traveled. She has never been permitted to return to the United States since.

Terrorist Screening Database and Related Watchlists

18. The government maintains a web of interlocking watchlists, all now centered on the Terrorist Screening Database ("TSDB"). This web and how they interlock are important to the relief sought and awarded herein. The present tense is used but the findings accurately describe the

procedures in place at the time in question (except as indicated otherwise).

19. The Terrorist Screening Center ("TSC") is a multi-agency organization administered by the FBI. The TSC is staffed by officials from various agencies, including the FBI, the Department of Homeland Security, and the Department of State. The TSC manages the Terrorist Screening Database. The TSC and TSDB were created after September 11 so that information about known and suspected terrorists could be more centralized and then exported as appropriate to various "customer databases" operated by other agencies and government entities. In this way, "the dots could be connected." Information in the TSDB is *not* classified, although a closely allied and separate database called the Terrorist Identities Datamart Environment ("TIDE") does contain classified information. (The predecessor to TIDE was called TIPOFF.) The National Counterterrorism Center ("NCTC"), a branch of the Office of the Director of National Intelligence, places classified substantive "derogatory" information supporting a nomination to the TSDB in TIDE. These terrorist watchlists, and others, provide information to the United States intelligence community, a coalition of 17 agencies and organizations within the Executive Branch, including the Office of the Director of National Intelligence and the FBI.

20. FBI agents and other government employees normally nominate individuals to the TSDB using a "reasonable suspicion standard," meaning articulable facts which, taken together with rational inferences, reasonably warrant the determination that an individual is known or suspected to be or has been engaged in conduct constituting, in preparation for, in aid of, or related to terrorism and terrorist activities. Unlike a standard codified by Congress or rendered by judicial decision, this "reasonable suspicion" standard was adopted by internal Executive Branch policy and practice. From 2004 to 2007, there was no uniform standard for TSDB nominations. Each agency promulgated its own nominating procedures for inclusion in the TSDB based on its interpretation of homeland security presidential directives and the memorandum of opinion that established the TSC. One such directive was Homeland Security Presidential Directive 6 ("HSPD-6") which stated, "[t]his directive shall be implemented in a manner consistent with the provisions of the Constitution and applicable laws, including those protecting the rights of all Americans". Agents now interpret this guideline, and others, as meaning that it would not be appropriate to

watchlist someone based upon their religion, religious practices, and any other First Amendment activity.

21. For each nominee, the TSDB calls out which particular watchlists the nominee should be on and which he or she should not be on. It is a box-check procedure, then computerized. There are several watchlists affected by the TSDB, namely:

- the no-fly list (TSA),
- the selectee list (TSA),
- Known and Suspected Terrorist File ("KSTF," previously known as the Violent Gang and Terrorist Organizations File), Consular Lookout and Support System ("CLASS," including CLASS-Visa and CLASS-Passport) (Department of State),
- TECS (not an acronym, but the successor of the Treasury Enforcement Communications System) (Department of Homeland Security), Interagency Border Inspection System ("IBIS") (Department of Homeland Security),
- TUSCAN (used by Canada), and
- TACTICS (used by Australia).

If nominated, designations in the TSDB are then exported to the nominated downstream customer watchlists operated by various government entities. For example, information in the TSDB (if selected) is sent to the Department of State for inclusion in CLASS-Visa or CLASS-Passport.

22. Due to Agent Kelley's mistake, Dr. Ibrahim was nominated to the no-fly REDACTED. She was placed in the TSDB and her information was exported to the no-fly list REDACTED Thus, when she arrived at the ticket counter, the airline (which has and had access to the no-fly list), was obligated to deny her boarding (and then called the police).

23. When persons are placed on the no-fly list or any other watchlist, they receive no formal notice of such placement and may never learn of such placement until, if ever, they attempt to board a plane or do any other act covered by the watchlist.

24. When an agency "encounters" an individual via a visa application, airport boarding, border entry, to take three examples, the agency official searches for the individual's identity on applicable watchlists. If there is a potential name match, the individual's name is forwarded to the TSC. The TSC, in turn, reviews the TSDB record and an appropriate counterterrorism response may be made.

Travel Redress Inquiry Program (Trip)

25. Under Section 44926(a) of Title 49 of the United States Code:

The Secretary of Homeland Security shall establish a timely and fair process for individuals who believe they have been delayed or prohibited from boarding a commercial aircraft because they were wrongly identified as a threat under the regimes utilized by the Transportation Security Administration, United States Customs and Border Protection, or any other office or component of the Department of Homeland Security.

Prior to 2007, individuals who claimed they were denied or delayed boarding or entry to the United States or repeatedly subjected to additional screening or inspection could submit a Passenger Identity Verification Form (PIVF) to the TSA. This program was succeeded by the DHS's TRIP process in 2007.

26. If DHS determines that the complainant is an exact or near match to an identity in the TSDB, the match is referred to the TSC's redress unit.

27. The TSC's redress unit reviews the information available to determine (1) whether the individual's status is an exact match to an identity in the TSDB; (2) if an exact match, whether the traveler should continue to be in the TSDB; and (3) if the traveler should continue to be in the TSDB, whether the traveler meets additional criteria for placement on the no-fly or selectee lists.

28. The TSC's redress unit does not undertake additional fieldwork in determining whether an individual was properly placed in the TSDB or customer databases. The review is based on existing records and may (or may not) include contacting the nominating agency to obtain any new derogatory information that supports a nomination. The TSC's redress unit then notifies DHS TRIP of any modification or removal of the individual's record.

29. A letter responding to the request for redress is eventually sent to the complainant. Dr. Ibrahim attempted to use this redress method and received a vague and inconclusive response, described below.

Department of State and Visa Procedure

30. A visa is permission for an alien, also known as a foreign national, to approach the borders of the United States and ask to enter.

There are several types of visas, based primarily on the purpose of the alien's travel to the United States.

31. The procedure for obtaining a visa is as follows. *First*, the alien applies for a visa by submitting a visa application to a consular officer. The consular officer then evaluates whether the individual is eligible for a visa and what type of visa he or she may be eligible to receive. *Second*, the applicant makes an appointment for a visa interview with a consular officer at the United States embassy or a consulate abroad. Consular officers are employees of the Department of State who are authorized to adjudicate visa applications overseas. *Third*, an interview is conducted. *Fourth*, after the interview, the consular officer grants or denies the application. Consular officers are required to refuse a visa application if the alien has failed to demonstrate eligibility for the visa under the Immigration and Nationality Act, including under 8 U.S.C. 1182.

32. In ruling on applications, consular officers review the CLASS database, maintained by the Department of State, for information that may inform the visa application and adjudication process. Information is entered into CLASS directly by the Department of State or indirectly from other agencies. For example, entries in the Department of Homeland Security's TECS database can be electronically transferred over to CLASS to inform the visa adjudication process. CLASS also obtains information from the TSDB.

33. If the consular officer determines that further information is needed or if there is insufficient information to make an adjudication, the consular officer may refuse an individual's visa application under 8 U.S.C. 1201(g), request further information from the applicant, and/or request a Security Advisory Opinion ("SAO") from the Department of State. A SAO request initiates an interagency review of information about the applicant available to the Department of State and other agencies, including classified intelligence in TIDE, to determine whether the alien is inadmissible under 8 U.S.C. 1182(a)(3)(A) or (B) or otherwise ineligible for a visa. If requested, a SAO opinion is rendered and the consular officer reviews the SAO opinion. The consular officer then decides whether to issue the visa or refuse the visa application.

34. Once a visa issues, if pertinent information comes to the attention of the Department of State that was not available to the consular officer at the time of issuance, an additional review of the alien's eligibility and admissibility may be conducted. Section 1201(i) states: "After the issuance of a visa or other documentation to any alien, the consular officer or the Secretary of State may at any time, in his

discretion, revoke such visa or other documentation . . . ." The visa may be "prudentially" revoked, thereby making the individual ineligible to approach the borders of the United States. Within the Department of State, such a revocation is called "prudential." Such a prudential revocation forces the alien to reapply for a new visa, so that a new evaluation of the applicant's eligibility and admissibility can be made. When an alien's visa is revoked, the alien is informed of his or her right to establish their qualification for a visa through a new visa application.

35. The visa office in the Department of State keeps "revocation files" that explain the basis for an entry in the CLASS database until the applicant reaches age ninety and has no visa application within the past ten years.

Plaintiff and the Watchlists

36. Dr. Ibrahim obtained a F-1 student visa to attend Stanford University for her Ph.D. for at least the duration of 2000 to 2005. . . .

39. In an e-mail dated January 3, 2005, between two officials in the coordination division of the visa office, one wrote (emphasis in original):

> As I mentioned to you, I have a stack of pending revocations that are based on VGTO entries. These revocations contain virtually no derogatory information. After a *long* and frustrating game of phone tag with INR, TSC, and Steve Naugle of the FBI's VGTO office, finally we're going to revoke them.
>
> Per my conversation with Steve, there is no practical way to determine what the basis of the investigation is for these applicants. The only way to do it would be to contact the case agent for each case individually to determine what the basis of the investigation is. Since we don't have the time to do that (and, in my experience, case agents don't call you back promptly, if at all), we will accept that the opening of an investigation itself is a prima facie indicator of potential ineligibility under 3(B) . . . .

40. A pending revocation for Dr. Ibrahim was in the above-referenced stack. (Again, VGTO referred to the FBI's Violent Gang and Terrorist Organization office; INR refers to the Department of State's Bureau of Intelligence and Research; and the term 3(B) referred to Section 212(a)(3)(B) of the Immigration and Nationality Act, 8 U.S.C. 1182(a)(3)(B).)

41. Dr. Ibrahim's F-1 student visa was revoked on January 31, 2005. The certificate of revocation stated: "subsequent to visa issuance, information has come to light indicating that the alien may be inadmissable to the United States and ineligible to receive a visa under section 212(a)(3)(B) of the Immigration and Nationality Act, such that the alien should reappear before a U.S. Consular Officer to establish his eligibility for a visa before being permitted to apply for entry to the United States". The trial record does not explain what "information" had come to light. After Dr. Ibrahim's visa was revoked, the Department of State entered a record into CLASS that would notify any consular officer adjudicating a future visa application submitted by Dr. Ibrahim that Dr. Ibrahim may be inadmissible under 8 U.S.C. 1182(a)(3)(B).

42. The revocation was pursuant to Section 212(a)(3)(B) of the Immigration and Nationality Act, 8 U.S.C. 1182(a)(3)(B). The revocation itself was on January 31, 2005, and Dr. Ibrahim learned of the revocation in March 2005.

43. In an e-mail dated February 8, 2005, between the chief of the consular section at the United States Embassy in Kuala Lumpur and an official in the coordination division of the visa office of the Department of State, the chief asked about a prudential visa revocation cable he had received concerning the events Dr. Ibrahim experienced in January 2005. The Department of State employee replied in e-mail stating:

> Paul asked me to respond to you on this case, as I handle revocations in VO/L/C. The short version is that this person's visa was revoked because there is law enforcement interest in her as a potential terrorist. This is sufficient to prudentially revoke a visa but doesn't constitute a finding of ineligibility. The idea is to revoke first and resolve the issues later in the context of a new visa application . . . . My guess based on past experience is that she's probably issuable. However, there's no way to be sure without putting her through the interagency process. I'll gin up the revocation. VO/L/C is the designation of the coordination division within the visa office.

44. After she tried unsuccessfully to return to the United States in March 2005, using what she thought was a valid student visa, a letter arrived for Dr. Ibrahim, dated April 2005, stating: "[t]he revocation of your visa does not necessarily indicate that you are ineligible to receive a U.S. visa in future [sic]. That determination can only be made at such time as you apply for a new visa. Should you choose to do so,

instructions can be found on the Embassy web site at http://malaysia.
usembassy.gov". . . .

46. In March 2005, Dr. Ibrahim filed a Passenger Identity
Verification Form (PIVF). . . .

50. In 2006, the government determined that Dr. Ibrahim did not
meet the reasonable suspicion standard. On September 18, 2006, Dr.
Ibrahim was REDACTED   The trial record, however, does not show
whether she was REDACTED

51. In a letter dated March 1, 2006, the TSA responded to Dr.
Ibrahim's PIVF submission as follows:

> The Transportation Security Administration (TSA) has received your
> Passenger Identity Verification Form (PIVF) and identity documentation. In
> response to your request, we have conducted a review of any applicable
> records in consultation with other federal agencies, as appropriate. Where it
> has been determined that a correction to records is warranted, these records
> have been modified to address any delay or denial of boarding that you may
> have experienced as a result of the watchlist screening process . . . . This
> letter constitutes TSA's final agency decision, which is reviewable by the
> United States Court of Appeals under 49 U.S.C. §46110. If you have any
> further questions, please call the TSA Contact Center Office of
> Transportation Security Redress (OTSR) toll-free at (866) 289-9673 or
> locally at (571) 227-2900, send an [e]-mail to TSA-
> ContactCenter@dhs.gov, or write to the following address . . . .

The response did not indicate Dr. Ibrahim's status with respect to the
TSDB and no-fly and selectee lists.

REDACTED . . . .

54. Dr. Ibrahim did not apply for a new visa from 2005 to 2009. In
2009, however, she applied for a visa to attend proceedings in this
action. On September 29, 2009, Dr. Ibrahim was interviewed at the
American Embassy in Kuala Lumpur for her visa application

REDACTED . . . .

59. The SAO [Security Advisory Opinion from the Department of
State requested by the consular officer] stated: "Information on this
applicant surfaced during the SAO review that would support a [Section]
212(a)(3)(B) inadmissibility finding. Post should refuse the case
accordingly. Since the Department reports all visa refusals under INA
section 212(a)(3)(B) to Congress, post should notify CA/VO/L/C when
the visa refusal is effected. There has been no request for an INA section
212(d)(3)(A) waiver at this time". (INA means Immigration and

Nationality Act.) Based on the SAO, the visa was denied. Dr. Ibrahim was thus not permitted to attend proceedings in this action or return to the United States.

60. On December 14, 2009, Dr. Ibrahim's visa application was denied. Dr. Ibrahim was given a letter by the consular officer informing her that the Department of State was unable to issue her a visa pursuant to Section 212(a)(3)(B). The consular officer wrote the word "(Terrorist)" on the form beside Section 212(a)(3)(B) to explain why she was deemed inadmissible. [She was not informed of her right to apply for a waiver.] . . .

65. In September 2013, Dr. Ibrahim submitted a visa application so that she could attend the trial on this matter. She attended a consular officer interview in October 2013. At the interview, she was asked to provide supplemental information via e-mail. Trial in this action began on December 2 and ended on December 6. As of December 6, Dr. Ibrahim had not received a response to her visa application. At trial, however, government counsel stated verbally that the visa had been denied. Plaintiff's counsel said that they had not been so aware and that Dr. Ibrahim had not been so notified.

Dr. Ibrahim Today

66. Dr. Ibrahim has been successful at the Universiti Putra Malaysia. She was selected as Deputy Dean in 2006 and Dean for the Faculty of Design and Architecture in 2011.

67. One grant that Dr. Ibrahim received accounted for 75% of the grant funding received for the entire faculty.

68. Due to her inability to travel to the United States, Dr. Ibrahim has resorted to collaborating with her United States colleagues via e-mail, Skype, and telephone.

69. Dr. Ibrahim desires to visit the United States to attend conferences, collaborate on projects, and visit venture capitalists.

70. Since 2005, Dr. Ibrahim has never been permitted to enter the United States. . . .

CONCLUSIONS OF LAW

Due Process

At long last, the government has conceded that plaintiff poses no threat to air safety or national security and should never have been placed on the no-fly list. She got there by human error within the FBI. This too is conceded. This was no minor human error but an error with palpable impact, leading to the humiliation, cuffing, and incarceration of an innocent and incapacitated air traveler. That it was human error may seem hard to accept — the FBI agent filled out the nomination form in a way *exactly* opposite from the instructions on the form, a bureaucratic analogy to a surgeon amputating the wrong digit — human error, yes, but of considerable consequence. Nonetheless, this order accepts the agent's testimony.

Since her erroneous placement on the no-fly list, plaintiff has endured a litany of troubles in getting back into the United States. Whether true or not, she reasonably suspects that those troubles are traceable to the original wrong that placed her on the no-fly list. Once derogatory information is posted to the TSDB, it can propagate extensively through the government's interlocking complex of databases, like a bad credit report that will never go away. As a post-deprivation remedy, therefore, due process requires, and this order requires, that the government remediate its wrong by cleansing and/or correcting all of its lists and records of the mistaken 2004 derogatory designation and by certifying that such cleansing and/or correction has been accurately done as to every single government watchlist and database. This will not implicate classified information in any way but will give plaintiff assurance that, going forward, her troubles in returning to the United States, if they continue, are unaffected by the original wrong.

The basic issue is what due process of law requires in these circumstances. The Supreme Court has stated that "[d]ue process . . . is a flexible concept that varies with the particular situation." *Zinermon v. Burch*, 494 U.S. 113, 127 (1990). To determine what process is constitutionally due, the Supreme Court in *Mathews v. Eldridge*, 424 U.S. 319, 335 (1976), set forth the following three-factor test:

> First, the private interest that will be affected by the official action; second, the risk of an erroneous deprivation of such interest through the procedures

used, and the probable value, if any, of additional or substitute procedural safeguards; and finally, the Government's interest.

Due process provides heightened protection against government interference when certain fundamental rights and liberty interests are involved. *Washington v. Glucksberg*, 521 U.S. 702,720 (1997).

With respect to Dr. Ibrahim, the private interests at stake in her 2005 deprivations were the right to travel, *Kent v. Dulles*, 357 U.S. 116, 125 (1958), and the right to be free from incarceration, *Hamdi v. Rumsfeld*, 542 U.S. 507, 529 (2004), and from the stigma and humiliation of a public denial of boarding and incarceration, *Paul v. Davis*, 424 U.S. 693, 701, 711 (1976), any one of which would be sufficient and all three of which apply on this record.

With respect to the government's interest, all would surely agree that our government must and should track terrorists who pose a threat to America — not just to its air travel — but to any aspect of our national security. In this connection, however, the government concedes that Dr. Ibrahim herself poses no such threat (nor did she in 2005).

The final *Mathews* factor is the risk of an erroneous deprivation through the procedures used and the probable value, if any, of additional or substitute procedural safeguards. FBI Agent Kelley made a plain, old-fashioned, monumental error in filling out the VGTOF nomination form for Dr. Ibrahim. He checked the boxes *in exactly the opposite way* from the instructions on the form, thus nominating Dr. Ibrahim to the no-fly list (against his intention). This was the start of all problems in Dr. Ibrahim's case. Surprisingly, Agent Kelley first learned of this mistake eight years later at his deposition.

Significantly, therefore, our case involves a conceded, proven, undeniable, and serious error by the government — not merely a risk of error. Consequently, this order holds that due process entitles Dr. Ibrahim to a correction in the government's records to prevent the 2004 error from further propagating through the various agency databases and from causing further injury to Dr. Ibrahim. By this order, all defendants shall specifically and thoroughly query the databases maintained by them, such as the TSDB, TIDE, CLASS, KSTF, TECS, IBIS, TUSCAN, TACTICS, and the no-fly and selectee lists, and to remove all references to the designations made by the defective 2004 nomination form or, if left in place, to add a correction in the same paragraph that the designations were erroneous and should not be relied upon for any purpose. To be clear, no agency should even rely on Agent Kelley's actual unexpressed intention to nominate to certain lists in 2004, for the form instructions were not properly followed. The designations in the November 2004 form should be disregarded for all purposes. The government is always free to make a new nomination doing it the right way. A deadline will be set for defendants to file declarations under oath attesting to compliance.

It is perhaps true that the error has already been corrected, at least in part, but there is reason to doubt that the error and all of its echoes have been traced and cleansed from all interlocking databases. A correction in the TSDB REDACTED would *not* have automatically expunged incorrect data previously exported from the TSDB REDACTED to the customer agency databases. For example, the Department of State separately maintains its CLASS database. If the bad information was transferred from the TSDB REDACTED to CLASS in the 2004 period, then that bad information may remain there and may linger on there notwithstanding a correction in the TSDB REDACTED. This order will require defendants to trace through each agency database employing the TSDB REDACTED and make sure the correction or deletion has actually been made.

This order finds that suspicious adverse effects continued to haunt Dr. Ibrahim in 2005 and 2006, even though the government claims to have learned of and corrected the mistake. For example, after her name was removed from the no-fly list, the next day, Dr. Ibrahim was issued a bright red "SSSS" pass. Less than a month after she was removed from the no-fly list, her visa was "prudentially" revoked. In March 2005, she was not permitted to fly to the United States. Her daughter was not allowed to fly to the United States even to attend this trial despite the fact that her daughter is a United States citizen. After so much gnashing of teeth and so much on-the-list-off-the-list machinations, the government is ordered to provide the foregoing relief to remediate its wrong. If the government has already cleansed its records, then no harm will be done in making sure again and so certifying to the Court.

With respect to the government's TRIP program, which does provide a measure of post-deprivation relief, this order holds that it is inadequate, at least on this record. After Dr. Ibrahim was denied boarding on January 2, 2005, and denied boarding to return in March 2005, she submitted a Passenger Identity Verification Form (PIVF), a program that eventually morphed into the TRIP program by 2007. Approximately one year later, the TSA responded to her PIVF form with the following vague response:

> Where it has been determined that a correction to records is warranted, these records have been modified to address any delay or denial of boarding that you may have experienced as a result of the watchlist screening process.

Noticeably missing from the response to Dr. Ibrahim was whether there had been errors in her files and whether all errors in customer databases had been corrected. This vague response fell short of providing any assurance to Dr. Ibrahim — who the government concedes is not a national security threat and was the victim of concrete, reviewable adverse government action caused by government error — that the mistake had been traced down in all its forms and venues and corrected.

This order provides only a post-deprivation remedy, to be sure, but post-deprivation remedies are efficacious, especially where, as here, it would be impractical and harmful to national security to routinely provide a pre-deprivation opportunity to be heard of the broad and universal type urged by plaintiff's counsel. *Haig v. Agee*, 453 U.S. 280, 309-10 (1981). Such advance notice to all nominees would aid terrorists in their plans to bomb and kill Americans. Moreover, at the time of listing, the government would have no way of knowing which nonimmigrant aliens living abroad would enjoy standing under *Ibrahim II*. Instead, any remedy must await the time when, if ever, concrete, reviewable adverse action is taken against the nominee.

Put differently, until concrete, reviewable adverse action occurs against a nominee, the Executive Branch must be free to maintain its watchlists in secret, just as federal agents must be able to maintain in secret its investigations into organized crime, drug trafficking organizations, prostitution, child-pornography rings, and so forth. To publicize such investigative details would ruin them. Once concrete, reviewable adverse action is taken against a target, then there is and will be time enough to determine what post-deprivation process is due the individual affected. In this connection, since the reasonable suspicion standard is an internal guideline used within the Executive Branch for watchlisting and not imposed by statute (or by specific judicial holding), the Executive Branch is free to modify its own standard as needed by exception, even if the exception is cloaked in state secrets. Any other rule requiring reviewability before concrete adverse action would be manifestly unworkable.[*]

Given the Kafkaesque REDACTED treatment imposed on Dr. Ibrahim, the government is further ordered expressly to tell Dr. Ibrahim REDACTED (always subject, of course, to future developments and evidence that might REDACTED). This relief is appropriate and warranted because of the confusion generated by the government's own mistake and the very real misapprehension on her part that the later visa denials are traceable to her erroneous 2004 placement on the no-fly list, suggesting (reasonably from her viewpoint) that she somehow remains on the no-fly list.

It is true, as the government asserts as part of its ripeness position, that she cannot fly to the United States without a visa, but she is entitled to try to solve one hurdle at a time and perhaps the day will come when all hurdles are cleared and she can fly back to our country. The government's legitimate interest in keeping secret the composition of the no-fly list should yield, on the facts of this case, to a particularized remedy isolated by this order only to someone even the government concludes poses no threat to the United States. Everyone else in this case knows it. As a matter of remedy, she should be told that REDACTED.

*   *   *

---

[*] In the instant case, the nomination in 2004 to the no-fly list was conceded at trial to have been a mistake. In this sense, this is an easier case to resolve. Harder no-fly cases surely exist. For example, the government uses "derogatory" information to place individuals on the no-fly list. When an individual is refused boarding, does he or she have a right to know the specific information that led to the listing? Certainly in some (but not all) cases, providing the specifics would reveal sources and methods used in our counterterrorism defense program and disclosure would unreasonably jeopardize our national security. Possibly, instead, a general summary might provide a degree of due process, allowing the nominee an opportunity to refute the charge. Or, agents might interview the nominee in such a way as to address the points of concern without revealing the specifics. Possibly (or possibly not), even that much process would betray our defense systems to our enemies. This order need not and does not reach this tougher, broader issue, for, again, the listing of Dr. Ibrahim was concededly based on human error. Revealing this error could not and has not betrayed any worthwhile methods or sources.

No relief granted herein implicates state secrets. The foregoing relief does nothing more than order the government to delete or to correct in all its agency systems any ongoing effects of its own admitted inexcusable error and reconfirm what she was told in 2005, REDACTED The government has no defense, classified or not, against their conceded error in 2004. In complying with this relief, the government will not have to reveal any classified information. It merely has to certify that it has cleansed its record of its own error and reveal to plaintiff her current no-fly list status, a non-classified item that the Department of Homeland Security itself revealed to Dr. Ibrahim in 2005.

In sum, after what our government has done by error to Dr. Ibrahim, this order holds that she is entitled to the post-deprivation remedy described above, that the government's post-deprivation administrative remedies fall far short of such relief, and to deny her such relief would deprive her of due process of law. This order will supply the due process that otherwise has been denied to plaintiff.

The Visa Issues

In December 2009, Dr. Ibrahim was informed that her visa application was denied pursuant to Section 212(a)(3)(B) of the Immigration and Nationality Act, 8 U.S.C. 1182(a)(3)(B). The consular officer wrote the word "(Terrorist)" on the denial form. It is undisputed, moreover, that the visa refusal form did not have a check mark next to the box stating, "You are eligible to apply for a waiver on the ground(s) of ineligibility". It is also undisputed that the Immigration and Naturalization Act provides that nonimmigrant visa applicants may apply for a waiver of many of the grounds of visa ineligibility under 8 U.S.C. 1182(a).

The Court has REDACTED, that led to the visa denials. REDACTED Therefore, under the state secrets privilege, any challenge to the visa denials in 2009 and 2013 must be denied. *Mohamed v. Jeppesen Dataplan, Inc.*, 614 F.3d 1070, 1080, 1086-89 (9th Cir. 2010) (en banc). In any event, denial of visas may *not* be reviewed by district courts. *Kleindienst v. Mandel*, 408 U.S. 2 753, 769-70 (1972).

Nonetheless, this order grants other limited relief as follows. The government must inform Dr. Ibrahim of the specific subsection of Section 212(a)(3)(B) that rendered her ineligible for a visa in 2009 and 2013. This is pursuant to the on-point holding of *Din v. Kerry*, 718 F.3d 856, 863 (9th Cir. 2013). As quoted above in the findings, subpart B has nine subsections and is lengthy. The pertinent subsections should have been identified to plaintiff, according to *Din*. Doing so would have assisted her in understanding the particular provision of law that barred her entry. Merely citing to a lengthy collection of grounds collected together under the heading "Terrorist activities" will not do under *Din*. Under the law of our circuit, this precise error is reviewable and relief is warranted by the record.

One might wonder why, if Dr. Ibrahim herself is concededly not a threat to our national security, the government would find her inadmissible under the Act. In this connection, please remember that the Act includes nine ineligible categories. Some of them go beyond whether the applicant herself poses a national security threat.

Keeping in mind the government's concession that Dr. Ibrahim herself is not a threat to the United States, this order further holds that the consular officer erred in indicating that Dr. Ibrahim was ineligible to *apply* for a waiver of the ground(s) for ineligibility. . . .

_____

[NSL p. 694, CTL p. 307. Insert after Note 4.]

5. *The Paradigm Case?* *Ibrahim* provides a chilling case study for each problem identified in the foregoing Notes. First, notwithstanding the nominal "reasonable suspicion" standard for watch listing, Ibrahim was listed by error, after which the error propagated to other lists without any further review. In her case, the false positive arose from human error and not an over-inclusion under the standard. But had the standard been applied correctly, can you confidently say that she would not have been listed?

The initial listing was for the purpose of screening airline passengers, but the propagation of the listing soon saw it used almost casually to revoke Dr. Ibrahim's visa and then deny her renewal application, apparently because running down the case agent to confirm the cause of the listing was just be too much trouble. One can argue that this is not mission creep, as visa control *is* one of the missions of the related lists, yet the initial listing was based on a different criterion than those applied to visa determinations.

The front-end corrective for Ibrahim's case might involve independent review or confirmation of the reason for the listing, if not initially, then when the list is used for a purpose other than the original no-fly decision. These added checks could have intercepted the original human error, although it would still have taken some conscientious human initiative to correct it once it left the original agent's hands. But each check would also add time and expense to the listing process.

    6. *The Process Due?* The back-end corrective for Dr. Ibrahim's case was the TRIP program in the first instance. Was that an effective process (as measured by its potential for correction rather than just by the result in Dr. Ibrahim's case)?

    Clearly, the only effective back-end process *for Dr. Ibrahim* was judicial review of her due process claim. But such a claim requires a threshold constitutionally protected interest. In *Gilmore*, the Ninth Circuit held that there was no fundamental right to travel by airplane (or by the most convenient mode of transportation), and the Supreme Court has held that government-imposed "stigma" alone is not enough to trigger procedural due process protections without some change in legal status. *Paul v. Davis,*424 U.S. 693 (1976). *See Latif v. Holder*, No. 3:10-CV-00750-BR, 2014 WL 2871346 (D. Ore. June 24, 2014) ("Although placement on the No-Fly List carries with it the significant stigma of being a suspected terrorist and Defendants do not contest the fact that the public disclosure involved may be sufficient to satisfy the stigma-plus test, the Court notes the limited nature of the public disclosure in this case mitigates Plaintiffs' claims of injury to their reputations.").

    So how was Dr. Ibrahim different? One answer is that Gilmore was a domestic air traveler; Dr. Ibrahim was an international traveler without any convenient alternative to air travel. *See Tarhuni v. Holder*, No. 3:13-cv-00001-BR, 2014 WL 1269655 (D. Ore. Mar. 26, 2014) (right to international air travel is protected when air travel is only practical means of passenger travel); *Latif v. Holder*, 969 F. Supp. 2d 1293 (D. Ore. 2013) (burden on international travel is greater than on interstate travel). Another is that the government did not "just" stigmatize Dr. Ibrahim, it also prevented her from flying and then revoked her visa. *Latif,* 969 F. Supp. 2d at 1304. Moreover, these actions cost her money and altered her job status.

    Once the court found a constitutionally protected liberty interest, it then balanced the private interest and the government interest in light of the risk of erroneous deprivation from the existing procedures afforded Dr. Ibrahim by the government. *See Matthews v. Eldridge*, 424 U.S. 319 (1976). As the court noted, her case presented an unusually clear example of that risk, given the case agent's admission of a straightforward error. On the other hand, if this was human error, does it really prove that *the procedures* pose too great a risk of error, or just that sloppy bureaucrats make occasional errors even under good procedures? And if the availability of judicial review is part of the process, is the total package enough to guard against too many errors? *See Tarhuni*, 2014 WL 1269655, at *15 (finding, on motion to dismiss, that plaintiff had "plausibly alleged the procedures in the DHS TRIP process and subsequent judicial review do not strike the proper balance under *Mathews* and, therefore, violate due process").

The 2014 decision in *Latif* also noted the apparent inefficacy of the TRIP regime for correcting No-Fly listings, citing *Ibrahim*. But it added this:

> [T]he DHS TRIP process suffers from an even more fundamental deficiency. As noted, the reasonable suspicion standard used to accept nominations to the TSDB is a low evidentiary threshold. This low standard is particularly significant in light of Defendants' refusal to reveal whether travelers who have been denied boarding and who submit DHS TRIP inquiries are on the No–Fly List and, if they are on the List, to provide the travelers with reasons for their inclusion on the List. "Without knowledge of a charge, even simple factual errors may go uncorrected despite potentially easy, ready, and persuasive explanations." *Al Haramain Islamic Found., Inc. v. United States Dep't of Treasury*, 686 F.3d 965, 982 (9th Cir. 2012).
>
> The availability of judicial review does little to cure this risk of error. While judicial review provides an independent examination of the existing administrative record, that review is of [sic] the same one-sided and potentially insufficient administrative record that TSC relied on in its listing decision without any additional meaningful opportunity for the aggrieved traveler to submit evidence intelligently in order to correct anticipated errors in the record. Moreover, judicial review only extends to whether the government reasonably determined the traveler meets the minimum substantive derogatory criteria; i.e., the reasonable suspicion standard. Thus, the fundamental flaw at the administrative-review stage (the combination of a one-sided record and a low evidentiary standard) carries over to the judicial-review stage.

2014 WL 2871346, at *15.

7. *The Remedy Due?* In *Ibrahim*, the remedy was straightforward and dictated by the very specific human error that cascaded through the watchlisting system: purging the error. In *Latif*, the court was more ambitious:

Because due process requires Defendants to provide Plaintiffs (who have all been denied boarding flights and who have submitted DHS TRIP inquiries without success) with notice regarding their status on the No–Fly List and the reasons for placement on that List, it follows that such notice must be reasonably calculated to permit each Plaintiff to submit evidence relevant to the reasons for their respective inclusions on the No–Fly List. In addition, Defendants must include any responsive evidence that Plaintiffs submit in the record to be considered at both the administrative and judicial stages of review. As noted, such procedures could include, but are not limited to, the procedures identified by the Ninth Circuit in *Al Haramain*; that is, Defendants may choose to provide Plaintiffs with unclassified summaries of the reasons for their respective placement on the No–Fly List or disclose the classified reasons to properly-cleared counsel.

Although this Court cannot foreclose the possibility that in some cases such disclosures may be limited or withheld altogether because any such disclosure would create an undue risk to national security, Defendants must make such a determination on a case-by-case basis including consideration of, at a minimum, the factors outlined in *Al Haramain*; i.e., (1) the nature and extent of the classified information, (2) the nature and extent of the threat to national security, and (3) the possible avenues available to allow the Plaintiff to respond more effectively to the charges. *See Al Haramain*, 686 F.3d at 984. Such a determination must be reviewable by the relevant court.

Latif, 2014 WL 2871346, at *24. What other procedural remedies might be better or sufficient to reduce the risk of error?

_____

[NSL p. 720, CTL p. 333. Insert at end of Note 5.]

More recently the Fifth Circuit Court of Appeals held itself bound by *Verdugo* to reject a Fourth Amendment claim based on the shooting of a Mexican national who was located on the Mexican side of the U.S.-Mexico border by a U.S. Border Patrol agent who was standing on the U.S. side. The court acknowledged the "practical necessities" caveat and *Boumediene*, but concluded:

[W]e cannot ignore a decision from the Supreme Court unless directed to do so by the Court itself. While the *Boumediene* Court appears to repudiate the formalistic reasoning of *Verdugo-Urquidez*'s sufficient connections test, courts have continued to rely on the sufficient connections test and its related interpretation of the Fourth Amendment text. Other circuits have relied on *Verdugo-Urquidez*'s interpretation to limit the Fourth Amendment's extraterritorial effect. [*Hernandez v. United States*, No. 11-50792, 2014 WL 2932598, at *11 (5th Cir. June 30, 2014).]

Judge Dennis agreed with the plaintiffs that *Boumediene* had repudiated *Verdugo*'s formalistic analysis, but concurred in the judgment "out of concern for pragmatic and political questions rather than on a formal classification of the litigants involved." *Id.* at *25.

However, the court went on to find that the Fifth Amendment was different, as applied (using the *Boumediene* factors) to the cross-border shooting by a U.S. agent.

> The Fourth Amendment protects against unreasonable searches and seizures, while, in this context, the Fifth Amendment protects against arbitrary conduct that shocks the conscience. The level of egregiousness required to satisfy the latter standard militates against protecting conduct that reaches it. We abstained from placing Fourth Amendment limits on actions across the border in part to allow officials to preserve our national interest in self-protection. A reasonableness limitation would have injected uncertainty into the government's decision-making process, perhaps resulting in adverse consequences for U.S. actions abroad. That interest, however, plays no role in determining whether an alien is entitled to protection against arbitrary, conscience-shocking conduct across the border. This principle protecting individuals from arbitrary conduct is consistent with those our government has recognized internationally, and applying it here would hardly cause friction with the host government. . . .
>
> Because Agent Mesa was inside our territory when he allegedly acted unconstitutionally, the United States, like in *Boumediene*, "is, for all practical purposes, answerable to no other sovereign for its acts." If the Constitution does not apply here, the only check on unlawful conduct would be that which the Executive Branch applies. Indeed, a strict territorial approach would allow agents to move in and out of constitutional strictures, creating zones of lawlessness. [*Id.* at *16.]

Refusing to create a "zone of lawlessness" at the border, the court allowed a *Bivens* challenge based on the Fifth Amendment. Judge DeMoss dissented from the panel's Fifth Amendment holding, arguing that the United States' relationship with Mexico bears no resemblance whatsoever to its relationship with Guantánamo, and that "the Fifth Amendment does not protect a non-citizen with no connections to the United States who suffered an injury in Mexico where the United States has no formal control or de facto sovereignty." *Id.* at *26 (DeMoss, J., concurring in part and dissenting in part).

[NSL p. 810, CTL p. 424. Insert after *Rasul v. Myers*.]

Al-Zahrani v. Rodriguez

United States Court of Appeals, District of Columbia Circuit, Feb. 21, 2012
669 F.3d 315

[Relatives of two non-citizens who died while detained as "enemy combatants" at Guantánamo Bay brought suit seeking damages arising from the alleged mistreatment and eventual death of the detainees. In its earlier decision in *Rasul v. Myers*, 563 F.3d 527 (D.C. Cir. 2009) (per curiam) (*Rasul II*), the Court of Appeals held that Guantánamo detainees could not pursue damages claims for constitutional violations against federal officials because (1) no clearly established law existed with respect to the detainees' constitutional rights (and so the defendants were entitled to qualified immunity), and, in any event, (2) "special factors" counseled hesitation with respect to recognizing a *Bivens* remedy for Guantánamo detainees. In another earlier decision, *Ali v. Rumsfeld*, 649 F.3d 762 (D.C. Cir. 2011), the Court of Appeals likewise concluded that Guantánamo detainees could not pursue claims under the Alien Tort Statute, 28 U.S.C. §1350. The district court relied on these decisions in dismissing the plaintiffs' claims. In the following opinion, the Court of Appeals affirmed, albeit for different — and broader — reasons.]

SENTELLE, Chief Judge: . . .

Background

. . . Beginning in January of 2002, Yasser Al-Zahrani, Jr., a citizen of Saudi Arabia, and Salah Ali Abdullah Ahmed Al-Salami, Jr., a citizen of Yemen, were detained at the United States military base at Guantanamo Bay, Cuba, as "enemy combatants." In 2004, under the then-current procedure of the United States military, [CSRTs] reviewed the detention of the two and confirmed the earlier determination that both detainees were enemy combatants. On June 10 of 2006, both men, along with a third detainee, died. Although the cause of death is the subject of dispute in the current litigation, a Naval Criminal Investigative Service report concluded that the deaths were the result of suicide by hanging.

On January 7, 2009, the plaintiffs, as fathers of the two named decedents, filed an action against the United States, twenty-four named, current, or former officials of the United States, and one hundred unnamed "John Doe" officials of the United States, seeking money damages relating to the deaths of the two detainees and alleging that the defendants had subjected the decedents to torture, arbitrary detention, and ultimately, wrongful death. The defendants moved for the dismissal of plaintiffs' by-then amended complaint. The district court dismissed the complaint pursuant to Rule 12(b)(6) of the Federal Rules of Civil Procedure for failure to state a claim upon which relief could be granted.

For the reasons more fully set forth below, we affirm the judgment of dismissal, although we further hold that the dismissal is for a lack of jurisdiction rather than the failure to state a claim for relief.

Analysis

. . . Because a federal court without jurisdiction cannot perform a law-declaring function in a controversy, "the Supreme Court [has] held 'that Article III jurisdiction is always an antecedent question' to be answered prior to any merits inquiry." *Public Citizen v. U.S. District Court for the District of Columbia*, 486 F.3d 1342, 1346 (D.C. Cir. 2007) (quoting *Steel Co. v. Citizens for a Better Env't*, 523 U.S. 83, 101 (1998)). Therefore, rather than proceed to weigh the adequacy of the complaint to state a claim, as did the District Court, we first examine the jurisdiction of the courts to entertain plaintiffs' claims and find that jurisdiction wanting.

In October of 2006, Congress enacted the Military Commissions Act. Section 7 of the MCA included an amendment to the habeas corpus statute. The amended statute reads:

> (1) No court, justice, or judge shall have jurisdiction to hear or consider an application for a writ of habeas corpus filed by or on behalf of an alien detained by the United States who has been determined by the United States to have been properly detained as an enemy combatant or is awaiting such determination.
>
> (2) Except as provided in [section 1005(e)(2) and (e)(3) of the Detainee Treatment Act of 2005], no court, justice, or judge shall have jurisdiction to hear or consider any other action against the United States or

its agents relating to any aspect of the detention, transfer, treatment, trial, or conditions of confinement of an alien who is or was detained by the United States and has been determined by the United States to have been properly detained as an enemy combatant or is awaiting such determination.

28 U.S.C. §2241(e)(1) and (2).

The present litigation rather plainly constitutes an action other than habeas corpus brought against the United States and its agents relating to "aspect[s] of the detention . . . treatment . . . [and] conditions of confinement of an alien" as described in the MCA. Therefore, as the District Court noted, this action is excluded from the jurisdiction of this court by the "plain language" of an Act of Congress. This ends the litigation and requires that we affirm the dismissal of the action.

. . . It is true that the Supreme Court, in its review of our decision in *Boumediene*, found §7 of the MCA to be constitutionally defective. *Boumediene v. Bush*, 553 U.S. 723, 787-92 (2008). However, the *Boumediene* appeal involved a decision applying the first subsection of §7 governing and barring the hearing of applications for writs of habeas corpus filed by detained aliens. . . . Subsection 2 of the MCA, which governs and bars the present litigation, has no effect on habeas jurisdiction. The Suspension Clause is not relevant and does not affect the constitutionality of the statute as applied in "treatment" cases [such as this one]. . . .

Appellants argue that §2241(e)(2)'s jurisdictional bar is unconstitutional because it fails to provide a proper remedy for violations of their constitutional rights. But the only remedy they seek is money damages, and, as the government rightly argues, such remedies are not constitutionally required. The Supreme Court has made this eminently clear in its jurisprudence finding certain of such claims barred by common law or statutory immunities, and applying its "special factors" analysis in preclusion of *Bivens* claims. Further, the Court applies that analysis to preclude *Bivens* claims even in cases such as the present one, where damages are the sole remedy by which the rights of plaintiffs and their decedents might be vindicated. For example, in *United States v. Stanley*, the Court refused to create a *Bivens* cause of action for a military serviceman who had been secretly administered doses of LSD; in doing so, the Court noted that it was "irrelevant to [the analysis] whether the laws currently on the books afford Stanley . . . an 'adequate' federal remedy for his injuries." 483 U.S. 669, 683 (1987). As we have recently said, "Not every violation of a right yields a remedy, even when the right is constitutional." *Kiyemba v. Obama*, 555 F.3d 1022, 1027 (D.C. Cir. 2009), *reinstated as amended by Kiyemba v. Obama*, 605 F.3d 1046 (D.C. Cir. 2010) [(per curiam)]. In light of this, we see no basis on which to invalidate Congress's decision to foreclose such claims as plaintiffs'.

Conclusion

. . . [W]e hold that 28 U.S.C. §2241(e)(2) deprives this court of jurisdiction over appellants' claims. We further hold that the Supreme Court did not declare §2241(e)(2) unconstitutional in *Boumediene* and the provision retains vitality to bar those claims. We therefore conclude that the decision of the District Court dismissing the claims should be affirmed, although for a lack of jurisdiction under Rule 12(b)(1) rather than for failure to state a claim under Rule 12(b)(6).

———————

[NSL p. 810, CTL p. 424. Insert after Note 2.]

3. *Jurisdiction-Stripping and Bivens Claims. Al-Zahrani* holds that Congress validly took away federal jurisdiction over *Bivens* suits for damages by former Guantánamo detainees because, unlike the habeas remedy at issue in *Boumediene v. Bush*, 553 U.S. 723 (2008), "such remedies are not constitutionally required." Two years later, the D.C. Circuit extended *Al-Zahrani* to *Bivens* suits by former detainees who had *won* their habeas petitions. *See Al Janko v. Gates*, 741 F.3d 136 (D.C. Cir. 2014). Although the Supreme Court has never identified a case in which the Constitution *does* require a damages remedy for a violation of a specific constitutional provision, it has never expressly forsworn such a possibility, either. Indeed, it has repeatedly alluded to the "'serious constitutional question' that would arise if a federal statute were construed to deny any judicial forum for a colorable constitutional claim," *Webster v. Doe*, 486 U.S. 592, 603 (1988), as the D.C. Circuit construes the MCA to do in *Al-Zahrani* and *Al Janko*. Given that, should the D.C. Circuit have done more to explain why the MCA validly divested the courts of jurisdiction? More fundamentally, why didn't *Al-Zahrani* simply rely on *Rasul II*, which declined to infer a *Bivens* remedy in a suit brought by former Guantánamo detainees?

———————

[NSL p. 876, CTL p. 490. Insert after Note 5.]

National Defense Authorization Act for Fiscal Year 2012

Pub. L. No. 112–81, 125 Stat. 1298, 1562-1564 (2011)

§1021. Affirmation of Authority of the Armed Forces of the United States to Detain Covered Persons Pursuant to the Authorization for Use of Military Force.

(a) In General. — Congress affirms that the authority of the President to use all necessary and appropriate force pursuant to the Authorization for Use of Military Force (Public Law 107–40; 50 U.S.C. 1541 note) includes the authority for the Armed Forces of the United States to detain covered persons (as defined in subsection (b)) pending disposition under the law of war.

(b) Covered Persons. — A covered person under this section is any person as follows:

(1) A person who planned, authorized, committed, or aided the terrorist attacks that occurred on September 11, 2001, or harbored those responsible for those attacks.

(2) A person who was a part of or substantially supported al-Qaeda, the Taliban, or associated forces that are engaged in hostilities against the United States or its coalition partners, including any person who has committed a belligerent act or has directly supported such hostilities in aid of such enemy forces.

(c) Disposition under Law of War. — The disposition of a person under the law of war as described in subsection (a) may include the following:

(1) Detention under the law of war without trial until the end of the hostilities authorized by the Authorization for Use of Military Force.

(2) Trial under chapter 47A of title 10, United States Code (as amended by the Military Commissions Act of 2009).

(3) Transfer for trial by an alternative court or competent tribunal having lawful jurisdiction.

(4) Transfer to the custody or control of the person's country of origin, any other foreign country, or any other foreign entity.

(d) Construction. — Nothing in this section is intended to limit or expand the authority of the President or the scope of the Authorization for Use of Military Force.

(e) Authorities. — Nothing in this section shall be construed to affect existing law or authorities relating to the detention of United States citizens, lawful resident aliens of the United States, or any other persons who are captured or arrested in the United States. . . .

§1022. Military Custody for Foreign Al-qaeda Terrorists.

(a) Custody Pending Disposition under Law of War. —

(1) In General. — Except as provided in paragraph (4), the Armed Forces of the United States shall hold a person described in paragraph (2) who is captured in the course of hostilities authorized by the Authorization for Use of Military Force (Public Law 107–40) in military custody pending disposition under the law of war.

(2) Covered Persons. — The requirement in paragraph (1) shall apply to any person whose detention is authorized under section 1021 who is determined —

(A) to be a member of, or part of, al-Qaeda or an associated force that acts in coordination with or pursuant to the direction of al-Qaeda; and

(B) to have participated in the course of planning or carrying out an attack or attempted attack against the United States or its coalition partners.

(3) Disposition under Law of War. — For purposes of this subsection, the disposition of a person under the law of war has the meaning given in section 1021(c) . . . .

(4) Waiver for National Security. — The President may waive the requirement of paragraph (1) if the President submits to Congress a certification in writing that such a waiver is in the national security interests of the United States.

(b) Applicability to United States Citizens and Lawful Resident Aliens. —

(1) United States Citizens. — The requirement to detain a person in military custody under this section does not extend to citizens of the United States.

(2) Lawful Resident Aliens. — The requirement to detain a person in military custody under this section does not extend to a lawful resident alien of the United States on the basis of conduct

taking place within the United States, except to the extent permitted by the Constitution of the United States.

(c) Implementation Procedures. — ...

(2) ...

(B) ... [T]he requirement for military custody under subsection (a)(1) does not require the interruption of ongoing surveillance or intelligence gathering with regard to persons not already in the custody or control of the United States.

(C) ... [A] determination under subsection (a)(2) is not required to be implemented until after the conclusion of an interrogation which is ongoing at the time the determination is made and does not require the interruption of any such ongoing interrogation. ...

(d) Authorities. — Nothing in this section shall be construed to affect the existing criminal enforcement and national security authorities of the Federal Bureau of Investigation or any other domestic law enforcement agency with regard to a covered person, regardless whether such covered person is held in military custody. ...

Statement by the President on H.R. 1540
Dec. 31, 2011

Today I have signed into law H.R. 1540, the "National Defense Authorization Act for Fiscal Year 2012." ...

... I have signed this bill despite having serious reservations with certain provisions that regulate the detention, interrogation, and prosecution of suspected terrorists. ...

Section 1021 affirms the executive branch's authority to detain persons covered by the 2001 Authorization for Use of Military Force (AUMF) (Public Law 107-40; 50 U.S.C. 1541 note). This section breaks no new ground and is unnecessary. The authority it describes was included in the 2001 AUMF, as recognized by the Supreme Court and confirmed through lower court decisions since then. ... I want to clarify that my Administration will not authorize the indefinite military detention without trial of American citizens. ...

Section 1022 seeks to require military custody for a narrow category of non-citizen detainees who are "captured in the course of hostilities authorized by the Authorization for Use of Military Force." This section is ill-conceived and will do nothing to improve the security of the United

States. The executive branch already has the authority to detain in military custody those members of al-Qa'ida who are captured in the course of hostilities authorized by the AUMF, and as Commander in Chief I have directed the military to do so where appropriate. I reject any approach that would mandate military custody where law enforcement provides the best method of incapacitating a terrorist threat. While section 1022 is unnecessary and has the potential to create uncertainty, I have signed the bill because I believe that this section can be interpreted and applied in a manner that avoids undue harm to our current operations. . . .

. . . [U]nder no circumstances will my Administration accept or adhere to a rigid across-the-board requirement for military detention. . . .

Barack Obama

———————

Hedges v. Obama

United States Court of Appeals, Second Circuit, July 17, 2013
724 F.3d 170, *cert. denied*, 134 S. Ct. 1936 (2014)

[One of the most difficult questions raised by Section 1021 of the NDAA for Fiscal Year 2012 is its relationship to the 2001 Authorization for Use of Military Force (AUMF). Does the NDAA *expand* the scope of the government's existing detention authority? Does it merely *codify* the understanding of the AUMF embraced by the Obama administration and endorsed by the D.C. Circuit in the Guantánamo litigation prior to the NDAA's passage? Or something else? And do the answers to these questions depend upon the citizenship of the detainee and/or whether he is captured within or without the territorial United States?

Because of the D.C. Circuit's Guantánamo jurisprudence (*see* NSL pp. 876-887, CTL pp. 490-501), these questions have not arisen (and likely will not arise) in litigation concerning prisoners held at Guantánamo. Instead, shortly after the NDAA was signed into law, a group of writers, journalists, and activists — whose work routinely brings them into contact with persons engaged in conduct the government regards as "material support" for terrorist organizations under 18 U.S.C. §2339B — brought suit seeking to enjoin the enforcement of §1021(b). The plaintiffs included both U.S. citizens and non-citizens.

The lead plaintiff was described by the lower court in part as follows:

> Christopher Hedges has been a foreign correspondent and journalist for more than 20 years. During that time, he has published numerous articles and books on topics such as al-Qaeda, Mohammad Atta, and the Paris bombing plot; he is a Pulitzer Prize winner. . . .
>
> . . . His work has involved interviewing al-Qaeda members who were later detained. He has reported on 17 groups contained on a list of known terrorist organizations prepared by the U.S. Department of State. . . .
>
> Hedges's work has involved investigating, associating with and reporting on al-Qaeda. . . .
>
> Hedges has recently spoken at events in Belgium and France, and could encounter people associated with groups that are "hostile to the U.S. government." *Id.* at 174. . . .
>
> Hedges testified that his oral and written speech as well as associational activities have been chilled by §1021: he does not understand what conduct is covered by §1021(b)(2), but does understand that the penalty of running afoul of it could be indefinite military detention. He anticipated having to change his associational activities at speeches he was giving as a result of §1021. Hedges testified that prior to the passage of §1021, he never feared his activities could subject him to indefinite military detention by the United States. [*Hedges v. Obama*, 890 F. Supp. 2d 424, 432-433 (S.D.N.Y. 2012).]

Plaintiffs argued that the statute authorized military detention on the basis of activities protected by the First and Fifth Amendments. The district court agreed and granted the injunction. Specifically, the court held that "[m]ilitary detention based on allegations of 'substantially supporting' or 'directly supporting' the Taliban, al-Qaeda or associated forces, is not encompassed within the AUMF." *Id.* at 472. The court then ruled that because such amorphous detention power in the NDAA might subject individuals to detention based upon constitutionally protected speech, and because of vagueness of terminology in the statute, it violated the First and Fifth Amendments. The government immediately obtained a stay pending appeal. In the decision that follows, the Second Circuit reversed — albeit not on the merits.]

Lewis A. Kaplan, District Judge [sitting by designation]: . . . The government contends that Section 1021 simply reaffirms authority that the government already had under the AUMF, suggesting at times that the statute does next to nothing at all. Plaintiffs take a different view. . . . They contend that Section 1021 is a dramatic expansion of the

President's military detention authority, supposedly authorizing the military, for the first time, to detain American citizens on American soil. As one group of amici has noted, "[r]arely has a short statute been subject to more radically different interpretations than Section 1021." . . .

We conclude that plaintiffs lack standing to seek preenforcement review of Section 1021 and [we] vacate the permanent injunction. The American citizen plaintiffs lack standing because Section 1021 says nothing at all about the President's authority to detain American citizens. And while Section 1021 does have a real bearing on those who are neither citizens nor lawful resident aliens and who are apprehended abroad, the non-citizen plaintiffs also have failed to establish standing because they have not shown a sufficient threat that the government will detain them under Section 1021. Accordingly, we do not address the merits of plaintiffs' constitutional claims. . . .

II. Discussion . . .

B. The Proper Construction of Section 1021 . . .

The AUMF authorized the President to "use all necessary and appropriate force against those nations, organizations, or persons he determines planned, authorized, committed, or aided the terrorist attacks that occurred on September 11, 2001, or harbored such organizations or persons." Section 1021(a) "affirms" that the AUMF authority includes the detention of a "covered person[ ]," which under Section 1021(b) means (1) a "person who planned, authorized, committed, or aided the terrorist attacks that occurred on September 11, 2001, or harbored those responsible for those attacks" or (2) a "person who was a part of or substantially supported al-Qaeda, the Taliban, or associated forces that are engaged in hostilities against the United States or its coalition partners, including any person who has committed a belligerent act or has directly supported such hostilities in aid of such enemy forces."

At first blush, Section 1021 may seem curious, if not contradictory. While Section 1021(b)(1) mimics language in the AUMF, Section 1021(b)(2) adds language absent from the AUMF. Yet Section 1021(a) states that it only "affirms" authority included under the AUMF, and Section 1021(d) indicates that Section 1021 is not "intended to limit or expand the authority of the President or the scope of the [AUMF]."

Fortunately, this apparent contradiction — that Section 1021 merely affirms AUMF authority even while it adds language not used in the

AUMF — is readily resolved. It is true that the language regarding persons who "planned, authorized, committed, or aided" the 9/11 attacks (or harbored those who did) is identical in the AUMF and Section 1021(b)(1). The AUMF, however, does not merely define persons who may be detained, as does Section 1021(b). Instead, it provides the President authority to use "force" against the "nations, organizations, or persons" responsible for 9/11. Section 1021(b)(1) (read with Section 1021(a)) affirms that the AUMF authority to use force against the persons responsible for 9/11 includes a power to detain such persons. But it does not speak to what additional detention authority, if any, is included in the President's separate AUMF authority to use force against the organizations responsible for 9/11.

This is where Section 1021(b)(2), a provision concerned with the organizations responsible for 9/11 — al-Qaeda and the Taliban — plays a role. Section 1021(b)(2) naturally is understood to affirm that the general AUMF authority to use force against these organizations includes the more specific authority to detain those who were part of, or those who substantially supported, these organizations or associated forces. Because one obviously cannot "detain" an organization, one must explain how the authority to use force against an organization translates into detention authority. Hence, it is not surprising that Section 1021(b)(2) contains language that does not appear in the AUMF, notwithstanding Section 1021(d). Plaintiffs create a false dilemma when they suggest that either Section 1021 expands the AUMF detention authority or it serves no purpose.

Indeed, there are perfectly sensible and legitimate reasons for Congress to have affirmed the nature of AUMF authority in this way. To the extent that reasonable minds might have differed — and in fact very much did differ — over whether the administration could detain those who were part of or substantially supported al-Qaeda, the Taliban, and associated forces under the AUMF authority to use force against the "organizations" responsible for 9/11, Section 1021(b)(2) eliminates any confusion on that particular point. At the same time, Section 1021(d) ensures that Congress' clarification may not properly be read to suggest that the President did not have this authority previously — a suggestion that might have called into question prior detentions. This does not necessarily make the section a "'legislative attempt at an ex post facto "fix" . . . to try to ratify past detentions which may have occurred under an overly-broad interpretation of the AUMF,'" as plaintiffs contend.

Rather, it is simply the 112th Congress' express resolution of a previously debated question about the scope of AUMF authority.

It remains to consider what effect Section 1021(e) has on this understanding. That provision states that "[n]othing in this section shall be construed to affect existing law or authorities relating to the detention of United States citizens, lawful resident aliens of the United States, or any other persons who are captured or arrested in the United States." Although this provision may appear superficially similar to Section 1021(d), nuances in the text and the legislative history make clear that Section 1021(e) actually is a significantly different provision.

As discussed above, in stating that Section 1021 is not intended to limit or expand the scope of the detention authority under the AUMF, Section 1021(d) mostly made a statement about the original AUMF — that is, it indicated that the specific power to detain those who were part of or who substantially supported the enumerated forces had been implicit in the more generally phrased AUMF. By contrast, in saying that Section 1021 shall not be construed to affect "existing law or authorities" relating to citizens, lawful resident aliens, or any other persons captured or arrested in the United States, Section 1021(e) expressly disclaims any statement about existing authority. Rather, it states only a limitation about how Section 1021 may be construed to affect that existing authority, whatever that existing authority may be. . . .

We thus conclude, consistent with the text and buttressed in part by the legislative history, that Section 1021 means this: With respect to individuals who are not citizens, are not lawful resident aliens, and are not captured or arrested within the United States, the President's AUMF authority includes the authority to detain those responsible for 9/11 as well as those who were a part of, or substantially supported, al-Qaeda, the Taliban, or associated forces that are engaged in hostilities against the United States or its coalition partners — a detention authority that Section 1021 concludes was granted by the original AUMF. But with respect to citizens, lawful resident aliens, or individuals captured or arrested in the United States, Section 1021 simply says nothing at all. . . .

C. American Citizen Plaintiffs

With this understanding of Section 1021, we may dispose of the claims of the citizen plaintiffs . . . . As discussed above, Section 1021 says nothing at all about the authority of the government to detain citizens. There simply is no threat whatsoever that they could be detained pursuant to that section. While it is true that Section 1021(e) does not foreclose the possibility that previously "existing law" may permit the detention of American citizens in some circumstances — a possibility that *Hamdi* [*v. Rumsfeld*, 542 U.S. 507 (2004), *see* NSL p. 831; CTL p. 445] clearly envisioned in any event — Section 1021 cannot itself be challenged as unconstitutional by citizens on the grounds advanced by plaintiffs because as to them it neither adds to nor subtracts from whatever authority would have existed in its absence. For similar reasons, plaintiffs cannot show that any detention [citizens] may fear would be redressable by the relief they seek, an injunction of Section 1021. . . .

D. Non-citizen Plaintiffs

The claims of [the non-citizen plantiffs] stand differently. Whereas Section 1021 says nothing about the government's authority to detain citizens, it does have real meaning regarding the authority to detain individuals who are not citizens or lawful resident aliens and are apprehended abroad. It provides that such individuals may be detained until the end of hostilities if they were part of or substantially supported al-Qaeda, the Taliban, or associated forces. To be sure, Section 1021 in substance provides also that this authority was implicit in the original AUMF. But . . . [i]t is not immediately apparent on the face of the AUMF alone that the President had the authority to detain those who substantially supported al-Qaeda, and indeed many federal judges had concluded otherwise prior to Section 1021's passage. Hence, Section 1021(b)(2) sets forth an interpretation of the AUMF that had not previously been codified by Congress. Where a statute codifies an interpretation of an earlier law that is subject to reasonable dispute, the interpretive statute itself may affect the rights of persons under the earlier law.

As the standing inquiry as to these [non-citizen] plaintiffs is more involved, we discuss the . . . applicable law in detail. . . .

2. Fear-based Standing Law

We have no occasion to disturb the factual findings of the district court, which are well-supported by the record, or to question the truth of the factual testimony of the plaintiffs, which the district court found credible. Rather, we are faced only with a question of law: whether the non-citizen plaintiffs' fears of enforcement, as well as any present costs they have incurred as a result of those fears, establish their standing to bring this challenge.

. . . [T]he Supreme Court has recognized that such fears may support standing when the threat creating the fear is sufficiently imminent. The Supreme Court's jurisprudence regarding how imminent a threat must be in order to support standing, however, has been less than clear. [Here the court discusses the Supreme Court's decision in *Clapper v. Amnesty International USA*, 133 S. Ct. 1138 (2013), p. 7 in this *Supplement*, and other decisions.] . . .

3. Coverage Under Section 1021(b)(2)

. . . Plaintiffs never articulate a precise theory on which they fear detention under Section 1021(b)(2) — that is, in what sense the government may conclude that they were a "part of or substantially supported al-Qaeda, the Taliban, or associated forces that are engaged in hostilities against the United States or its coalition partners." The strongest argument would seem to be a contention that the work of [the non-citizen plaintiffs] substantially, if indirectly, supports al-Qaeda and the Taliban as the term "support" is understood colloquially. The record demonstrates a number of ways in which the government has concluded, or would have a basis to conclude, that WikiLeaks has provided some support to al-Qaeda and the Taliban. . . . One perhaps might fear that [the non-citizen plaintiffs'] efforts on behalf of WikiLeaks could be construed as making them indirect supporters of al-Qaeda and the Taliban as well.

The government rejoins that the term "substantial support" cannot be construed so in this particular context. Rather, it contends that the term must be understood — and limited — by reference to who would be detainable in analogous circumstances under the laws of war. It points to (1) the *Hamdi* plurality's limitation of the duration of the detention authority it recognized based on the laws of war, (2) the March 2009 Memo's repeated invocation of law-of-war limiting principles[1] and the

---

[1. The reference here is to Respondents' Memorandum Regarding the Government's Detention Authority Relative to Detainees Held at Guantanamo Bay, *In re Guantanamo Bay Detainee Litigation*, Misc. No. 08-442 (TFH) (D.D.C. Mar 13, 2009), in which the government "refin[ed]" its position regarding its detention authority for persons held at Guantánamo Bay.]

legislative history suggesting that Section 1021 was meant to codify the interpretation that the Memo set forth, (3) Section 1021(d), to the extent that *Hamdi* and the administration suggested that the laws of war inform AUMF authority, as bearing on how broadly "substantial support" may be construed, and (4) the references to "law of war" in Section 1021 itself, albeit not in Section 1021(b)(2). The government then contends that individuals like [the non-citizen plaintiffs] are civilians who are not detainable under these law-of-war principles and so cannot reasonably fear detention under Section 1021.

In these circumstances, we are faced with a somewhat peculiar situation. The government has invited us to resolve standing in this case by codifying, as a matter of law, the meaningful limits it has placed on itself in its interpretation of Section 1021. We decline the government's invitation to do so. Thus, we express no view regarding whether the laws of war inform and limit detention authority under Section 1021(b)(2) or whether such principles would foreclose the detention of individuals like [the non-citizen plaintiffs]. This issue presents important questions about the scope of the government's detention authority under the AUMF, and we are wary of allowing a preenforcement standing inquiry to become the vehicle by which a court addresses these matters unless it is necessary. Because we conclude that standing is absent in any event, we will assume without deciding that Section 1021(b)(2) covers [the non-citizen plaintiffs] in light of their stated activities.

4. Threat of Enforcement

We next consider whether there is a sufficient threat of enforcement even given this assumption. . . . As noted above, however, neither this Court nor the Supreme Court has required much to establish this final step in challenges to ordinary criminal or civil punitive statutes. Rather, we have presumed that the government will enforce the law.

The question is the extent to which such a presumption is applicable here. The district court concluded that it was, reasoning that Section 1021 "is equivalent to a criminal statute" because "the possibility of being placed in indefinite military detention is the equivalent of a criminal penalty." Certainly we agree that military detention until the termination of hostilities would be severe and that the prospect of such detention can be "as inhibiting of speech as can trepidation in the face of threatened criminal prosecution." But that is a separate question from whether it is appropriate to presume that Section 1021 will be enforced as would any criminal or civil punitive statute.

On this point, there are several important differences between Section 1021 and a typical statute imposing criminal or civil penalties. Section 1021 is not a law enforcement statute, but an affirmation of the President's military authority.[172] As discussed above, it applies only to individuals who are not citizens, are not lawful resident aliens, and are apprehended outside the United States. It thus speaks entirely to the authority of the President in the context of military force, national security, and foreign affairs, areas in which the President generally enjoys "unique responsibility"[173] and "broad discretion."[174] The Supreme Court has recognized that "Congress cannot anticipate and legislate with regard to every possible action the President may find it necessary to take" in the fields of national security and foreign affairs.[175] As a result, "Congress — in giving the Executive authority over matters of foreign affairs — must of necessity paint with a brush broader than that it customarily wields in domestic areas."[176]

Moreover, Section 1021 "at most *authorizes* — but does not *mandate* or *direct*" — the detention that plaintiffs fear. To be sure, the executive branch enjoys prosecutorial discretion with regard to traditional punitive statutes. Congress generally does not mandate or direct criminal prosecution or civil enforcement. But we can distinguish between Congress, on the one hand, proscribing a certain act and then leaving it to the President to enforce the law under his constitutional duty to "take Care that the Laws be faithfully executed" and Congress,

---

172. The *Hamdi* plurality observed that military detention "'is neither a punishment nor an act of vengeance, but merely a temporary detention which is devoid of all penal character. A prisoner of war is no convict; his imprisonment is a simple war measure.'" 542 U.S. at 518.

173. Am. Ins. Ass'n v. Garamendi, 539 U.S. 396, 415 (2003) (internal quotation marks omitted).

174. Olegario v. United States, 629 F.2d 204, 233 (2d Cir. 1980).

175. Dames & Moore v. Regan, 453 U.S. 654, 678 (1981).

176. Haig v. Agee, 453 U.S. 280, 292 (1981) (emphasis and internal quotation marks omitted).

on the other hand, authorizing the President to use a certain kind of military force against non-citizens abroad.

Consequently, there is a world of difference between assuming that a state executive will enforce a statute imposing civil penalties for certain campaign finance violations — or even that the executive branch will enforce a federal criminal statute barring provision of material support to terrorists — and assuming that the President will detain any non-citizen abroad that Congress authorizes him to detain under the AUMF. *Clapper* further supports this understanding, as it made clear that plaintiffs cannot establish standing on the basis of speculation about how the government may choose to utilize its authority to engage in foreign surveillance. In short, while it generally may be appropriate to presume for standing purposes that the government will enforce the law against a plaintiff covered by a traditional punitive statute, such a presumption carries less force with regard to a statute concerned entirely with the President's authority to use military force against non-citizens abroad. Thus, in the circumstances of this case, [the non-citizen plaintiffs] must show more than that the statute covers their conduct to establish preenforcement standing.

We need not quantify precisely what more is required because [the non-citizen plaintiffs] have shown nothing further here. Indeed, they have not established a basis for concluding that enforcement against them is even remotely likely. We reach this conclusion independent of the government's litigation position on appeal that plaintiffs are "in no danger whatsoever" of being detained on the basis of their stated activities.

First, even assuming that [the non-citizen plaintiffs] fall within the ambit of authority provided by the statute, this is certainly not a case in which "the law is aimed directly at plaintiffs."[186] They point to nothing in the record, or in the text or legislative history of Section 1021, that suggests that the statute was passed to facilitate the military detention of individuals specifically like them.

Second, while we do not hold that a specific threat of enforcement is necessary, neither [of the non-citizen plaintiffs] has adduced any evidence that the government intends or has threatened to place them in military detention.

---

186. [Virginia v. Am. Booksellers Ass'n, Inc., 484 U.S. 383 (1988),] at 392.

Third, they have not put forth evidence that individuals even remotely similarly situated have been subjected to military detention. The government argues that this latter failure is particularly meaningful because, it contends, Section 1021 codified an interpretation "that the President had long articulated and exercised and that the Judiciary had repeatedly recognized."

To be sure, the government overstates its case on this point. As the history of litigation regarding the scope of AUMF detention authority shows, numerous courts criticized or rejected the government's reliance on substantial support in the March 2009 Memo. Prior to that, a divided Fourth Circuit set forth a number of different interpretations of executive detention authority, none of which resembled the government's position. While the D.C. Circuit's decision in *Al-Bihani* [*v. Obama*, 590 F.3d 866 (D.C. Cir. 2010), *see* NSL p. 877; CTL p. 491] is supportive of the government's standard, it focused primarily on a "purposeful and material support" standard, the relationship of which to "substantial support" is not clear. Simply put, to the extent that Congress resolved a previously debated question about the scope of AUMF detention authority in passing Section 1021, it was not obvious that the answer it provided is the one that ultimately would have prevailed had Congress not passed anything at all. In light of this uncertainty, at least in principle Section 1021's codification of the "substantial support" standard could place the administration on stronger footing to detain individuals under such a theory than it might have been willing to risk previously.

Nevertheless, plaintiffs bear the burden of establishing standing. Whether Section 1021 can or will alter executive practice, particularly with regard to individuals like them, is purely a matter of speculation. The fact remains that — despite the executive at least nominally asserting the authority to detain on the basis of "support" since the 2004 CSRT enemy combatant definition,[2] and on the basis of "substantial support" since the March 2009 Memo, and despite the D.C. Circuit recognizing the lawfulness of detention at least on the basis of "purposeful and material support" since 2010 — plaintiffs have provided no basis for believing that the government will place [the non-citizen plaintiffs] in military detention for their supposed substantial support. In

---

[2. Memorandum from Deputy Secretary of Defense Paul Wolfowitz re: *Order Establishing Combatant Status Review Tribunal* §a (July 7, 2004), *available at* http://www.defense.gov/news/ Jul2004/d20040707review.pdf.]

all the circumstances, plaintiffs have not shown a sufficient threat of enforcement to establish standing. Moreover, they cannot "manufacture standing" based on any present injuries incurred due to their expressed fears.

Nothing in this decision should be confused as deference to the political branches because the case involves national security and foreign affairs. We adhere to the principle that courts have a vigorous and meaningful role to play in assessing the propriety of military detention, as the Supreme Court has made clear in cases from *Hamdi* to *Boumediene* [*v. Bush*, 553 U.S. 723 (2008), *see* NSL p. 787; CTL p. 401]. We hold only that a court first must satisfy itself that the case comports with the "irreducible constitutional minimum" of Article III standing. This inquiry is rooted in fundamental separation-of-powers principles and must be "especially rigorous" where, as here, the merits of the dispute require the court to "decide whether an action taken by one of the other two branches of the Federal Government was unconstitutional."[197] Section 1021 is concerned entirely with the military authority of the President with respect to non-citizens abroad — a context in which Congress provides the President broad authority to exercise with considerable discretion. Particularly after *Clapper*, plaintiffs must show more than that they fall within the ambit of this authority to establish the sufficient threat of enforcement necessary for Article III standing. They have failed to do so here. . . .

III. Conclusion

In sum, [the citizen plaintiffs] do not have Article III standing to challenge the statute because Section 1021 simply says nothing about the government's authority to detain citizens. While Section 1021 does have meaningful effect regarding the authority to detain individuals who are not citizens or lawful resident aliens and are apprehended abroad, [the non-citizen plaintiffs] have not established standing on this record. We VACATE the permanent injunction and remand for further proceedings consistent with this opinion.

---

197. *Clapper*, 133 S. Ct. at 1147 (internal quotation marks omitted).

NOTES AND QUESTIONS

1. *The Government's Rejected Invitation: Substantial Support and the Laws of War.* The heart of the issue in *Hedges* is the language of §1021(b)(2) that authorizes detention of individuals who "substantially support" al Qaeda or its affiliates in hostilities against the United States. What does "substantial[]" support *mean*? In enjoining the enforcement of §1021(b)(2), the district court held that the phrase was unconstitutionally vague because a reasonable person would not know what activity would actually subject them to detention. *See Hedges* v. *Obama*, 890 F. Supp. 2d 424, 466-471 (S.D.N.Y. 2012).

On appeal, the government argued that one way to understand the term is by reference to the laws of war: the NDAA clearly did not authorize detention of civilians (such as the *Hedges* plaintiffs). So understood, *Hedges* would be an easy case, as the court could have held that, since the NDAA expressly incorporated the laws of war, individuals who were not belligerents under the laws of war clearly lack standing to challenge it. *See also* Marty Lederman & Steve Vladeck, *The NDAA: The Good, the Bad, and the Laws of War — Part I*, Lawfare, Dec. 31, 2011, http://www.lawfareblog.com/2011/12/the-ndaa-the-good-the-bad-and-the-laws-of-war-part-i/; Marty Lederman & Steve Vladeck, *The NDAA: The Good, the Bad, and the Laws of War — Part II*, Lawfare, Dec. 31, 2011, http://www.lawfareblog.com/2011/12/the-ndaa-the-good-the-bad-and-the-laws-of-war-part-ii/.

Why did the Second Circuit reject the government's invitation? Isn't the actual holding in *Hedges* — that, for the non-citizen plaintiffs, the threat of enforcement was insufficient to confer standing — itself open to substantial questioning? By that logic, the government could arguably control who has standing to challenge its detention authority merely by disclaiming a general desire to detain certain groups of individuals. Why do you suppose the court balked?

2. *The NDAA vs. the AUMF.* By far, the most significant passage of the Second Circuit's opinion comes where Judge Kaplan summarizes the relationship between the NDAA and the AUMF:

> With respect to individuals who are not citizens, are not lawful resident aliens, and are not captured or arrested within the United States, the President's AUMF authority includes the authority to detain those responsible for 9/11 as well as those who were a part of, or substantially supported, al-Qaeda, the Taliban, or associated forces that are engaged in

hostilities against the United States or its coalition partners — a detention authority that Section 1021 concludes was granted by the original AUMF. But with respect to citizens, lawful resident aliens, or individuals captured or arrested in the United States, Section 1021 simply says nothing at all.

In one sense, this language merely restates the plain language of the NDAA. But is there more going on here? Why does the relationship between the AUMF and NDAA actually *matter*? Put another way, can you describe an individual who was not subject to military detention on the day before the NDAA was enacted, but who is subject to military detention now? If not, what's all the fuss about?

3. *U.S. Citizens and the Feinstein Amendment.* To explain why the citizen plaintiffs in *Hedges* lack standing, the Second Circuit held that §1021(e) — the "Feinstein Amendment" — means what it says (or what it doesn't say): that, "with respect to citizens, lawful resident aliens, or individuals captured or arrested in the United States, Section 1021 simply says nothing at all." Does that mean that citizens, "lawful resident aliens" (a term nowhere defined in U.S. law), or anyone else "captured or arrested in the United States" *cannot* be subjected to military detention under the AUMF? Or does it merely codify the pre-NDAA status quo? If the latter, what *was* the pre-NDAA status quo in these cases? *See* Steve Vladeck, *The Problematic NDAA: On Clear Statements and Non-Battlefield Detention*, Lawfare, Dec. 13, 2011, http://www.lawfareblog.com/2011/12/the-problematic-ndaa-on-clear-statements-and-non-battlefield-detention/. Is it clear that the government may *not* detain someone covered by the Feinstein Amendment on the ground that they "substantially supported" al Qaeda or its affiliates in its hostilities against the United States? If not, why *didn't* the U.S. citizen plaintiffs in *Hedges* have standing? Was their challenge too narrow?

4. *Did Hedges Get Clapper'd?* In between the district court's decision in *Hedges* and the Second Circuit opinion excerpted above, the Supreme Court handed down its 5-4 decision in *Clapper v. Amnesty International USA*, 133 S. Ct. 1138 (2013) (this *Supplement* p. 7), holding that plaintiffs could not challenge secret governmental surveillance programs without demonstrating that actual injury to them (through interception of their communications) was "certainly impending." Might *Hedges* have come out differently before *Clapper*? Note the very different issues complicating the standing analysis in the

two cases: In *Clapper*, the problem arises from the secret nature of the government's surveillance programs, which will make it difficult for most plaintiffs to prove that they are actually injured by the challenged government conduct. In *Hedges*, by contrast, the problem arises from the lack of clarity surrounding the permissible scope of the government's detention power. In the end, does that difference make the case for standing stronger in *Hedges*? Weaker? Or is the problem in *Hedges* not *standing* so much as it is *ripeness* (*see* NSL p. 140)?

—————————

[NSL p. 892; CTL p. 506. Insert at end of chapter.]

E. The Next Generation of Guantánamo Litigation

Despite his repeated pledges to close Guantánamo, President Obama has thus far been unable to do so, and 149 detainees remain at the base as of July 15, 2014. Part of the difficulties have resulted from a series of spending restrictions that Congress began imposing in 2011 on the transfer of detainees either into the United States or to foreign countries. The following provision, for example, was enacted as part of the National Defense Authorization Act for FY2013:

> None of the funds authorized to be appropriated by this Act for fiscal year 2013 may be used to transfer, release, or assist in the transfer or release to or within the United States, its territories, or possessions of Khalid Sheikh Mohammed or any other detainee who —
>
> > (1) is not a United States citizen or a member of the Armed Forces of the United States; and
> >
> > (2) is or was held on or after January 20, 2009, at United States Naval Station, Guantanamo Bay, Cuba, by the Department of Defense.

National Defense Authorization Act for Fiscal Year 2013, Pub. L. No. 112-239, §1027, 126 Stat. 1632, 1914 (2012).

And Section 1028 of that Act prohibited the transfer of detainees elsewhere unless ordered by a court, or unless the Secretary of Defense certified, at least 30 days in advance of the transfer, that the country to which the detainee was to be transferred:

> (A) is not a designated state sponsor of terrorism oris not a designated state sponsor of terrorism or designated foreign terrorist organization;

(B) maintains control over each detention facility in which the individual is to be detained if the individual is to be housed in a detention facility;

(C) is not, as of the date of the certification, facing a threat that is likely to substantially affect its ability to exercise control over the individual;

(D) has taken or agreed to take effective actions to ensure that the individual cannot take action to threaten the United States, its citizens, or its allies in the future;

(E) has taken or agreed to take such actions as the Secretary of Defense determines are necessary to ensure that the individual cannot engage or reengage in any terrorist activity; and

(F) has agreed to share with the United States any information that —

(i) is related to the individual or any associates of the individual; and

(ii) could affect the security of the United States, its citizens, or its allies . . . .

Id. §1028(b)(1), 126 Stat. at 1915. Although the measure included authority for the Secretary to waive some of these certifications, *see id.* §1028(d), 126 Stat. at 1915-16, the difficulties inherent in making these showings may have helped to account for the total absence of such certifications — and, as such, of non-court-ordered foreign transfers — between 2011 and 2013. These restrictions also provoked annual signing statements from President Obama, who objected that the provisions

hinder[] the executive's ability to carry out its military, national security, and foreign relations activities and . . . would, under certain circumstances, violate constitutional separation of powers principles. The executive branch must have the flexibility to act swiftly in conducting negotiations with foreign countries regarding the circumstances of detainee transfers. In the event that the statutory restrictions . . . operate in a manner that violates constitutional separation of powers principles, my Administration will interpret them to avoid the constitutional conflict.

Statement by the President on H.R. 1540 (Dec. 31, 2011), http://www.whitehouse.gov/the-press-office/2011/12/31/statement-president-hr-1540.

In the NDAA for Fiscal Year 2014, Congress, while leaving the ban on transfers into the United States intact, relaxed the foreign transfer restrictions. Instead of requiring onerous certifications from the Secretary of Defense before detainees could be transferred, Section 1035 authorized transfers if (1) "the Secretary determines, following a review conducted in accordance with [prior statutes and Executive Orders] that the individual is no longer a threat to the national security of the United States"; *or* (2) if he determines that:

> (1) actions that have been or are planned to be taken will substantially mitigate the risk of such individual engaging or reengaging in any terrorist or other hostile activity that threatens the United States or United States persons or interests; and
>
> (2) the transfer is in the national security interest of the United States.

National Defense Authorization Act for Fiscal Year 2014, Pub. L. No. 113-66, §1035(b), 127 Stat. 622, 851 (2013). In all such cases, Section 1035(d) mandated that "[t]he Secretary of Defense shall notify the appropriate committees of Congress of a determination of the Secretary under subsection (a) or (b) not later than 30 days before the transfer or release of the individual under such subsection." *Id*. §1035(d), 127 Stat. at 853. Thanks in part to these more relaxed provisions, 10 detainees were transferred out of Guantánamo between December 2013 and April 2014.

On May 31, 2014, the Executive Branch announced the transfer of five additional Taliban detainees at Guantánamo to Qatar as part of an exchange for Sergeant Bowe Bergdahl, the one U.S. soldier held by Taliban forces in Afghanistan as a prisoner of war. Whatever the policy merits of the exchange, many objected that the transfer was unlawful, insofar as the government had failed to satisfy the notice requirements of §1035(d). In response, the National Security Council issued a statement explaining that

> the Administration determined that the notification requirement should be construed not to apply to this unique set of circumstances, in which the transfer would secure the release of a captive U.S. soldier and the Secretary of Defense, acting on behalf of the President, has determined that providing notice as specified in the statute could endanger the soldier's life.
>
> In these circumstances, delaying the transfer in order to provide the 30-day notice would interfere with the Executive's performance of two related functions that the Constitution assigns to the President: protecting the lives of Americans abroad and protecting U.S. soldiers. Because such interference would significantly alter the balance between Congress and the President, and could even raise constitutional concerns, we believe it is fair to conclude that Congress did not intend

that the Administration would be barred from taking the action it did in these circumstances.

E-Mail from NSC Press Office (June 3, 2014, 1:27 p.m.), *available at* http://www.scribd.com/doc/228207506/NSC-Statement-On-30-Day-Transfer-Notice-Requirement-In-2014-NDAA.

NOTES AND QUESTIONS

1. *A Statutory Argument, or a Constitutional One?* Re-read the NSC statement about the Bergdahl swap carefully. Is this a rare example of the Obama administration asserting that a statute unconstitutionally interferes with executive power? Or is the argument, instead, that the statutory notice requirement shouldn't be read to apply to unique cases like Bergdahl's — that Congress wasn't contemplating either (1) prisoner exchanges generally; or (2) cases where the notice requirement might negatively affect the health of a service member, specifically. Are you convinced by either or both of these arguments? Does it make a difference that the provision President Obama arguably violated was a procedural, rather than substantive, constraint on detainee transfers? Could anyone bring a lawsuit challenging President Obama's allegedly unlawful conduct?

2. *A Good Deal?* The five detainees who were exchanged for Sergeant Bergdahl were all held based upon their connection to the Taliban, *not* al Qaeda. As a result, many — including former State Department Legal Adviser John Bellinger — believed that the government's authority to continue to detain them would have lapsed not long after the withdrawal of combat troops from Afghanistan, perhaps as early as the end of 2014. *See, e.g.,* John Bellinger, *Released Taliban Detainees: Not So "Innocent" After All?*, Lawfare, June 1, 2014, http://www.lawfareblog.com/2014/06/released-taliban-detainees-not-so-innocent-after-all/.

This argument — that detention authority under the 2001 Authorization for the Use of Military Force (AUMF) may began to expire as combat troops are withdrawn from Afghanistan — is considered in more detail below. Insofar as it is accurate, though, does it affect your view on the merits of the exchange and/or your interpretation of §1035's notice requirement?

As a result of the transfer restrictions, along with the diplomatic difficulties that the government has encountered in transferring detainees, the continuing detention of these individuals has provoked a series of additional (and, in many cases, novel) legal claims largely unrelated to the litigation over the legality of the detainees' confinement discussed above in Section C. This "next generation" of Guantánamo litigation is significant not only in helping to set the terms upon which these detainees will continue to be held, but also in setting precedents that may apply far beyond the factual and legal context of military detention of non-citizens captured outside the United States.

Aamer v. Obama

United States Court of Appeals, District of Columbia Circuit, Feb. 11, 2014
742 F.3d 1023

TATEL, Circuit Judge: Petitioners Ahmed Belbacha, Abu Dhiab, and Shaker Aamer are detainees who, although cleared for release, remain held at the United States Naval Station at Guantanamo Bay, Cuba. Protesting their continued confinement, they and other similarly situated detainees have engaged in a hunger strike, refusing to eat unless and until released. In response, the government instituted a force-feeding protocol. Petitioners, each of whom had already sought release via a writ of habeas corpus, moved in those habeas actions for a preliminary injunction preventing the government from subjecting them to force-feeding. Two separate district judges denied their requests, each concluding that the Military Commissions Act (MCA) stripped federal courts of jurisdiction to consider such challenges brought by Guantanamo detainees. For the reasons set forth in this opinion, we conclude that under the law of this circuit petitioners' challenges to the conditions of their confinement properly sound in habeas corpus and thus are not barred by the MCA. We also conclude, however, that although their claims are not insubstantial, petitioners have failed to establish their entitlement to preliminary injunctive relief.

I. . . .

In June, petitioners . . . invoked the district court's habeas jurisdiction and moved for a preliminary injunction prohibiting the authorities from force-feeding them. According to petitioners, the

practice violated both their constitutional rights and the Religious
Freedom Restoration Act (RFRA), 42 U.S.C. §2000bb-1. . . .

II. . . .

A.

   . . . After the Supreme Court held that [the jurisdiction-stripping
provisions of the Detainee Treatment Act (DTA)] could not apply
retroactively to cases pending at the time the DTA was enacted, *see
Hamdan v. Rumsfeld*, 548 U.S. 557, 575-76 (2006), Congress responded
by passing the MCA, the statute at issue in this case, whose
jurisdiction-stripping provisions unequivocally applied to *all* claims
brought by Guantanamo detainees. *See Boumediene v. Bush*, 553 U.S.
723, 736-39 (2008). MCA section 7 provides:

> (1) No court, justice, or judge shall have jurisdiction to hear or
> consider an application for a writ of habeas corpus filed by or on behalf of
> an alien detained by the United States who has been determined by the
> United States to have been properly detained as an enemy combatant or is
> awaiting such determination.
>   (2) Except as provided [in section 1005(e) of the DTA], no court,
> justice, or judge shall have jurisdiction to hear or consider any other action
> against the United States or its agents relating to any aspect of the detention,
> transfer, treatment, trial, or conditions of confinement of an alien who is or
> was detained by the United States and has been determined by the United
> States to have been properly detained as an enemy combatant or is awaiting
> such determination.

28 U.S.C. §2241(e).
   Passage of the MCA required the Supreme Court to confront the
constitutional question it had until then successfully avoided: may
Congress eliminate federal habeas jurisdiction over Guantanamo without
complying with the requirements of the Suspension Clause? In
Boumediene v. Bush, 553 U.S. 723 (2008), the Court answered this
question in the negative. It first held that the Suspension Clause "has full
effect at Guantanamo Bay." *Id.* at 771. The Court then concluded that
the substitute procedures Congress had developed for Guantanamo
detainees — review in this court of military tribunal decisions — were
"an inadequate substitute for habeas corpus," *id.* at 792, which at the
very least "entitles the prisoner to a meaningful opportunity to

demonstrate that he is being held pursuant to 'the erroneous application or interpretation' of relevant law" before a court that "must have the power to order the conditional release of an individual unlawfully detained," *id.* at 779 (quoting *INS v. St. Cyr*, 533 U.S. 289, 302 (2001)). Thus, the Court held, MCA section 7 "operates as an unconstitutional suspension of the writ." *Id.* at 733, 792.

This court addressed *Boumediene*'s effect on the relevant jurisdictional statutes in *Kiyemba v. Obama*, 561 F.3d 509 (D.C. Cir. 2009) ["*Kiyemba II*"]. In petitions for habeas corpus, nine detainees had sought to bar the government from transferring them to a country where they might be tortured or detained. *Id.* at 511. The government contended that the district court lacked jurisdiction to consider such claims, arguing that *Boumediene* held MCA section 7 to be "unconstitutional only insofar as it purported to deprive the district court of jurisdiction to hear a claim falling within the 'core' of the constitutional right to habeas corpus, such as a challenge to the petitioner's detention or the duration thereof." *Id.* at 512. Rejecting that argument, we held — in language central to this case — that *Boumediene* "invalidate[d] §2241(e)(1) with respect to all habeas claims brought by Guantanamo detainees, not simply with respect to so-called 'core' habeas claims." *Id.* Thus, the Supreme Court's decision had "necessarily restored the status quo ante, in which detainees at Guantanamo had the right to petition for habeas under §2241." *Id.* at 512 n.2. Because the federal courts' statutory habeas jurisdiction had been restored, we saw "no need to decide . . . whether the . . . petitions c[a]me within the contours and content of constitutional habeas." *Id.* (internal quotation marks omitted). Rather, the question was simply whether the petitioners had "allege[d] a proper claim for habeas relief." *Id.* at 513. We concluded that they had. *Id.*

Subsequently, in *Al-Zahrani v. Rodriguez*, 669 F.3d 315 (D.C.Cir. 2012), we clarified that section 2241(e)(2) — the *other* subsection of MCA section 7 — continues in force. In *Al-Zahrani,* which involved a suit brought by families of detainees who had died at Guantanamo, *id.* at 316-17, we held that the district court lacked jurisdiction because the "litigation rather plainly constitute[d] an action other than habeas corpus brought against the United States and its agents relating to 'aspect[s] of the detention . . . treatment . . . [and] conditions of confinement of an alien' as described in the MCA," *id.* at 319. *Boumediene*, we explained, dealt with section 2241(e)(1), which stripped federal courts of habeas jurisdiction. *Id.* By contrast, section 2241(e)(2) "has no effect on habeas jurisdiction," and thus the "Suspension Clause is not relevant and does not affect the constitutionality of the statute." *Id.* We went on to reject the plaintiffs' claim that section 2241(e)(2) was itself unconstitutional, observing that the only remedy sought by the plaintiffs was money damages and that "such remedies are not constitutionally required." *Id.*

B.

Kiyemba and *Al-Zahrani* make clear that the jurisdictional question we consider here is relatively narrow: are petitioners' claims the sort that may be raised in a federal habeas petition under section 2241? As the government emphasizes, petitioners challenge neither the fact nor the duration of their detention, claims that would lie at the heart of habeas corpus. *See, e.g., Preiser v. Rodriguez*, 411 U.S. 475, 484 (1973) ("[T]he traditional function of the writ is to secure release from illegal custody."). Instead, they attack the conditions of their confinement, asserting that their treatment while in custody renders that custody illegal — claims that state and federal prisoners might typically raise in federal court pursuant to 42 U.S.C. §1983 and *Bivens v. Six Unknown Named Agents*, 403 U.S. 388 (1971). But although petitioners' claims undoubtedly fall outside the historical core of the writ, that hardly means they are not a "proper subject of statutory habeas." *Kiyemba*, 561 F.3d at 513. "Habeas is not 'a static, narrow, formalistic remedy; its scope has grown to achieve its grand purpose.'" *Boumediene*, 553 U.S. at 780 (quoting *Jones v. Cunningham*, 371 U.S. 236 (1963)).

If, as petitioners assert, their claims fall within the scope of habeas, then the district courts possessed jurisdiction to consider them because the federal habeas corpus statute extends, in its entirety, to Guantanamo. *See Kiyemba*, 561 F.3d at 512 & n.2. But if petitioners' claims do not sound in habeas, their challenges "constitute[ ] an action other than habeas corpus" barred by section 2241(e)(2). *Al-Zahrani,* 669 F.3d at 319.

Contrary to the contentions of the government and the dissent, in order to resolve this jurisdictional question we have no need to inquire into Congress's intent regarding federal court power to hear Guantanamo detainees' claims. Although Congress undoubtedly intended to preclude federal courts from exercising jurisdiction over *any* claims brought by Guantanamo detainees, it chose to do so through a statute that separately proscribes two different sorts of challenges: "habeas" actions, *see* 28 U.S.C. §2241(e)(1), and all "other" actions, *see id.* §2241(e)(2).

Boumediene struck down the first of these — the provision that would, but for *Boumediene,* preclude Guantanamo detainees from bringing habeas actions. *See Kiyemba*, 561 F.3d at 512. The remaining, lawful subsection of MCA section 7 has, by its terms, "no effect on habeas jurisdiction." *Al-Zahrani,* 669 F.3d at 319. In the wake of *Boumediene* and this court's interpretation of that decision in *Kiyemba,* Congress might very well want to preclude Guantanamo detainees from bringing particular types of habeas actions. But even assuming that Congress intends to again strip federal courts of habeas jurisdiction, it has yet to do so. Because we are unable to give effect to a non-existent statute, any such unmanifested congressional intent has no bearing on whether petitioners may bring their claims. Instead, given that statutory habeas extends to Guantanamo, the issue now before us is not Guantanamo-specific. We ask simply whether a challenge such as that advanced by petitioners constitutes "a proper claim for habeas relief" if brought by an individual in custody in Guantanamo or elsewhere. *Kiyemba*, 561 F.3d at 513.

For the same reasons, we have no need to explore the reach or breadth of the Suspension Clause. Simply put, there is no longer any statute in place that might unconstitutionally suspend the writ. We express no view on whether Congress could constitutionally enact legislation designed to preclude federal courts from exercising jurisdiction over the particular species of habeas claim petitioners advance. For our purposes, it suffices to say that Congress has not done so. . . . It is to the question of the current scope of statutory habeas corpus that we now turn.

C. . . .

Since *Preiser* [*v. Rodriguez*, 411 U.S. 475 (1973)], the Court has continued — quite expressly — to leave [whether habeas can be used to challenge conditions of confinement] open. In *Bell v. Wolfish*, 441 U.S. 520 (1979), the Court left "to another day the question of the propriety of using a writ of habeas corpus to obtain review of the conditions of confinement, as distinct from the fact or length of the confinement itself." *Id.* at 527 n.6. More recently, in *Boumediene* itself, the Court declined to "discuss the reach of the writ with respect to claims of unlawful conditions of treatment or confinement." 553 U.S. at 792. . . .

. . . [A]lthough the Supreme Court has left the question open, the law of this circuit — which is consistent with the weight of the reasoned precedent in the federal Courts of Appeal — compels us to conclude that a prisoner may, in a federal habeas corpus petition, "challenge the conditions of his confinement." [*United States v.*] *Wilson*, 471 F.2d [1072,] 1081 [(D.C. Cir. 1972)]. Petitioners here advance just such a challenge. They raise claims that their force-feeding at the hands of their jailers constitutes an "additional and unconstitutional restraint[ ] during [their] lawful custody," *Preiser*, 411 U.S. at 499, and violates their fundamental right to religious freedom, *see* 42 U.S.C. §2000bb-1, thus rendering their "imprisonment more burdensome than the law allows or curtail[ing] [their] liberty to a greater extent than the law permits." *Miller* [*v. Overholser*], 206 F.2d [415,] 420 [(D.C. Cir. 1953)] (quoting *Coffin* [*v. Reichard*], 143 F.2d [443,] 445 [(6th Cir. 1944)]). They have therefore brought "a proper claim for habeas relief" over which the district courts possess subject-matter jurisdiction. *Kiyemba*, 561 F.3d at 513. We thus turn to the question of whether petitioners have established their entitlement to injunctive relief.

III.

"'A plaintiff seeking a preliminary injunction must establish [1] that he is likely to succeed on the merits, [2] that he is likely to suffer irreparable harm in the absence of preliminary relief, [3] that the balance of equities tips in his favor, and [4] that an injunction is in the public interest.'" *Sherley v. Sebelius*, 644 F.3d 388, 392 (D.C. Cir. 2011) (alteration in original) (quoting *Winter v. Natural Resources Defense Council, Inc.*, 555 U.S. 7, 20 (2008)). We review the district court's balancing of these four factors for abuse of discretion, while reviewing de novo the questions of law involved in that inquiry. *Id.* at 393.

A.

We begin with the first and most important factor: whether petitioners have established a likelihood of success on the merits. Petitioners advance two separate substantive claims regarding the legality of force-feeding.

Their first and central claim is that the government's force-feeding of hunger-striking detainees violates their constitutionally protected liberty interest — specifically, the right to be free from unwanted medical treatment, *see Cruzan v. Director, Missouri Department of Health*, 497 U.S. 261, 278-79 (1990) — and that the government is unable to justify the practice of force-feeding under the standard established in *Turner v. Safley*, 482 U.S. 78 (1987). In *Turner*, the Supreme Court set forth the general test for assessing the legality of a prison regulation that "impinges on" an inmate's constitutional rights, holding that such a regulation is "valid if it is reasonably related to legitimate penological interests." *Id.* at 89. As the government does not press the issue, we shall, for purposes of this case, assume without deciding that the constitutional right to be free from unwanted medical treatment extends to nonresident aliens detained at Guantanamo and that we should use the *Turner* framework to evaluate petitioners' claim. . . .

For petitioners to be entitled to injunctive relief, . . . it is not enough for us to say that force-feeding may cause physical pain, invade bodily integrity, or even implicate petitioners' fundamental individual rights. This is a court of law, not an arbiter of medical ethics, and as such we must view this case through *Turner*'s restrictive lens. The very premise of *Turner* is that a "prison regulation [that] impinges on inmates' constitutional rights" may nonetheless be "valid." *Turner*, 482 U.S. at 89. That is, although "[p]rison walls do not form a barrier separating prison inmates from the protections of the Constitution," they do substantially change the nature and scope of those constitutional protections, as well as the degree of scrutiny that courts will employ in assessing alleged violations. *Id.* at 84. Thus, even if force-feeding "burdens fundamental rights," *Turner*, 482 U.S. at 87. *Turner* makes clear that a federal court may step in only if the practice is not "reasonably related to legitimate penological interests," *id.* at 89.

The government has identified two penological interests at stake here: preserving the lives of those in its custody and maintaining security and discipline in the detention facility. As the government emphasizes, many courts have concluded that such interests are legitimate and justify prison officials' force-feeding of hunger-striking inmates. The New York Court of Appeals recently explained that prison officials faced with a hunger-striking inmate whose behavior is life-threatening would, absent force-feeding, face two choices: (1) give in to the inmate's demands, which would lead other inmates to "copy the same tactic, manipulating the system to get a change in conditions"; or (2) let the inmate die, which is a harm in its own right, and would often "evoke[ ] a strong reaction from the other inmates and create[ ] serious safety and security concern[s]." *Matter of Bezio* [*v. Dorsey*], 989 N.E.2d [942,] 951 [(N.Y. 2013)] (internal quotation marks omitted). Although a handful of state appellate courts have rejected prison officials' attempts to force-feed particular inmates, those courts have largely done so while applying state law and under unique factual circumstances. But such an approach is not constitutionally compelled because it fails to similarly achieve the government's legitimate penological interests — including, most obviously, the interest in preserving the inmate's life.

Thus, the overwhelming majority of courts have concluded, as did Judge Collyer and as we do now, that absent exceptional circumstances prison officials may force-feed a starving inmate actually facing the risk of death. Petitioners point to nothing specific to their situation that would give us a basis for concluding that the government's legitimate penological interests cannot justify the force-feeding of hunger-striking detainees in Guantanamo.

Instead, petitioners attempt to distinguish the many decisions upholding the lawfulness of force-feeding by tying their challenge to an attack on the legality of the fact of their detention itself, arguing that "[t]here cannot be a legitimate penological interest in force-feeding the Guantanamo Bay detainees to prolong their indefinite detention" because force-feeding then simply "facilitates the violation of a fundamental human right." Appellants' Br. 40. But this court has repeatedly held that under the Authorization for the Use of Military Force, Pub. L. No. 107-40, 115 Stat. 224 (2001), individuals may be detained at Guantanamo so long as they are determined to have been part of Al Qaeda, the Taliban, or associated forces, and so long as hostilities are ongoing. *See, e.g., Al-Bihani v. Obama,* 590 F.3d 866, 873-74 (D.C. Cir. 2010). Given that such continued detention is lawful, force-feeding that furthers this detention serves the same legitimate penological interests as it would if petitioners were serving determinate sentences in state or federal prison.

In reaching this conclusion, we emphasize that we are addressing only petitioners' *likelihood* of success on the merits, not the actual merits of their claim. It is conceivable that petitioners could establish that the government's interest in preserving the lives of those detained at Guantanamo is somehow reduced, or demonstrate that the government has such complete control over Guantanamo detainees that hunger-striking inmates present no threat to order and security, or even show that there are "ready alternatives" to force-feeding that the government might employ to achieve these same legitimate interests. *Turner,* 482 U.S. at 90. We leave it to the district court to decide in the first instance what procedures may be necessary to provide petitioners a "meaningful opportunity" to make this showing. *Boumediene,* 553 U.S. at 779.

Finally, we reject petitioners' attempt to advance for the first time in their reply brief, and then again at oral argument, a very different ground for relief — that the government's force-feeding protocol must be enjoined not because force-feeding is inherently unconstitutional, but because the government subjects detainees to such treatment before they are actually at risk. As petitioners' counsel phrased this contention at oral argument: "[A] reasonable alternative would be to not force feed them until . . . they're at risk of death or permanent organ injury." Oral Arg. Tr. 16. But prior to their reply brief, the only "alternative" petitioners identified to the current force-feeding protocol was that the government bring petitioners to trial or set them free. Appellants' Br. 40. Accordingly, this argument is forfeited. In any event, record evidence appears to contradict petitioners' contentions. According to the declaration submitted by the government, Guantanamo medical staff will enterally feed a detainee "only . . . when it becomes medically necessary to preserve a detainee's life and health." Decl. of Commander [Redacted], M.D., 4. Of course, petitioners may seek to press this claim — as well as other claims related to particular aspects of the force-feeding protocol employed at Guantanamo — before the district court. . . .

[Judge Tatel next held that the Court of Appeals' earlier decision in *Rasul*, 563 F.3d 527 (D.C. Cir. 2009), foreclosed the plaintiffs' RFRA claim on the merits.]

B.

. . . [T]he remaining factors do not . . . weigh in petitioners' favor. The primary "purpose of a preliminary injunction is to preserve the object of the controversy in its then existing condition — to preserve the status quo." *Doeskin Products, Inc. v. United Paper Co.*, 195 F.2d 356, 358 (7th Cir. 1952). In this case, even if petitioners might eventually prevail in their challenge to the government's force-feeding protocol, we see especially good reasons for preserving the status quo by denying petitioners' request. Were we to now conclude that a preliminary injunction should issue, and then the district court, this court, or the Supreme Court later determined that the petitioners' claims lacked merit, the petitioners could very well die before the government would ever receive the benefit of that decision. But were we to uphold the district court's denial of a preliminary injunction, and it was later determined that force-feeding as practiced at Guantanamo violates petitioners' rights, petitioners would suffer by being compelled to endure force-feeding or the threat of force-feeding in the interim, but they would ultimately be able to engage in an uninterrupted hunger strike as they wish. Given that the risk of error is greater if a preliminary injunction is granted than if it is denied, we conclude, as did Judge Collyer, that the balance of equities and public interest support denying petitioners' request for interim relief.

IV.

For the forgoing reasons, we affirm the district courts' denials of petitioners' applications for a preliminary injunction.

So ordered.

WILLIAMS, Senior Circuit Judge, dissenting: [In his omitted dissent, Judge Williams disputed Judge Tatel's claim that D.C. Circuit precedent established that the plaintiffs' claims properly sounded in habeas, and argued that, in light of Congress's clear intent to circumscribe judicial review of Guantánamo detainees' claims, he would not so hold as a matter of first impression.]

NOTES AND QUESTIONS

1. *The Significance of the Jurisdictional Holding.* Judge Tatel reads the D.C. Circuit's earlier decision in *"Kiyemba II"* as holding that *Boumediene* invalidated §2241(e)(1) — the "habeas-stripping" provision of the Military Commissions Act — in *all* cases. As evidenced by the district court decisions at issue in *Aamer*, however, *Kiyemba II*'s "holding" in this regard was largely overlooked, whether because it came in a cryptic footnote, *see Kiyemba v. Obama*, 561 F.3d 509, 512 n.2 (D.C. Cir. 2009); or because that case involved a claim far closer to the "core" of the Suspension Clause; or both. Regardless, do you *agree* with this reading of *Boumediene* — as categorically invalidating §2241(e)(1) even in cases in which the Suspension Clause does *not* require access to habeas corpus? Wouldn't the Congress that enacted §2241(e)(1) have wanted to preclude habeas claims in every case in which such preclusion *is* constitutional? If so, what might explain the D.C. Circuit's conclusions to the contrary?

Regardless of the merits of *Aamer*'s jurisdictional analysis, consider the consequences of restoring the pre-2005 status quo with respect to habeas jurisdiction: Not only does *Aamer* suggest that the D.C. courts will have jurisdiction to entertain *any* claim from a Guantánamo detainee that can properly be brought through a habeas petition, but it also suggests that the D.C. courts may now entertain habeas petitions from individuals in U.S. custody *anywhere in the world*, notwithstanding the D.C. Circuit's prior opinions rejecting habeas jurisdiction over non-citizens detained in Afghanistan. *See Maqaleh v. Hagel*, 738 F.3d 312 (D.C. Cir. 2013); *Al Maqaleh v. Gates*, 605 F.3d 84 (D.C. Cir. 2010). After all, both of those decisions only considered whether the Suspension Clause mandated the availability of habeas in such cases. *See* Steve Vladeck, *Global (Statutory) Habeas After Aamer*, Lawfare, June 25, 2014, http://www.lawfareblog.com/2014/06/global-statutory-habeas-after-aamer/.

2. *Turner v. Safley at Guantánamo.* The D.C. Circuit ruled against the detainees on the merits because it concluded that "force-feeding that furthers this detention serves the same legitimate penological interests as it would if petitioners were serving determinate sentences in state or federal prison," and because the detainees' other claim — "that the government's force-feeding protocol must be enjoined not because force-feeding is inherently unconstitutional, but because the government subjects detainees to such treatment before they are actually at risk" — wasn't properly raised on appeal. Leaving aside the second point (which became the focus of the proceedings on remand), do you agree with the analogy Judge Tatel draws with regard to the first point, i.e., that the government's "penological interests" vis-a-vis the Guantánamo detainees are the same as its interests with respect to ordinary criminal prisoners? Aren't there fairly significant *differences* between the goals (and the government's interests) in military versus criminal detention? If there are, which way would that cut under *Turner*?

3. *The Proceedings on Remand.* Thus far, the remand in *Aamer* has produced a series of orders by Judge Kessler in Dhiab's case — a May 16, 2014 temporary restraining order halting "forcible cell extractions" (FCEs) and force-feeding at Guantánamo until a May 21 status conference; a May 22 order in which Judge Kessler refused to reissue the May 16 TRO after the status conference, because of the "Hobson's choice" the government had forced upon her: "Thanks to the

intransigence of the Department of Defense, Mr Dhiab may well suffer unnecessary pain from certain enteral feeding practices and forcible cell extractions. However, the Court simply cannot let Mr Dhiab die," *see Dhiab v. Obama*, No. 05-1457, 2014 WL 2134491, at *1 (D.D.C. May 22, 2014); and a separate May 23 order demanding that the government produce 34 videotapes of FCEs and force-feeding of Dhiab, along with copies of all of its force-feeding protocols and Dhiab's medical records, by early June, to allow Judge Kessler to fully resolve the merits of Dhiab's claims, *see Dhiab v. Obama*, No. 05-1457, 2014 WL 2178140 (D.D.C. May 23, 2014). A final decision on the merits remained pending when this *Supplement* went to press.

4. *Genital Searches and the Detainees' Access to Counsel.* The hunger strikes that precipitated the force-feeding at issue in *Aamer* were themselves provoked by a shift in the search policies utilized by guards — including mandatory searches of the detainees' Qurans and genitals — before the detainees were allowed to leave their cell areas for any purpose, including meeting (or communicating by telephone) with their counsel. Many detainees refused to comply with the searches (thereby effectively prohibiting them from meeting with counsel) and/or began hunger strikes in protest. At the same time, detainee lawyers were also requested to sign a new "Memorandum of Understanding" (MOU) that, they alleged, further restricted their ability to meet with their clients. Both of these developments were challenged as interfering with the detainees' right of access to their counsel. After ruling that the new MOU violated the detainees' *constitutional* right of access to counsel, *see In re Guantanamo Bay Detainee Continuing Access to Counsel*, 892 F. Supp. 2d 8 (D.D.C. 2012), then-Chief Judge Lamberth also concluded, in the decision excerpted below, that the genital searches *themselves* were unlawful.

————————————

In re Guantanamo Bay Detainee Litigation

United States District Court, District of Columbia, 2013
953 F. Supp. 2d 40

ROYCE C. LAMBERTH, Chief Judge:

I. INTRODUCTION

On May 23, 2013, President Obama promised, concerning detainees held at Guantanamo Bay, that "[w]here appropriate, we will bring terrorists to justice in our courts and our military justice system. And we will insist that judicial review be available for every detainee." Remarks by the President at the National Defense University (May 23, 2013) (transcript available at http:// www.whitehouse.gov/the- press-office/ 2013/05/23/remarks-president- national-defense-university). This matter concerns whether the President's insistence on judicial review may be squared with the actions of his commanders in charge of the military prison at Guantanamo Bay. Currently, it cannot.

Petitioners are detainees at Guantanamo Bay who are in the process of seeking habeas corpus relief and whose access to counsel is governed by this Court's 2008 Protective Order. Petitioners allege that the Joint Detention Group ("JDG"), the group responsible for detention operations within Joint Task Force-Guantanamo ("JTF-GTMO"), has instituted new search and procedures that impair petitioners' access to legal counsel.

The petitioners' unique circumstances render this case no ordinary challenge to prison regulations: At its heart, this case is about petitioners' ability to invoke the writ of habeas corpus through access to the Court and access to counsel.

. . . [F]or the reasons set forth below, the Court finds the JDG's new procedures invalid as they pertain to access to counsel and will GRANT petitioners' motions in part and DENY petitioners' motions in part.

II. BACKGROUND

A. Procedural Background

. . . All the petitioners request that this Court order the government to discontinue the use of certain procedures that petitioners allege inhibit their access to legal counsel. Specifically, petitioners request the Court to order (1) that they may meet with counsel in person or by phone without being subject to the new search protocol instituted by the JDG, (2) that they may meet with counsel in person or by phone within their housing camps, and (3) that the government may not transport detainees within the detention facility for attorney meetings or phone calls using new vans that petitioners contend force them into painful stress positions. . . .

B. Factual Background

Petitioners are housed within two separate "camps" within the Guantanamo detention facility. These camps — known as Camps 5 and 6 — are modeled after, and comparable to, maximum security prisons in the United States. Previously, meetings between petitioners and habeas counsel took place in Camps 5 and 6, though the government contends that attorney-client meetings have not taken place in Camps 5 and 6 for some time.

Currently, to meet with counsel or speak with counsel by phone, petitioners must travel from their housing camp to other buildings — known as Camps Delta and Echo — located nearby within the Guantanamo detention facility. Petitioners are transported to Camp Delta for all phone calls with counsel and to Camp Echo for all in-person meetings with counsel. . . .

The process of transporting detainees from their housing camps to Camps Delta and Echo requires that they be searched and then transported by van to the relevant camp. Previously, the search protocol in effect for detainees at GTMO did not allow guards to frisk the area between a detainee's waist and mid-thigh except with authorization from the JDG Commander. Instead, guards used a modified search procedure whereby a guard would grasp the waistband of a detainee's trousers and shake the detainee's pants in order to dislodge any contraband. The purpose of this modified search procedure was "to avoid actions that could be construed as disrespectful" of detainees' religious or cultural sensitivities. The use of the modified procedures represented a considered policy judgment on the part of the former JDG commanders: The commanders recognized that the modified search procedures "carrie[d] a level of risk," but they "accepted that risk out of an elevated respect for the religious concerns of the detainees." [Review of

Department Compliance with President's Executive Order on Detainee
Conditions of Confinement 26 ("Walsh Report").]

. . . On May 3, 2013, JDG revised its search procedures for detainees
to comport with the standard army search procedure. This standard
procedure includes frisking and wanding of the detainee's groin area. As
before, the search involves the guard grasping the detainee's waistband
and shaking it vigorously to dislodge contraband. The new search
protocol, however, adds several additional elements: First, the guard
gathers and crushes the fabric of the detainee's pants pockets to detect
any objects in the pockets. Second, the guard will search the detainee's
groin area "by placing the guard's hand as a wedge between the
[detainee's] scrotum and thigh . . . and using [a] flat hand to press
against the groin to detect anything foreign attached to the body." Third,
the guard uses a flat hand to frisk the detainee's buttocks to ensure no
contraband is hidden there. Fourth, "a hand-held 'wand' metal detector . . .
is passed over the [detainee's] body." The wand search includes the
detainee's groin and buttocks area, and guards hold the wand about one
to two inches from the detainee's body while conducting the wand
search.

Under the JDG's standard procedure, detainees are searched
whenever (1) they are moved to a facility external to their housing camp
or (2) they meet with any non-JTF-GTMO personnel. . . . The JDG's
standard procedure requires searching detainees for all movements or
meetings, including attorney meetings, phone calls with attorneys or
family members, or medical appointments.

For phone calls or attorney-client meetings, detainees must travel
outside of Camps 5 and 6 to Camps Delta and Echo. The JDG transports
detainees from Camps 5 and 6 to Camps Delta and Echo by van. While
traveling in the vans, detainees are restrained following standard military
procedure using a 5-point fabric seatbelt harness. On April 1, 2013, the
JDG introduced several new vans as part of a routine equipment upgrade
and to address detainee complaints about a lack of air conditioning in the
vans. The new vans include larger air ducts to improve air conditioning,
but lower ceilings. Petitioners contend that, as a result, the lower ceilings
in the vans force detainees to sit in crouched and painful stress positions
for the duration of the van ride.

C. Legal Background

In a litany of rulings, this Court and the Supreme Court have affirmed that the federal courts are open to Guantanamo detainees who wish to prove that their indefinite detentions are illegal. . . . This Court and the Supreme Court also held that Guantanamo detainees have a concomitant right to the assistance of counsel. *Hamdi v. Rumsfeld*, 542 U.S. 507, 539 (2004); *Al Odah v. United States*, 346 F. Supp. 2d 1, 5 (D.D.C. 2004). . . .

. . . In light of the *Boumediene* decision in 2008, the members of this Court again determined that a single judge should rule on common procedural issues to facilitate the expeditious resolution of Guantanamo habeas cases. *In re Guantanamo Bay Detainee Litig.*, Miscellaneous No. 08-442 (TFH), Order [1] at 1-2, July 2, 2012. The Court designated Judge Thomas F. Hogan . . . "to coordinate and manage proceedings in all cases involving petitioners presently detained at Guantanamo Bay, Cuba." *Id.* . . . After considering the parties' positions espoused both in written submissions and at a status conference, Judge Hogan issued a carefully crafted and thorough protective order that contained procedures for counsel access to detainees and to classified information. *In re Guantanamo Bay Detainee Litig.*, 577 F. Supp. 2d 143 (D.D.C. 2008) ("Protective Order" or "P.O."). . . .

This Court recently revisited Judge Hogan's protective order as it pertained to detainees without any pending habeas petition before the Court. *In re Guantanamo Bay Detainee Continued Access to Counsel*, 892 F. Supp. 2d 8 (D.D.C. 2012). At that time, the government argued "that the Protective Order cease[d] to control counsel-access in the absence of a pending or imminent habeas petition" and sought to enter into Memoranda of Understanding (MOUs) with detainees that would set the terms for counsel access. *Id.* at 11. The terms of the MOUs proposed by the government differed substantially from those of Judge Hogan's Protective Order and would have hampered both petitioners' access to counsel and counsels' access to classified information. *Id.* at 13-14. This Court rejected the government's argument and the proposed MOUs. Instead, the Court held that Judge Hogan's protective order governed counsel-access issues for all petitioners, including those without any pending habeas action. *Id.* at 28.

III. STANDARD OF REVIEW

The foundation of the Supreme Court's habeas jurisprudence is that the Great Writ lies at the core of this nation's constitutional system and that it is the duty of the courts to remedy lawless executive detention. . . . Moreover, the separation of powers also points to the fundamental importance of the Great Writ. Indeed, under our Constitution it is the Suspension Clause that "protects the rights of the detained by affirming the duty and authority of the Judiciary to call the jailer to account." [*Boumediene*, 553 U.S.] at 745 (citing *Preiser v. Rodriguez*, 411 U.S. 475, 484 (1973)).

The duty imposed by the Great Writ requires the Judiciary to ensure that access to the courts is "adequate, effective, and meaningful." *Bounds v. Smith*, 430 U.S. 817, 822 (1977). Practically, this means "that the privilege of habeas corpus entitles the prisoner to *a meaningful opportunity to demonstrate* that he is being held pursuant to 'the erroneous application or interpretation' of relevant law." *Boumediene*, 553 U.S. at 779 (quoting *INS v. St. Cyr*, 533 U.S. 289, 302) (emphasis added).

In the context of Guantanamo Bay habeas litigation, "access to the Court means nothing without access to counsel." *Al–Joudi v. Bush*, 406 F. Supp. 2d 13, 22 (D.D.C. 2005). They are inseparable concepts and must run together. . .

IV. JURISDICTION

The government contends that this Court lacks jurisdiction to address petitioners' emergency motions. "Federal courts are courts of limited subject-matter jurisdiction. A federal court created by Congress pursuant to Article III of the Constitution has the power to decide only those cases over which Congress grants jurisdiction." *Al-Zahrani v. Rodriguez*, 669 F.3d 315, 317 (D.C. Cir. 2012). . . .

[Chief Judge Lamberth next explains that *Al-Zahrani* forecloses jurisdiction over *non-habeas* claims by Guantánamo detainees.]

The instant litigation, however, is not a general challenge to petitioners' treatment or conditions of confinement. Instead, it is a narrow challenge to alleged government interference to petitioners' access to counsel that prevents them from prosecuting habeas cases before this Court. Petitioners' challenge falls squarely within the Court's jurisdiction. The Supreme Court implicitly recognized that counsel access issues relating to habeas cases fall within the district court's jurisdiction over habeas petitions. In *Boumediene*, the Supreme Court explained that it "ma[de] no attempt to anticipate all of the evidentiary and access-to-counsel issues that will arise during the course of the detainees' habeas corpus proceedings . . . . These and . . . other remaining questions are within the expertise and competence of the District Court to address in the first instance." 553 U.S. at 796. Logically, the Supreme Court would not refer counsel-access issues to the expertise of the District Court if it lacked jurisdiction to consider the issues in the first place.

Indeed, all the cases the government cites where this Court or the D.C. Circuit has concluded it lacked jurisdiction under §2241(e)(2) are inapposite. . . . This action focuses solely on what rules will govern counsel access for the Guantanamo detainees during their habeas cases and whether the government, in contravention of Judge Hogan's protective order and numerous other rulings, may interfere with detainees' access to counsel. Of course, it may not. . . .

V. ANALYSIS

A. The *Turner v. Safley* Standard is Logically Inapplicable to this Case

The government contends that the new search procedures instituted by Col. Bogdan pass muster under the deferential standard for prison regulations identified by the Supreme Court in *Turner v. Safley*, 482 U.S. 78 (1987). The government's reliance on the *Turner* standard is misplaced, however, as *Turner* is logically inapplicable to regulations impinging on a detainee's right to petition for a writ of habeas corpus.

The logical foundation of the *Turner* line of cases lies in striking a balance between a circumscribed constitutional right and the judgment of prison administrators. . . .

The logical progression of the Court's analysis . . . is clear and simple: Prisoners retain basic constitutional rights, but those rights may be necessarily limited in the prison context. Further, the government, acting as prison administrator, may limit prisoners' constitutional rights to accomplish valid penological objectives. Finally, given the Executive and Legislative branches' particular roles and expertise in prison administration, the Judiciary should give deference to the Executive and Legislature in how they chose to circumscribe prisoners' rights to achieve legitimate penological ends. . . .

This logical analysis, however, is inapplicable to the right of habeas corpus itself. The notion that habeas corpus, like the freedoms of association or speech, may necessarily be limited or withdrawn in the penological context is absurd: "the essence of habeas corpus is an attack by a person in custody upon the legality of that custody, and . . . the traditional function of the writ is to secure release from illegal custody." *Preiser v. Rodriguez*, 411 U.S. 475 (1973). The right of habeas corpus is neither limited nor withdrawn in the prison context — indeed it is most valuable as a right to one who is incarcerated. To restrict a detainee's access to habeas corpus solely by virtue of his detention would run counter to the writ's purpose and would eviscerate the writ.

Moreover, the particular circumstances of the petitioners in this case strengthen, rather than weaken, the power of the writ. As the Supreme Court recognized in *Boumediene,* "where[, as here,] a person is detained by executive order, rather than, say, after being tried and convicted in a court, the need for collateral review is most pressing. . . . In this context the need for habeas corpus is more urgent." 553 U.S. at 783. Any effort by the Executive or Legislature to limit a detainee's right to seek habeas corpus, just as they might limit the detainee's freedoms of speech or association, would be antithetical to the purpose of the writ. . . .

B. The New Search Procedures Fail Under the *Turner* Standard . . .

In order to balance the competing considerations between prisoners' rights and prison administration, the Supreme Court formulated its test as follows: "when a prison regulation impinges on inmates' constitutional rights, the regulation is valid if it is reasonably related to legitimate penological interests." [*Turner*, 482 U.S.] at 89. By contrast, a prison regulation is invalid if it represents an "exaggerated response" to legitimate penological concerns. *Id.* at 87. To aid its analysis, the Supreme Court identified "four factors [that] are relevant in deciding whether a prison regulation affecting a constitutional right that survives incarceration withstands constitutional challenge: whether the regulation has a 'valid, rational connection' to a legitimate governmental interest; whether alternative means are open to inmates to exercise the asserted right; what impact an accommodation of the right would have on guards and inmates and prison resources; and whether there are 'ready alternatives' to the regulation." *Overton v. Bazzetta*, 539 U.S. 126, 132 (2003) (quoting and citing *Turner*, 482 U.S. at 89-91). . . .

. . . As petitioners' counsel correctly noted during this Court's hearing, "[t]he government is a recidivist when it comes to denying counsel access." Sealed Hrg. Tr. 11. The government, seemingly at every turn, has acted to deny or to restrict Guantanamo detainee's access to counsel. The government designated Guantanamo as a "detention facility" rather than as a "corrections facility" because, under the Navy's own regulations, those incarcerated at a corrections facility have unconditional access to their attorneys. *See In re Guantanamo Bay Detainee Continued Access to Counsel*, 892 F. Supp. 2d at 17. The government sought to require detainees without pending habeas petitions to sign memoranda of understanding that would have removed them from the ambit of the Court's Protective Order and only allowed access to counsel at the government's whim. *See id.* at 13–14. The government has severely curtailed the number of flights to Guantanamo. *See* Order at 4, *Al–Zarnougi v. Obama,* No. 06-CV-1767 (RCL) (D.D.C. May 6, 2013), ECF No. 415. Predictably, given the limited number of commercial flights to Guantanamo, counsel must now wait in queue for at least two months before they may meet with their clients. Open Hr'g Tr. 20–21, June 5, 2013; *see also* Hatim Reply Ex. K ¶¶ 11-12 (noting that the limited flight schedule — counsel may only fly in on Mondays and out on Fridays — increases costs since counsel and translators must travel to Guantanamo for a full week). The government has, in some instances, withheld legal mail from petitioners without notifying the Court or petitioners' counsel. *See* Order at 4, *Al-Zarnougi v. Obama,* No. 06-CV-1767 (RCL) (D.D.C. May 6, 2013), ECF No. 415. And this is to say nothing of the multiple instances this Court has identified where the government sought to inhibit counsel access in individual cases. *See In re Guantanamo Bay Detainee Continued Access to Counsel*, 892 F. Supp. 2d at 24-26 (collecting cases). The government's repeated actions substantially increase the likelihood that its justification is mere pretext and that the new searches represent an "exaggerated response" to its legitimate interest in security of the detention facility. Thus, a thorough examination of the government's proffered justification is appropriate.

While the Court agrees that the presence of improvised weapons and contraband is logically related to the need for searches generally, the Court finds the new genital search procedure to be yet another exaggerated response by the JDG that is presently inhibiting petitioners' access to counsel. Since implementation of the new search procedure, multiple petitioners have foregone, some for the first time, phone calls or meetings with counsel. This does not represent, as the government argues, "mere voluntary refusal" on each petitioner's part. Instead, the Court finds that the new search procedures actively discourage petitioners from taking phone calls or meeting with counsel. As petitioners' counsel argued, the choice between submitting to a search procedure that is religiously and culturally abhorrent or foregoing counsel effectively presents no choice for devout Muslims like petitioners. The relationship between the searches and petitioners' choices to refuse phone calls and counsel meetings is clear and predictable. Indeed, petitioners also find searches of the Quran abhorrent, and many petitioners have chosen to forego having a Quran in their cells rather than having their Qurans subject to search.

That this relationship is so clear and predictable makes it easy for the government to exploit. Given that detainees are already shackled and under guard whenever they are moved, the added value of the new genital search procedure vis-à-vis the prior search procedure is reduced. In this context, the court finds searching the genitals of petitioners up to four times for every phone call or attorney-client meeting — as petitioners have described — to be excessive. Searching detainees up to four times in this manner for every movement, meeting, or phone call belies any legitimate interest in security given the clear and predictable effects of the new searches. Moreover, as petitioners note, nothing in the record indicates that detainees have received any contraband from their attorneys or that detainees have attempted to pass contraband to each other during phone calls or meetings with attorneys. The motivation for the searches is not to enhance security but to deter counsel access. Thus, the Court finds the search procedure an "excessive response" under the first *Turner* factor.

Turning to the remaining factors identified in *Turner,* the second factor considers "whether there are alternative means of exercising the right that remain open to prison inmates." *Turner*, 482 U.S. at 90. . . . As petitioners' counsel noted, the predicable consequences of the government's actions are "the breaking [and] severing of attorney-client communication except by letter which is by slow boat." Open Hrg. Tr. 19. The Court recognizes that, as petitioners argue, it would be untenable to prepare a habeas case for trial or appeal where counsel could only contact petitioners by legal mail. Absent face-to-face meetings and telephone calls, petitioners' habeas cases will not go forward. Thus, the new search procedures effectively leave petitioners without alternative avenues to exercise their right to habeas corpus.

The third *Turner* factor looks at "the impact [that] accommodation of the asserted constitutional right will have on guards and other inmates, and on the allocation of prison resources generally." *Turner*, 482 U.S. at 90. Here, the government contends that "[r]everting to the old search policy . . . would mean restoration of the same security risks to detainees, guards, and counsel, and the same operational disruptions and difficulties." Opp'n 24. But, as petitioners correctly argue, the record presents no connection between the prior search procedures and any such "disruptions or difficulties." . . .

The fourth *Turner* factor looks to the "absence" or "existence" of "ready alternatives" to the challenged regulation. *Turner*, 482 U.S. at 90. . . . As this court counseled in its previous counsel-access opinion, "if it ain't broke, don't fix it." *In re Guantanamo Bay Detainee Continued Access to Counsel*, 892 F. Supp. 2d at 16. Given its many years of use at the Guantanamo detention facility, the old modified search procedure represents an "obvious, easy," and proven alternative to the challenged new search procedure. . . .

In summary, the Court finds the evidence submitted by petitioners and contained in the record sufficient to carry their burden to show that the new search procedure is an "exaggerated response" to the JDG's concerns. Further, the Court finds the government's proffered justifications for the new search procedure unpersuasive in light of the evidence in the record. Thus, the Court will order that the modified search procedure be used for in-person detainee meetings with counsel and for detainee phone calls with counsel.

C. The JDG Must Allow Certain Detainees to Meet with Counsel in the Housing Camps

The Court now turns to the petitioners' request that the Court order JTF–GTMO to allow detainees to meet with counsel in their housing camps. . . .

. . . [After analyzing this issue under *Taylor*, Chief Judge Lamberth found] the JDG's policy of forbidding attorney-client meetings in the housing camps to be an exaggerated response to the government's penological interests in security and orderly operations. The Court will amend Judge Hogan's Protective Order to require that the JDG allow attorney-client meetings in Camps 5 and 6 for those detainees who are in a weakened physical state due to participation in the hunger strike or who have a medical condition that similarly makes travel outside the housing camps difficult. Given the limited space available for attorney-client meetings in Camps 5 and 6, counsel for petitioners and government counsel shall meet to establish procedures to ensure that the limited availability for attorney-client meetings in the housing camps is apportioned fairly amongst the detainees.

D. The JDG Must Allow Certain Petitioners to Use the Old Vans for Transport to Camps Echo and Delta

Due to the limited space for attorney-client meetings at Camps 5 and 6, some detainees may still need to travel to Camps Echo and Delta for attorney-client meetings and phone calls. Thus, the Court now turns to petitioners' challenge to the vans used by JDG to transport detainees from their housing camps to Camps Echo and Delta. Applying the same considerations that it applied to the regulations concerning attorney-client meetings in the housing camps, the Court concludes under *Turner* that detainees engaged in the hunger strike should be allowed to use the old vans for transport to Camps Echo or Delta. . . .

VI. CONCLUSION

In closing his speech at the National Defense University, the President quoted Judge William Young. *See* Remarks by the President at the National Defense University. In sentencing Richard Reid, the shoe bomber, Judge Young told him that "[t]he way we treat you . . . is the measure of our own liberties." *Id.* Judge Young's comment is equally apt when applied to the detainees at Guantanamo.

This Court is duty bound to protect the writ of habeas corpus as a fundamental prerequisite of liberty by ensuring that all those who seek it have meaningful and effective access to the courts. For Guantanamo detainees, it is undisputed that access to the courts means nothing without access to counsel. The JDG's behavior, exemplified by the new search and meeting procedures, flagrantly disregards the need for a light touch on religious and cultural matters that Admiral Walsh recognized years ago. Further, the search procedures discourage meetings with counsel and so stand in stark contrast to the President's insistence on judicial review for every detainee. The Court, whose duty it is to call the jailer to account, will not countenance the jailer's interference with detainees' access to counsel.

For the foregoing reasons, the Court finds the challenged procedures and regulations invalid as they pertain to counsel access. The Court further concludes, pursuant to ¶I.E.34 of the Protective Order, that this Memorandum Opinion and the accompanying Order issued this date should not be designated as protected, but will be available on the public record. Given the limits of this Court's jurisdiction, the Court's holding does not affect the ability of the JDG to continue to administer the Guantanamo detention facility as it finds appropriate with respect to issues unrelated to counsel access. . . .

So Ordered.

NOTES AND QUESTIONS

1. *Genital Searches as Access to Counsel.* Chief Judge Lamberth seems to take it as given that the genital searches necessarily implicate the detainees' access to counsel. This conclusion is critical not just to the merits of Chief Judge Lamberth's analysis, but also to his holding for why he has jurisdiction to *reach* the merits (a holding that might have been overtaken by *Aamer*). Do you agree? Doesn't the fact that some of the detainees are continuing to meet with their counsel undermine that conclusion? How important to Chief Judge Lamberth's analysis were the prior examples of government interference with access to counsel? How important was Col. Bogdan's *motive* in imposing the genital searches? *Should* the government's motive matter under *Turner*?

The government sought — and obtained — a stay of Chief Judge Lamberth's decision pending its appeal to the D.C. Circuit, which was argued before a three-judge panel on December 9, 2013. The decision remained pending as this *Supplement* went to print.

2. *Access to Counsel Before and After Boumediene.* Chief Judge Lamberth makes much out of Judge Kollar-Kotelly's decision in *Al Odah*, which first recognized the Guantánamo detainees' right of access to counsel. But that decision was grounded in the federal habeas statute, which the Supreme Court had just held to apply to Guantánamo in the *Rasul* case. Does Chief Judge Lamberth identify the *source* of the right of access to counsel in his opinion (keep in mind, he was writing before *Aamer*)? If so, where is it?

Put another way, is Chief Judge Lamberth's jurisdictional analysis narrow, merely reaffirming that the judge-made protective orders in the

Guantánamo cases continue to apply to the detainees even after their cases have been terminated? Or, as the repeated allusions to *Boumediene* suggest, is it a broad — and potentially momentous — holding that the Constitution's Suspension Clause (the source of the right to seek habeas relief) might also *itself* confer a right of access to counsel in at least some cases, as part of the "meaningful opportunity" to challenge detention that *Boumediene* held it to require? Wouldn't such a holding have significant consequences far beyond the specific issue in this case — indeed, far beyond Guantánamo?

3. *The Genital Search Decision and the Future of Guantánamo.* Critics of Chief Judge Lamberth's opinion have seized upon the argument that continuing access to counsel, at least for those detainees whose cases have been dismissed, is futile, whether because *Boumediene* only requires one bite at the judicial-review apple, or because, on the merits, a Guantánamo detainee who has already lost his habeas petition is doomed to fail should he try again, based upon res judicata and other considerations. *See, e.g.*, Andrew Kent, *Do Boumediene Rights Expire?*, 161 U. Penn. L. Rev. PENNumbra 20 (2012).

On the former point, should the Guantánamo cases follow "ordinary" rules of habeas litigation, including the well-established principle that res judicata does not apply, *see, e.g.*, *Sanders v. United States*, 373 U.S. 1, 8 (1963), meaning that there is no inherent bar on second-or-successive habeas petitions challenging executive detention? Indeed, under *Boumediene*, might executive detention cases present even *stronger* arguments against res judicata, because, unlike detention in the post-conviction context, the length of executive detention is not usually fixed *ab initio,* and the same source of detention authority may, in fact, vary as time goes on? *See, e.g.*, Stephen I. Vladeck, *Access to Counsel, Res Judicata, and the Future of Habeas at Guantanamo*, 161 U. Penn. L. Rev. PENNumbra 78 (2012).

On the latter point, *might* there come a point when detainees whose detention has already been upheld will nevertheless be able to argue that the government's authority to hold them under the 2001 Authorization for Use of Military Force (AUMF) has expired? Could such an argument be advanced if and when the remaining U.S. ground troops in Afghanistan are removed, at least with respect to Taliban — as opposed to al Qaeda — detainees? If and when the AUMF is repealed? Does either of these possibilities help to explain why Chief Judge Lamberth was at such pains to preserve these detainees' right to continue to have access to counsel — and, therefore, to the courts? Consider the following excerpt from an opinion by Justice Breyer, concurring in the Supreme Court's denial of certiorari in another Guantánamo case:

> The Court has not directly addressed whether the AUMF authorizes, and the Constitution permits, detention on the basis that an individual was part of al Qaeda, or part of the Taliban, but was not "engaged in an armed conflict against the United States" in Afghanistan prior to his capture. Nor have we considered whether, assuming detention on these bases is permissible, either the AUMF or the Constitution limits the duration of detention.

Hussain v. Obama, 134 S. Ct. 1621, 1622 (2014) (Breyer, J., respecting the denial of certiorari). Justice Breyer nevertheless voted to deny certiorari because "[t]he circumstances of Hussain's detention may involve these unanswered questions, but his petition does not ask us to answer them." *Id.* Does his opinion nevertheless suggest that these two questions will become fertile ground for future Guantánamo habeas cases — in which the detainees' continuing access to their counsel will be critical? If so, how would you resolve these questions?

————————

[NSL p. 944, CTL p. 558. Insert at the end of Note 2.]

Department of Justice, Office of Public Affairs, Statement of Attorney General Eric Holder on Closure of Investigation into the Interrogation of Certain Detainees

Aug. 30, 2012
available at http://www.justice.gov/opa/pr/2012/August/12-ag-1067.html

The Attorney General announced today the closure of the criminal investigations into the death of two individuals while in United States custody at overseas locations. Below is some background on the investigation and the Attorney General's statement.

BACKGROUND ON INVESTIGATION:

On Jan. 2, 2008, Attorney General Michael Mukasey selected Assistant U.S. Attorney (AUSA) John Durham of the District of

Connecticut to conduct a criminal investigation into the destruction of interrogation videotapes by the Central Intelligence Agency (CIA).

On Aug. 24, 2009, based on information the Department received pertaining to alleged CIA mistreatment of detainees, Attorney General Eric Holder announced that he had expanded Mr. Durham's mandate to conduct a preliminary review into whether federal laws were violated in connection with the interrogation of specific detainees at overseas locations. Attorney General Holder made clear at that time, that the Department would not prosecute anyone who acted in good faith and within the scope of the legal guidance given by the Office of Legal Counsel regarding the interrogation of detainees. Accordingly, Mr. Durham's review examined primarily whether any unauthorized interrogation techniques were used by CIA interrogators, and if so, whether such techniques could constitute violations of the torture statute or any other applicable statute.

In June of last year, the Attorney General announced that Mr. Durham recommended opening full criminal investigations regarding the death of two individuals while in United States custody at overseas locations, and closing the remaining matters. The Attorney General accepted that recommendation. Today, the Attorney General announced that those two investigations conducted over the past year have now been closed.

ATTORNEY GENERAL STATEMENT:

"AUSA John Durham has now completed his investigations, and the Department has decided not to initiate criminal charges in these matters. In reaching this determination, Mr. Durham considered all potentially applicable substantive criminal statutes as well as the statutes of limitations and jurisdictional provisions that govern prosecutions under those statutes. Mr. Durham and his team reviewed a tremendous volume of information pertaining to the detainees. That review included both information and matters that were not examined during the Department's prior reviews. Based on the fully developed factual record concerning the two deaths, the Department has declined prosecution because the admissible evidence would not be sufficient to obtain and sustain a conviction beyond a reasonable doubt.

"During the course of his preliminary review and subsequent investigations, Mr. Durham examined any possible CIA involvement with the interrogation and detention of 101 detainees who were alleged to have been in United States custody subsequent to the terrorist attacks of September 11, 2001. He determined that a number of the detainees were never in CIA custody. Mr. Durham identified the matters to include within his review by examining various sources including the Office of Professional Responsibility's report regarding the Office of Legal Counsel memoranda related to enhanced interrogation techniques, the 2004 CIA Inspector General's report on enhanced interrogations, additional matters investigated by the CIA Office of Inspector General, the February 2007 International Committee of the Red Cross Report on the Treatment of Fourteen 'High Value Detainees' in CIA Custody, and public source information.

"Mr. Durham and his team of agents and prosecutors have worked tirelessly to conduct extraordinarily thorough and complete preliminary reviews and investigations. I am grateful to his team and to him for their commitment to ensuring that the preliminary review and the subsequent investigations fully examined a broad universe of allegations from multiple sources. I continue to believe that our Nation will be better for it.

"I also appreciate and respect the work of and sacrifices made by the men and women in our intelligence community on behalf of this country. They perform an incredibly important service to our nation, and they often do so under difficult and dangerous circumstances. They deserve our respect and gratitude for the work they do. I asked Mr. Durham to conduct this review based on existing information as well as new information and matters presented to me that I believed warranted a thorough examination of the detainee treatment issue.

"I am confident that Mr. Durham's thorough reviews and determination that the filing of criminal charges would not be appropriate have satisfied that need. Our inquiry was limited to a determination of whether prosecutable offenses were committed and was not intended to, and does not resolve, broader questions regarding the propriety of the examined conduct."

On December 13, 2012, Senator Dianne Feinstein, chair of the Senate Intelligence Committee, released a statement, excerpted here, concerning the issuance of a classified report, *Study of the Central Intelligence Agency's Detention and Interrogation*, initiated by the committee in March 2009:

The committee's report is more than 6,000 pages long. It is a comprehensive review of the CIA's detention program that includes details of each detainee in CIA custody, the conditions under which they were detained, how they were interrogated, the intelligence they actually provided and the accuracy — or inaccuracy — of CIA descriptions about the program to the White House, Department of Justice, Congress and others. . . .

The report is based on a documentary review of more than 6 million pages of CIA and other records, extensively citing those documents to support its findings. There are more than 35,000 footnotes in the report. I believe it to be one of the most significant oversight efforts in the history of the United States Senate, and by far the most important oversight activity ever conducted by this committee.

. . . I will provide the report to President Obama and key executive branch officials for their review and comment. The report will remain classified and is not being released in whole or in part at this time. The committee will make those decisions after receiving the executive branch comments.

The report uncovers startling details about the CIA detention and interrogation program and raises critical questions about intelligence operations and oversight. . . .

Conducting oversight is sometimes a difficult and unpleasant task for all involved, but I am confident the CIA will emerge a better and more able organization as a result of the committee's work. I also believe this report will settle the debate once and for all over whether our nation should ever employ coercive interrogation techniques such as those detailed in this report.

I strongly believe that the creation of long-term, clandestine "black sites" and the use of so-called "enhanced-interrogation techniques" were terrible mistakes. The majority of the Committee agrees. . . . [*available at* http://www.feinstein.senate.gov/public/index.cfm/2012/12/feinstein-statement-on-cia-detention-interrogation-report.]

In April 2014, the Senate Intelligence Committee voted to declassify portions of the report, even while the Committee engaged in a public dispute with the CIA based on alleged electronic eavesdropping *of Committee staff* by the CIA during the investigation. The CIA is conducting the declassification review for President Obama, who will decide whether to release the excerpts of the report. Greg Miller & Adam Goldman, *Senate Panel Votes to Release CIA Interrogation Report*, Wash. Post, Apr. 3, 2014.

[NSL p. 951; CTL p. 565. Insert as new Note 4.]

4. *Contractor Liability After Kiobel.* After the Supreme Court decided *Kiobel v. Royal Dutch Petroleum Co.*, this *Supplement* p. 19, the district court threw out *Al Shimari* on the ground that the Alien Tort Statute does not encompass *any* claims arising outside the territorial United States, even if the defendants were U.S. contractors operating on a U.S. military base. *See Al Shimari v. CACI Int'l, Inc.*, 951 F. Supp. 2d 857 (E.D. Va. 2013). The Fourth Circuit vacated and remanded the district court decision in June 2014. *Al-Shimari v. CACI Premier Technology, Inc.*, No. 13-1937, 2014 WL 2922840 (4th Cir. 2014). Applying *Kiobel*, the court held that plaintiffs' claims "touch and concern" the territory of the United States with sufficient force to displace the presumption against extraterritorial application of the ATS. Because it was unable to determine from the record before it whether the claims present nonjusticiable political questions, the court did not reach the district court's dismissal of the plaintiffs' common law claims.

[NSL p. 951, CTL p. 565. Insert at end of chapter.]

Padilla v. Yoo
United States Court of Appeals, Ninth Circuit, May 2, 2012
678 F.3d 748

FISHER, Circuit Judge: After the September 11, 2001 attacks on the United States, the government detained Jose Padilla, an American citizen, as an enemy combatant. Padilla alleges that he was held incommunicado in military detention, subjected to coercive interrogation techniques and detained under harsh conditions of confinement, all in violation of his constitutional and statutory rights. In this lawsuit, plaintiffs Padilla and his mother, Estela Lebron, seek to hold defendant John Yoo, who was the Deputy Assistant Attorney General in the U.S. Department of Justice's Office of Legal Counsel (OLC) from 2001 to 2003, liable for damages they allege they suffered from these unlawful actions. Under recent Supreme Court law, however, we are compelled to conclude that, regardless of the legality of Padilla's detention and the wisdom of Yoo's judgments, at the time he acted the law was not "sufficiently clear that every reasonable official would have understood that what he [wa]s doing violate[d]" the plaintiffs' rights. We therefore hold that Yoo must be granted qualified immunity, and accordingly reverse the decision of the district court.

As we explain below, we reach this conclusion for two reasons. First, although during Yoo's tenure at OLC the constitutional rights of convicted prisoners and persons subject to ordinary criminal process were, in many respects, clearly established, it was not "beyond debate" at that time that Padilla — who was not a convicted prisoner or criminal defendant, but a suspected terrorist designated an enemy combatant and confined to military detention by order of the President — was entitled to the same constitutional protections as an ordinary convicted prisoner or accused criminal. Second, although it has been clearly established for decades that torture of an American citizen violates the Constitution, and we assume without deciding that Padilla's alleged treatment rose to the level of torture, that such treatment *was* torture was not clearly established in 2001-03.

I. BACKGROUND

A. . . .

[For the background of Padilla's initial arrest, military detention, and subsequent transfer to civilian custody, see NSL pp. 855-857 or CTL pp. 469-471.]

Padilla and his mother, Estela Lebron, filed this civil action against John Yoo, in his individual capacity, on January 4, 2008, two years after Padilla's military detention ended. . . . Padilla and Lebron alleged that Padilla was imprisoned in the military brig without charge and without the ability to defend himself or to challenge his conditions of confinement. They alleged that during Padilla's detention, he suffered gross physical and psychological abuse upon the orders of high-ranking government officials as part of a systematic program of abusive interrogation mirroring the alleged abuses committed at Guantanamo Bay, including extreme isolation; interrogation under threat of torture, deportation and even death; prolonged sleep adjustment and sensory deprivation; exposure to extreme temperatures and noxious odors; denial of access to necessary medical and psychiatric care; substantial interference with his ability to practice his religion; and incommunicado detention for almost two years, without access to family, counsel or the courts. . . .

. . . From 2001 to 2003, Yoo was Deputy Assistant Attorney General at OLC. Padilla and Lebron alleged that Yoo set in motion Padilla's allegedly illegal interrogation and detention, both by formulating unlawful policies for the designation, detention and interrogation of suspected "enemy combatants" and by issuing legal memoranda designed to evade legal restraints on those policies and to immunize those who implemented them. They alleged that, in doing so, Yoo abdicated his ethical duties as a government attorney and abandoned his office's tradition of providing objective legal advice to the President.

The complaint alleged that Yoo publicly acknowledged in his book, *War By Other Means,* that he stepped beyond his role as a lawyer to participate directly in developing policy in the war on terrorism. It alleged that Yoo shaped government policy in his role as a key member of a small, secretive and highly influential group of senior administration officials known as the "War Council," which met regularly "to develop policy in the war on terrorism." It alleged that Yoo acted outside the scope of his employment at OLC by taking instructions directly from White House Counsel Alberto Gonzales and providing Gonzales with verbal and written advice without first consulting Attorney General John Ashcroft. The complaint alleged that, in his role as the de facto head of war-on-terrorism legal issues, Yoo wrote and promulgated a series of memoranda that ultimately led to Padilla's allegedly unlawful treatment . . . .

The complaint alleged that these memoranda advised that there were no legal constraints on the Executive's policies with respect to the detention and interrogation of suspected terrorists. It alleged that the memoranda "did not provide the fair and impartial evaluation of the law required by OLC tradition and the ethical obligations of an attorney to provide the client with an exposition of the law adequate to make an informed decision." Rather, it alleged that Yoo "intentionally used the Memos to evade well-established legal constraints and to justify illegal policy choices that he knew had already been made — sometimes by virtue of his own participation in the War Council."

The complaint also alleged that Yoo personally participated in Padilla's unlawful military detention. Quoting from Yoo's book, it alleged that Yoo "personally 'reviewed the material on Padilla to determine whether he could qualify, legally, as an enemy combatant, and issued an opinion to that effect.'" It alleged that Ashcroft relied on Yoo's opinion in recommending to the President that Padilla be taken into military custody.

The complaint alleged that Padilla's designation as an enemy combatant, military detention, conditions of confinement and program of interrogation violated his rights to procedural and substantive due process, not to be subjected to cruel or unusual punishment or treatment that shocks the conscience, to freely exercise his religion, of access to information, to association with family members and friends, of access to legal counsel, of access to the courts, against compelled self-incrimination and against arbitrary and unconstitutional seizure and military detention. It alleged violations of the First, Fourth, Fifth, Sixth and Eighth Amendments to the United States Constitution, Article III of the Constitution, the Habeas Suspension and Treason Clauses of the Constitution and the Religious Freedom Restoration Act (RFRA), 42 U.S.C. §2000bb. . . .

B.

Yoo moved to dismiss the action for failure to state a claim upon which relief could be granted. He argued that the complaint failed to state a claim for money damages on three grounds. First, he argued that the plaintiffs could not state an action for damages because *Bivens* . . . did not apply. [In *Lebron v. Rumsfeld*, 670 F.3d 540 (4th Cir. 2012), the Fourth Circuit relied on this argument in dismissing Padilla's damages suit against those military and law enforcement officials directly involved in his detention and alleged mistreatment]. Second, Yoo argued that he was entitled to qualified immunity because the complaint failed to allege facts sufficient to establish his personal responsibility for the constitutional and statutory violations alleged in the complaint. Third, Yoo argued that he was entitled to qualified immunity because the complaint failed to allege a violation of clearly established constitutional or statutory rights. . . .

II. DISCUSSION

A.

The outcome of this appeal is governed by the Supreme Court's decision in *Ashcroft v. al-Kidd,* 131 S. Ct. 2074 (2011) [NSL p. 754; CTL p. 368]. . . .

The Court [in *al-Kidd*] began by reaffirming the general principle that "[q]ualified immunity shields federal and state officials from money damages unless a plaintiff pleads facts showing (1) that the official violated a statutory or constitutional right, and (2) that the right was 'clearly established' at the time of the challenged conduct." *Id.* at 2080. Significant here, under the second prong, a "Government official's conduct violates clearly established law when, at the time of the challenged conduct, '[t]he contours of [a] right [are] sufficiently clear' that every 'reasonable official would have understood that what he is doing violates that right.'" *Id.* at 2083. "We do not require a case directly on point, but existing precedent must have placed the statutory or constitutional question beyond debate." *Id.* The Court emphasized that "[q]ualified immunity gives government officials breathing room to make reasonable but mistaken judgments about open legal questions," *id.* at 2085, and admonished us "not to define clearly established law at a high level of generality." *Id.* at 2084. . . .

Here, the complaint alleged that Yoo, as a Justice Department attorney, participated in policy decisions and rendered legal opinions that ultimately authorized federal officials to designate Padilla as an enemy combatant, take him into military custody, hold him incommunicado without access to the courts or counsel and subject him to both coercive interrogation techniques and harsh conditions of confinement, in violation of his constitutional and statutory rights.

Padilla and Lebron acknowledge that at the time Yoo served as Deputy Assistant Attorney General at OLC, there did not exist a "single judicial opinion," holding that a United States citizen held in military detention as an enemy combatant possessed rights against the kind of treatment to which Padilla was subjected. They argue, however, that it was clearly established that Padilla possessed such rights because any reasonable official would have understood during 2001 to 2003 that a citizen detained as an enemy combatant had to be afforded at least the constitutional protections to which convicted prisoners and ordinary criminal suspects were entitled. That argument is foreclosed by *al-Kidd*, which compels us "not to define clearly established law at a high level of generality." . . .

Here, of course, the Supreme Court had not, at the time of Yoo's tenure at OLC, declared that American citizens detained as enemy combatants had to be treated at least as well, or afforded at least the same constitutional and statutory protections, as convicted prisoners. On the contrary, the Supreme Court had suggested in *Ex parte Quirin*, 317 U.S. 1 (1942), the most germane precedent in existence at the time of Yoo's tenure at OLC, that a citizen detained as an unlawful combatant could be afforded *lesser* rights than ordinary prisoners or individuals in ordinary criminal proceedings. . . .

Padilla and Lebron alternatively rely on the Supreme Court's decision in *Hamdi v. Rumsfeld*, 542 U.S. 507 (2004) [NSL p. 831, CTL p. 445], to establish that Padilla's treatment violated clearly established law. . . . When measured against [at least some of the] language in *Hamdi*, Padilla's alleged cruel and degrading treatment appears to have been a violation of his constitutional rights.

Hamdi, however, was not decided until 2004, so it could not have placed Yoo on clear notice of Padilla's constitutional rights in 2001-03 when Yoo was at the Department of Justice. Even after *Hamdi*, moreover, it remains murky whether an enemy combatant detainee may be subjected to conditions of confinement and methods of interrogation that would be unconstitutional if applied in the ordinary prison and criminal settings. Although *Hamdi* recognized that citizens detained as enemy combatants retain constitutional rights to due process, the Court suggested that those rights may not be coextensive with those enjoyed by other kinds of detainees. On the contrary, the Court held that the rights afforded to an enemy combatant detainee "may be tailored" to the circumstances, because "the full protections that accompany challenges to detentions in other settings may prove unworkable and inappropriate in the enemy-combatant setting." *Id.* at 535.

In sum, the plaintiffs did not, through their reliance on either *Hamdi* or cases involving ordinary prison and criminal settings, allege violations of constitutional and statutory rights that were clearly established in 2001-03. During that relevant time frame, the constitutional rights of convicted prisoners and persons subject to *ordinary* criminal process were, in many respects, clearly established. But Padilla was not a convicted prisoner or criminal defendant; he was a suspected terrorist designated an enemy combatant and confined to military detention by order of the President. He was detained as such because, in the opinion of the President — albeit allegedly informed by his subordinates, including Yoo — Padilla presented a grave danger to national security and possessed valuable intelligence information that, if communicated to the United States, could have been helpful to the United States in staving off further terrorist attacks. We express no opinion as to whether those allegations were true, or whether, even if true, they justified the extreme conditions of confinement to which Padilla says he was subjected. In light of Padilla's status as a designated enemy combatant, however, we cannot agree with the plaintiffs that he was just another detainee — or that it would necessarily have been "apparent" to someone in Yoo's position that Padilla was entitled to the same constitutional protections as an ordinary convicted prisoner or accused criminal. Given the unique circumstances and purposes of Padilla's detention, and in light of *Quirin,* an official could have had some reason to believe that Padilla's harsh treatment fell within constitutional bounds. . . .

B.

The absence of a decision defining the constitutional and statutory rights of citizens detained as enemy combatants need not be fatal to the plaintiffs' claims. The Supreme Court has long held that "officials can still be on notice that their conduct violates established law even in novel factual circumstances." *Hope v. Pelzer,* 536 U.S. 730, 741 (2002).

The plaintiffs invoke this principle here. They argue that, even if there is no specific judicial decision holding that the Fifth Amendment's prohibition on government conduct that "shocks the conscience" is violated when the government tortures a United States citizen designated as an enemy combatant, torture of a United States citizen is the kind of egregious constitutional violation for which a decision "directly on point" is not required. We agree with the plaintiffs that the unconstitutionality of torturing a United States citizen was "beyond debate" by 2001.[9] Yoo is entitled to qualified immunity, however, because it was not clearly established in 2001-03 that the treatment to which Padilla says he was subjected amounted to torture.

In 2001-03, there was general agreement that torture meant the intentional infliction of severe pain or suffering, whether physical or mental. The meaning of "severe pain or suffering," however, was less clear in 2001-03. *See, e.g.,* Michael W. Lewis, *A Dark Descent into Reality: Making the Case for an Objective Definition of Torture,* 67 Wash. & Lee L. Rev. 77, 82-83 (2010); Judith Resnik, *Detention, the War on Terror, and the Federal Courts,* 110 Colum. L. Rev. 579, 633-34 (2010); Sanford Levinson, *In Quest of a "Common Conscience":*

---

9. That substantive due process under the Fifth Amendment prohibits the government from engaging in conduct that "shocks the conscience" has long been clearly established. What has not been clearly established is how that standard applies to citizens detained as enemy combatants.

Reflections on the Current Debate About Torture, 1 J. Nat'l Security L. & Pol'y 231, 231-52 (2005).

In several influential judicial decisions in existence at the time of Yoo's tenure at OLC, for example, courts had declined to define certain severe interrogation techniques as torture:

Ireland v. United Kingdom, 25 Eur. Ct. H.R. (ser. A) (1978), is the European Court of Human Rights' leading decision on torture. The court considered whether five interrogation techniques used by the United Kingdom to interrogate suspected members of the Irish Republican Army violated Article 3 of the European Convention of Human Rights, which prohibits both torture and "inhuman or degrading treatment or punishment." The five techniques at issue were wall standing (i.e., stress positions), hooding, subjection to noise, sleep deprivation and deprivation of food and drink. . . . The court concluded that "[a]lthough the five techniques, as applied in combination, undoubtedly amounted to inhuman and degrading treatment," in violation of Article 3, "they did not occasion suffering of the particular intensity and cruelty implied by the word torture as so understood." *Id.* at 80.

In *HCJ 5100/94 Public Committee Against Torture in Israel v. Israel* 53(4) PD 817 [1999] (Isr.), the Israeli Supreme Court considered whether coercive techniques used by Israeli security forces violated international law. The techniques included hooding, violent shaking, painful stress positions, exposure to loud music and sleep deprivation. The court concluded that each of these techniques was illegal, although the court did not address whether they constituted torture rather than cruel, inhuman and degrading treatment, which was also prohibited by international law.

In *Price v. Socialist People's Libyan Arab Jamahiriya*, 294 F.3d 82 (D.C. Cir. 2002), the plaintiffs were two American citizens imprisoned in Libya, allegedly for political reasons. They alleged that they endured deplorable conditions while incarcerated, including urine-soaked mattresses, a cramped cell with substandard plumbing they were forced to share with seven other inmates, a lack of medical care and inadequate food. They also alleged that they were "kicked, clubbed and beaten" by prison guards, and "interrogated and subjected to physical, mental and verbal abuse." The plaintiffs sued Libya under the Foreign Sovereign Immunities Act, alleging torture. The court held that the plaintiffs had failed to adequately allege torture because they did not allege sufficiently *severe* pain or suffering, noting that "[t]he critical issue is the degree of pain and suffering that the alleged torturer intended to, and actually did, inflict upon the victim. The more intense, lasting, or heinous the agony, the more likely it is to be torture." *Id.* at 93. Although the plaintiffs alleged that they suffered "kicking, clubbing, and beatings," there was "no way to determine from the present complaint the severity of plaintiffs' alleged beatings — including their frequency, duration, the parts of the body at which they were aimed, and the weapons used to carry them out." *Id.*

In other decisions in existence at the time of Yoo's OLC tenure, this Circuit found torture, but the treatment at issue was more severe than that to which Padilla was allegedly subjected:

In *Al-Saher v. INS*, 268 F.3d 1143 (9th Cir. 2001), *amended on another ground*, 355 F.3d 1140 (9th Cir. 2004), an immigration case, we concluded that the petitioner was entitled to relief under the Convention Against Torture and Other Cruel, Inhuman or Degrading Treatment or Punishment (CAT) because he had been tortured in Iraq. On one occasion, the petitioner was detained, interrogated and severely beaten for one month. During his interrogations, he was blindfolded and his hands were tied behind his back. On another occasion, he was blindfolded, restrained, beaten and burned with cigarettes over an 8- to 10-day period. Noting that these actions "were specifically intended by officials to inflict severe physical pain" on the petitioner, we held, under CAT, that he suffered torture. *Id.* at 1147-48.

In *Hilao v. Estate of Marcos*, 103 F.3d 789 (9th Cir. 1996), an Alien Tort Statute case, we held that two plaintiffs, Sison and Piopongco, were tortured in the Philippines during the regime of Ferdinand Marcos. Sison had been interrogated by members of the military, who blindfolded and severely beat him while he was handcuffed and fettered; threatened him with electric shock and death; denied him sleep; and imprisoned him for seven months in a suffocatingly hot and unlit cell, measuring 2.5 meters square, during which time he was shackled to his cot, his handcuffs often so tight that the slightest movement made them cut into his flesh. During this period, Sison felt "extreme" and "almost undescribable" pain. After his seven months shackled to his cot, Sison spent more than eight years in detention, approximately five of them in solitary confinement and the rest in near-solitary confinement. In one round of interrogation, lasting six hours, Sison's limbs were shackled to a cot, a towel was placed over his nose and mouth and his interrogators then poured water down his nostrils so that he felt as though he were drowning. The other plaintiff — Piopongco — was arrested, held incommunicado, interrogated, subjected to mock executions and threatened with death.

Here, Padilla alleged that he was subjected to prolonged isolation; deprivation of light; exposure to prolonged periods of light and darkness, including being "periodically subjected to absolute light or darkness for periods in excess of twenty-four hours"; extreme variations in temperature; sleep adjustment; threats of severe physical abuse; death threats; administration of psychotropic drugs; shackling and manacling for hours at a time; use of "stress" positions; noxious fumes that caused pain to eyes and nose; loud noises; withholding of any mattress, pillow, sheet or blanket; forced grooming; suspensions of showers; removal of religious items; constant surveillance; incommunicado detention, including denial of all contact with family and legal counsel for a 21-month period; interference with religious observance; and denial of medical care for "serious and potentially life-threatening ailments, including chest pain and difficulty breathing, as well as for treatment of the chronic, extreme pain caused by being forced to endure stress positions." The complaint also alleged, albeit in conclusory fashion, that Padilla "suffered and continues to suffer severe mental and physical harm as a result of the forty-four months of unlawful military detention and interrogation." It also alleged that Padilla suffered "severe physical pain" and "profound disruption of his senses and personality."

We assume without deciding that Padilla's alleged treatment rose to the level of torture. That it *was* torture was not, however, "beyond debate" in 2001-03. There was at that time considerable debate, both in and out of government, over the definition of torture as applied to specific interrogation techniques. In light of that debate, as well as the judicial decisions discussed above, we cannot say that any reasonable official in 2001-03 would have known that the specific interrogation techniques allegedly employed against Padilla, however appalling, necessarily amounted to torture. Thus, although we hold that the unconstitutionality of torturing an American citizen was beyond debate in 2001-03, it was not clearly established at that time that the treatment Padilla alleges he was subjected to amounted to torture.

C.

For these reasons, we hold that Yoo is entitled to qualified immunity on the plaintiffs' claims.[16] Because we reverse on that basis, we do not address Yoo's alternative arguments that the complaint does not adequately allege his personal responsibility for Padilla's treatment and that a *Bivens* remedy is unavailable.

Our conclusion that Yoo is entitled to qualified immunity does not address the propriety of Yoo's performance of his duties at OLC otherwise. As amici point out, the complaint alleges that Yoo "*intentionally* violated professional standards reflected in OLC practice and *willfully* disregarded the obligations attendant on his office." Amici argue that "[s]uch conduct, if proven, would strike at the very heart of OLC's mission and seriously compromise the ability of the executive to make informed, even lawful, decisions." These allegations have been the subject of an internal Department of Justice investigation of Yoo's compliance with professional standards and are not at issue here.

III. CONCLUSION

Yoo is entitled to qualified immunity. The order of the district court denying Yoo's motion to dismiss is therefore reversed in pertinent part.

Reversed.

NOTES AND QUESTIONS

1. *"Clearly Established" Law.* In *Harlow v. Fitzgerald*, 457 U.S. 800 (1982), the Supreme Court articulated the modern standard for qualified immunity. Under *Harlow*, "government officials performing discretionary functions generally are shielded from liability for civil damages insofar as their conduct does not violate clearly established statutory or constitutional rights of which a reasonable person would have known." Thus, damages suits like *Padilla* raise two different

---

16. We have discretion to decide which of the two prongs of qualified immunity analysis to address first. *See al-Kidd*, 131 S. Ct. at 2080 (citing *Pearson v. Callahan*, 555 U.S. 223, 236 (2009)). Here, we consider only the second prong.

questions: the "illegality" question (whether the plaintiff's rights actually *were* violated) and the "liability" question (whether the defendant officer should have known that his conduct violated the plaintiff's "clearly established" rights). Do you see why the plaintiff must prevail on both questions in order to recover, whereas the defendant prevails if either question is resolved in his favor?

2. *Torture vs. CIDT.* Given the *Harlow* standard, what did the Ninth Circuit actually hold in *Padilla*? Did the Court of Appeals decide that Padilla's alleged mistreatment did or did not constitute torture? That it did or did not constitute cruel, inhuman, or degrading treatment (CIDT)? Why does the torture/CIDT distinction seem to matter so much to the Court of Appeals? Was it clear from 2001 to 2003 that torture was prohibited by U.S. law? Was it clear during the same time period that CIDT was unlawful? Was it clear during that time period on which side of the torture/CIDT line Padilla's alleged mistreatment fell? Is it clear today?

3. *The Specificity of the Legal Claim.* In *Padilla*, the court notes the Supreme Court's decision in *Hope v. Pelzer*, 536 U.S. 730 (2002), which rejected the argument that a defendant is entitled to qualified immunity unless the individual right at issue has been clearly established by a prior case squarely on point both legally *and* factually. Instead, *Hope* framed the inquiry as asking whether "in the light of pre-existing law the unlawfulness [should have been] apparent." 536 U.S. at 739. Given that standard, are you convinced by the *Padilla* court's analysis of prior case law, including the foreign and international decisions discussed earlier? After *Hope*, is the question whether Padilla's alleged mistreatment was as bad as that suffered by the plaintiffs in those cases, or rather whether those cases *should have* established the unlawfulness of the measures that were allegedly authorized against Padilla? Is this a distinction worth a difference?

4. *Footnote 16 and the Order of Battle.* In its decision in *Saucier v. Katz*, 533 U.S. 194 (2001), the Supreme Court mandated an "order of battle" in qualified immunity cases, pursuant to which courts had to first decide the illegality question before turning to the liability question. The justification for such an approach was to ensure that, even in cases in which the unlawfulness of the defendant's conduct was *not* clearly established (where the defendant therefore prevailed on liability), the

law *would be* established going forward. Lower-court judges, who were often left to decide constitutional questions that were not necessary to the result, complained bitterly, leading the Supreme Court to abandon the "*Saucier* sequence" in *Pearson v. Callahan*, 555 U.S. 223 (2009). Under *Pearson*, courts *may*, but need not, resolve the illegality question in cases in which the law was not clearly established. In footnote 16, the *Padilla* court cites *Pearson* to explain why it can sidestep whether Padilla's rights were *actually* violated. Do you see why *Padilla* will therefore have virtually no precedential effect? *Should* the Ninth Circuit have decided whether, going forward, Padilla's alleged mistreatment actually *was* a violation of his rights?

5. *National Security Litigation and the Pearson Problem.* Many damages suits against government officers arise out of conduct that can be challenged through other forms of litigation, including suits for prospective relief while the allegedly unlawful conduct is occurring, or as defenses to criminal prosecutions. In those contexts, *Pearson*'s effect on law-formation may not be significant, since judges will have numerous chances to articulate forward-looking principles of constitutional law in similar cases. But the same may not be true in national security litigation, given the far smaller number of putative victims, the uniqueness of many of the claims in such cases, and the government's prosecutorial discretion. Indeed, as the *Padilla* litigation itself demonstrates, the government will often take affirmative steps to *avoid* a judicial decision on the merits in national security cases. One of us has suggested that "the general rule articulated in *Pearson* will wreak particular havoc in the national security context, potentially freezing (or, at a minimum, substantially slowing) the development of constitutional law with regard to the surveillance, detention, and treatment of terrorism suspects." Stephen I. Vladeck, *The New National Security Canon*, 61 Am. U. L. Rev. 1295, 1328 (2012). If so, and if this is a problem worth a solution, should courts in cases like *Padilla* feel impelled to decide the illegality question even if they are not required to do so? Is there a better solution to this "*Pearson* problem"?

[NSL p. 974, CTL p. 588. Insert after Note 5.]

6. *Remedies from International Courts?* Khaled el-Masri, a German citizen of Lebanese descent, was pulled off a bus at the Macedonian border on New Year's eve 2003 after border guards apparently confused him with an Al Qaeda operative who had a similar name. He was locked in a hotel room in Skopje for 23 days and told that he would be shot if he attempted to leave. He was then taken to the Skopje airport, where he was transferred to a CIA team. CIA operatives stripped al-Masri, then beat, shackled, hooded, and allegedly sodomized him, before flying him to Afghanistan, where he was detained in solitary confinement for more than four months. Once the mistaken identity was confirmed, he was flown to Albania and left on the side of a road.

When el-Masri sought relief in U.S. courts against the CIA for his rendition and mistreatment, his claims were dismissed on state secrets doctrine grounds (*see* NSL pp. 142-158). *El-Masri v. United States*, 479 F.3d 296 (4th Cir. 2007), *cert. den.*, 552 U.S. 947 (2007). However, his claim against the government of Macedonia was vindicated when, in December 2012, the seventeen judges of the European Court of Human Rights ruled unanimously that Macedonia violated Article 5 the European Convention on Human Rights, which prohibits torture and inhuman or degrading treatment. *Case of El-Masri v. The Former Yugoslav Republic of Macedonia*, Grand Chamber, Dec. 13, 2012, *available at* http://www.aclu.org/files/assets/ el_masri_ruling.pdf. The Court awarded el-Masri about $78,000 in damages, finding that his extraordinary rendition was "by its deliberate circumvention of due process . . . anathema to the rule of law and the values protected by the Convention." *Id.*, para. 239. Macedonian officials should have known, said the Court, that when el-Masri was handed over to U.S. authorities he faced a considerable risk that his Article 5 rights would be violated. The Macedonian government thus failed in its duty to protect el-Masri from such violations, and it actively facilitated his detention in Afghanistan by handing him over to the CIA. Macedonia also violated Article 5 by holding el-Masri for 23 days in the Skopje hotel.

[NSL p. 1015; CTL p. 629. Insert after Note 8.]

United States v. Brehm

United States Court of Appeals, Fourth Circuit, 2012
691 F.3d 547, *cert. denied*, 133 S. Ct. 808 (2012)

KING, Circuit Judge: Sean Theodore Brehm, a citizen of South Africa, pleaded guilty in the Eastern District of Virginia to a federal charge of assault resulting in serious bodily injury, on condition that he be allowed to challenge through appeal the jurisdictional basis of the indictment underlying his conviction. The grand jury accused Brehm of stabbing a British subject, "J.O.," during an altercation at Kandahar Airfield ("KAF"), while both men were employed with private contractors supporting the NATO war effort in Afghanistan.

On appeal, Brehm maintains that the indictment's reliance on the Military Extraterritorial Jurisdiction Act ("MEJA") was misplaced, in that the statute — which Brehm admits is valid on its face — cannot be applied to him in a manner consistent with the Constitution. Brehm also asserts that the government has failed to establish a sufficient nexus between him and the United States to support the exercise of criminal jurisdiction, pointing out that, prior to his arrival in Virginia as an accused, neither he nor his victim had ever set foot in this country. For that and other reasons, according to Brehm, his prosecution does not comport with due process. As described below, we reject Brehm's challenges to his conviction and affirm the district court's judgment.

I.

KAF is a NATO-operated military base that, in 2010, was home to about 19,000 troops, more than 15,000 of which were American. Brehm was employed by DynCorp International LLC, a domestic military contractor headquartered in Falls Church, Virginia. On Thanksgiving Day, November 25, 2010, Brehm was at KAF to process arriving DynCorp employees, when he encountered J.O. The latter was an employee of Global Strategies Group, a United Kingdom entity also providing support services. J.O. had just returned from a vacation with his American wife, who was likewise employed at KAF. The two men engaged in a heated altercation concerning an ongoing and rancorous dispute, which ended calamitously with Brehm stabbing J.O. in the left arm and stomach, seriously injuring him. Afterward, Brehm was taken into custody by United States military police.

Brehm had signed a "Foreign Service Employment Agreement" with DynCorp in July 2010. The agreement provided, in pertinent part, that Brehm "has been informed of, understands and accepts that [he] may be subject to U.S. . . . federal civilian criminal jurisdiction under the [MEJA] by accompanying the U.S. Armed Forces outside the United States." J.A. 121. . . .

Brehm promptly filed a pair of motions seeking dismissal of the indictment. The first motion, on February 25, 2011, asserted that "Brehm's connection to the United States is so lacking" that the district court could not, "consistent with the requirements of the Due Process Clause, exercise jurisdiction under MEJA." J.A. 19. The second, on March 4, 2011, insisted that MEJA, as applied to Brehm, was unconstitutional in that "the framers did not grant Congress the power to police routine assaults between foreigners that occur abroad and do not harm the United States." *Id.* at 44. The court conducted a hearing on the motions on March 29, 2011, and it denied them both by memorandum opinion the following day. *See United States v. Brehm,* No. 1:11–cr–00011, 2011 WL 1226088 (E.D. Va. Mar. 30, 2011) (the "Opinion").

Facing trial on the indictment, Brehm agreed with the government to conditionally plead guilty to Count Two in return for, inter alia, being permitted to appeal the district court's denial of his motions to dismiss. *See* Fed. R. Crim. P. 11(a)(2). . . .

III.

A.

[In this part of the opinion, Judge King held that MEJA does not exceed Congress's powers under Article I, §8.] . . .

B.

Though a criminal statute having extraterritorial reach is declared or conceded substantively valid under the Constitution, its enforcement in a particular instance must comport with due process. Some courts have, as a proxy for due process, required "a sufficient nexus between the defendant and the United States, so that such application would not be arbitrary or fundamentally unfair." *United States v. Davis,* 905 F.2d 245, 248-49 (9th Cir. 1990) (citation omitted); *see also United States v. Yousef,* 327 F.3d 56, 111 (2d Cir. 2003). The court of appeals in *Davis* concluded that the requisite nexus was present in a prosecution under the Maritime Drug Law Enforcement Act ("MDLEA"), where the British defendant and his boat were seized off the coast of California while attempting to smuggle marijuana into the United States. *See* 905 F.2d at 249. In *Yousef,* the Second Circuit arrived at the same result with respect to Middle Eastern terrorists tried for multiple federal crimes associated with their plot to bomb American commercial aircraft in Southeast Asia. *See* 327 F.3d at 118.

It is undoubtedly the case that, unlike the defendants in *Davis* and *Yousef,* Brehm did not target his conduct toward American soil or American commerce. Nevertheless, his actions affected significant American interests at KAF, not the least of which were the preservation of law and order on the base, the maintenance of military-related discipline, and the reallocation of DOD resources to confine Brehm, provide care for J.O., and investigate the incident. Indeed, Brehm's very presence inside KAF was possible only pursuant to an official DOD Letter of Authorization, entitling him to DOD-furnished transportation, meals, and equipment. Although KAF was not technically territory of the United States, the American influence was so pervasive that we think it a suitable proxy for due process purposes, such that the imposition of American criminal law there is not arbitrary.

On occasion, the connection between the United States and a putative criminal defendant may properly be more fluid, as was the case in *United States v. Angulo-Hernandez,* 565 F.3d 2 (1st Cir. 2009). In *Angulo-Hernandez,* a MDLEA prosecution, the court of appeals rejected the challenge of drug smugglers whose Bolivian-flagged boat was intercepted by the Coast Guard in international waters. The smugglers were prosecuted pursuant to an agreement between the United States and Bolivia to enforce the former's drug laws against the latter's maritime fleet members. Under the circumstances, the First Circuit had little difficulty concluding that due process is satisfied even absent a discernible jurisdictional nexus where "the flag nation has consented to the application of United States law to the defendants." *Id.* at 11.

The American presence at KAF and throughout Afghanistan is regulated in part by a written arrangement similar in respects to the one in *Angulo-Hernandez. See* Agreement regarding the Status of United States Military and Civilian Personnel of the U.S. Department of

Defense Present in Afghanistan in connection with Cooperative Efforts in Response to Terrorism, Humanitarian and Civic Assistance, Military Training and Exercises, and Other Activities, U.S.-Afg., May 28, 2003, 42 I.L.M. 1500, 2003 WL 21754316 [hereinafter the "Agreement"]. Within the Agreement, the Afghan government, in recognition of "the particular importance of disciplinary control by the United States military authorities," authorized the American government "to exercise its criminal jurisdiction over the personnel of the United States." 2003 WL 21754316, at *4.

The Agreement refers to "personnel" without limiting the term to those serving in the military, and without purporting to exclude civilians. It is reasonable, then, to interpret "personnel of the United States" to include employees of DynCorp and other American contractors and subcontractors. With Afghanistan having disclaimed any interest in prosecuting criminal conduct at KAF by those situated similarly to Brehm, due process is not offended by the United States stepping into the jurisdictional void. Indeed, absent the credible threat of American prosecution of civilian crimes at KAF, it is conceivable that such conduct would go unpunished. The risk of that sort of random lawlessness is readily seen as inimical to the success of the military mission in Afghanistan, and thus contrary to the American interest in that mission. Insofar as the enactment of MEJA serves to legitimately advance that interest, its application is unlikely to be arbitrary. . . .

IV.

In accordance with the foregoing, we affirm Brehm's conviction in the district court.

Affirmed.

NOTES AND QUESTIONS

1. *Due Process, Indeed.* In essence, the Fourth Circuit answers the question we posed in Note 8 on NSL p. 1015, CTL p. 629: Whether or not it's necessary, due process (through minimum contacts) is *sufficient* to support the prosecution of a non-citizen for offenses committed outside the territorial United States under the "passive personality" principle. But do you agree that Brehm's contacts with the United States — through his employer — were sufficient to *satisfy* ordinary "minimum contacts"

analysis? Isn't the Fourth Circuit's analysis more focused on the sufficiency of the U.S. government's contacts with Afghanistan? Isn't that backwards?

2. *A One-Way Ratchet?* *Brehm* was decided just three weeks after the Court of Appeals for the Armed Forces, in *United States v. Ali*, 72 M.J. 128 (C.A.A.F. 2012), held that a non-citizen military contractor could be tried by court-martial for offenses committed in Iraq entirely because his contacts with the United States were *insufficient* to trigger Fifth and Sixth Amendment protections. In *Ali*, however, the defendant had also participated in pre-deployment training *within* the territorial United States before deploying to Iraq. Is it possible that contacts sufficient to support a civilian criminal prosecution could be *less* than those that are insufficient to trigger the *protections* of the Fifth and Sixth Amendments? Or are *Brehm* and *Ali* irreconcilable?

3. *The Implications of Brehm.* Whatever the merits of the Fourth Circuit's analysis, it certainly supports exceptionally broad assertions of criminal jurisdiction by the United States — especially in the context of military, and potentially terrorism-related, offenses. The upside is obvious: the more expansive our extraterritorial criminal jurisdiction, the more civilian criminal prosecution becomes a means of incapacitating terrorism suspects (and other criminals) anywhere in the world. But might there be downsides, as well? Put another way, have we forgotten why, as Note 5 asserts, the "passive-personality theory traditionally has been anathema to U.S. law and practice"? Other than the defendants (who arguably become subject to criminal prosecution in a far greater number of jurisdictions, perhaps without fair notice), who — or what — is negatively affected by extraterritorial criminal jurisdiction premised on the passive personality principle?

[NSL p. 1032; CTL p. 646. Replace *United States v. Rosen* with the following two cases.]

While *Abu Ali* was a criminal prosecution, the concern about secret evidence carries over to civil cases and immigration proceedings, as the following case shows.

Ibrahim v. Department of Homeland Security (*Ibrahim II*)

United States District Court, Northern District of California, Dec. 20, 2012
2012 WL 6652362

WILLIAM ALSUP, District Judge. . . .

[The background of this case is described *supra*, p. 189 in this *Supplement*.]

1. Secret and *Ex Parte* Communications.

The analysis begins by addressing the request by the government to dismiss this case based on secret evidence the government wishes to show the judge *ex parte* and extra record. It came about as follows:

After the government's second reversal by the court of appeals in this six-year old action, the government again moved to dismiss under Rule 12, again moving on lack-of-standing grounds, even though the standing issue had gone the other way on appeal. While the briefing was in progress, a telephone call came into the court staff saying that a federal agent was on his way from Washington to San Francisco to show the judge confidential records about this case, all to be relied upon by the government in support of its motion to dismiss (but not to be disclosed to the other side). The officer would take back the records after the judge reviewed them and would leave no record behind of what he had shown the judge. Upon hearing of this, the judge suspended this proposed process and called for the briefing that is the subject of this order, namely the extent to which the government may rely on secret *ex parte* communication in connection with its motion to move to dismiss. Pending resolution of that issue, the Court has not reviewed any such *ex parte* communications (and believes they are not even in the courthouse). Nor has it read any of the redacted passages in the briefing (and believes unredacted versions are not even in the courthouse).

Our court of appeals has not spoken directly to our circumstance so this order will review the three most pertinent decisions. In essence, those decisions strongly favor maintenance of our traditional system of fair play in which both sides have notice of the arguments and evidence being used against them. Nonetheless, for good cause, the judge may receive *ex parte* secret communications for deciding ancillary matters, such as discovery privileges, but only in the rarest of circumstances should the judge do so to resolve or to end a case. It is a matter of discretion for the district judge. Now follows an analysis of the three appellate decisions.

In a 1991 appellate decision that our court of appeals was "careful to limit" to the "precise facts of this case," the district judge had reviewed *ex parte* and *in camera* an FBI declaration stating that an FBI agent had been acting within the course and scope of his employment for the United States and then, based thereon, dismissed a civil suit brought by a criminal-investigation target against the agent. This decision is the government's best authority. The plaintiff there challenged the *ex parte/in camera* procedure. The court of appeals was clearly troubled by it, stating:

> While in our judicial system adversary proceedings are the norm and ex parte proceedings the exception, this court has generally recognized the capacity of a district judge to "fashion and guide the procedures to be followed in cases before him." *United States v. Thompson,* 827 F.2d 1254, 1257 (9th Cir. 1987) (finding, in a criminal context, that district court erred in considering government's reasons for utilization of peremptory challenges ex parte). "[D]istrict judges are able to consider matters that may be unique to particular fact situations and tailor procedures to serve the ends of justice. . . ." *Id.* at 1258. We find that the procedure used by the court in the instant case was proper, it adequately balanced the rights of the Government and Meridian. The Government's interest in having FBI documents, which relate to an ongoing investigation, remain confidential was clearly satisfied by the court's action; and although Meridian did not have the opportunity to conduct discovery and cross-examine the Government's witnesses, its interests as a litigant are satisfied by the ex parte/in camera decision of an impartial district judge. However, because procedures such as these should be used only in unique situations, we are careful to limit our holding to the precise facts of this case.

Meridian Intern. Logistics, Inc. v. United States, 939 F.2d 740, 745 (9th Cir. 1991). Although there was no reversal per se on the procedural ground, the court of appeals reversed on the merits, holding that the generalized *ex parte* declarations were insufficient to establish that all agent acts had been within the scope of FBI authority.

Meridian is distinguishable for several reasons. First, the dismissal by the district judge was pursuant to a statutory (and public) certification by the Attorney General that the FBI actions involved had all been within the scope and course of FBI employment. . . . The only role of the *ex parte/in camera* declarations was to supply proof to back up the certification as to scope. So, the first point of distinction is the limited role that the declarations played in *Meridian.*

Second, despite its limited role, our court of appeals nonetheless reversed on the merits and held that the declarations were too inadequate and too conclusory to support the scope certification. It remanded for reconsideration and instructed the district judge to "entertain further documentary proof by the parties." *Id.* at 745. This meant that, on remand, both sides would have an opportunity to submit evidence on the scope issue, not just the government.

Third, our court of appeals described the substantive declarations in its public order, stating that they only generally asserted that the agent's investigation had been proper without addressing the specific factual allegation of Meridian's complaint. Put differently, under our system of law, the court felt obliged to explain the basis for its ruling, even if that meant revelation of some of the information in the secret submission.

Fourth, unlike here, the government there at least had the declarations filed in the court record, even if under seal, so that there would be a precise judicial record for appeal. Here, by contrast, the government wishes to whisk away all of its secret evidence and leave no trace behind in our district court records for appellate review. Our court of appeals would have to depend upon an agency bureaucratic process to recreate the same material shown to the district judge.

In short, *Meridian* provides guidance and a word of caution. Our court of appeals limited its holding there "to the precise facts" of that case. Our facts are much different. Here, we have no public statutory certification. We would have no district court record for appellate review. We would have no proceeding where both sides were given a chance to submit documentary proof on the issue, for here no one has a clue what the government's secret evidence purports to address.

In *Gilmore v. Gonzales,* 435 F.3d 1125 (9th Cir. 2006), our court of appeals itself ordered the government to file under seal and *ex parte* materials sufficient to show that a TSA Security Directive was a "final order." This was done on appeal in a suit by someone who refused to give his identification at the airport security check-in and sued to challenge the authority of the TSA to condition the right to travel on showing proper identification. If the TSA Security Directive was a "final order," then the district court lacked subject-matter jurisdiction and only the court of appeals could hear a petition for review. After reviewing the Security Directive *in camera* and *ex parte,* our court of appeals described the directive sufficiently in its ruling to demonstrate that it was indeed a "final order" and then transferred the matter to itself under its own original review jurisdiction. Nothing in this *ex parte* procedure was used to make a ruling on the merits and, indeed, our court of appeals went on to reach the merits in the next passage in the opinion. By contrast, here the government seeks to use *ex parte* communications to defeat plaintiff's case altogether.

Finally, let's turn to a decision of our appellate court most on point. Although Congress later enacted a provision to strip federal courts of subject-matter jurisdiction to review certain immigration proceedings, our court of appeals held — in an action commenced *before* the jurisdiction-stripping enactment — that due process was violated when the government uses secret, classified information to deny resident illegal aliens the privilege of legalization, that is, temporary or permanent resident status. *American-Arab Anti-Discrimination Committee v. Reno,* 70 F.3d 104, 1066-71 (9th Cir. 1995), *vacated on other grounds,* 525 U.S. 471 (1999). This part of the decision by our court of appeals remains good law. Given that in our very case, our court of appeals has now held that Ibrahim, even though voluntarily outside our country, is entitled to assert claims to the same extent as an alien within our borders, it is hard to avoid the *Reno* principle in the instant civil action.

To be sure, there are circumstances where a district judge must and should examine *ex parte* materials *in camera.* When claims of privilege are made in discovery matters to shield material from revelation, we do so to rule on the privilege. But there no one is yet trying to end or to win a case on the merits in secret — rather, the issue is whether the other side has a right to obtain the allegedly privileged evidence. In contrast, where the holder affirmatively seeks to use the evidence to win or to end the case, then, of course, any privilege must be deemed waived and both sides then have access to it, at least under an appropriate protective order. Here the government seeks to affirmatively use allegedly privileged information to dispose of the case entirely without ever revealing to the other side what its secret evidence might be.

Similarly, in the *Rovario* context in criminal cases, we are sometimes called on to hold an *in camera* hearing to examine a confidential informant under oath to determine the extent to which the informant has sufficient evidence helpful to the defense so as to overcome the *Rovario* privilege and require disclosure to the defense of the identity of the witness. *Rovario v. United States,* 353 U.S. 53, 59 (1957). Again, however, in that context, the government is *not* trying to use secret information to convict. It does not wish to use the evidence at all. It is the *other side* that wants to have access to the evidence for potential use in court. And, it might be added, when this is done, the proceeding is reported and the transcript is made part of the record, albeit under seal, for the review by the court of appeals. Before the *in camera* review, moreover, it is the practice of at least this district judge to ask defense counsel to submit a list of questions to be covered by the judge during the *in camera* proceeding.

Similarly, a district judge sometimes reviews potential *Brady* material *in camera* and *ex parte* to rule on whether it must be turned over. Again, in those circumstances, the government does not seek to affirmatively rely on the material. Rather, the question is whether to disclose it for potential use by the other side. These are only examples. There are other *ex parte* circumstances known to the courts but the main point is now evident.

In the exercise of its discretion, here is how the Court concludes such issues should be determined. Where the government seeks to end or win a case entirely based on secret evidence via an *ex parte* communication, it should first submit a precis available to both sides (i) laying out the general purport of the argument and evidence such that the other side will have an opportunity to respond to the general tenor of the proposed submission and (ii) explaining why more detail should not be made available to the other side. Then both sides may address the fairness and need for the *ex parte* procedure and, if it is to be done at all, the parameters for it. The more case dispositive the proposed submission, the more justification should be shown. In sum, only in the rarest of circumstances should a district judge, in his or her discretion, receive *ex parte* argument and evidence in secret from only one side aimed at winning or ending a case over the objection of the other side. Here, the government has not justified its sweeping proposal. It has gone so far as even to redact from its table of authorities some of the reported caselaw on which it relies! This is too hard to swallow.

This order holds that the government has not justified and may not affirmatively seek to dismiss this civil action based upon proposed secret *ex parte* communications with the district judge. If the government seeks to make affirmative use of evidence to end the case, then it must disclose that information — under an appropriate protective order, of course, but nonetheless disclose it. If it does not wish to make such affirmative use, then it may withhold it subject only to the possibility that plaintiff's counsel may eventually seek discovery of it, in which case it may or may not be kept under wraps depending on the strength of the competing discovery consideration at that time and the strength of the privilege asserted.

Therefore, the Court will ignore all of the redacted material in the government briefs on this set of motions and will rule on the same paperwork made available to both sides, which is totally redacted as to the standing issue. The government's latest motion based on lack of standing, being a complete mystery, is DENIED. . . .

United States v. Rosen

United States District Court, Eastern District of Virginia, 2007
520 F. Supp. 2d 786

T.S. ELLIS, III, District Judge. At issue in this Espionage Act prosecution is the government's second motion pursuant to §6(c) of the Classified Information Procedures Act (CIPA), 18 U.S.C. App. 3, to introduce certain summaries, redactions, and substitutions at trial in lieu of certain specific classified information, and to use the "silent witness rule" (SWR) with respect to portions of certain documents and recordings. . . .

I. CIPA Proceedings to Date

Defendants Steven Rosen and Keith Weissman are charged with conspiracy to violate the Espionage Act, in violation of 18 U.S.C. §§793(g) and (e). Rosen is also charged with one count of aiding and abetting alleged co-conspirator Larry Franklin's unauthorized disclosure of national defense information, in violation of 18 U.S.C. §[§]2, 793(d). The Superseding Indictment generally charges that defendants cultivated sources of information within the United States government, obtained or sought to obtain NDI [National Defense Information] from those sources, and disclosed that information to a variety of other individuals not authorized to receive it, including American Israel Public Affairs Committee (AIPAC) staffers, journalists, and foreign government officials. . . .

The government . . . filed a motion, ostensibly pursuant to CIPA §6(c), in which it sought application of the SWR to most of the classified information at issue in the case. The Court struck this motion in its entirety, finding, *inter alia,* that the government's proposed extensive use of the SWR effectively closed the trial to the public and that the government had not adequately justified this trial closure under the applicable standard of *Press-Enterprise Co. v. Superior Court of California,* 464 U.S. 501 (1984). The government has now filed a second CIPA §6(c) motion in which the proposed use of the SWR is significantly reduced, and in which the government also proposes numerous conventional CIPA §6(c) substitutions to be provided to the public and the jury in the same form. The motion has been fully briefed and argued, and is now ripe for resolution.

II. Applicable Law . . .

C. The Silent Witness Rule

In addition to conventional CIPA substitutions, *i.e.* redactions, admissions, and summaries, the government also proposes use of the SWR, a procedure whereby certain evidence designated by the government is made known to the judge, the jury, counsel, and witnesses, but is withheld from the public. Under this procedure, a witness referring to this evidence would not specifically identify or describe it, but would instead refer to it by reference to page and line numbers of a document or transcript, or more commonly by use of codes such as "Person 1," "Country A," etc. The jury, counsel, and the judge would have access to a key alerting them to the meaning of these code designations; the public, however, would not have access to this key.10 Any recordings containing the portions designated for SWR treatment would be played in open court, but would revert to static when the portions designated to be treated under the SWR are reached; thus, the public would not hear these portions. At the same time, however, jurors, counsel, and the judge would listen on headphones to the unredacted recording. This SWR procedure is in sharp contrast to the CIPA procedure, which contemplates that any substitutions, summaries, and redactions will be made available to the public and jury in identical form. . . .

The SWR is a novel evidence presentation technique that has received little judicial attention in the context of the use of classified information in trials. . . . This paucity of judicial precedent on the SWR's use in CIPA cases counsels caution with respect to its use in this context.

The threshold question that must be resolved with respect to the SWR's use in this case is whether it is even permissible to use in the CIPA context. Put differently, the question is whether CIPA provides the exclusive means of dealing with classified information in criminal trials and, even if so, whether the SWR can be said to be authorized by CIPA §6(c) as constituting a species of "summary" or "substitution" under that provision. These are not easily answered questions. Substantial arguments exist on both sides of these questions. Defendants point chiefly to CIPA's comprehensiveness in its prescriptions for the handling of classified information in trial. This comprehensiveness, defendants argue, manifests Congress' intent to forbid the use of any trial presentation techniques not specifically authorized by CIPA, including the SWR. A closely-related statutory construction argument defendants advance relies on the familiar interpretive canon *expressio unius est exclusio alterius,* namely that "[w]hen a statute limits a thing to be done in a particular mode, it [the statute] includes the negative of any other mode." *Diaz v. Va. Hous. Dev. Auth.,* 117 F. Supp. 2d 500, 504 (E.D. Va. 2000). Defendants point further in support of their argument to Rule 26, Fed. R. Crim. P., which in general terms states that trial testimony "must be taken in open court, unless otherwise provided by a statute or by rules adopted under 28 U.S.C. §§2072-2077."

Although not insubstantial, these arguments, in the end, fail to persuade. CIPA, while undeniably detailed in some respects, is neither explicitly nor implicitly exclusive as to the trial treatment of classified information. CIPA provides no answer, for example, to the question whether the classification markings on relevant documents should be removed as inadmissible hearsay as to the issue whether the document's contents are NDI within the meaning of the Espionage Act. Nor does CIPA provide any guidance on whether it might either be appropriate or required to issue a jury instruction limiting the purposes for which the jury might consider a document's classification markings. Similarly, CIPA does not address the question, presented in this case, whether it is appropriate to allow disparate access by experts to certain classified information redacted from a relevant classified trial document. Also not addressed by CIPA is whether witnesses whose identity is classified may appear to testify using a pseudonym, a mask or some other device to conceal the witness's identity. . . .

In sum, CIPA is neither exhaustive nor explicitly exclusive with respect to the presentation of classified testimony or documents at trial. It follows that CIPA cannot be said to exclude the use of the SWR at trial. And, indeed, while no court has squarely addressed this precise question, a few courts have implicitly approved the use of the SWR at trial. Other courts, without using the "SWR" term, have approved the presentation of evidence in one form to the jury and in another form to the public. In doing so, these courts have given effect to Congress' express intent in enacting CIPA that federal district judges "must be relied on to fashion creative and fair solutions to these problems," *i.e.,* the problems raised by use of classified information in trials. S. Rep. 96-823, *reprinted in* 1980 U.S.C.C.A.N. 4294. In short, the SWR is precisely the sort of judicially-created fair solution envisioned by Congress.

Nor is Rule 26 of any aid to defendants' argument. The Rule is general and aspirational and suffers the fate of all general rules: It has well-established exceptions. Courts in criminal cases have in a variety of circumstances partially closed proceedings to accommodate overriding interests, such as the safety of confidential informants and undercover officers. The SWR is simply another of these exceptions. Of course, the SWR should be used sparingly and only where the standards governing trial closures are met. It may not be used excessively, as was true with the government's first motion pursuant to CIPA §6(c).

Less difficult to answer is the second question posed, namely whether the SWR is merely a species of redaction or substitution authorized by CIPA §6(c). It is not. CIPA §6(c) redactions and substitutions, unlike the SWR, do not effect any closing of the trial to the public. To the contrary, CIPA plainly envisions that substitutions and redactions will be made available in the same form to the public as to the trial participants. This is confirmed not only by the plain meaning of CIPA's text, but also by the absence of any statutory language or legislative history concerning the First Amendment considerations raised by the partial closing of the trial that results from the SWR's use. It is difficult to believe that this important constitutional consequence went unnoticed by CIPA's drafters. It went unnoticed because it was not present; CIPA's redactions and substitutions do not close the trial. The

SWR is not part of CIPA. To conclude otherwise impermissibly engrafts on CIPA a judicial gloss of constitutional magnitude never envisioned, discussed, or provided for by CIPA's architects.

Given that the SWR is not part of CIPA and is neither foreclosed by CIPA nor by Rule 26, the question now presented is what standards apply for its application. As explained in [*United States v. Rosen (Rosen VII)*, 487 F. Supp. 2d 703 (E.D. Va. 2007)], use of the SWR constitutes a partial closure of the trial — or, if used extensively, a complete closure of the trial — because it prevents the public from seeing and hearing the complete body of evidence in the case. Of course, the SWR is not *per se* impermissible because it closes the trial, but use of the procedure is permissible only after a searching analysis, both because the rights of the public and defendants to a public trial are constitutionally guaranteed, and also because erroneous deprivation of the right to a public trial is *per se* prejudicial. Specifically, because the SWR effects a partial closure of the trial, the use of the rule must survive scrutiny under *Press-Enterprise. Press-Enterprise* requires that before a trial may be closed to the public, the proponent of the closure must demonstrate, and the court must find, (i) that a compelling interest exists to justify the closure, (ii) that the closure is no broader than necessary to protect that interest, and (iii) that no reasonable alternatives exist to closure. Additionally, the court must also make findings concerning these determinations on the record. Importantly, as applied to a trial closure premised on the need to protect classified information, the *Press-Enterprise* inquiry into reasonable alternatives must consider whether a conventional CIPA substitution is feasible in the circumstances.

Although *Press-Enterprise* does not require an explicit finding that a trial closure is fair to defendants, it is appropriate to reject any use of the SWR that is unfair to defendants. This is so for several reasons. First, defendants have a due process right to a fundamentally fair trial. Second, *Press-Enterprise* and its progeny are concerned with conventional sealing of proceedings and simply did not foresee or address this novel procedure, which is a "highly artificial" means of presenting evidence that could, in many circumstances, inhibit the ability of witnesses and counsel to communicate with the jury, to the detriment of defendants' ability to present their defense fairly. In other words, conventional sealing of a courtroom under *Press-Enterprise* does not alter the manner in which evidence and argument are presented, but merely restricts who is physically present to hear the evidence and argument. The SWR is different. It has some features of both a trial closure, in that some evidence presented to the jury is kept from the public, and of a CIPA substitution, in that some evidence is discussed in open court only via codes or euphemisms, which, in a limited way, may be viewed as analogous to substitutions allowed by §6(c). Thus, even though the SWR is not a substitution or redaction authorized by CIPA, it is only sensible that both *Press-Enterprise* analysis and a CIPA-like fairness analysis should be undertaken before the SWR's use is authorized. Yet the potential for unfairness from a conventional substitution and from the SWR are different in important ways, a point that merits further elaboration.

Because the SWR, unlike a conventional summary or redaction, permits the jury to view the actual evidence the government seeks to protect from public disclosure, there is no potential for unfairness based on the factfinder's inability to learn relevant, classified facts which have been summarized or redacted out. Yet there is potential for unfairness in the SWR's use; it lies (i) in the awkwardness of presentation and resulting jury confusion, (ii) in witnesses' and counsel's inability to explore fully and argue about the facts protected by the SWR, and (iii) in the prejudice from employing a procedure that suggests to the jury that the information being discussed is a closely-held government secret when the jury itself must decide that very issue. Assessing unfairness of this sort is more difficult than assessing the fairness of a conventional CIPA substitution. Under CIPA §6(c), a court need only consider whether defendants, in making their defense, need to introduce into evidence factual details present in the classified information, but not in the substitution. In other words, §6(c) calls for a focused evidentiary ruling: Are particular facts contained in the classified material, but not in the substitution relevant and significantly exculpatory? In contrast, fairness under the SWR must consider all the mechanics of the SWR's use at trial, including whether the defendants can fairly present evidence, cross-examine, and argue to the jury about the facts protected by the SWR, whether an ordinary juror will be able to follow the evidence and argument if presented by the SWR, and whether the prejudice from the rule's use is curable by an instruction or otherwise. This fairness analysis is no easy task, but it is required.

The SWR's use may entail a second type of potential unfairness to a defendant, namely infringement of a defendant's Sixth Amendment right to a public trial. This right helps ensure that the public sees the evidence and proceedings so that it can make its own assessment about the fairness of the proceedings. This public scrutiny of a trial provides some insurance against an unfair prosecution or proceeding. The public's assessment of the fairness of a trial may be impaired by the use of the SWR if that use distorts the meaning of the underlying evidence. Thus, even if an SWR proposal does not hinder the defense in presenting its case, it may, in certain circumstances not present here, be appropriate to reject or modify an SWR "substitution" or code if the code significantly distorts the meaning of the underlying information. Unlike the effect the SWR may have on a defendant's right to cross-examine, this public trial concern is adequately accommodated by the *Press-Enterprise* test for trial closure, as the analysis for closing a trial under the First Amendment is the same as the analysis required for closing a trial under the Sixth Amendment.

To summarize, because the concerns animating both *Press-Enterprise* and CIPA are present when the SWR is used, it is appropriate to approve use of the SWR only when both tests are satisfied, that is only when the government establishes (i) an overriding reason for closing the trial, (ii) that the closure is no broader, (iii) that no reasonable alternatives exist to closure, and (iv) that the use of the SWR provides defendants with substantially the same ability to make their defense as full public disclosure of the evidence, presented without the use of codes. . . .

This Memorandum Opinion outlines the legal principles governing the disposition of the government's second motion pursuant to CIPA §6(c). A separate classified, sealed order will issue applying the principles elucidated here and setting forth the specific rulings made with respect to the government's second CIPA §6(c) motion.

[NSL p. 1051; CTL p. 665. Insert before Section D.]

C1. National Security Criminal Procedure: *Miranda*, Presentment, and Speedy Trial

Recent events such as the 2013 Boston Marathon bombings and the June 2014 capture of Abu Khattala — the alleged ringleader of the 2012 Benghazi attacks — have rekindled debates over whether captured terrorism suspects should be detained without trial, tried by civilian court, or tried by military commission. Some have argued, as well, that the government should be able to interrogate these suspects without advising them of their rights to counsel and to remain silent under *Miranda v. Arizona*, 384 U.S. 436 (1966), at least for some time before criminal proceedings formally begin. *See, e.g.*, Charlie Savage, *Debate Over Delaying of Miranda Warning*, N.Y. Times, Apr. 20, 2013. Senator Lindsey Graham, among others, urged the Obama administration not to Mirandize Dzokhar Tsarnaev, one of the Boston bombers, and instead to hold him as an enemy combatant in order to interrogate him for intelligence gathering purposes. *See, e.g.*, Wells Bennett, *Senator Graham on Tsarnaev and Miranda*, Lawfare, Apr. 23, 2013, *available at* http://www.lawfareblog. com/2013/04/senator-graham-on-tsarnaev-and-miranda/. Similar calls followed the capture of Abu Khattala.

The Supreme Court has already recognized an exception to *Miranda* for interrogations motivated by concern for "public safety," as opposed to ordinary law enforcement. *See New York v. Quarles*, 467 U.S. 649 (1984). As you review the materials that follow, consider how, if at all, the *Quarles* exception — and the range of issues that have arisen alongside *Miranda*'s applicability to terrorism cases — illuminates this debate.

U.S. Department of Justice, Federal Bureau of Investigation, Custodial Interrogation for Public Safety and Intelligence-Gathering Purposes of Operational Terrorists Inside the United States[1]

Oct. 21, 2010

Identifying and apprehending suspected terrorists, interrogating them to obtain intelligence about terrorist activities and impending terrorist attacks, and lawfully detaining them so that they do not pose a continuing threat to our communities are critical to protecting the American people. The Department of Justice and the FBI believe that we can maximize our ability to accomplish these objectives by continuing to adhere to FBI policy regarding the use of *Miranda* warnings for

---

1. This guidance applies only to arrestees who have not been indicted and who are not known to be represented by an attorney. . . .

custodial interrogation of operational terrorists[2] who are arrested inside the United States:

1. If applicable, agents should ask any and all questions that are reasonably prompted by an immediate concern for the safety of the public or the arresting agents without advising the arrestee of his *Miranda* rights.[3]

2. After all applicable public safety questions have been exhausted, agents should advise the arrestee of his *Miranda* rights and seek a waiver of those rights before any further interrogation occurs, absent exceptional circumstances described below.

3. There may be exceptional cases in which, although all relevant public safety questions have been asked, agents nonetheless conclude that continued unwarned interrogation is necessary to collect valuable and timely intelligence not related to any immediate threat, and that the government's interest in obtaining this intelligence outweighs the disadvantages of proceeding with unwarned interrogation.[4] . . . Presentment of an arrestee may not

---

2. For these purposes, an operational terrorist is an arrestee who is reasonably believed to be either a high-level member of an international terrorist group; or an operative who has personally conducted or attempted to conduct a terrorist operation that involved risk to life; or an individual knowledgeable about operational details of a pending terrorist operation.

3. The Supreme Court held in *New York v. Quarles*, 467 U.S. 649 (1984), that if law enforcement officials engage in custodial interrogation of an individual that is "reasonable prompted by a concern for the public safety," any statements the individual provides in the course of such interrogation shall not be inadmissible in any criminal proceeding on the basis that the warnings described in *Miranda v. Arizona*, 384 U.S. 436 (1966), were not provided. The court noted that this exception to the *Miranda* rule is a narrow one and that "in each case it will be circumscribed by the [public safety] exigency which justifies it." 467 U.S. at 657.

4. The Supreme Court has strongly suggested that an arrestee's Fifth Amendment right against self-incrimination is not violated at the time a statement is taken without *Miranda* warnings, but instead may be violated only if and when the government introduces an unwarned statement in a criminal

be delayed simply to continue the interrogation, unless the defendant has timely waived prompt presentment.

The determination whether particular unwarned questions are justified on public safety grounds must always be made on a case-by-case basis based on all the facts and circumstances. In light of the magnitude and complexity of the threat often posed by terrorist organizations, particularly international terrorist organizations, and the nature of their attacks, the circumstances surrounding an arrest of an operational terrorist may warrant significantly more extensive public safety interrogation without *Miranda* warnings than would be permissible in an ordinary criminal case. Depending on the facts, such interrogation might include, for example, questions about possible impending or coordinated terrorist attacks; the location, nature, and threat posed by weapons that might post an imminent danger to the public; and the identities, locations, and activities or intentions of accomplices who may be plotting additional imminent attacks. . . .

NOTES AND QUESTIONS

1. *Quarles and the Origin of the "Public Safety" Exception.* Although *Quarles* has come to serve as the fountainhead for the "public safety" exception, it was a fairly unexceptional case. There, a rape victim told the police that the perpetrator (who was armed) had just entered a nearby supermarket. When officers arrested the suspect inside the supermarket, they found an empty holster, leading one of the officers to ask the suspect what had happened to the gun. The suspect's answer, which led the officers to where he had hidden the gun, was subsequently suppressed by the trial court on the ground that it obtained in violation of *Miranda*; it was, after all, a statement made in response to an unwarned

---

proceeding against the defendant. *See* Chavez v. Martinez, 538 U.S. 760, 769 (2003) (plurality op.); *id.* at 789 (Kennedy, J., concurring in part and dissenting in part); *cf. also id.* at 778-79 (Souter, J., concurring in the judgment); *see also* United States v. Patane, 542 U.S. 630, 641 (2004) (plurality opinion) ("[V]iolations [of the Fifth Amendment right against self-incrimination] occur, if at all, only upon the admission of unwarned statements into evidence at trial."); United States v. Verdugo-Urquidez, 494 U.S. 259, 264 (1990) ("[A] violation [of the Fifth Amendment right against self-incrimination] occurs only at trial.").

custodial interrogation. *See New York v. Quarles*, 467 U.S. 649, 651-653 (1984). But the Supreme Court reversed. As then-Justice Rehnquist explained for a 5-4 majority, "Whatever the motivation of individual officers in such a situation, we do not believe that the doctrinal underpinnings of *Miranda* require that it be applied in all its rigor to a situation in which police officers ask questions reasonably prompted by a concern for the public safety." *Id*. at 656.

In other words, where questioning in a custodial interrogation focuses on ongoing concern for public safety, rather than the suspect's specific culpability, statements made by the suspect in response are admissible against him even if they were obtained prior to the administration of the *Miranda* warnings. Otherwise, Rehnquist explained, law enforcement officers would be forced to make a difficult choice — to decide on the spur of the moment and under exigent circumstances

> whether it best serves society for them to ask the necessary questions without the *Miranda* warnings and render whatever probative evidence they uncover inadmissible, or for them to give the warnings in order to preserve the admissibility of evidence they might uncover but possibly damage or destroy their ability to obtain that evidence and neutralize the volatile situation confronting them. [*Id*. at 657-658.]

2. *Justice O'Connor's Objection*. In an unusually strident dissent, Justice O'Connor criticized this reasoning as presenting a false dichotomy grounded in a misunderstanding of *Miranda* — as a bar on interrogations, rather than as an exclusionary rule. (As the FBI guidelines note in footnote 3, the Supreme Court has all but held that *Miranda* is only the latter, and does not bar unwarned interrogations in the abstract.) As she elaborated,

> *Miranda* has never been read to prohibit the police from asking questions to secure the public safety. Rather, the critical question *Miranda* addresses is who shall bear the cost of securing the public safety when such questions are asked and answered: the defendant or the State. *Miranda*, for better or worse, found the resolution of that question implicit in the prohibition against compulsory self-incrimination and placed the burden on the State. When police ask custodial questions without administering the required warnings, *Miranda* quite clearly requires that the answers received be presumed compelled and that they be excluded from evidence at trial. [*Quarles*, 467 U.S. at 665 (O'Connor, J., concurring in the judgment in part and dissenting in part).]

Isn't Justice O'Connor correct that *Quarles* would allow law enforcement officers to have their cake and eat it, too? Is that simply a necessary compromise in situations in which there is a serious threat to "public safety"? If so, was *Quarles* (where the threat to public safety consisted of a handgun hidden in a grocery store) an appropriate case *for* the "public safety" exception?

3. *The FBI's "Exceptional Cases" Category.* The FBI guidelines reproduced above are mostly devoted to implementing *Quarles* in practice. But consider the suggestion under point "3" that "[t]here may be exceptional cases in which, although all relevant public safety questions have been asked, agents nonetheless conclude that continued unwarned interrogation is necessary to collect valuable and timely intelligence not related to any immediate threat, and that the government's interest in obtaining this intelligence outweighs the disadvantages of proceeding with unwarned interrogation." Are the guidelines suggesting that such statements may nevertheless be admissible under *Quarles*? Or are they suggesting that there will be cases in which the potential fruits of such statements outweigh the government's need to be able to introduce them against the suspect at trial? If these considerations are already applied by the government, doesn't that undermine Justice Rehnquist's reasoning in *Quarles*, which sought to free the government from such calculus? Or might it suggest, in the alternative, that the FBI has a narrower view of the "public safety" exception than the courts?

4. *The Scope of the "Public Safety" Exception in Terrorism Cases.* How should courts measure the threat to public safety in terrorism cases, where the potential risk to public safety may be far greater than that posed by a single gun hidden in a grocery store, but where it also may be far less imminent and specific? Is there a principled way to define "public safety" in this context? Or was Justice O'Connor correct in *Quarles* when she warned that "[t]he end result will be a finespun new doctrine on public safety exigencies incident to custodial interrogation, complete with the hair-splitting distinctions that currently plague our Fourth Amendment jurisprudence"? 467 U.S. at 663-664 (O'Connor, J., concurring in the judgment in part and dissenting in part). The following case presents this question rather starkly.

United States v. Abdulmutallab

United States District Court, Eastern District of Michigan, 2011
2011 WL 4345243

NANCY G. EDMUNDS, District Judge:

[Omar Farouk Abdulmutallab, the "underwear bomber," sustained significant burns while attempting to ignite explosives concealed in his underwear in order to blow up Northwest Flight 253 as it was approaching Detroit, Michigan, on December 25, 2009. He was interrogated by the FBI after his arrest while under treatment at the University of Michigan Hospital, but before advising him of his rights under *Miranda v. Arizona*, 384 U.S. 436 (1966). In the criminal prosecution that followed, Abdulmutallab moved to suppress statements made by him prior to the administration of the *Miranda* warnings. The government replied by arguing that the statements were admissible under the "public safety" exception to *Miranda* articulated in *New York v. Quarles*, 467 U.S. 649 (1984). The district court denied Abdulmutallab's motion to suppress.]

I. Facts — Evidentiary Hearing

On December 25, 2009, when Northwest-Delta Flight 253 landed, U.S. Customs and Border Protection officers met the plane at the gate, having been advised of an incident on board the plane. . . . After assessing the severity of Defendant's burns, U.S. Customs officers transported Defendant to the U of M Hospital for treatment and informed the FBI's Joint Terrorism Task Force of the situation. . . .

Around 3:35 p.m., after he was moved to a room, Defendant was questioned by FBI Special Agent Timothy Waters. Other federal agents were present, including FBI Special Agent Peissig, and U.S. Customs Officer Steigerwald. Before the 3:35 interview began, Special Agent Waters had learned from U.S. Customs and Border Protection Officer Steigerwald that Defendant had admitted that he had detonated an explosive device hidden in his underwear while on Flight 253 and that he was acting on behalf of al-Qaeda. He had also learned from other federal agents that an explosive device similar to the one used by Defendant had been used previously, although not on a plane. He also knew that the explosive device had no mechanical devices associated with it and was thus problematic because it could defeat airport security and, indeed, had done so in this instance. Mindful of Defendant's self-proclaimed association with al-Qaeda and knowing the group's past history of large, coordinated plots and attacks, the agents feared that there could be additional, imminent aircraft attacks in the United States and elsewhere in the world. For these reasons, Agent Waters questioned Defendant for about 50 minutes without first advising him of his *Miranda* rights.

During that interview, . . . Agent Waters asked Defendant where he traveled, when he had traveled, how, and with whom; the details of the explosive device; the details regarding the bomb-maker, including where Defendant had received the bomb; his intentions in attacking Flight 253; and who else might be planning an attack. Every question sought to identify any other potential attackers and to prevent another potential attack. Defendant answered, providing information that helped the agents to determine where to go next and investigate if anyone else might be planning to or was already in the process of carrying a similar device on an aircraft. At the end of the interview, once they received the public safety information, the agents turned their attention to immediately sharing the information with law enforcement and intelligence agencies worldwide.

II. Analysis

A. Voluntariness of Defendant's Statements

[In this part of the opinion, Judge Edmunds concluded that Abdulmutallab's statements were voluntarily given, despite his medical condition at the time of his interrogation.]

B. *Quarles* Exception

Defendant argues that his statements to the federal agents on December 25, 2009 at U of M Hospital should be suppressed because the federal agents failed to first advise him of his *Miranda* rights. The Court disagrees. The circumstances present at the time of Defendant's questioning fall within the public safety exception to *Miranda* recognized in *Quarles*, 467 U.S. at 657. The Sixth Circuit has applied the *Quarles* exception. *See United States v. Talley*, 275 F.3d 560, 564 (6th Cir. 2001) (applying the *Quarles* public safety exception).

The federal courts have extended the logic of *Quarles* to the questioning of terrorism suspects. *See* [*United States v. Khalil*, 214 F.3d 111 (2d Cir. 2000)], at 121. In *Khalil*, the district court determined that the *Quarles* exception to *Miranda* applied when, after a raid on the defendant's apartment where he was injured, officers questioned the defendant at the hospital "about the construction and stability of the bombs" discovered in his apartment and included within the *Quarles* exception the defendant's response to the officer's inquiry "whether he had intended to kill himself in detonating the bombs." *Id.* On appeal, the defendant challenged the district court's "ruling only insofar as the court failed to suppress" his response to the question about his intent to kill himself, arguing that "that question was unrelated to the matter of public safety." *Id.* The Second Circuit resolved the issue as follows:

> We are inclined to disagree, given that [the defendant]'s vision as to whether or not he would survive his attempt to detonate the bomb had the potential for shedding light on the bomb's stability. In any event, even if we were to take a different view as to the relevance of that question, we would conclude that the admission of [the defendant's] response at trial was, at worst, harmless error.

Id. See also In re Terrorist Bombings of U.S. Embassies in E. Africa, 552 F.3d 177, 203 n.19, 204 (2d Cir. 2008) (assuming *Quarles* would apply to exigent circumstances in a terrorism case).

In light of the testimony provided at the evidentiary hearing, the logic of *Quarles* extends to the questioning of Defendant, a terrorism suspect at the time of his December 25, 2009 questioning. The agents' questions were intended to shed light on the obvious public safety concerns in this case and were "necessary to secure . . . the safety of the public[.]" *Quarles*, 467 U.S. at 659. Defendant was asked where he traveled, when he had traveled, how, and with whom; the details of the explosive device; the details regarding the bomb-maker, including where Defendant had received the bomb; his intentions in attacking Flight 253; who else might be planning an attack; whether he associated with, lived with, or attended the same mosque with others who had a similar mind-set as Defendant about jihad, martyrdom, support for al-Qaeda, and a desire to attack the United States by using a similar explosive device on a plane, and what these individuals looked like — all in an attempt to discover whether Defendant had information about others who could be on planes or about to board planes with explosive devices similar to the one Defendant used because, based upon his training, experience, and knowledge of earlier al-Qaeda attacks, this was not a solo incident and the potential for a multi-prong attack existed even if Defendant was unaware of any specific additional planned attack.

Special Agent Waters reiterated that, before he interviewed Defendant, he was aware that Defendant claimed to be acting on behalf of al-Qaeda. The agents were also well aware that on September 11, 2001, al-Qaeda operatives hijacked four airplanes in an attack on the United States that killed almost 3,000 people. Mindful of Defendant's self-proclaimed association with al-Qaeda and knowing the group's past history of large, coordinated plots and attacks, the agents logically feared that there could be additional, imminent aircraft attacks in the United States and elsewhere in the world. . . .

The circumstances present at the time of Defendant's questioning fall within the public safety exception to *Miranda* recognized in *Quarles*. Accordingly, the fact that he was questioned by federal agents at U of M Hospital on December 25, 2009 before receiving *Miranda* warnings does not warrant suppression of his challenged statements. Doing so here was fully justified. . . .

NOTES AND QUESTIONS

1. *Easy Cases and the Public Safety Exception.* In one sense, *Abdulmutallab* is a remarkably easy case for the public safety exception, given that he was arrested while attempting to commit an act of terrorism — and one which could potentially have been part of a larger series of coordinated, imminent attacks. But don't the unique facts of his case also make invocation of the exception especially *unnecessary*, since the government is hardly lacking for physical and other testimonial evidence to use against him at trial? Indeed, isn't the public safety exception only really at issue in cases in which the defendant's statements are a critical part of the government's case-in-chief?

2. *Terrorism Prosecutions and the Public Safety Exception.* How useful a precedent is *Abdulmutallab* for other terrorism cases? On one hand, Judge Edmunds heartily endorses the view that concerns about related terrorist attacks will generally justify application of the exception. On the other hand, *Abdulmutallab* is atypical insofar as the defendant is being prosecuted for an act of terrorism *after* it was attempted. Most terrorism prosecutions are focused instead on inchoate

liability — where no actual act of terrorism has yet taken place. In such cases, where any threat to public safety arises from an impending plot in which the suspect is allegedly involved, won't preserving "public safety" and establishing the suspect's culpability necessarily merge? If so, doesn't *Abdulmutallab* suggest that the government will have wide latitude in interrogating such suspects free from the dictates of *Miranda*, in a manner that won't be true for other classes of crimes (where the distinction between public safety and culpability will remain more evident)?

3. *The Other Shoe: Presentment.* Even *Abdulmutallab* only upholds 50 minutes of "public safety" questioning, suggesting, at least implicitly, that the temporal scope of the *Quarles* exception is quite limited. If it is not, then the other relevant consideration is "presentment" — the requirement that arrestees be brought before a neutral magistrate "without unnecessary delay," Fed. R. Crim. P. 5(a)(1)(A), at which point a suspect will be advised of his rights to counsel and to remain silent, if he has not been already. As a result, under *McNabb v. United States*, 318 U. S. 332 (1943), and *Mallory v. United States*, 354 U.S. 449 (1957), an arrestee's confession is inadmissible if it is given after an unreasonable delay in presentment. *See Corley v. United States*, 556 U.S. 303 (2009). And under *County of Riverside v. McLaughlin*, 500 U.S. 44 (1991), the Fourth Amendment itself requires a probable cause finding by a grand jury or neutral magistrate within 48 hours of arrest (if no such finding had previously been made). Taken together, these cases might be read to suggest that the government would be entitled to no more than 48 hours of "public safety" questioning of a suspect before he would have to be apprised of his *Miranda* rights. Is there any argument that the presentment requirement might itself have a "public safety" exception? Would such an exception ever be necessary?

4. *Does Quarles Apply Once a Suspect Invokes? Quarles* clearly allows law enforcement officers to begin to question a suspect without advising him of his *Miranda* rights. But what if, without being so warned, a suspect nevertheless invokes his right to remain silent and/or consult with an attorney? Of course, the government could continue to question a suspect even after he has invoked his rights; *Miranda*, after all, is only an exclusionary rule. But would *Quarles* apply in such a case to allow for the admission of statements made in response to such post-invocation questioning? What little case law there is on this question

suggests that the answer is "no." *See Williams v. Jacquez*, No. S-05-0058, 2011 WL 703616, at *14 (E.D. Cal. Feb. 18, 2011) ("The rationale for the *Quarles* exception does not justify continuing a broad ranging interview after the suspect invokes her right to silence."). If *Quarles* means what it says, why should it matter whether or not the suspect has invoked his rights?

5. *How Quarles Fits into the Terrorism Disposition Debate.* Return to the debate described at the beginning of these materials. Doesn't *Quarles* strongly support those who favor trying most (if not all) terrorism suspects in civilian courts (who might otherwise object to *Quarles*), insofar as it allows the government both to interrogate terrorism suspects about ongoing threats to public safety without advising them of their *Miranda* rights *and* to use anything the suspects say in response against them at trial? On the flip side, for those who support military detention and/or trial by military commission for new terrorism suspects, and who might otherwise be more sympathetic to *Quarles*, doesn't it militate *against* such arguments insofar as it demonstrates the ability of the civilian courts adequately to accommodate the government's interests in terrorism cases? *See generally* Joanna Wright, Note, *Mirandizing Terrorists?: An Empirical Analysis of the Public Safety Exception*, 111 Colum. L. Rev. 1296 (2011). Ultimately, does *Quarles*' utility in this area — and in preserving the government's flexibility in terrorism cases — help to explain why, despite its controversial nature, its overruling has never been sought?

6. *When Do the Relevant Clocks "Start"?* One of the questions not raised in *Quarles* or *Abdulmuttalab* is when the relevant *Miranda* and presentment clocks "start." In cases in which suspects are arrested within the United States, the assumption has always been that the clocks begin to run at the moment of arrest. Is that necessarily true in cases in which the suspect is arrested *outside* the United States? What if the suspect is initially held in *military*, rather than *civilian*, detention? Consider how the Second Circuit handles this issue in the following case.

———————————

United States v. Ghailani

United States Court of Appeals, Second Circuit, Oct. 24, 2013

733 F.3d 29, *cert. denied*, 134 S. Ct. 1523 (2014)

JOSÉ A. CABRANES, Circuit Judge: Defendant Ahmed Khalfan Ghailani appeals his judgment of conviction, entered January 25, 2011, after a trial by jury in the United States District Court for the Southern District of New York (Lewis A. Kaplan, *Judge*), of conspiring to bomb the United States embassies in Nairobi, Kenya, and Dar es Salaam, Tanzania. The bombings, which occurred simultaneously on August 7, 1998, killed over two hundred people, and injured thousands more.

This appeal presents a question bound to arise from the government's efforts to obtain actionable and time-sensitive intelligence necessary to thwart acts of terror, while still bringing those charged with committing crimes of terrorism against Americans to justice in an orderly fashion under the laws of our country. We are asked whether the Speedy Trial Clause of the Sixth Amendment of the Constitution prevents the United States from trying, on criminal charges in a district court, a defendant who was held abroad for several years by the Central Intelligence Agency ("CIA") and the Department of Defense while his indictment was pending. . . .

We conclude that . . . the District Court correctly determined that, in the circumstances presented here, there was no violation of Ghailani's right under the Speedy Trial Clause of the Sixth Amendment. In so holding, we reject Ghailani's claim that the government may never, no matter how expeditiously it acts, bring a defendant to trial after detaining him for national security purposes. We also reject Ghailani's argument that the delay occasioned by national security concerns and preparations for trial before a military commission was so excessive as to bar the government from thereafter proceeding to trial. For well over a century, the Supreme Court has repeatedly held that the government may purposely delay trials for significant periods of time, so long as, on balance, the public and private interests render the delay reasonable. We also reject Ghailani's argument that he was prejudiced *for constitutional speedy trial purposes* by his treatment during his detention by the CIA. The Speedy Trial Clause protects defendants against prejudice caused by delays in their trials, not against the harms of interrogation. . . .

BACKGROUND

On August 7, 1998, operatives of al Qaeda simultaneously detonated explosives at the United States embassies in Nairobi, Kenya, and Dar es Salaam, Tanzania. In Nairobi, the bombs killed two hundred and thirteen people, and injured approximately four thousand more. In Dar es Salaam, eleven died and eighty-five were injured. . . .

Although Ghailani was indicted along with his associates in 1998, he eluded authorities for the next six years. Throughout that time — which included the attacks on the World Trade Center on September 11, 2001 — Ghailani remained an active and engaged member of al Qaeda. He was finally captured abroad on July 25, 2004, and was held outside of the United States for approximately two years by the CIA. Judge Kaplan made the following factual findings regarding this period:

> Ghailani was detained and interrogated by the CIA outside of the United States for roughly two years. Many details of the [CIA's interrogation program] and its application to specific individuals remain classified. Nevertheless, it may be said that it sought to obtain critical, real-time intelligence about terrorist networks and plots by using a combination of so-called "standard" and "enhanced" interrogation techniques to question detainees thought to have particularly high-value intelligence information. These techniques were "designed to psychologically 'dislocate' the detainee, maximize his feeling of vulnerability and helplessness, and reduce or eliminate his will to resist [the United States government's] efforts to obtain critical intelligence."
>
> An individualized interrogation program was developed and approved for each detainee based on the unique personal, physical, and psychological characteristics of that individual. Not all interrogation techniques were used on all detainees. To the extent that they are relevant to the disposition of this motion, the details of Ghailani's experience in the CIA [interrogation program] — in particular, the specific interrogation techniques applied to him — are described in [a separate classified supplement]. Suffice it to say here that, on the record before the Court and as further explained in the [classified supplement], the CIA Program was effective in obtaining useful intelligence from Ghailani throughout his time in CIA custody.

United States v. Ghailani, 751 F. Supp. 2d 515, 522-23 (S.D.N.Y. 2010).

In September 2006, the CIA transferred Ghailani to the custody of the Department of Defense at Guantanamo Bay. . . .

[His status as "enemy combatant" was subsequently confirmed by a Combatant Status Review Tribunal (CSRT), and he was charged by a military commission with violating the laws of war. When President Obama suspended the military commissions, the government announced that it would try Ghailani in federal court on the original 1998 indictment, and he was arraigned in 2009.]

Ghailani . . . subsequently moved to dismiss the indictment on the ground that the Speedy Trial Clause of the Sixth Amendment precluded the government from proceeding against him, inasmuch as he had been held for nearly five years by the United States before being presented for trial. . . .

[The motion was denied, and Ghailani was tried and convicted by a jury on one of the 282 counts and sentenced to life in prison. This appeal followed.].

DISCUSSION . . .

A. The Speedy Trial Clause

1. Applicable Law

The Sixth Amendment guarantees that "[i]n all criminal prosecutions, the accused shall enjoy the right to a speedy . . . trial." . . .

. . . [Over time,] the Supreme Court has formulated a four-factor balancing test for evaluating a defendant's claim that his or her speedy trial right has been violated. In particular, we must consider: "(1) the length of the delay; (2) the reasons for the delay; (3) whether the defendant asserted his right in the run-up to the trial; and (4) whether the defendant was prejudiced by the failure to bring the case to trial more quickly." *United States v. Cain*, 671 F.3d 271, 296 (2d Cir. 2012).

As we recently explained, "[t]he first of the *Barker* factors, the length of the delay, is in effect a threshold question: 'by definition, a defendant cannot complain that the government has denied him a speedy trial if it has, in fact, prosecuted his case with customary promptness.'" *Id.* (quoting *Doggett v. United States*, 505 U.S. 647, 652 (1992)) (brackets omitted). That is to say that we will only consider the other *Barker* factors when the defendant makes a showing . . . "that the interval between accusation and trial has crossed the threshold dividing ordinary from 'presumptively prejudicial' delay." *Doggett,* 505 U.S. at 651-52 (quoting *Barker v. Wingo*, 407 U.S. [514,] 530-31 (1972)).

Once the defendant has demonstrated a "presumptively prejudicial" delay, we must proceed to balance the four *Barker* factors, remaining mindful that "they are related factors" with "no talismanic qualities" that "must be considered together with such other circumstances as may be relevant." *Barker,* 407 U.S. at 533. . . .

3. Analysis

Ghailani now asserts that the District Court made two principal errors in evaluating his speedy trial claim. First, he contends that national security interests and preparation for his then-intended trial before a military commission cannot justify the delay incurred. Second, he argues that the District Court was incorrect in finding that he did not suffer prejudice as a result of the delay. Ultimately, of course, he claims that the *Barker* factors demonstrate a violation of his rights under the Speedy Trial Clause, and, thus, require us to reverse his conviction.

Ghailani's claim is based on the delay from the time he first came into the exclusive custody of the United States following his July 25, 2004 capture until his June 9, 2009 arraignment in the District Court. The period he protests covers approximately five years and can be viewed as divided into two segments based on the changing concerns that caused the delay. The delay from the beginning of his custody until his transfer to Guantanamo was caused by national security concerns. The delay from his transfer until his arraignment was caused by preparations for trial before a military commission. We agree with Judge Kaplan that this period was long enough to trigger the *Barker* analysis. Accordingly, we discuss each *Barker* factor in turn, paying particular attention to the errors claimed by Ghailani in the District Court's analysis.

i. Reasons for Delay

a. National Security

As for his claim that the interests of national security cannot justify delaying his trial, Ghailani proposes that "[u]pon seizing [him], the government had a choice: It could either choose to accord him his Constitutional right to a speedy trial on the existing indictment, or it could choose to strip him of an array of Constitutional rights and hold him in a Black Site for questioning. Emphatically, however, the government could not do both." Appellant Br. 56. In other words, according to Ghailani's brief and presentation at oral argument, his detention for national security purposes may well have been proper, but it precluded the government from *ever* bringing him to justice in our civilian courts for his crimes under United States law because, in Ghailani's view, it constituted an automatic violation of his rights guaranteed by the Speedy Trial Clause. *Id.* Ghailani offers no case law or other authority that supports this view, and for good reason — the Speedy Trial Clause of the Sixth Amendment does not create any such rule.

To the extent that Ghailani suggests generally that the government may not choose, for policy reasons, to delay his trial, his claim is rebutted by an unbroken line of cases going back well over a century, each of which has permitted the government purposely to delay trials for significant periods of time, so long as, on balance, the public and private interests rendered the delay reasonable. For example, the Supreme Court has approved delays for the government to prosecute the defendant in another jurisdiction first, for the government to pursue interlocutory appeals, and for the government to prosecute a separate defendant in order to secure his testimony at trial. Following these precedents, we have, upon balancing the *Barker* factors, allowed delays for the government to keep co-defendants from fleeing, avoid risk to informants, and protect the integrity of an investigation, for the government to persuade a witness to testify, and for the government to decide whether to pursue the death penalty.

In each of these cases, the government made a deliberate choice to sacrifice proceeding to trial more quickly in favor of what it deemed to be in the public interest. Indeed, although a delay intended unfairly to interfere with the defense or purely to harass the defendant would count quite heavily in favor of a violation of the Speedy Trial Clause, the Speedy Trial Clause prohibits only trial delays that, on balance, are unreasonable in light of the public and private interests at stake *in the particular case.* In other words, a delay does not render a trial not "speedy" under the Constitution merely because the government intended to cause the delay.

To the extent that Ghailani nonetheless contends specifically that national security cannot justify pretrial delay, his argument is no more convincing. As we have now made abundantly clear, the definition of a "speedy" trial under the Sixth Amendment depends in each case in part upon the public interest that may weigh in favor of delay. And the Supreme Court has stated in no uncertain terms that "[i]t is 'obvious and unarguable' that no governmental interest is more compelling than the security of the Nation." *Haig v. Agee,* 453 U.S. 280, 307 (1981) (quoting *Aptheker v. Secretary of State,* 378 U.S. 500, 509 (1964)). Indeed, we have previously invoked "our traditional deference to the judgment of the executive department in matters of foreign policy" in denying a claim that the government's failure to extradite a defendant violated his right to a speedy trial. *United States v. Diacolios,* 837 F.2d 79, 83 (2d Cir. 1988) (internal quotation marks omitted). We see little reason not to accord a similar deference — at least when the government has made a showing that, on balance, the other *Barker* factors do not outweigh the reason for delay — in the context of national security.

It is true that national security is a somewhat unusual cause for trial delay in that it is not related to the trial itself. But we observe nothing in the text or history of the Speedy Trial Clause that requires the government to choose between national security and an orderly and fair justice system. To the contrary, the Speedy Trial Clause preserves both the interests of defendants and the societal interest in the integrity of the justice system by balancing those interests to determine whether the requirements of the Clause have been violated. We observe no basis for, and reject in full, Ghailani's argument that, once having detained a defendant as a national security intelligence asset, the government can no longer bring the defendant to trial. Ghailani's suggestion that the government *must* detain defendants who pose a threat to national security indefinitely rather than bring them to trial for their crimes in the manner consistent with our traditional notions of justice would hardly advance the interests of defendants or the values underpinning the Speedy Trial Clause.

We reject also Ghailani's fallback position that the delay occasioned by national security concerns was so excessive as to bar the government from thereafter proceeding to trial. There is no simple bright-line answer to the question of how much delay by reason of national security concerns is consistent with the government's right to proceed thereafter to trial. In previous cases, the Supreme Court has held that delays of upwards of five and seven years did not violate the Speedy Trial Clause in the circumstances presented. We have previously found circumstances which permitted delays of five, six, and seven years.

While the delay here was undoubtedly considerable, the District Court correctly determined that other factors strongly favor the government. As the District Court found, "the decision to place Ghailani in the CIA Program was made in the reasonable belief that he had valuable information essential to combating Al Qaeda and protecting national security" and "the evidence show[ed] that the government had reason to believe that this valuable intelligence could not have been obtained except by putting Ghailani into that program and that it could not successfully have done so and prosecuted him in federal court at the same time." *Ghailani*, 751 F. Supp. 2d at 535. In this context — and we emphasize that this question must be considered in the specific factual circumstances of each case — we do not think that the approximately two-year delay caused by national security concerns was so excessive as to bar Ghailani's prosecution.

Ghailani further contends that "once the specter of a national security threat has been raised, there [will be] no necessity for a further *Barker* analysis." Appellant Br. 56. We are not concerned that permitting a delay based on the weighty national security interests present in this case will somehow undo the Speedy Trial Clause for all future cases. Judge Kaplan's opinion in this case — which carefully and thoroughly weighed the evidence presented by the government before concluding that the delay did not amount to a speedy trial violation — did not announce any such general rule, nor does this Opinion. The District Court did not forgo the *Barker* analysis in deference to national security concerns. To the contrary, it addressed each factor and determined that, on balance, the speed with which the government brought Ghailani to trial was constitutionally sufficient. The District Court's analysis (and this Opinion) confirms that, under the *Barker* analysis, the weight of a national security justification for delay — just like any other justification — will depend on the facts and circumstances of each case.

In the final analysis, the Sixth Amendment right to a speedy trial is just that: a right to proceed to trial in a manner that is sufficiently expeditious under the circumstances presented in the particular case. In this case, proceedings were permissibly and reasonably delayed by weighty considerations relating to national security. Accordingly, the delay of Ghailani's trial while he was in CIA custody was justified under the *Barker* framework, and does not weigh against the government in the balancing of the factors.

b. Preparations for Trial before a Military Commission

In September 2006 Ghailani was placed in Department of Defense custody and transferred to Guantanamo Bay to be detained as an alien enemy combatant. On March 17, 2007, a CSRT hearing was held and

Ghailani's classification as an alien enemy combatant sustained. He was thereafter held at Guantanamo Bay while military authorities prepared to prosecute him before a military commission. Upon President Obama's inauguration in January 2009, the military commission was suspended and the government altered course, preparing instead to try Ghailani in civilian court. Soon thereafter, on June 9, 2009, he was arraigned in the District Court.

Once again, while recognizing that the duration of the delay at Guantanamo Bay was substantial, we conclude that the pertinent factors sufficiently favor the government. We reject Ghailani's contention that the delay from September 2006 until June 9, 2009 requires dismissal of the charges against him.

The job of preparing to prosecute Ghailani before the military commission was unquestionably difficult. Although much of the difficulty was a product of the government's own choices, the trial was proceeding under a new, untested legal regime and all events relevant to the charges occurred outside the United States and involved foreign actors and witnesses. Some significant period of delay was therefore reasonable. Ghailani contends this is rebutted by the government's acknowledgment that all of its preparation for the criminal trial was concluded prior to Ghailani coming into exclusive United States custody. This misconstrues the government's concession. The government indeed acknowledged that "every percipient witness called at Ghailani's [district court] trial was discovered and interviewed by federal law-enforcement officials before the defendant was captured in 2004 [and that] every piece of evidence offered at the . . . trial . . . was obtained before the defendant was captured." Appellee Br. 93. But the fact that the witnesses eventually called had already been interviewed, and the physical evidence eventually used had already been obtained, does not mean that all investigation had been accomplished, much less that trial preparation was complete. After all, preparation for trial in any case as complex as this case remains a huge undertaking.

We also agree with Judge Kaplan's determination that "there is no evidence that the government ever acted in bad faith to gain a tactical advantage over or to prejudice Ghailani with respect to his defense of th[e] indictment." *Ghailani*, 751 F. Supp. 2d at 534. Indeed, the record demonstrates that the government was not acting with the intent to cause prejudicial delay but, until President Obama took office in January 2009 and suspended the military commissions, was acting under the good faith belief that Ghailani would be tried by military commission. Undoubtedly, however, the delay caused by the government's original strategy to try Ghailani before a military commission was long, and largely a product of the government's own choices. We agree, therefore, with the District Court's conclusion that the reasons for this delay weigh against the government. However, as explained more fully below, on balance, consideration of all the pertinent factors favors the government and requires denial of Ghailani's claim that he is entitled to have the indictment dismissed.

ii. Invocation of the Right

We note that throughout the period of delay at issue, Ghailani never demanded a speedy trial. His March 2009 petition for habeas corpus did not seek a speedy trial, but rather, demanded his release and dismissal of the indictment with prejudice. Generally, failure to demand a speedy trial makes it difficult for a defendant to prove that he was denied a speedy trial. *See Barker*, 407 U.S. at 532. Here, the District Court addressed Ghailani's invocation of his right to a speedy trial and determined that "*Barker*'s demand factor does not cut one way or the other in this case [because] Ghailani cannot be faulted for having failed to invoke his right to a speedy trial earlier than he did[, n]or can the government be criticized for ignoring demands for a trial." *Id.* at 530. We agree with Judge Kaplan's conclusion that this factor does not affect the balancing test he was required to apply.

iii. Prejudice

Ghailani next argues that the District Court erred in its consideration of whether he was prejudiced by the delay in his case. Most significantly, Ghailani contends that the District Court should have considered the physical and psychological harm he endured while in CIA custody as prejudice supporting his speedy trial claim. The District Court concluded, however, that whatever treatment Ghailani endured at the hands of the CIA was not caused by the delay in his trial and therefore not relevant to the *Barker* analysis. *See Ghailani*, 751 F. Supp. 2d at 531–32.

We agree with Judge Kaplan. The Supreme Court has consistently emphasized three interests of a defendant that may be prejudiced by trial delay: "'oppressive pretrial incarceration,' 'anxiety and concern of the accused,' and 'the possibility that the accused's defense will be

impaired' by dimming memories and loss of exculpatory evidence."
Doggett, 505 U.S. at 654 (quoting *Barker*, 407 U.S. at 532) (brackets
omitted). Ghailani complains of oppressive pretrial incarceration, but
notably, his detention by the CIA was not "pretrial," as it was not
incarceration for the purpose of awaiting trial. In other words, Ghailani
would have been detained by the CIA for the purpose of obtaining
information whether or not he was awaiting trial, and the conditions of
his detention were a product of the CIA's investigation, not incarceration
as a prelude to trial.

We have denied a speedy trial claim in similar circumstances,
explaining that the defendant could not "claim prejudice traceable to any
oppressive pretrial incarceration, because he would have been serving
his state sentence in any event." *United States v. Lainez–Leiva*, 129 F.3d
89, 92 (2d Cir. 1997). . . . In sum, the Speedy Trial Clause protects
defendants against prejudice caused by delays in their trials, not against
the harms of interrogation of enemy combatants.

Finally, Ghailani contends that the District Court incorrectly
determined that his defense was not prejudiced by the pretrial delay.
Notably, Ghailani fails to make any argument addressing the prejudice at
the core of the Speedy Trial right — that the delay of the trial itself (as
opposed to other government conduct occurring during the delay) caused
prejudice, such as through the fading of memories or unavailability of
witnesses. Ghailani makes other arguments, however, including a
number related to the idea that the government gained an informational
advantage from Ghailani's interrogation, that he was denied a fair and
impartial jury due to pretrial publicity, that he was denied the
opportunity to gain the benefit of a cooperation agreement, and that
federal agents interfered with his military lawyer's efforts to contact
witnesses.

These claims of prejudice all fail, however. Several were not raised
below and are thus not properly before us on appeal. Many are cursory,
completely unsupported, or were not caused by the delay and were
properly remedied in other ways. As Ghailani has not demonstrated any
substantial prejudice resulting from the delay in his trial, we find that
this factor weighs in the government's favor. Although Ghailani points
to several theoretical effects the delay might have had on his preparation
for trial, he has identified nothing that would lead us to conclude that the
District Court erred. . . .

Accordingly, the judgment of the District Court is **AFFIRMED**.

NOTES AND QUESTIONS

1. *The Two Relevant Time Periods*. Both the district court and the
Second Circuit bifurcated Ghailani's speedy trial claim into two time
periods: the period during which he was in CIA detention, and the period
during which he was detained at Guantánamo. Does this allow the courts
to skirt the real issue — and to effectively cut in half the duration of
Ghailani's "pre-trial" detention? Alternatively, are you convinced that
these two periods raise two very different speedy trial issues, especially
insofar as only the latter period seemed to be with an eye toward
potential criminal prosecution?

2. *National Security Delays*. One of the key innovations in the
Second Circuit's analysis is its holding that "national security" can
justify a trial delay that is "not related to the trial itself." To justify this
conclusion, Judge Cabranes writes that "nothing in the text or history of
the Speedy Trial Clause that requires the government to choose between
national security and an orderly and fair justice system." Is *that* the
relevant choice here? Shouldn't there have come a point where
Ghailani's continuing detention by the military precluded the
government from eventually subjecting him to civilian criminal trial?
More generally, shouldn't the delay have to have *something* to do with
the trial? If not, will anything prevent the government from holding
other terrorism suspects in potentially long-term military detention
before transferring them to civilian criminal trial?

3. *When Would Miranda and Rule 5 Have Kicked In?* The Second
Circuit's ruling suggests that any such constraints will not come from the
Speedy Trial Clause. Might they come from *Miranda* and/or Rule 5, as
discussed above? Although the Second Circuit didn't consider these
questions, at what point in Ghailani's case should *Miranda* and Rule 5
have kicked in? When he was initially captured? When he was
transferred to Guantánamo? When he was transferred to New York? If
not until then, wouldn't that allow the government to control the timing
of *Miranda* and Rule 5 simply by having most terrorism suspects picked
up initially by the military? Shouldn't there be some other factor, besides
the government's whim, that helps to explain when these procedural
protections begin to kick in?

4. *What If Ghailani's Military Detention Was Unlawful?* Partly because his detention was upheld by a CSRT, the Second Circuit sidesteps the argument that the Speedy Trial Clause might have been violated if Ghailani's military detention was, in fact, unlawful. But in other cases, including those of Ahmed Warsame and Abu Anas al-Libi, defendants who were initially captured overseas by the military never had a chance to contest their military detention before being transferred to civilian criminal trials. In such a case, does the criminal defendant have any means of objecting to their military detention? Habeas is generally unavailable to challenge the legality of custody that has ceased; and damages remedies are not likely to be available given the courts' hostility to *Bivens* suits — especially in national security cases. Might the Speedy Trial Clause constrain the government's power to hold such individuals in military custody for some indefinite period (perhaps until and unless the detainee wins their habeas petition), and only file criminal charges at *that* point? If the Speedy Trial Clause doesn't prevent such "constitutional cross-ruffing," does *any* constitutional provision? *See* Stephen I. Vladeck, *Terrorism Prosecutions and the Problem of Constitutional Cross-Ruffing*, 36 Cardozo L. Rev. (forthcoming 2015).

5. *What If Ghailani's Arrest Was Unlawful?* Finally, as the frequency of cases in which the government arrests terrorism suspects overseas has increased, questions have begun to arise about whether the legality of the *capture* has any bearing on the subsequent criminal proceedings. For example, in June 2014, members of the U.S. special forces, in conjunction with the FBI, captured Abu Khattala — the alleged ringleader of the September 11, 2012 Benghazi attacks — in Libya, and then transported him (slowly) to New York by way of a U.S. Navy ship. Unlike Ghailani, Warsame, and al-Libi, however, Abu Khattala has no alleged connection to Al Qaeda or to any other group whose members are subject to military detention under the September 2001 Authorization for the Use of Military Force. It is therefore debatable whether U.S. military personnel had any domestic law authority to even *arrest* him. Moreover, unless the operation was a valid exercise of self-defense authorities, it almost certainly constituted a violation of Libyan sovereignty. Could Khattala challenge his capture, transfer, or subsequent criminal trial on the ground that the underlying operation was unlawful under domestic and/or international law? Unless the government's conduct "shocked the conscience," *United States v.*

Toscanino, 500 F.2d 267 (2d Cir. 1974), the answer is usually "no," thanks to a body of U.S. cases known as the "*Ker-Frisbie* doctrine." *See* Jennifer Daskal & Steve Vladeck, *The Case of Abu Anas al-Libi: The Domestic Law Issues*, Just Security, Oct. 10, 2013, http://justsecurity. org/1850/case-abu-anas-al-libi-domestic-law-issues/.

     6. *Revisiting the Terrorism Disposition Debate.* Note the conflicting tensions that the existing precedents outlined in this Section (and these Notes) create: On the one hand, they suggest that, in contrast to frequent statements from key politicians, there is no legal barrier preventing the government from arresting terrorism suspects and subjecting them to military detention and interrogation for some *non-de mimimis* period prior to their transfer to civilian criminal trial — even if the military's arrest and detention of the suspect were unlawful. On the other hand, *shouldn't* there be such a barrier?

––––––––––––––––

[NSL p. 1104; CTL p. 718. Insert after Note 6.]

     After Congress enacted the 2006 MCA, the government again sought to try Hamdan, the petitioner in *Hamdan v. Rumsfeld*, 548 U.S. 557 (2006) (NSL p. 1075; CTL p. 689), before a military commission. Hamdan was charged with the two offenses discussed in Notes 2 and 3 above, conspiracy and "providing material support to terrorism." In August 2008, the commission convicted Hamdan on the material support charges but acquitted on conspiracy, sentencing him to 66 months' imprisonment, including time served. Hamdan was then repatriated to Yemen in late 2008 (and released shortly thereafter), while an appeal of his conviction remained pending. Following a long and unexplained delay, the intermediate appellate court created by the MCA, the Court of Military Commission Review, unanimously upheld his conviction, holding that "providing material support to terrorism" was a recognized violation of the international laws of war. *See United States v. Hamdan*, 801 F. Supp. 2d 1247 (Ct. Mil. Comm'n Rev. 2011) (en banc). That conviction was subsequently reversed by a three-judge panel of the D.C. Circuit in *Hamdan v. United States* (*"Hamdan II"*), 696 F.3d 1238 (D.C. Cir. 2012), which held that (1) the MCA did not intend to authorize prosecutions for pre-MCA offenses that were not clearly recognized as international war crimes at the time of their commission; and (2) material support was not clearly recognized as an international war crime at the time of Hamdan's conduct.

Because the government conceded that "conspiracy" was also not recognized as an international war crime prior to the MCA's enactment, *Hamdan II* compelled a three-judge panel to reach the same result as applied to conspiracy in a second case, *Al Bahlul v. United States*, No. 11-1324, 2013 WL 297726 (D.C. Cir. Jan. 25, 2013) (mem.). The D.C. Circuit then granted the government's petition for rehearing en banc in *Al Bahlul*, and issued the following decision:

Al Bahlul v. United States
United States Court of Appeals, District of Columbia Circuit, July 14, 2014
No. 11-1324

KAREN LECRAFT HENDERSON, Circuit Judge: Ali Hamza Ahmad Suliman al Bahlul (Bahlul) served as a personal assistant to Osama bin Laden, produced propaganda videos for al Qaeda and assisted with preparations for the attacks of September 11, 2001 that killed thousands of Americans. Three months after 9/11, Bahlul was captured in Pakistan and transferred to the United States Naval Base at Guantanamo Bay, Cuba. Military prosecutors charged him with three crimes: conspiracy to commit war crimes, providing material support for terrorism and solicitation of others to commit war crimes. A military commission convicted him of all three crimes and sentenced him to life imprisonment. The United States Court of Military Commission Review (CMCR) affirmed his conviction and sentence. Bahlul appeals. For the reasons that follow, we reject Bahlul's *ex post facto* challenge to his conspiracy conviction and remand that conviction to the original panel of this Court for it to dispose of several remaining issues. In addition, we vacate his material support and solicitation convictions. . . .

II. Standard of Review

[In this section, Judge Henderson concludes for a 4-3 majority that al Bahlul forfeited his *ex post facto* challenges to his conspiracy conviction by failing to make them before the military commission itself. As a result, the appropriate standard of review, she concludes, is the "plain error" rule outlined by Fed. R. Crim. P. 52(b), even though the majority "need not decide whether Rule 52(b) applies directly to this proceeding," "because plain-error review is appropriate whether or not Rule 52(b) directly governs." In a footnote, Judge Henderson also rejects the three dissenters' suggestion that plain error review is inappropriate because the ex post facto challenge is "jurisdictional." As she concludes, "the 2006 MCA explicitly confers jurisdiction on military commissions to try the charged offenses. The question whether that Act is unconstitutional does not involve 'the courts' statutory or constitutional power to adjudicate the case.'"]

III. Statutory Analysis

. . . *Hamdan II* held that the 2006 MCA "does not authorize retroactive prosecution for conduct committed before enactment of that Act unless the conduct was already prohibited under existing U.S. law as a war crime triable by military commission." 696 F.3d at 1248. Because we conclude, for the reasons that follow, that the 2006 MCA is unambiguous in its intent to authorize retroactive prosecution for the crimes enumerated in the statute — regardless of their pre-existing law-of-war status — we now overrule *Hamdan II*'s statutory holding.[7]

A. The 2006 MCA is Unambiguous

[In this section, Judge Henderson holds, contra *Hamdan II*, that Congress was unambiguous in the Military Commissions Act of 2006 that the listed offenses could be tried based upon conduct that *pre-dated* the MCA's October 17, 2006 enactment — because "[i]n enacting the military commission provisions of the 2006 MCA, the Congress plainly intended to give the President the power which *Hamdan [I]* held it had not previously supplied."]

---

7. Although perhaps uncommon, overruling our precedent on plain-error review is within the authority of the *en banc* court. *See, e.g., United States v. Padilla,* 415 F.3d 211, 217–18 (1st Cir. 2005) (en banc) (recognizing power of *en banc* court to overrule circuit precedent under plain-error review but declining to do so).

B. The Avoidance Canon is Inapplicable

[In this section, Judge Henderson concludes that the constitutional avoidance canon does not counsel an alternative construction of the MCA because of the conclusion that the MCA was unambiguous.]

IV. Bahlul's *Ex Post Facto* Challenge . . .

. . . [W]e will assume without deciding that the Ex Post Facto Clause applies at Guantanamo. In so doing, we are "not to be understood as remotely intimating in any degree an opinion on the question." *Petite v. United States*, 361 U.S. 529, 531 (1960) (per curiam); *see also Casey v. United States*, 343 U.S. 808, 808 (1952) (per curiam) ("To accept in this case [the Solicitor General's] confession of error would not involve the establishment of any precedent."); *United States v. Bell*, 991 F.2d 1445, 1447–48 (8th Cir. 1993).[9]

A. Conspiracy

We reject Bahlul's *ex post facto* challenge to his conspiracy conviction for two independent and alternative reasons. First, the conduct for which he was convicted was already criminalized under 18 U.S.C. §2332(b) (section 2332(b)) when Bahlul engaged in it. It is not "plain" that it violates the *Ex Post Facto* Clause to try a pre-existing federal criminal offense in a military commission and any difference between the elements of that offense and the conspiracy charge in the 2006 MCA does not seriously affect the fairness, integrity or public reputation of judicial proceedings. Second, it is not "plain" that conspiracy was not already triable by law-of-war military commission under 10 U.S.C. §821 when Bahlul's conduct occurred.

---

9. Were we to decide this issue *de novo*, Judge Henderson would conclude that the *Ex Post Facto* Clause does not apply in cases involving aliens detained at Guantanamo, for the reasons stated in her separate concurring opinion. Chief Judge Garland and Judges Tatel and Griffith would conclude that the Clause does apply in such cases, for the reasons stated in the first two paragraphs of Part II.B of Judge Rogers's opinion and in Note 3 of Judge Kavanaugh's opinion.

1. Section 2332(b)

Bahlul was convicted of conspiracy to commit seven war crimes enumerated in the 2006 MCA, including the murder of protected persons. Although the 2006 MCA post-dates Bahlul's conduct, section 2332(b) has long been on the books, making it a crime to, "outside the United States," "cngage[] in a conspiracy to kill[] a national of the United States." 18 U.S.C. §2332(b); see Omnibus Diplomatic Security and Antiterrorism Act of 1986, Pub. L. No. 99-399, §1202(a), 100 Stat. 853, 896. Section 2332(b) is not an offense triable by military commission but, the Government argues, "[t]he fact that the MCA provides a different forum for adjudicating such conduct does not implicate ex post facto concerns." E.B. Br. of United States 67. We agree.

The right to be tried in a particular forum is not the sort of right the *Ex Post Facto* Clause protects. *See Collins* [*v. Youngblood*, 497 U.S. 37 (1990),] at 51. In *Collins*, the Supreme Court sifted through its *Ex Post Facto* Clause precedent, noting that some cases had said that a "procedural" change — *i.e.*, a "change[] in the procedures by which a criminal case is adjudicated" — may violate the Ex Post Facto Clause if the change "affects matters of substance" by "depriving a defendant of substantial protections with which the existing law surrounds the person accused of crime or arbitrarily infringing upon substantial personal rights." *Id.* at 45 (citations, brackets and quotation marks omitted). . . .

It is therefore not a plain *ex post facto* violation to transfer jurisdiction over a crime from an Article III court to a military commission because such a transfer does not have anything to do with the definition of the crime, the defenses or the punishment. . . .

Our inquiry is not ended, however, because the 2006 MCA conspiracy-to-murder-protected-persons charge and section 2332(b) do not have identical elements. The difference is a potential problem because the *Ex Post Facto* Clause prohibits "retrospectively eliminating an element of the offense" and thus "subvert[ing] the presumption of innocence by reducing the number of elements [the government] must prove to overcome that presumption." *Carmell*, 529 U.S. at 532. Both statutes require the existence of a conspiracy and an overt act in furtherance thereof. *See* 18 U.S.C. §2332(b)(2); 10 U.S.C. §950v(b)(28) (2006); *see also* Trial Tr. 846, 849–50 (military judge's instructions to commission). The 2006 MCA conspiracy charge is in one sense more difficult to prove than section 2332(b) because it applies only to alien unlawful enemy combatants engaged in hostilities against the United States. *See* 10 U.S.C. §§948b(a), 948c, 948d; *see also* Trial Tr. 843–45 (instructions). But the 2006 MCA charge is in two ways easier to prove than a section 2332(b) charge. It does not require that the conspiracy occur "outside the United States" or that the conspiracy be to kill a "national of the United States," as section 2332(b) does. It simply requires a conspiracy to murder "one or more protected persons." Trial Tr. 850–51 (instructions); *see supra* n.10 (providing MCA's definition of "protected person"). Although the two statutes are quite similar, then, the 2006 MCA conspiracy charge eliminates two elements required to convict a defendant under section 2332(b).

Nevertheless, Bahlul cannot bear his burden of establishing that the elimination of the two elements "seriously affect[ed] the fairness, integrity or public reputation of judicial proceedings." [*United States v.*] *Olano*, 507 U.S. [725 (1993),] at 732 (quotation marks omitted). He cannot satisfy the fourth prong because the charges against him and the commission's findings necessarily included those elements and the evidence supporting them was undisputed. . . .

2. Section 821

When Bahlul committed the crimes of which he was convicted, section 821 granted — and still grants — military commissions jurisdiction "with respect to offenders or offenses that by statute or by the law of war may be tried by military commissions." 10 U.S.C. §821. Section 821 and its predecessor statute have been on the books for nearly a century. *See* Pub. L. No. 64-242, 39 Stat. 619, 653 (1916); Pub. L. No. 66-242, 41 Stat. 759, 790 (1920); Pub. L. No. 81-506, 64 Stat. 107, 115 (1950); *Madsen v. Kinsella*, 343 U.S. 341, 350–51 & n.17 (1952). We must therefore ascertain whether conspiracy to commit war crimes was a "law of war" offense triable by military commission under section 821 when Bahlul's conduct occurred because, if so, Bahlul's *ex post facto* argument fails.

In answering this question, we do not write on a clean slate. . . . [But] we need not resolve *de novo* whether section 821 is limited to the international law of war. It is sufficient for our purpose to say that, at the time of this appeal, the answer to that question is not "obvious." *Olano*, 507 U.S. at 734; *see Henderson v. United States*, 133 S. Ct. 1121, 1130–31 (2013) (plainness of error determined at time of appeal). As seven justices did in *Hamdan*, we look to domestic wartime precedent to determine whether conspiracy has been traditionally triable by military commission. That precedent provides sufficient historical pedigree to sustain Bahlul's conviction on plain-error review. . . .

[The court next reviews a series of historical precedents.]

We do not hold that these precedents conclusively establish conspiracy as an offense triable by military commission under section 821. After all, four justices examined the same precedents and found them insufficiently clear. *Hamdan*, 548 U.S. at 603–09 (plurality). But there are two differences between *Hamdan* and this case. First, the elements of the conspiracy charge were not defined by statute in *Hamdan* and therefore the plurality sought precedent that was "plain and unambiguous." 548 U.S. at 602. Here, the Congress has positively identified conspiracy as a war crime. We need not decide the effect of the Congress's action, however, because we rely on the second difference: The *Hamdan* plurality's review was *de novo*; our review is for plain error. We think the historical practice of our wartime tribunals is sufficient to make it not "obvious" that conspiracy was not traditionally triable by law-of-war military commission under section 821. *Olano*, 507 U.S. at 734. We therefore conclude that any *Ex Post Facto* Clause error in trying Bahlul on conspiracy to commit war crimes is not plain. *See United States v. Vizcaino*, 202 F.3d 345, 348 (D.C. Cir. 2000) (assuming error to decide it was not plain).

B. Material Support

A different result obtains, however, regarding Bahlul's conviction of providing material support for terrorism. The Government concedes that material support is not an international law-of-war offense, see Oral Arg. Tr. 15; Panel Br. of United States 50, 57, and we so held in *Hamdan II*, 696 F.3d at 1249–53. But, in contrast to conspiracy, the Government offers little domestic precedent to support the notion that material support or a sufficiently analogous offense has historically been triable by military commission. Although Bahlul carries the burden to establish plain error, *see United States v. Brown*, 508 F.3d 1066, 1071 (D.C. Cir. 2007), we presume that in the unique context of the "domestic common law of war" — wherein the Executive Branch shapes the relevant precedent and individuals in its employ serve as prosecutor, judge and jury — the Government can be expected to direct us to the strongest historical precedents. What the Government puts forth is inadequate. . . .

[Judge Henderson proceeds to explain why "the Civil War field precedent is too distinguishable and imprecise to provide the sole basis for concluding that providing material support for terrorism was triable by law-of-war military commission at the time of Bahlul's conduct."]

. . . We therefore think it was a plain *ex post facto* violation — again, assuming without deciding that the protection of the *Ex Post Facto* Clause extends to Bahlul — to try Bahlul by military commission for that new offense. The error is prejudicial and we exercise our discretion to correct it by vacating Bahlul's material support conviction.[23]

C. Solicitation

[For similar reasons, the court next concluded that Bahlul's conviction for solicitation was also plainly erroneous, and must be vacated.]

V. Remaining Issues

In his brief to the panel, Bahlul raised four challenges to his convictions that we have not addressed here. He argued that (1) the Congress exceeded its Article I, §8 authority by defining crimes triable by military commission that are not offenses under the international law of war; (2) the Congress violated Article III by vesting military commissions with jurisdiction to try crimes that are not offenses under the international law of war; (3) his convictions violate the First Amendment; and (4) the 2006 MCA discriminates against aliens in

---

23. Unlike with conspiracy, the Government has not identified a pre-existing federal criminal statute that might cure any *ex post facto* aspect of Bahlul's material support conviction. The Government cites 18 U.S.C. §2339A, which criminalizes providing material support or resources knowing they are to be used in a violation of section 2332, but that offense was not made extraterritorial until October 26, 2001. See Pub. L. No. 107-56, §805(a)(1)(A), 115 Stat. 272, 377. Although Bahlul was not captured until December 2001, nearly all of the conduct of which he was convicted took place before September 11, 2001. The only overt act that necessarily occurred after September 11 was Bahlul's research on the economic effects of the attack. The record does not reflect, however, whether Bahlul committed that or any other act of material support constituting a violation of section 2339A after October 26, 2001. This charge, then, is unlike the conspiracy charge, where Bahlul expressly conceded and the jury necessarily found the two omitted elements.

violation of the equal protection component of the Due Process Claus. We intended neither the *en banc* briefing nor argument to address these four issues. And with the exception of a few passages regarding the first two, we received none from the parties. We therefore remand the case to the original panel of this Court to dispose of Bahlul's remaining challenges to his conspiracy conviction. . . .

So ordered.

KAREN LeCRAFT HENDERSON, Circuit Judge, concurring: [In a concurring opinion omitted here, Judge Henderson argued that, had the government not conceded that the Ex Post Facto Clause applied, she would have held that it did not protect non-citizens detained outside the territorial United States.]

ROGERS, Circuit Judge, concurring in the judgment in part and dissenting: [Judge Rogers' opinion began with a lengthy discussion of why the government cannot meet its burden to demonstrate that the three offenses of which Bahlul was convicted were triable by a military commission at the time of his underlying conduct, before turning to why that shortcoming gives rise to an Ex Post Facto Clause violation.] . . .

II.

A.

. . . Bahlul's *Ex Post Facto* Clause challenge to his convictions is properly reviewed *de novo* for any one of three reasons. In applying a plain error standard of review, the majority imposes a magic-words requirement nowhere to be found in the precedent of the Supreme Court or in the Uniform Code of Military Justice as interpreted by the Court of Appeals for the Armed Forces. *See, e.g., Olano v. United States*, 507 U.S. 725 (1993).

Bahlul unambiguously objected to his trial on the grounds he was being charged with offenses that did not exist at the time of his alleged conduct. Although he did not refer specifically to the *Ex Post Facto* Clause, his pretrial colloquy with the presiding military judge invoked its principles and alerted the military commission to the substance of his objection, which is all that is required to preserve an objection. *See, e.g., United States v. Breedlove*, 204 F.3d 267, 270 (D.C. Cir. 2000). . . .

Even if Bahlul had forfeited his ex post facto challenge, *de novo* review of a forfeited issue is permitted where the lower court has "nevertheless addressed the merits of the issue." *Blackmon-Malloy v. Capitol Police Bd.*, 575 F.3d 699, 707 (D.C. Cir. 2009). This principle applies in both criminal and civil cases. *See [United States v.] Williams*, 504 U.S. [36 (1992),] at 41. The Court of Military Commission Review considered Bahlul's constitutional *Ex Post Facto* Clause objection on the merits, 820 F. Supp. 2d 1141, 1218 (C.M.C.R. 2011), and this court may as a matter of discretion consider Bahlul's challenge under a *de novo* standard of review. Given that Bahlul's objections go to the fundamental issue of the military commission's jurisdiction, this court should apply *de novo* review. . . .

B.

The government concedes that the *Ex Post Facto* Clause applies in military commission prosecutions under the 2006 Act of detainees at Guantanamo Bay. *See* Resp't's Br. 64. This conclusion follows from *Boumediene [v. Bush]*, 553 U.S. [723 (2008),] at 766–71. . . .

Tellingly, when ratified and now, the Ex Post Facto Clause addresses the risk that, in response to political pressures, the legislature "may be tempted to use retroactive legislation as a means of retribution against unpopular groups or individuals." *Landgraf [v. USI Film Products]*, 511 U.S. [244 (1994),] at 266. By safeguarding the boundaries between the branches of government, the Clause promises that accusations that this country has, in Bahlul's words, "put [our laws] on the side" and "established a new law" for our enemies, Trial Tr. 23–24, will lack merit. Yet in an odd turn of phase for addressing "one of the most basic presumptions of our law," *Johnson [v. United States]*, 529 U.S. [694 (2000),] at 701, the government urges that the Clause "should apply flexibly" here "because of the common law nature of military proceedings" and "because Bahlul's conduct was criminal when done," albeit under statutes providing for prosecution in an Article III court. Resp't's Br. 62–63, 67. The government's "flexible" approach to the Ex Post Facto Clause, relying on the position that Bahlul's conduct may have been proscribed by laws other than those under which he was charged and convicted, "is a standardless exercise in crime by analogy," Pet'r's Reply Br. 21, that the Supreme Court has condemned, see, e.g., *Papachristou v. Jacksonville*, 405 U.S. 156, 168–69 (1972), and the law of war forbids, *see, e.g.*, Rome Statute of the International Criminal

Court art. 22, July 17, 1998, 2187 U.N.T.S. 90; 6 Law Reports of Trials of War Criminals at 95 (practices such as "application of principles of law condemned by the practice of civilised nations such as punishment by analogy . . . are all properly classed as war crimes").

C. . . .

Accordingly, the inchoate conspiracy charge of which Bahlul was convicted under the 2006 Act does not support the jurisdiction of the military commission and this conviction must be vacated as well as the two convictions vacated by the court. All three convictions must be vacated as violations of the Ex Post Facto Clause. It remains for the Administration to decide whether to bring other charges against Bahlul before a military commission or whether to charge him in an Article III court. To the extent that Congress has created an obstacle to bringing Bahlul to the United States, Congress can remove it. The question whether Congress has impermissibly intruded upon the President's Article II powers is not before the court. . . . I concur in the judgment vacating Bahlul's convictions for material support and solicitation, and I respectfully dissent with regard to affirmance of Bahlul's conviction for inchoate conspiracy.

BROWN, Circuit Judge, concurring in the judgment in part and dissenting in part: [Judge Brown's lengthy opinion begins by noting (1) her agreement with Judge Henderson that, but for the government's concession, she would have held the *Ex Post Facto* Clause inapplicable to the Guantánamo detainees; and (2) her disagreement with the majority over the applicability of plain error. Although, like Judge Rogers, she therefore believed Bahlul's *ex post facto* claims had to be resolved *de novo*, she would have reached a different result from Judge Rogers even if the *Ex Post Facto* Clause applied, for reasons she summarized at the beginning of her (otherwise omitted) opinion.] . . .

. . . I would reject Bahlul's *Ex Post Facto* Clause challenge as it concerns his conspiracy conviction. As Judge Kavanaugh explains, prior to 2006, the "law of war" provision of 10 U.S.C. §821 (Article 21 of the Uniform Code of Military Justice) preserved the jurisdiction of military commissions to try offenses that (1) were codified in federal statutes and explicitly made triable by military commission, (2) were recognized by the international law of war, or (3) were, according to domestic tradition and practice, triable by military commission. Furthermore, as the Lincoln conspirators' cases, *Quirin*, *Colepaugh*, and the Korean War decisions demonstrate, domestic practice traditionally treated conspiracy as an offense triable by military commission. Because conspiracy was an offense triable by military commission before the 2006 MCA, Bahlul's prosecution for that offense did not violate the *Ex Post Facto* Clause.[1] . . .

KAVANAUGH, Circuit Judge, concurring in the judgment in part and dissenting in part: . . .

I . . .

Bahlul's argument that Section 821's "law of war" prong consists *exclusively* of international law offenses is inconsistent with the text and textually stated purpose of Section 821, as well as with Supreme Court precedents such as *Madsen* and *Yamashita* interpreting Section 821. Perhaps most tellingly for present purposes, Bahlul's interpretation of Section 821 conflicts with what the Supreme Court actually did in *Hamdan*. Seven Justices in *Hamdan* analyzed the "law of war" embodied in Section 821 as the international law of war *supplemented by established U.S. military commission precedents*. Indeed, that is the only interpretation of Section 821 that squares with how the seven Justices analyzed the question in *Hamdan*.

In short, at the time of Bahlul's conduct, Section 821 authorized military commissions to try offenses drawn from three bodies of law: federal statutes defining offenses triable by military commission, the international law of war, and historical U.S. military commission

---

1. In upholding Bahlul's conspiracy conviction, I would not rely on 18 U.S.C. §2332(b). Indeed, by relying on *Olano*'s fourth prong, the court practically concedes that the existence of the conspiracy provision in Title 18 would not save Bahlul's conviction if not for the court's application of a plain error standard. I am also reluctant to rely on that provision, however, because of the significant procedural differences between criminal prosecutions in Article III civilian courts and prosecutions before military commissions. The parties have not fully briefed the issue, and I would be reluctant without such briefing to hold that a law retroactively transferring jurisdiction to try an offense from an Article III court to a military commission does not violate the *Ex Post Facto* Clause. Because the court utilizes a plain error standard, the court also does not fully embrace this novel and potentially far-reaching result.

tradition and practice as preserved by Congress when it enacted Section 821 in 1916 and 1950.

At the time of Bahlul's conduct, neither any federal statute nor the international law of war proscribed conspiracy as a war crime triable by military commission. So the question we must decide is whether U.S. military commission precedents treated conspiracy as an offense triable by military commission. In other words, we must decide the question that was addressed by seven Justices in *Hamdan* but not decided by the Court. The answer, in my view, is yes: U.S. military commission precedents have treated conspiracy as an offense triable by military commission. . . .

[Judge Kavanaugh proceeds to explain why the military commission trial of the Lincoln assassination conspirators provides an "especially clear and significant" historical precedent for trying conspiracy before a military commission, along with the commission upheld in *Ex parte Quirin*, 317 U.S. 1 (1942). He then concludes that no similar precedents support trying material support or solicitation before a commission.]

II

In challenging his convictions, Bahlul also advances a far more sweeping constitutional argument. He contends that Congress lacks constitutional authority to make conspiracy, material support for terrorism, or solicitation war crimes triable by military commissions, *even prospectively*, because those offenses are not proscribed under the international law of war. Bahlul's argument, in essence, is that the U.S. Constitution (as relevant here) incorporates international law and thereby interposes international law as a constitutional constraint on what crimes Congress may make triable by military commission. On its face, that is an extraordinary argument that would, *as a matter of U.S. constitutional law*, subordinate the U.S. Congress and the U.S. President to the dictates of the international community — a community that at any given time could be unsupportive of or even hostile to U.S. national security interests as defined by Congress and the President. And because conspiracy is not and has not been an offense under the international law of war, the argument would render the Lincoln conspirators and Nazi saboteur convictions for conspiracy illegitimate and unconstitutional. I would reject the argument. . . .

Bahlul says that Congress may enact offenses triable by U.S. military commissions only under Congress's Article I, Section 8 power to "define and punish . . . Offences against the Law of Nations." U.S. Const. art. I, §8, cl. 10. Because conspiracy is not an offense under international law, Bahlul argues that Congress lacked power under Article I, Section 8 to make the offense triable by military commission.

The premise of this argument is incorrect. As the Supreme Court has repeatedly stated, Congress's authority to establish military commissions to try war crimes does not arise exclusively from the Define and Punish Clause. On the contrary, as the Supreme Court has explained, Congress also has authority to establish military commissions to try war crimes under the Declare War and Necessary and Proper Clauses of Article I, Section 8. See U.S. Const. art. I, §8, cls. 11, 18; *Hamdan v. Rumsfeld*, 548 U.S. 557, 591-92 & n.21 (2006); *Madsen v. Kinsella*, 343 U.S. 341, 346 n.9 (1952); *Ex parte Quirin*, 317 U.S. 1, 26-31 (1942). And unlike the Define and Punish Clause, the Declare War Clause and the other Article I war powers clauses do not refer to international law and are not defined or constrained by international law. In other words, at least as a matter of U.S. constitutional law (as distinct from international law), the United States is not subject to the whims or dictates of the international community when the United States exercises its war powers. Therefore, under the text of Article I, international law is not a constitutional constraint when Congress proscribes war crimes triable by military commission. . . .

III

Citing the jury trial protections of Article III and the Fifth and Sixth Amendments, Bahlul reprises the same basic argument that U.S. military commissions may try only international law of war offenses. This version of Bahlul's argument begins with the premise that the Constitution requires all crimes to be tried by jury. Bahlul recognizes, as he must, that the Supreme Court in *Quirin* nonetheless permitted trial by military commission for war crimes. *See Ex parte Quirin*, 317 U.S. 1, 38-45 (1942); *see also Hamdan v. Rumsfeld*, 548 U.S. 557, 592-93 (2006). But Bahlul says that this exception to the jury trial right extends only to international law of war offenses.

To begin with, there is no textual support for Bahlul's theory. There is no textual reason to think that the exception to the jury trial protections for military commissions is somehow confined to international law of war offenses. That exception, as the Supreme Court has explained, stems from the various war powers clauses in Article I and Article II. And those war powers clauses are not defined or constrained by international law. *See Hamdan*, 548 U.S. at 591-92; *Quirin*, 317 U.S. at 25-27.

Moreover, Bahlul's novel theory contravenes precedent: It is inconsistent with the Lincoln conspirators and Nazi saboteurs conspiracy convictions, and it cannot be squared with *Quirin*. . . .

For present purposes, two things are notable about *Quirin*. First, in reaching its conclusion on the jury trial issue, the Court relied on the fact that Congress had made spying an offense triable by military commission since the earliest days of the Republic. The Court said that the early Congress's enactment of the spying statute "must be regarded as a contemporary construction" of both Article III and the Fifth and Sixth Amendments "as not foreclosing trial by military tribunals, without a jury, of offenses against the law of war committed by enemies not in or associated with our Armed Forces." *Id.* at 41. "Such a construction," the Court said, "is entitled to the greatest respect." *Id.* at 41-42. To reiterate, the offense of spying on which the Court relied was not and has never been an offense under the international law of war. It thus makes little sense to read *Quirin* as barring military commission trial of non-international-law-of-war offenses when *Quirin*, in rejecting a jury trial objection to military commissions, relied expressly on a longstanding statute making a non-international-law-of-war offense triable by military commission. Second, nothing about the Court's reasoning in *Quirin* on this point depended on whether the offense tried before a military commission was an international law of war offense or, by contrast, was a military commission offense recognized only by U.S. law. In other words, the Court never stated that military commissions are constitutionally permitted only for international law of war offenses, which one would have expected the Court to say if the Court believed that military commissions are constitutionally permitted only for international law of war offenses. . . .

VI . . .

. . . [L]ike Judge Brown (as well as Judge Rogers), I too respectfully have serious doubts about the majority opinion's suggestion that the Ex Post Facto Clause may allow military commissions to retroactively prosecute crimes that were previously triable as federal crimes in federal court even when they were not previously triable by military commission. Can Congress, consistent with the Ex Post Facto

Clause, really just pull out the federal criminal code and make offenses retroactively triable before military commissions? I am aware of no commentator who has taken that position or even analyzed the question. I have found no precedent taking that position or analyzing the question. And even Congress, hardly in a passive mode when it enacted the 2006 Act, did not go so far as the majority opinion about the meaning of the Ex Post Facto Clause. The text of the 2006 Act reveals that Congress thought there was no ex post facto problem because the listed offenses were previously triable by military commission. See 10 U.S.C. §950p(a) (2006). If Congress had thought it enough that there were some prior federal criminal statutes on the books, Congress no doubt would have relied on that point to respond to the ex post facto concerns. But as best as I can tell, no Member said as much. On the contrary, the text of the Act itself demonstrates that Congress thought it necessary, in order to overcome ex post facto objections, to show that the offenses had been previously triable *by military commission. . . .*

Second, from the other direction, I am also surprised by what the majority opinion does *not* decide. We took this case en banc specifically to decide whether, consistent with the Ex Post Facto Clause, a military commission could try conspiracy for conduct that occurred before the 2006 Act. Yet the majority opinion does not actually decide that question.

That is because the majority opinion applies the plain error standard of review. The majority opinion thus does not decide whether there was error in the conspiracy conviction; instead, it decides only whether any alleged error was plain.

Like Judge Brown (as well as Judge Rogers), I too disagree with the majority opinion's use of a plain error standard of review. . . .

. . . [But] even if the issue had been forfeited and plain error review applied, the majority opinion still would possess discretion to decide the ex post facto issue under the first prong of the plain error test as defined by the Supreme Court and conclude that there was no "error" in the conspiracy conviction. *See United States v. Olano*, 507 U.S. 725, 732 (1993). The majority opinion should do so. Courts have an appropriate role in times of war to decide certain justiciable disputes — but we should do so "with as much clarity and expedition as possible." *Kiyemba v. Obama*, 561 F.3d 509, 522 (D.C. Cir. 2009) (Kavanaugh, J., concurring). The majority opinion's failure to decide the ex post facto question with respect to conspiracy does not comport with that principle, in my respectful view. Given the various pending cases raising the same question and the need for guidance in those wartime tribunals, I believe that the majority opinion should decide the issue.

On top of not deciding how the ex post facto principle applies to conspiracy trials before military commissions, the majority opinion also does not decide Bahlul's Article I, jury trial, equal protection, or First Amendment challenges, but rather sends those four issues back to a three-judge panel for resolution. I also respectfully disagree with that approach. The remaining issues are not that complicated; we have the requisite briefing; and we could request supplemental briefing if need be. . . . Sending the case back to a three-judge panel will delay final resolution of this case, likely until some point in 2015, given the time it will take for a decision by the three-judge panel and then resolution of any future petitions for panel rehearing or rehearing en banc. Like Judge Brown, I believe that we should resolve the case now, not send it back to the three-judge panel. . . .

NOTES AND QUESTIONS

1. *The Significance of "Plain Error" Review.* Leaving aside the fight between the majority and the dissenters (Judges Rogers, Brown, and Kavanaugh) over whether "plain error" review *should* have applied to al Bahlul's ex post facto claim, note the significance to the result of the majority's conclusion that it does: What were the majority's two explanations for why al Bahlul's conspiracy conviction doesn't violate the Ex Post Facto Clause? Does either of those arguments strike you as one that would hold up under *de novo* review (that is, if plain error didn't apply)? Note that there are clearly three (out of seven) judges who *would* have rejected the ex post facto challenge even under *de novo* review, albeit for different reasons (Henderson, Brown, and Kavanaugh). But is there a fourth? Might the absence of a fourth vote on the merits help to explain why the majority relied on such a debatable and hypertechnical basis for rejecting Bahlul's ex post facto claim?

2. *What "Precedent" Does Al Bahlul Set?* As Judge Kavanaugh laments in his separate opinion, note how little the decision excerpted above actually resolves. Although the en banc Court of Appeals rejects al Bahlul's ex post facto challenge to his conviction, it does so pursuant to a standard (plain error) that shouldn't apply to any other cases, thereby leaving for another day whether, under *de novo* review, a military commission conviction for pre-MCA conspiracy *would* violate

the Ex Post Facto Clause. At the same time, the majority remands *all* of al Bahlul's other challenges to his conviction to the original three-judge panel, which includes Judges Henderson, Tatel, and Rogers (a procedural move that draws unusual objections from both Judges Brown and Kavanaugh). At the same time, the majority overrules *Hamdan II*, and all but Judges Henderson and Brown appear to hold (Judge Henderson's protestations to the contrary notwithstanding) that the Ex Post Facto Clause *does* apply to the Guantánamo detainees. As a result, al Bahlul's appeal may still *succeed*, especially in light of the Article III issues discussed in Note 3, below. Given that, consider the sentiment expressed by Judge Brown:

> Bahlul was first charged before a military commission ten years ago. Today, this court again leaves the government without any definitive answers. The court does not express respect to the coordinate branches of government by further delaying the executive's prosecutorial efforts and thwarting the legislative's expressed preference that detainees be tried by military commission. [Slip op. at 24 (Brown, J., concurring in the judgment and dissenting in part).]

Do you share Judge Brown's (and Judge Kavanaugh's) exasperation? Or might such frustration be colored by a view as to the underlying validity and legitimacy of the commissions?

3. *The Article III Elephant in the Room.* One of the arguments that the three-judge panel will now have to confront in *Al Bahlul* is his claim that Article III precludes the exercise of military jurisdiction over offenses not recognized as "international war crimes." This argument relies on *Ex parte Quirin*, 317 U.S. 1 (1942), which recognized an exception from Article III only for "offenses committed by enemy belligerents against the law of war," *id.* at 41, and on the Supreme Court's more recent admonitions that exceptions to Article III ought to be narrowly construed, *see, e.g., Stern v. Marshall*, 131 S. Ct. 2594 (2011). Thus, although Article III *would* sanction military commission trials for recognized violations of the international laws of war (as in the 9/11 trial, for example), al Bahlul's claim is that Article III limits the trial of violations of the "domestic" common law of war (whatever the source of Congress's power to proscribe such conduct) to the civilian courts.

Like al Bahlul's other challenges to his conviction, the majority sidestepped the Article III issue. Only Judge Kavanaugh addressed it —

concluding that Article III does not so confine the jurisdiction of military courts, largely because U.S. military courts have long had jurisdiction to try two outlier offenses (spying and aiding the enemy) that are not recognized as international war crimes. But note two objections to this view: First, it is limitless; on Judge Kavanaugh's logic, Congress can subject to trial by military commission any offense *it* deems a violation of the U.S. common law of war (at least so long as it does so prospectively — to avoid ex post facto concerns). Second, and in any event, no Supreme Court decision (including *Quirin*) has ever specifically *upheld* such jurisdiction. Instead, the only instances in which the Court has upheld military commission jurisdiction over offenses that were not international war crimes involved cases like *Madsen*, where the relevant international law (there, the law of belligerent occupation) specifically authorized military trials of non-military offenses. Might that suggest, then, that the exception to Article III recognized in *Quirin* is not for "offenses committed by enemy belligerents against the law of war," as *Quirin* suggested, but rather a slightly broader exception for "offenses triable by military courts under international law"? *See* Stephen I. Vladeck, *Military Courts and Article III*, 103 Geo. L.J. (forthcoming 2014). Given that, unlike his ex post facto challenge, al Bahlul's Article III challenge is almost certainly "jurisdictional" — and therefore not subject to "plain error" review — how *should* the three-judge panel resolve the Article III claim?

4. *War Crimes Without a War?* Another major jurisdictional challenge to the commissions has been lodged by Abd al-Rahim al-Nashiri, a Guantánamo detainee charged based upon his involvement in the 2000 bombing of the *USS Cole*. In Nashiri's case, the question is also whether the charged offenses were recognized as international war crimes at the time of their commission — not, as in *Al Bahlul*, because international law doesn't recognize the offenses in the abstract, but because the United States was not actually in an armed conflict with Al Qaeda prior to September 11, 2001. If the jurisdiction of the commissions does indeed turn on the existence of a state of armed conflict at the time of the relevant offense, what is the argument for the assertion of jurisdiction over Nashiri? As a matter of international humanitarian law, when did the non-international armed conflict with Al Qaeda *begin*?

5. *The Future of the Commissions.* For obvious reasons, *Al Bahlul* creates a fair amount of uncertainty as to the future utility of the commissions both as applied to the Guantánamo detainees and as potentially applied to future terrorism suspects. With regard to the Guantánamo detainees, *Al Bahlul* takes pre-MCA material support and solicitation charges off the table, and leaves the availability of pre-MCA conspiracy charges for another day. But what about charges for material support, solicitation, or conspiracy based upon *post*-MCA conduct?

Whereas virtually all of the Guantánamo detainees were captured prior to the MCA's October 17, 2006 enactment, in February 2014, the government referred charges against one of the detainees — Abdul Hadi al Iraqi — for conspiracy based at least in part upon *post*-MCA conduct. If al Iraqi were to challenge the inclusion of the conspiracy charge, he could not do so on ex post facto grounds. But he *could* raise the Article III argument described above in Note 3 — since that challenge applies equally to retrospective or prospective prosecutions. Thus, if the three-judge panel in *Al Bahlul* ends up ducking the Article III issue in his case, do you see why *Al Iraqi* would become the critical test case for the future of the commissions not just at Guantánamo, but for future terrorism suspects elsewhere?

————————

[NSL p. 1113, CTL p. 727. Insert at end of chapter.]

Eric Holder, Attorney General, Remarks at Northwestern University School of Law

Mar. 5, 2012,
available at
http://www.justice.gov/iso/opa/ag/speeches/2012/ag-speech-1203051.html

. . .

It's important to note that the reformed [military] commissions draw from the same fundamental protections of a fair trial that underlie our civilian courts. They provide a presumption of innocence and require proof of guilt beyond a reasonable doubt. They afford the accused the right to counsel — as well as the right to present evidence and cross-examine witnesses. They prohibit the use of statements obtained through torture or cruel, inhuman, or degrading treatment. And they secure the right to appeal to Article III judges — all the way to the United States

Supreme Court. In addition, like our federal civilian courts, reformed commissions allow for the protection of sensitive sources and methods of intelligence gathering, and for the safety and security of participants.

A key difference is that, in military commissions, evidentiary rules reflect the realities of the battlefield and of conducting investigations in a war zone. For example, statements may be admissible even in the absence of Miranda warnings, because we cannot expect military personnel to administer warnings to an enemy captured in battle. But instead, a military judge must make other findings — for instance, that the statement is reliable and that it was made voluntarily.

I have faith in the framework and promise of our military commissions, which is why I've sent several cases to the reformed commissions for prosecution. There is, quite simply, no inherent contradiction between using military commissions in appropriate cases while still prosecuting other terrorists in civilian courts. Without question, there are differences between these systems that must be — and will continue to be — weighed carefully. Such decisions about how to prosecute suspected terrorists are core Executive Branch functions. In each case, prosecutors and counterterrorism professionals across the government conduct an intensive review of case-specific facts designed to determine which avenue of prosecution to pursue.

Several practical considerations affect the choice of forum.

First of all, the commissions only have jurisdiction to prosecute individuals who are a part of al Qaeda, have engaged in hostilities against the United States or its coalition partners, or who have purposefully and materially supported such hostilities. This means that there may be members of certain terrorist groups who fall outside the jurisdiction of military commissions because, for example, they lack ties to al Qaeda and their conduct does not otherwise make them subject to prosecution in this forum. Additionally, by statute, military commissions cannot be used to try U.S. citizens.

Second, our civilian courts cover a much broader set of offenses than the military commissions, which can only prosecute specified offenses, including violations of the laws of war and other offenses traditionally triable by military commission. This means federal prosecutors have a wider range of tools that can be used to incapacitate suspected terrorists. Those charges, and the sentences they carry upon successful conviction, can provide important incentives to reach plea agreements and convince defendants to cooperate with federal authorities.

Third, there is the issue of international cooperation. A number of countries have indicated that they will not cooperate with the United States in certain counterterrorism efforts — for instance, in providing evidence or extraditing suspects — if we intend to use that cooperation in pursuit of a military commission prosecution. Although the use of military commissions in the United States can be traced back to the early days of our nation, in their present form they are less familiar to the international community than our time-tested criminal justice system and Article III courts. However, it is my hope that, with time and experience, the reformed commissions will attain similar respect in the eyes of the world. . . .

And we will continue to reject the false idea that we must choose between federal courts and military commissions, instead of using them both. If we were to fail to use all necessary and available tools at our disposal, we would undoubtedly fail in our fundamental duty to protect the Nation and its people. That is simply not an outcome we can accept. . . .

[NSL p. 1240. Insert as new Note 4a.]

4a. *Public Access to the Bradley Manning Court Martial.* The Guantánamo military commissions have yet to resolve on the merits the First Amendment questions raised in Note 4, holding in the context of the 9/11 trial that such claims have not yet become ripe. *See, e.g., ACLU v. United States*, No. 13-003 (Ct. Mil. Comm'n Rev. Mar. 27, 2013) (per curiam). But the Court of Appeals for the Armed Forces (CAAF) — the highest court in the military justice system — was confronted with an analogous challenge arising out of the Bradley Manning court martial. A coalition of journalists, advocacy organizations, and media enterprises sought a writ of mandamus to challenge the trial judge's presumptive closure of various of the pre-trial proceedings in Manning's case. In a 3-2 decision, CAAF held that it lacked jurisdiction to provide such relief, reasoning that military (as opposed to civilian) courts have no power to entertain such applications for "civil" relief from third parties. *See Ctr. for Const'l Rights v. United States*, 72 M.J. 126 (C.A.A.F. 2013). For harsh criticism of this reasoning, see Steve Vladeck, *CAAF Rejects Jurisdiction Over Bradley Manning Court-Martial Public Access Claims*, Lawfare, Apr. 17, 2013, *available at* http://www.lawfareblog. com/2013/04/caaf-rejects-jurisdiction-over-bradley-manning-court-martial-public-access-claims/. Shortcomings aside, at least one of the judges on the Court of Military Commission Review has endorsed a variation of this reasoning. *See ACLU*, slip op. at 2–5 (Silliman, J., concurring).

If the military commissions follow CAAF's lead and hold that they lack the power to entertain First Amendment challenges to closed proceedings, does that suggest that the right of public access identified by the Supreme Court in *Richmond Newspapers* and its progeny is one with no meaningful remedy in the military justice system? Could *civilian* courts entertain collateral pre-trial challenges to the closed nature of military proceedings? Would we want them to? *See, e.g., Ctr. for Const'l Rights*, 72 M.J. at 132 (Baker, C.J., dissenting) (describing the "untenable consequences" for military courts of such reliance upon collateral and interlocutory civilian judicial oversight); *cf. Ctr. for Const'l Rights v. Lind*, 954 F. Supp. 2d 389 (D. Md. 2013) (expressing reservations about enjoining ongoing court-martial proceedings).

[NSL p. 1262. Insert at the end of Note 5.]

Office of the Director of National Intelligence, Intelligence Community Directive 119: Media Contacts
Mar. 20, 2014

C. APPLICABILITY

1. This Directive applies to the IC [intelligence community], as defined by the National Security Act of 1947, as amended; Executive Order (EO) 12333, as amended; EO 13526; EO 13462; Presidential Policy Directive-19 (PPD-19); and other applicable provisions of law.

2. This Directive is limited to contact with the media about intelligence-related information, including intelligence sources, methods, activities, and judgments (hereafter, "covered matters"). . . .

4. For purposes of this Directive, media is any person, organization, or entity (other than Federal, State, local, tribal and territorial governments):

    a. primarily engaged in the collection, production, or dissemination to the public of information in any form, which includes print, broadcast, film and Internet; or

b. otherwise engaged in the collection, production, or dissemination to the public of information in any form related to topics of national security, which includes print, broadcast, film and Internet. . . .

D. POLICY

1. The IC is committed to sharing information responsibly with the public via the media to further government openness and transparency and to build public understanding of the IC and its programs, consistent with the protection of intelligence sources and methods. Appropriate IC element engagement with the media is encouraged.

2. The IC also is committed to protecting intelligence information from unauthorized disclosure. It is the responsibility of each individual IC employee not to disclose covered matters.

3. Contact by IC employees with the media on covered matters must be authorized by their IC element.

a. Within the IC, only the head or deputy head of an IC element, the designated public affairs official, and other persons designated in agency policy or authorized by that public affairs official are authorized to have contact with the media on covered matters, except as provided below.

b. IC employees, as defined in EO 12333, Section 3.5(d), not designated in accordance with Section D.3.a, must obtain authorization for contacts with the media on covered matters through the office responsible for public affairs for their IC element, and must also report to that office unplanned or unintentional contact with the media on covered matters.

4. No substantive information should be provided to the media regarding covered matters in the case of unplanned or unintentional contacts. . . .

9. IC employees who are found to be in violation of this IC policy may be subject to administrative actions that may include revocation of security clearance or termination of employment. If failure to comply with this policy results in an unauthorized disclosure of classified information, referral to the Department of Justice for prosecution may occur . . . . At a minimum, violation of this IC policy will be handled in the same manner as a security violation. . . .

If you were an employee of, say, the NSA, how would you respond to this directive? Do you understand what kind of information is included in "covered matters"? Does it include unclassified information? Can you tell from the directive who a member of the media is? Can you guess why the directive does not apply to IC contractors like Edward Snowden?

How do you suppose members of the media will be affected by the requirement to report "unplanned or unintentional contact with the media on covered matters"? *See* NSL p. 1308, Note 6; Ethan Bronner, Charlie Savage & Scott Shane, *Leak Inquiries Show How Wide a Net U.S. Cast*, N.Y. Times, May 26, 2013.

Does the directive violate the First Amendment free speech rights of IC employees? *See* NSL p. 1260, Note 2, and p. 1275, Note 2. Does it offend the First Amendment freedom of the press? *See* NSL pp. 1232-1242.

Do you think the directive strikes the right balance between national security and representative democracy? For analysis and criticism see *Intelligence Directive Bars Unauthorized Contacts with Media*, Secrecy News, Apr. 21, 2014, and Charlie Savage, *Intelligence Chief Issues Limits on Press Contacts*, N.Y. Times, Apr. 22, 2014.

[NSL p. 1274. Insert after Note 3.]

3a. *"Injury of the United States."* In May 2013, a federal judge ruled in a §793(d) case that while the prosecution had to prove that a defendant had "reason to believe" that the information could be damaging and that he nevertheless "willfully" communicated that information to someone not entitled to receive it, it was not necessary to prove that the information was "potentially damaging to the United States or useful to an enemy." *United States v. Kim* (No. CRIM. 10–255 CKK), slip op. at 10 (D.D.C. May 30, 2013), *available at* http://www.fas.org/sgp/jud/kim/072413-opinion3.pdf. It refused to follow the holding in *United States v. Morison*, 844 F.2d 1057, 1071 (4th Cir. 1988), that such proof was required, thus considerably easing the prosecution's burden under this provision of the Espionage Act. *See Court Eases Prosecutors' Burden of Proof in Leak Cases*, Secrecy News, July 29, 2013.

Can this ruling be squared with the *Rosen* court's reading of the term "national defense information"? With its balancing of the defendants' First Amendment interests?

————————————

[NSL p. 1309. Insert at the end of Note 6.]

Department of Justice, Report on Review of News Media Policies
July 12, 2013

In May 2013, at the President's direction, the Attorney General initiated a comprehensive evaluation of the Department of Justice's policies and practices governing the use of law enforcement tools, including subpoenas, court orders, and search warrants, to obtain information or records from or concerning members of the news media in criminal and civil investigations. . . . Based on this review, the Attorney General is making significant revisions to the Department's policies regarding investigations that involve members of the news media.

As an initial matter, it bears emphasis that it has been and remains the Department's policy that members of the news media will not be subject to prosecution based solely on newsgathering activities. Furthermore, in light of the importance of the constitutionally protected newsgathering process, the Department views the use of tools to seek evidence from or involving the news media as an extraordinary measure. The Department's policy is to utilize such tools only as a last resort, after all reasonable alternative investigative steps have been taken, and when the information sought is essential to a successful investigation or prosecution.

The changes in policy outlined in this report are intended to further ensure the Department strikes the appropriate balance between two vital interests: protecting the American people by pursuing those who violate their oaths through unlawful disclosures of information and safeguarding the essential role of a free press in fostering government accountability and an open society. As set forth in more detail below, the Department's policy revisions strengthen protections for members of the news media by, among other things, requiring more robust oversight by senior Department officials and by clarifying and expanding the presumption of negotiations with, and notice to, members of the news media when

Department attorneys request authorization to seek newsgathering records. . . .

Revisions to Department of Justice News Media Policies

I. Reversing the Existing Presumption Regarding Advance Notice

The first and most significant policy change would be to reverse and expand the presumption concerning notice to, and negotiations with, affected members of the news media whenever Department attorneys seek access to their records related to newsgathering activities. The presumption will ensure notice in all but the most exceptional cases.

. . . Under the new policy, the presumption of advance notice will be overcome only if the Attorney General affirmatively determines, taking into account recommendations from the newly established News Media Review Committee described below, that for compelling reasons, advance notice and negotiations *would* pose a clear and substantial threat to the integrity of the investigation, risk grave harm to national security, or present an imminent risk of death or serious bodily harm. The possibility that notice and negotiations with the media, and potential judicial review, may delay the investigation will not, on its own, be considered a compelling reason under this updated policy.

Advance notice will afford members of the news media the opportunity to engage with the Department regarding the proposed use of investigative tools to obtain communications or business records, and also provide the news media with the opportunity to challenge the government's use of such tools in federal court. . . .

It is expected that only the rare case would present the Attorney General with the requisite compelling reasons to justify a delayed notification. Under this updated policy, if a determination is made by the Attorney General to delay notification for an initial 45-day period, only the Attorney General may authorize a delay of notification for up to an additional 45 days, and even then, only if the Attorney General again determines, after an additional review by the News Media Review Committee, that, for compelling reasons, notice would pose a clear and substantial threat to the integrity of the investigation, grave harm to national security, or imminent risk of death or serious bodily harm. No further delays may be sought beyond the 90-day period. . . .

II. Enhanced Approvals and Heightened Standards for Use of Search Warrants and Section 2703(d) Orders

The Privacy Protection Act of 1980 (PPA), 42 U.S.C. §2000aa, generally prohibits the search or seizure of work product and documentary materials held by individuals who have a purpose to disseminate information to the public. The PPA, however, contains a number of exceptions to its general prohibition, including the "suspect exception" which applies when there is "probable cause to believe that the person possessing such materials has committed or is committing a criminal offense to which the materials relate," including "the receipt, possession, or communication of information relating to the national defense, classified information, or restricted data" under enumerated code provisions. . . .

. . . Under this revised policy, the Department would not seek search warrants under the PPA's suspect exception if the sole purpose is the investigation of a person other than the member of the news media.

Second, the Department would revise current policy to elevate the current approval requirements and require the approval of the Attorney General for all search warrants and court orders issued pursuant to 18 U.S.C. §2703(d) [regarding access to contents of stored electronic communications] directed at members of the news media. In addition, as part of the new approval process the Attorney General would consider the factors . . . [that include] demonstrating that the information sought is essential to a successful investigation, that other reasonable alternative investigative steps to obtain the information have been exhausted, and that the request has been narrowly tailored to obtain only the information necessary for the investigation . . . .

III. Establishment of News Media Review Committee

The Department will create a standing News Media Review Committee, akin to its Capital Case Review Committee and State Secrets Review Committee, to advise the Attorney General and Deputy Attorney General when Department attorneys request authorization to seek media-related records in investigations into the unauthorized disclosure of information; when Department attorneys request authorization to seek media-related records in any law enforcement investigation without providing prior notice to the relevant member of the media; and when Department attorneys request authorization to seek testimony from a member of the media that would disclose the identity of a confidential source. . . . This committee will ensure that senior Department officials with relevant expertise and experience, and who are neither directly involved nor playa supervisory role in the investigations involved, are engaged in the consideration of the use of investigative tools that involve members of the news media. . . .

V. Intelligence Community Certification

In investigations of unauthorized disclosures of national defense information or of classified information, under the Department's revised policy the Director of National Intelligence after consultation with the relevant Department or agency head, would certify to the Attorney General the significance of the harm that could have been caused by the unauthorized disclosure and reaffirm the intelligence community's continued support for the investigation and prosecution before the Attorney General authorizes the Department to seek media-related records in such investigations. . . . [C]urrent practice [provides] the Attorney General with information about whether the information disclosed was properly classified, whether the disclosure could have caused harm to the national security or foreign policy of the United States, and whether the victim Department or agency continues to support the investigation and potential prosecution of persons responsible for the unauthorized disclosure. . . .

United States v. Sterling

United States Court of Appeals, Fourth Circuit, July 19, 2013
724 F.3d 482, *rehearing en banc denied,* 732 F.3d 292,
cert. denied sub nom. Risen v. United States, 2014 WL 695068 (June 2, 2014)

[Jeffrey Sterling was a CIA case officer with a top secret security clearance, assigned to a highly classified program intended to impede Iran's efforts to acquire or develop nuclear weapons ("Classified Program No. 1"). Sterling also served as the case officer for a covert asset ("Human Asset No. 1") who was assisting the CIA with this program.

After unsuccessfully suing the CIA twice for employment discrimination, Sterling met with staff of the Senate Select Committee on Intelligence ("SSCI"), raised concerns about the CIA's handling of

Classified Program No. 1 and "threatened to go to the press," although it was unclear whether he was referring to the program or his lawsuits. He then called *New York Times* reporter James Risen seven times and emailed him, referencing an article from CNN's website entitled, "Report: Iran has 'extremely advanced' nuclear program," and asking, "quite interesting, don't you think? All the more reason to wonder . . . ."

Risen subsequently warned the Administration that he intended to publish an article about Classified Program No. 1. In response, senior administration officials met with Risen and *Times* officials, after which the *Times* advised the administration that the newspaper would not publish the story.

Subsequently, Sterling allegedly telephoned and emailed Risen on multiple occasions, and the emails revealed that Sterling and Risen were meeting and exchanging information. Risen then published a book, *State of War: The Secret History of the CIA and the Bush Administration* ("*State of War*"), which disclosed classified information about Classified Program No. 1, which he described as a "failed attempt by the CIA to have a former Russian scientist provide flawed nuclear weapon blueprints to Iran."

Sterling was thereafter indicted on six counts of unauthorized retention and communication of national defense information in violation of the Espionage Act, 18 U.S.C. §793(d) & (e), and other provisions. When the government subpoenaed Risen seeking testimony about the identity of and statements by his source, Risen moved to quash the subpoena and for a protective order, asserting that he was protected from compelled testimony by the First Amendment or, in the alternative, by a federal common-law reporter's privilege.]

TRAXLER, Chief Judge, writing for the court on [the First Amendment and reporter's privilege claims]:

II. The Reporter's Privilege Claim . . .

B. The First Amendment Claim

1.

There is no First Amendment testimonial privilege, absolute or qualified, that protects a reporter from being compelled to testify by the prosecution or the defense in criminal proceedings about criminal conduct that the reporter personally witnessed or participated in, absent a showing of bad faith, harassment, or other such non-legitimate motive, even though the reporter promised confidentiality to his source. In *Branzburg v. Hayes,* 408 U.S. 665 (1972), the Supreme Court "in no uncertain terms rejected the existence of such a privilege." *In re Grand Jury Subpoena, Judith Miller,* 438 F.3d 1141, 1146 (D.C. Cir. 2006).

Like Risen, the *Branzburg* reporters were subpoenaed to testify regarding their personal knowledge of criminal activity. One reporter was subpoenaed to testify regarding his observations of persons synthesizing hashish and smoking marijuana; two others were subpoenaed to testify regarding their observations of suspected criminal activities of the Black Panther Party. All resisted on the ground that they possessed a qualified privilege against being "forced either to appear or to testify before a grand jury or at trial." . . .

. . . [T]he Court proceeded to unequivocally reject [their claim]. Noting "the longstanding principle that the public . . . has a right to every man's evidence, except for those persons protected by a constitutional, common-law, or statutory privilege," *id.* at 688, the Court held as follows:

> Until now the only testimonial privilege for unofficial witnesses that is rooted in the Federal Constitution is the Fifth Amendment privilege against compelled self-incrimination. We are asked to create another by interpreting the First Amendment to grant newsmen a testimonial privilege that other citizens do not enjoy. *This we decline to do.*

Id. at 689-90 (emphasis added).

The First Amendment claim in *Branzburg* was grounded in the same argument offered by Risen — that the absence of such a qualified privilege would chill the future newsgathering abilities of the press, to the detriment of the free flow of information to the public. And the *Branzburg* claim, too, was supported by affidavits and amicus curiae memoranda from journalists claiming that their news sources and news reporting would be adversely impacted if reporters were required to testify about confidential relationships. However, the *Branzburg* Court rejected that rationale as inappropriate in criminal proceedings:

> The preference for anonymity of . . . confidential informants *involved in actual criminal conduct* is presumably a product of their desire to escape criminal prosecution, [but] this preference, while understandable, is hardly deserving of constitutional protection. It would be frivolous to assert — and

no one does in these cases — that the First Amendment, in the interest of securing news or otherwise, confers a license on either the reporter or his news sources to violate valid criminal laws. Although stealing documents or private wiretapping could provide newsworthy information, neither reporter nor source is immune from conviction for such conduct, whatever the impact on the flow of news. Neither is immune, on First Amendment grounds, from testifying against the other, before the grand jury or at a criminal trial.

Id. at 691 (emphasis added). . . .

Although the Court soundly rejected a First Amendment privilege in criminal proceedings, the Court did observe, in the concluding paragraph of its analysis, that the press would not be wholly without protection:

[N]ews gathering is not without its First Amendment protections, and grand jury investigations if *instituted or conducted other than in good faith,* would pose wholly different issues for resolution under the First Amendment. *Official harassment of the press undertaken not for purposes of law enforcement but to disrupt a reporter's relationship with his news sources would have no justification.*

Id. at 707-08 (majority opinion) (emphasis added). This is the holding of *Branzburg,* and the Supreme Court has never varied from it. . . .

. . . The *Branzburg* Court considered the arguments we consider today, balanced the respective interests of the press and the public in newsgathering and in prosecuting crimes, and held that, so long as the subpoena is issued in good faith and is based on a legitimate need of law enforcement, the government need not make any special showing to obtain evidence of criminal conduct from a reporter in a criminal proceeding. The reporter must appear and give testimony just as every other citizen must. We are not at liberty to conclude otherwise. . . .

3.

Like the *Branzburg* reporters, Risen has "direct information . . . concerning the commission of serious crimes." *Branzburg,* 408 U.S. at 709. Indeed, he can provide the *only* first-hand account of the commission of a most serious crime indicted by the grand jury — the illegal disclosure of classified, national security information by one who was entrusted by our government to protect national security, but who is charged with having endangered it instead. The subpoena for Risen's testimony was not issued in bad faith or for the purposes of harassment. *See id.* at 707-08. Risen is not being "called upon to give information bearing only a remote and tenuous relationship to the subject of the investigation," and there is no "reason to believe that his testimony implicates confidential source relationships without a legitimate need of law enforcement." *Id.* at 710 (Powell, J., concurring). Nor is the government attempting to "annex" Risen as its "investigative arm." *Id.* at 709. Rather, the government seeks to compel evidence that Risen alone possesses — evidence that goes to the heart of the prosecution.

The controlling majority opinion in *Branzburg* and our decision in [*In re Shain*, 978 F.2d 850 (4th Cir. 1992)] preclude Risen's claim to a First Amendment reporter's privilege that would permit him to resist the legitimate, good faith subpoena issued to him. The only constitutional, testimonial privilege that Risen was entitled to invoke was the Fifth Amendment privilege against self-incrimination, but he has been granted immunity from prosecution for his potential exposure to criminal liability. . . .

III. The Common-Law Privilege Claim

Risen next argues that, even if *Branzburg* prohibits our recognition of a First Amendment privilege, we should recognize a qualified, federal common-law reporter's privilege protecting confidential sources. We decline to do so.

A.

In the course of rejecting the First Amendment claim in *Branzburg,* the Supreme Court also plainly observed that the common law recognized no such testimonial privilege:

> It is thus not surprising that the great weight of authority is that newsmen are not exempt from the normal duty of appearing before a grand jury and answering questions relevant to a criminal investigation. At common law, courts consistently refused to recognize the existence of any privilege authorizing a newsman to refuse to reveal confidential information to a grand jury.

Branzburg, 408 U.S. at 685; *see also Judith Miller*, 438 F.3d at 1154 (Sentelle, J., concurring) (*Branzburg* is "as dispositive of the question of common law privilege as it is of a First Amendment privilege").

B.

Risen does not take issue with the clarity of *Branzburg's* statements regarding the state of the common law. Rather, he argues that Federal Rule of Evidence 501 . . . grants us authority to reconsider the question and now grant the privilege. We disagree.

Federal Rule of Evidence 501, in its current form, provides that:

> [t]he common law — *as interpreted by United States courts in the light of reason and experience* — governs a claim of privilege unless [the United States Constitution, a federal statute, or the rules prescribed by the Supreme Court] provide[ ] otherwise.

Fed. R. Evid. 501 (emphasis added). . . .

"In . . . enacting Rule 501, Congress manifested an affirmative intention not to freeze the law of privilege," but "rather . . . to provide the courts with the flexibility to develop rules of privilege on a case-by-case basis." *Trammel v. United States,* 445 U.S. 40, 47 (1980). Rule 501 thus leaves the door open for courts to adopt new common-law privileges, and modify existing ones, in appropriate cases. But nothing in Rule 501 or its legislative history authorizes federal courts to ignore existing Supreme Court precedent. . . .

Here, "[t]he Supreme Court has rejected a common law privilege for reporters" and "that rejection stands unless and until the Supreme Court itself overrules that part of *Branzburg." Judith Miller,* 438 F.3d at 1155 (Sentelle, J., concurring). Just as the Supreme Court must determine whether a First Amendment reporter's privilege should exist, *see Judith Miller,* 438 U.S. at 1166 (Tatel, J., concurring), "only the [Supreme Court] and not this one . . . may act upon th[e] argument" that a federal common-law privilege should now be recognized under Rule 501, *id.* at 1155 n.3 (Sentelle, J., concurring).

C.

Even if we were at liberty to reconsider the existence of a common-law reporter's privilege under Rule 501, we would decline to do so.

. . . [T]he federal courts' latitude for adopting evidentiary privileges under Rule 501 remains quite narrow indeed. Because they "contravene the fundamental principle that the public has a right to every man's evidence," *University of Pa.* [*v. EEOC,* 493 U.S. 182 (1990),] at 189, such privileges "are not lightly created nor expansively construed, for they are in derogation of the search for truth," [*United States v. Nixon,* 418 U.S. 683 (1974),] at 710. "When considering whether to recognize a privilege, a court must begin with 'the primary assumption that there is a general duty to give what testimony one is capable of giving, and that any exemptions which may exist are distinctly exceptional, being so many derogations from a positive general rule." *Virmani v. Novant Health Inc.,* 259 F.3d 284, 287 (4th Cir. 2001). New or expanded privileges "may be recognized 'only to the very limited extent that permitting a refusal to testify or excluding relevant evidence has a public good transcending the normally predominant principle of utilizing all rational means for ascertaining truth.'" [*United States v. Dunford,* 148 F.3d 385 (4th Cir. 1998),] at 391 (quoting *Trammel,* 445 U.S. at 50).

Risen contends that the public and private [interests] recognizing a reporter's privilege "are surely as significant [as the] public interest at stake in patient and psychotherapist communication." But we see several critical distinctions.

1.

First, unlike in the case of the spousal, attorney-client, and psychotherapist-patient privileges that have been recognized, the reporter-source privilege does not share the same relational privacy interests or ultimate goal. The recognized privileges promote the public's interest in full and frank communications between persons in special relationships by protecting the confidentiality of their private communications. A reporter's privilege might also promote free and full discussion between a reporter and his source, but Risen does not seek to protect from public disclosure the "confidential communications" made to him. Risen *published* information conveyed to him by his source or sources. His primary goal is to protect the *identity* of the person or persons who communicated with him because their communications violated federal, criminal laws. In sum, beyond the shared complaint that communications might be chilled in the absence of a testimonial privilege, Risen's proffered rationale for protecting his sources shares little in common with the privileges historically recognized in the common law and developed under Rule 501. . . .

We are admonished that refusal to provide a First Amendment reporter's privilege will undermine the freedom of the press to collect and disseminate news. But this is not the lesson history teaches us. As noted previously, the common law recognized no such privilege, and the constitutional argument was not even asserted until 1958. From the beginning of our country the press has operated without constitutional protection for press informants, and the press has flourished. The existing constitutional rules have not been a serious obstacle to either the development or retention of confidential news sources by the press.

Branzburg also weighed the public interest in newsgathering against the public's interest in enforcing its criminal laws:

> More important, it is obvious that agreements to conceal information relevant to commission of crime have very little to recommend them from the standpoint of public policy. Historically, the common law recognized a duty to raise the "hue and cry" and report felonies to the authorities. Misprison of a felony — that is, the concealment of a felony "which a man knows, but never assented to . . . [so as to become] either principal or accessory," 4 W. Blackstone, Commentaries, was often said to be a common-law crime. . . . It is apparent from [the federal statute defining the crime of misprison], as well as from our history and that of England, that concealment of crime and agreements to do so are not looked upon with favor. Such conduct deserves no encomium, and we decline now to afford it First Amendment protection. . . .

[408 U.S.] at 695-97.

We fail to see how these policy considerations would differ in a Rule 501 analysis. . . .

2.

Risen's reliance upon state statutes and decisions that have adopted a reporter's shield also fails to persuade us that we can or should create a federal common-law privilege. . . .

[The opinion of GREGORY, Circuit Judge, writing for the court on the admission of testimony from two government witnesses and on the withholding of witness information under the Classified Information Procedures Act, is omitted].

GREGORY, Circuit Judge, dissenting as to [the existence of a reporter's privilege]: . . .

A.

The freedom of the press is one of our Constitution's most important and salutary contributions to human history. Reporters are "viewed 'as surrogates for the public,'" *United States v. Criden,* 633 F.2d 346, 355 (3d Cir. 1980) (quoting *Richmond Newspapers, Inc. v. Virginia,* 448 U.S. 555, 573 (1980)), who act in the public interest by uncovering wrongdoing by business and government alike. Democracy without information about the activities of the government is hardly a democracy. The press provides "a constitutionally chosen means for keeping officials elected by the people responsible to all the people whom they were selected to serve." *Mills v. Alabama,* 384 U.S. 214, 219 (1966). A citizen's right to vote, our most basic democratic principle, is rendered meaningless if the ruling government is not subjected to a free press's "organized, expert scrutiny of government." Justice Potter Stewart, *Or of the Press,* 26 Hastings L.J. 631, 634 (1975).

The protection of confidential sources is "necessary to ensure a free and vital press, without which an open and democratic society would be impossible to maintain." *Ashcraft v. Conoco, Inc.,* 218 F.3d 282, 287 (4th Cir. 2000). If reporters are compelled to divulge their confidential sources, "the free flow of newsworthy information would be restrained and the public's understanding of important issues and events would be hampered in ways inconsistent with a healthy republic." *Id.*

Yet if a free press is a necessary condition of a vibrant democracy, it nevertheless has its limits. "[T]he reporter's privilege . . . is not absolute and will be overcome whenever society's need for the confidential information in question outweighs the intrusion on the reporter's First Amendment interests." *Ashcraft,* 218 F.3d at 287. And we must be mindful of the "fundamental maxim that the public . . . has a right to every man's evidence." *Jaffee v. Redmond,* 518 U.S. 1, 9 (1996).

The public, of course, does not have a right to see all classified information held by our government. But public debate on American military and intelligence methods is a critical element of public oversight of our government. Protecting the reporter's privilege ensures the informed public discussion of important moral, legal, and strategic issues. Public debate helps our government act in accordance with our Constitution and our values. . . .

A reporter's need for keeping sources confidential is not hypothetical. . . . Scott Armstrong, executive director of the Information Trust and former *Washington Post* reporter, points to three ways in which investigative journalism uses confidential sources: "developing factual accounts and documentation unknown to the public," "tak[ing] a mix of known facts and new information and produc[ing] an interpretation previously unavailable to the public," and "publiciz[ing] information developed in government investigations that has not been known to the public and might well be suppressed." Joint App'x (J.A.) 531. "It would be rare," Armstrong asserts, "for there not to be multiple sources — including confidential sources — for news stories on highly sensitive topics." *Id.* In turn, "[m]any sources require such guarantees of confidentiality before any extensive exchange of information is permitted." J.A. 350. Such guarantees of confidentiality enable sources to discuss "sensitive matters such as major policy debates, personnel matters, investigations of improprieties, and financial and budget matters." *Id.* Even in ordinary daily reporting, confidential sources are critical. "[O]fficial government pronouncements must be verified before they are published," and this is frequently done through discussion with officials not authorized to speak on the subject but who rely on assurances of confidentiality. J.A. 352. These discussions can often lead to "unique and relevant, contextual comments" made by the confidential source, comments that deepen the story. *Id.*

. . . [Affidavits submitted by the defendant] also recount numerous instances in which the confidentiality promised to sources was integral to a reporter's development of major stories critical to informing the public of the government's actions. *See, e.g.,* J.A. 378-80 (affidavit of Dana Priest) (noting, among many stories, her reporting on the existence and treatment of military prisoners at Guantanamo Bay, Cuba; the abuse of prisoners in Abu Ghraib, Iraq; the existence of secret CIA prisons in Eastern Europe; and the "systematic lack of adequate care" for veterans at Walter Reed Army Medical Center relied upon confidential sources). Carl Bernstein, who has worked for the *Washington Post* and ABC News, writes that without his confidential source known as "Deep Throat," the investigation into the Watergate scandal — the break-in of the Democratic National Committee's offices in the Watergate Hotel and Office Building that led to the resignation of President Nixon — would never have been possible. J.A. 361-62. "Total and absolute confidentiality" was essential for Bernstein to cultivate the source. J.A. 362. . . .

B.

Any consideration of the reporter's privilege must start with *Branzburg,* where the Supreme Court upheld, by a vote of five to four, the compulsion of confidential source information from reporters. *Branzburg v. Hayes,* 408 U.S. 665 (1972). . . . The opinion also stated that "news gathering is not without its First Amendment protections," *id.* at 707, but the Court did not specify exactly what those protections might encompass, although it indicated that "[o]fficial harassment of the press" and bad faith investigations might fall within the parameters of the First Amendment's protection of reporters. *Id.* at 707-08.

Further complicating matters is Justice Powell's "enigmatic concurring opinion," *id.* at 725 (Stewart, J., dissenting), which is in part at odds with the majority opinion he joined. In the concurrence, Justice Powell emphasized "the limited nature of the Court's holding," and endorsed a balancing test, according to which "if the newsman is called upon to give information bearing only a remote and tenuous relationship to the subject of the investigation," then courts should consider the applicability of the reporter's privilege on a "case-by-case basis" by "the striking of a proper balance between freedom of the press and the obligation of all citizens to give relevant testimony with respect to criminal conduct." *Id.* at 709-10 (Powell, J., concurring).

The full import of Justice Powell's concurrence continues to be debated. Some analogize the *Branzburg* majority opinion to a plurality opinion, and therefore assert Justice Powell's concurrence as the narrowest opinion is controlling. Others, like my good friends in the majority, treat Justice Powell's concurrence as ancillary . . . .

Given this confusion, appellate courts have subsequently hewed closer to Justice Powell's concurrence — and Justice Stewart's dissent — than to the majority opinion, and a number of courts have since recognized a qualified reporter's privilege, often utilizing a three-part balancing test. *See, e.g., United States v. Caporale,* 806 F.2d 1487, 1504 (11th Cir. 1986) (applying the reporter's privilege in the criminal context); *United States v. Burke,* 700 F.2d 70, 76-77 (2d Cir. 1983) (recognizing the qualified privilege in criminal cases); *Zerilli v. Smith,* 656 F.2d 705, 711-13 (D.C. Cir. 1981) (applying the reporter's privilege in a civil case). Indeed, a mere five years after *Branzburg,* a federal court of appeals confidently asserted that the existence of a qualified reporter's privilege was "no longer in doubt." *Silkwood v. Kerr-McGee Corp.,* 563 F.2d 433, 437 (10th Cir. 1977). In short, Justice Powell's concurrence and the subsequent appellate history have made the lessons of *Branzburg* about as clear as mud.

The Fourth Circuit, like our sister circuits, has applied Justice Powell's balancing test in analyzing whether to apply a reporter's privilege to quash subpoenas seeking confidential source information from reporters. We first explicitly adopted Justice Powell's balancing test in an en banc opinion in *United States v. Steelhammer,* 539 F.2d 373, 376 (4th Cir. 1976) (Winter, J., dissenting), *adopted by the court en banc,* 561 F.2d 539, 540 (4th Cir. 1977). Then in *LaRouche [v. National Broadcasting Co.*, 780 F.2d 1134 (4th Cir. 1986)], we applied the reporter's privilege doctrine to a civil case, again citing Justice Powell's concurrence in *Branzburg* for authority. 780 F.2d at 1139. Following the lead of the Fifth Circuit, we applied a three-part test to help us balance the interests at stake in determining whether the reporter's privilege should be applied; that is, we considered "(1) whether the information is relevant, (2) whether the information can be obtained by alternative means, and (3) whether there is a compelling interest in the information." *Id.* . . .

In a subsequent case in the criminal context, *In re Shain,* four reporters in South Carolina asserted the reporter's privilege to protect information gleaned from interviews with a state legislator. 978 F.2d 850, 851-52 (4th Cir.1992). But applying Justice Powell's principles, we rejected the reporters' claim on the ground that none of the reporters asserted that the interviews were confidential, that there were agreements to refuse revealing the identity of the interviewee, or that the government sought to harass the reporters. *Id.* at 853. Thus, although the reporter's privilege was not recognized in "the circumstances of this case," *see id.* at 854, it is clear to me that we have acknowledged that a reporter's privilege attaches in criminal proceedings given the right circumstances.

The most recent federal appellate court decision to address the reporter's privilege at length is *In re Grand Jury Subpoena, Judith Miller,* 438 F.3d 1141, 1145-49 (D.C. Cir. 2006). In that case, the court rejected the reporter's privilege claim asserted by Judith Miller of *The New York Times,* stating that the *Branzburg* decision was dispositive. The majority there — as in this case — reasoned that the Supreme Court had not revisited the question of a reporter's privilege under the First Amendment after *Branzburg,* and that Justice Powell's concurrence did not detract from the precedential weight of the majority's conclusion that there was no First Amendment reporter's privilege, at least when there was no suggestion that the reporter was being pressed for information as a means of harassment or intimidation. *Id.* at 1145-49. In a thoughtful concurrence, though, Judge Tatel pointed to the ambiguities of the *Branzburg* decision, and noted that nearly every state and the District of Columbia has recognized a reporter's privilege. Nevertheless, Judge Tatel concluded that "if *Branzburg* is to be limited or distinguished in the circumstances of this case, we must leave that task to the Supreme Court." *Id.* at 1166 (Tatel, J., concurring). And although he felt constrained to deny applying a First Amendment privilege, Judge Tatel would have held that Rule 501 of the Federal Rules of Evidence provides for a reporter's privilege (though on the facts of that case, the privilege would have given way due to the extraordinary national security issue involved). *See id.* at 1177-78 (Tatel, J ., concurring).

C.

. . . Are there circumstances in which a reporter may refuse to testify as to the identity of one of his confidential sources, when the government seeks this information as part of a criminal investigation, and there is no evidence of prosecutorial bad faith or harassment? Some appellate courts have used a three-part test, essentially identical to the test we announced in *LaRouche* in the civil context, to help determine whether to apply the reporter's privilege in criminal cases. They require the moving party, i.e. the government, "to make a clear and specific showing" that the subpoenaed information is "highly material and relevant, necessary or critical to the maintenance of the claim, and not obtainable from other available sources." [*United States v. Burke,* 700 F.2d 70 (2d Cir.1983),] at 77.

I, too, would recognize a qualified reporter's privilege in the criminal context, and evaluate the privilege using the three-part test enunciated in *LaRouche* as an "aid" to help "balance the interests involved." 780 F.2d at 1139. I would add a caveat to this general rule, however; in cases involving questions of national security, *if* the three-part *LaRouche* test is satisfied in favor of the reporter's privilege, I would require consideration of two additional factors: the harm caused by the public dissemination of the information, and the newsworthiness of the information conveyed. . . .

D.

[Here Judge Gregory reviews the record to conclude that the *LaRouche* test, augmented by his two additional factors, is satisfied.] . . .

E.

Even if I were not inclined to recognize a First Amendment privilege for a reporter in the criminal context given *Branzburg,* I would recognize a common law privilege protecting a reporter's sources pursuant to Federal Rule of Evidence 501. . . . In light of *Branzburg's* insistence that "Congress has freedom to determine whether a statutory newsman's privilege is necessary and desirable and to fashion standards and rules as narrow or broad as deemed necessary to deal with the evil discerned," 408 U.S. at 706, a full discussion of the reporter's privilege must reckon with Rule 501. . . .

The Supreme Court has stated that "the policy decisions of the States bear on the question [of] whether federal courts should recognize a new privilege or amend coverage of an existing one," and "[i]t is of no consequence that recognition of the privilege in the vast majority of States is the product of legislative action rather than judicial decision." [*Jaffee,* 518 U.S.] at 12-13. When the *Branzburg* decision issued, only seventeen states had recognized some protection for a reporter regarding his or her confidential sources. Today, only one state, Wyoming, has not enacted or adopted a reporter's privilege. Thirty-nine states and the District of Columbia have shield laws for reporters, whether those shields are absolute or qualified. In ten states without statutory shield laws, the privilege has been recognized in some form or another by the courts. . . . The landscape in regards to the reporter's privilege has changed drastically since *Branzburg.* The unanimity of the States compels my conclusion that Rule 501 calls for a reporter's privilege. . . .

6a. *A De Facto Reporter's Privilege?* Just days before the Supreme Court's denial of James Risen's appeal, Attorney General Eric Holder declared in a meeting with journalists, "As long as I'm attorney general, no reporter who is doing his job is going to go to jail. As long as I'm attorney general, someone who is doing their job is not going to get prosecuted." Charlie Savage, *Holder Hints Reporter May Be Spared Jail in Leak*, N.Y. Times, May 27, 2014. Whether the Justice Department might nevertheless seek a fine against Risen for contempt remains unclear. Also unclear is the willingness of future Attorneys General to seek imprisonment for reporters who refuse to reveal their sources.

6b. *A Statutory Reporter's Privilege?* On May 29, 2014, the House of Representatives approved a funding measure containing this language:

> None of the funds made available by this Act may be used to compel a journalist or reporter to testify about information or sources that the journalist or reporter states in a motion to quash the subpoena that he has obtained as a journalist or reporter and that he regards as confidential. [H.R. 4660, Commerce, Justice, Science, and Related Agencies Appropriations Act, 2015, 113th Cong. (2014).]

According to its sponsor, Rep. Alan Grayson (D-FL), "This amendment is to be construed liberally and broadly, to effectuate its purpose of protecting journalists and their sources from any coercive action taken by the government and the legal system." 160 Cong. Rec. E932 (June 9, 2014).

If this measure is signed into law, how extensive will the resulting protection be? Are you prepared to say who is a "journalist or reporter," or how long the protection would last?

[CTL p. 836. Insert at end of Note 1.]

The Second Circuit has now joined the Seventh in finding that the ATA's silence precludes common law aiding and abetting liability. *Rothstein v. UBS AG*, 708 F.3d 82, 97 (2d Cir. 2013). While it cited *Boim III* with approval for this conclusion, it did not address the question of "statutory secondary liability," which the Seventh Circuit substituted for common law aiding and abetting liability, as discussed in the next Note.

[CTL p. 837. Insert at end of Note 5.]

The Second Circuit has held that the ATA requires proximate causation, which it explained as "'the idea that a person is not liable to all those who may have been injured by his conduct, but only to those with respect to whom his acts were a substantial factor in the sequence of responsible causation and whose injury was reasonably foreseeable anticipated as a natural consequence.'" *Rothstein v. UBS AG*, 708 F.3d 82, 95-97 (2d Cir. 2013) (internal citation omitted). But how would a plaintiff show that a defendant's provision of funds to a terrorist is ever a "substantial factor," when the fungibility of money makes it impossibl for a plaintiff to trace the funds to any particular attack?

The Supreme Court may have suggested an answer by noting an exception to "but for" causation in fact:

> [w]hen the conduct of two or more actors is so related to an event that their combined conduct, viewed as a whole, is a but-for cause of the event, and application of the but-for rule to them individually would absolve all of them, the conduct of each is a cause in fact of the event.

Paroline v. United States, 134 S. Ct. 1710, 1723 (Apr. 23, 2014) (internal citation omitted). (Many first-year law students were exposed to that exception by *Summers v. Tice*, 33 Cal. 2d 80 (1948), in which several hunters had fired their guns in plaintiff's direction, and he was unable to identify who among them had inflicted his injuries.) The *Paroline* Court explained that "it would be nonsensical to adopt a rule whereby individuals hurt by the combined wrongful acts of many (and thus in many instances hurt more badly than otherwise) would have no redress, whereas individuals hurt by the acts of one person alone would have a remedy." *Id.* at 1724.

If this exception applies to defendants who fund terrorism, then ATA plaintiffs could prove causation by showing (a) that the defendant's contribution was a sufficient (even if not necessary and even if sufficient only in combination with other funds) cause of terror attacks like the one that injured the plaintiffs, and (b) that it was reasonably foreseeable that providing such funds to terrorists would result in attacks like the one that injured the plaintiffs.

[CTL p. 851. Insert as Note 3.]

3. *Finding the Property.* Discovery in aid of post-judgment execution is quite permissive. But does the Foreign Sovereign Immunities Act restrict it when the judgment-debtor is a foreign sovereign? The Supreme Court said no in *Argentina v. NML Capital, Ltd.*, 134 S. Ct. 2250 (June 16, 2014). But the ruling was limited to the

or

e

the Act. The Court noted that other sources of law
l bear on the propriety of discovery requests of this nature
h as 'settled doctrines of privilege and the discretionary
by the district court whether the discovery is warranted,
ppropriately consider comity interests and the burden that
y might cause to the foreign state.'" *Id.* at 2258 n.6 (internal
tted). Thus, the terror-victim who wins a judgment against a
ereign or sovereign entity is not out of the woods yet; she still
rcome such doctrines to obtain discovery identifying assets,
as to execute the judgment against those assets.